FROM VICTORY TO PEACE

A VOLUME IN THE NIU SERIES IN
SLAVIC, EAST EUROPEAN, AND EURASIAN STUDIES

Edited by Christine D. Worobec

For a list of books in the series, visit our website at cornellpress.cornell.edu.

From Victory to Peace

Russian Diplomacy after Napoleon

Elise Kimerling Wirtschafter

NORTHERN ILLINOIS UNIVERSITY PRESS

AN IMPRINT OF CORNELL UNIVERSITY PRESS

ITHACA AND LONDON

First published 2021 by Cornell University Press

Library of Congress Cataloging-in-Publication Data
Names: Wirtschafter, Elise Kimerling, author.
Title: From victory to peace: Russian diplomacy after Napoleon / by Elise Kimerling Wirtschafter.
Description: Ithaca [New York]: Northern Illinois University Press, an imprint of Cornell University Press, 2021. | Series: NIU series in Slavic, East European, and Eurasian studies | Includes bibliographical references and index. |
Identifiers: LCCN 2020037692 (print) | LCCN 2020037693 (ebook) | ISBN 9781501756016 (paperback) | ISBN 9781501756498 (pdf) | ISBN 9781501756030 (epub)
Subjects: LCSH: Russia—Foreign relations—1801–1825. | Russia—History—Alexander I, 1801–1825. | Europe—Foreign relations—1815–1871. | Russia—Foreign relations—Europe. | Europe—Foreign relations—Russia.
Classification: LCC DK197.W57 2021 (print) | LCC DK197 (ebook) | DDC 327.47009/034—dc23
LC record available at https://lccn.loc.gov/2020037692
LC ebook record available at https://lccn.loc.gov/2020037693

Cover image adapted by Valerie Wirtschafter.

To my soulshine, Landon and Papy

CONTENTS

Contrary to Russia's present-day position on the political and psychological periphery of Europe, the period from the end of the Napoleonic Wars to the Crimean War (1853–56), and arguably until the Bolshevik Revolution of October 1917, represented a time of full integration into European society and politics. During this period, the Quadruple Alliance, the general alliance, the grand alliance, and the European political system stood as cornerstones of Russian diplomacy. Russia had led the allied coalition that defeated Napoleon in 1813–14, its armies had performed heroically and honorably in 1812, and its emperor had come to be seen by his subjects and intimates as the divinely anointed savior of Europe. From the Russian point of view, the glorious victory of 1812 and the subsequent wars leading to Napoleon's dethronement showed that Emperor Alexander I (ruled 1801–25) and his people, together with their allies, served as God's instrument in human history. Not surprisingly, in the eyes of Russia's monarch and diplomats, the peace settlement reached in 1814–15, and the peacemaking that continued in subsequent years, appeared equally providential.

The basic contours of what contemporaries referred to as the European political system were forged at the "Congress" of Westphalia, where rulers and diplomats recognized state sovereignty (not empire, dynasty, or religious belief) as the foundation of European order. Based on the principle that state sovereignty gave to each government the right to choose a domestic religion and political structure, free from the threat of outside intervention, the peacemakers also embraced the principle of a balance of power between independent states that aimed to preserve European equilibrium and prevent any one country from becoming powerful enough to achieve hegemony. Ultimately, the treaties of Westphalia failed to stop revolutionary France from overturning the equilibrium or Napoleonic France from dominating Europe. Thus, once Napoleon had been defeated militarily, it became necessary to reconstruct the European state system. After roughly twenty-five years of brutal warfare, fragile coalitions, and exhausting diplomacy, the continent's rulers and diplomats were eager to establish an enduring peace and prepared to make substantive compromises to achieve that goal. In a series of multilateral treaties, conventions, and protocols—produced primarily but not exclusively in Paris and at the Congress of Vienna in 1814–15—political leaders reconstituted the public law of Europe, which then provided the legal framework for interstate diplomacy and relations between governments and peoples.

Generations of historians have researched the chess game of European politics during the French Revolution, the Napoleonic Empire, and the peacemaking that followed the victory over France. The quality of this scholarship is impressive, yet the diplomacy of the era continues to fascinate and baffle. In recent decades, the reconstruction of Europe at the Congress of Vienna has been seen as a model of multilateral diplomacy and collective security arrangements that established precedents for today's United Nations and European Union. In addition, historians have moved beyond simplistic characterizations of Russia's actions, recognizing instead the critical and often salutary role of Emperor Alexander I. Scholarly perspectives have become diversified; however, significant aspects of European politics in the Restoration era remain understudied. These include the conceptual apparatus developed in diplomatic discourse and the relationship of diplomacy to national or local political cultures.

Among the great powers of Restoration Europe, the Russian Empire is the least integrated into both past and current historiography. Through study of Russian diplomacy in the years 1815–23, this book broadens the knowledge base available to historians and helps to fill a striking historiographical gap. Beginning in the immediate aftermath of the Congress of Vienna and continuing through the Congress of Verona, Europe's statesmen worked tirelessly to implement the edifice of pacification and peace constructed in 1814, 1815, and 1818. They completed territorial negotiations, codified political arrangements, and brought a defeated France back into the alliance of great powers. Equally significant, they confronted dangerous revolts and military crises in Europe, the Ottoman Empire, and Spanish America. In response to these developments, Emperor Alexander's hopes for peace, his pragmatic adaptability, and his commitment to act in concert with the other great powers came fully into focus. Close attention to Russian diplomacy, based on sources of Russian provenance, challenges characterizations of Alexander's behavior as erratic and his foreign policy as heavy-handed and expansionist. Indeed, as historians assimilate the Russian perspective on European order (as well as the perspectives of other less well-studied countries and peoples), they encounter a multifaceted Restoration built upon the practices of enlightened reformism and direct experience of costly revolution and war.

Decades have passed since European historians began to reevaluate the European restorations and rebalance their understanding of the achievements and consequences of the French Revolution. The research presented here contributes in multiple ways to debates about the Restoration. As noted, this book highlights Russian diplomacy, which continues to occupy a peripheral and understudied position in European historiography. It does so, moreover, not by analyzing political maneuvers in the high stakes game of diplomatic chess, but by exploring the ideas and concepts that defined Russian foreign policy. The conceptual history of diplomacy leads in turn to emphasis on the dynamics of peacemaking over more familiar themes such as empire building, the emergence of ethno-nationalism, or the struggle between "progress" and "reaction." Finally, this book focuses on the intersection of principle and action in order to understand how Emperor Alexander and his diplomatic agents presented Russian foreign policy to Europe and the world, what they thought they were doing (or wanted others to think they were doing), and how they thought they were going to establish and preserve a durable peace.

Concrete investigation of what it meant to act in concert (*concerter*) encourages a deeper, more nuanced analysis of the Vienna settlement's outcomes and of Russia's role in European society than is suggested by current historiography. How did Russian statesmen interpret and represent the principles, problems, solutions, and goals of Alexander I's foreign policy? How did they respond to events on the ground as the process of implementing the peace unfolded? To address these questions, this book builds upon decades of research in Russian military and diplomatic archives. Archival access, especially since the end of the Cold War, has enhanced historians' knowledge of the socioeconomic, institutional, and cultural backdrop to foreign policy. As early as 1980, this author began to work in the Central State Military Historical Archive of the former Soviet Union. Scholars such as Patricia Kennedy Grimsted, whose 1969 book, *The Foreign Ministers of Alexander I*, remains foundational, lacked the opportunity to consult archives on a regular basis. Throughout the 1960s, the Military Historical Archive and the Archive of the Foreign Policy of the Russian Empire kept their doors closed to foreign researchers. Today, in the post-communist environment of open scholarly exchange, Grimsted's book continues to represent the most recent English-language study of the personnel and political thought behind Alexander's foreign policy. There is, in other words, much work to be done before the history of Russian diplomacy has been subjected to the same degree of scrutiny as Austrian, British, or French diplomacy. Nor is there a better way to gain insight into Russia's current foreign policy goals and ambitions than to study the diplomatic conduct and ideas that produced specific decisions in the past.

ACKNOWLEDGMENTS

The research for this book was conducted in the Russian State Archive of Ancient Acts (RGADA) and the Archive of the Foreign Policy of the Russian Empire (AVP RI) during trips to Moscow in 2013, 2017, and 2019. I am grateful to the administration and staff of these institutions for granting access to their rich archival holdings and for providing a professional work environment. I began this research as a visiting professor in the History Faculty of the National Research University Higher School of Economics in Moscow, where I enjoyed the privilege of teaching Russian students and interacting with Russian colleagues. I am particularly indebted to Alexander B. Kamenskii, dean of the faculty, for arranging this sojourn. In 2017 my research was further facilitated by an invitation to participate in the International Conference "What Is Enlightenment? New Answers to the Old Questions" held at the Kuskovo Estate Museum in Moscow.

In 2017–18, I benefited from writing time and discussions with colleagues thanks to a guest professorship at the University of Tübingen, sponsored by the German Academic Exchange Service (DAAD) and arranged by Ingrid Schierle. In Tübingen, as the guest of the Institute for East European History and Area Studies headed by Klaus Gestwa, I had the opportunity to teach, present my research, and co-organize an international workshop. I also benefited from multiple opportunities to make research presentations at other German universities: Munich, Freiburg, and Bonn. I am grateful to the institutional hosts, staff, colleagues, and students who made these activities possible.

I likewise wish to thank the organizers of two international conferences where I was able to present and discuss the research that went into this book: (1) "Russia and the Napoleonic Wars," sponsored by the Paulsen Foundation, the London School of Economics (LSE IDEAS), and the Russian State Historical Museum in Mezotnes, Latvia (May 2014); and (2) "The Price of Peace: Modernising the Ancien Régime? Europe 1815–1848," held at the University of Kent in Paris (August 2016).

Equally fruitful were research presentations and discussions organized by Valerie Kivelson at the University of Michigan in Ann Arbor (February 2019), Gail Lenhoff at the annual UCLA Winter Workshop in Medieval and Early Modern

Slavic Studies (February 2014, 2015, 2018), and Paul Werth at the Desert Workshop of Russian History at UNLV (March 2017).

Closer to home, I thank California State Polytechnic University in Pomona for the sabbatical and professional leaves that allowed me to teach in Moscow and Tübingen. I am also grateful to Amy Farranto of NIUP, Christine Worobec, Janet Hartley, and an anonymous reader—all paragons of professionalism and intellectual integrity—for the suggestions, comments, criticisms, and editorial advice that contributed to the publication of this book. Finally, I thank my daughter, Valerie Wirtschafter, for professional editing and for adapting the map used on the cover of this book.

ABBREVIATIONS

AVP RI	Arkhiv vneshnei politiki Rossiiskoi Imperii
d.	*delo*
f.	*fond*
l., ll.	*list, listy*
Martens, *Recueil*	F. F. Martens, *Recueil des traités et conventions, conclus par la Russie avec les puissances étrangères*
ob.	*oborotnaia storona* (verso)
op.	*opis'*
PSZ	*Polnoe sobranie zakonov Rossiiskoi Imperii*
RGADA	Rossiiskii gosudarstvennyi arkhiv drevnikh aktov
SIRIO	*Sbornik Imperatorskogo Rossiiskogo istoricheskogo obshchestva*
t.	*tom*
VPR	*Vneshniaia politika Rossii*

During the nineteenth century the Julian calendar used in Russia (Old Style dating) was twelve days behind the Gregorian calendar used by most states in Europe (New Style dating). Because Russian diplomatic sources generally indicated Old Style (OS) and New Style (NS) dates, I follow the dating of the Russian documents and try to give both dates. Where I do not use double dating, the New Style date presumably is given (though in Russian sources that lack double dating, it sometimes is unclear which date has been provided). When discussing Russia's domestic environment, I use the Old Style dates that are followed in the field of Russian Studies.

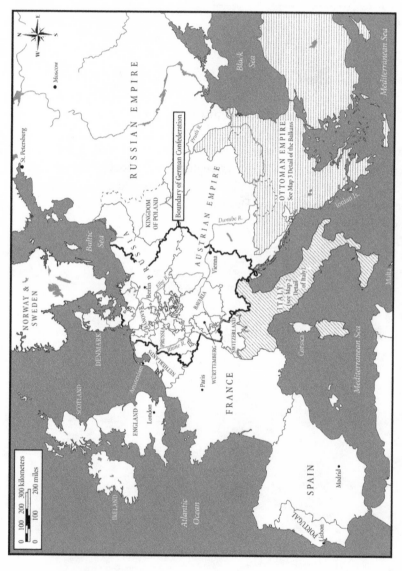

MAP 1. Europe in 1815. Map by Mike Bechthold (mike@blackflight.ca).

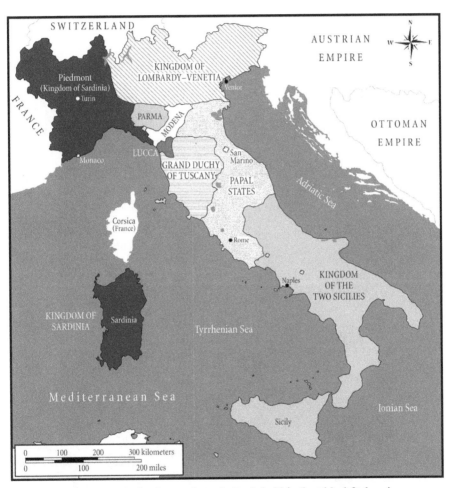

MAP 2. Detail of Italy. Map by Mike Bechthold (mike@blackflight.ca).

MAP 3. Detail of the Balkans. Map by Mike Bechthold (mike@blackflight.ca).

FROM VICTORY TO PEACE

Introduction

Russia as a Great Power in Europe

R USSIA'S RISE TO GREAT power status in modern Europe began with the military reforms and foreign policy ambitions of Tsar Peter I (ruled 1682/1689–1725), whose reign has for generations of historians embodied the transformation of the Muscovite tsardom into the Russian Empire. In October 1721, following the defeat of Sweden in the Great Northern War (1700–21), Tsar Peter assumed the titles "Father of the Fatherland, All-Russian Emperor, and Peter the Great." Scholars debate the meaning of Peter's greatness, and depending on the specific reform under investigation, they find varying degrees of continuity, change, and effectiveness.[1] With respect to military capability and foreign policy, Peter's reforms successfully addressed critical problems that Muscovite institutions could not overcome. These included the legal mechanisms connecting state service to social status and the relationships of authority binding the monarchy, church hierarchy, and nobility. As the monarchy embraced European-style military mobilization and Westphalian principles of sovereignty, the church and nobility accepted the need for a strong state to guarantee their own security and advancement. From Peter's reign onward, the monarchy and nobility also agreed that the importation and adaptation of European technology and cultural models offered the best means to confront European power. For this reason, Europeanization became the hallmark of government-directed reform and the symbol of social progress.

The lasting impact of Peter's reforms appeared most evident in the organization of the navy, standing army, officer corps, and apparatus of military administration and supply. But the growth of military power also required the reform of basic social and political institutions. The new arrangements, which would remain in place until the emancipation of the serfs in 1861, accounted for Russia's military success in the French Revolutionary and Napoleonic Wars. Indeed, decades before the emergence of France's citizen army, Russia implemented a system of mass conscription built upon the institution of serfdom and the ascription of individuals to local communities and social groups. Together with conscription, the ability to mobilize economic resources allowed the Russian government to support the large standing army that made possible Napoleon's defeat. In contrast to conditions in revolutionary Europe, Russia's military effort did not depend on the fusion of politics and war associated with an ideologically motivated nation in arms.[2] Rather, it sprang from sheer physical necessity, popular belief in God and Divine Providence, a willingness to serve the tsar, and devotion to household, community, and the Russian land—all bolstered by extraordinary endurance and the omnipresent threat of coercion.

BASED ON THE Muscovite Law Code (*Ulozhenie*) of 1649, all subjects of the Russian monarch belonged to legally defined social categories that performed prescribed service obligations and benefited from class-based privileges. Beginning in 1719, periodic censuses registered the male souls liable for conscription and payment of the capitation. Census registration, which also bound individuals to their communities of origin, placed the burden of defense primarily on Russia's laboring people, the overwhelming majority of whom were either state peasants or privately owned serfs. Townspeople also provided recruits and paid the capitation, though individuals who possessed sufficient capital to qualify for merchant status were exempted on an annual basis. Nobles and clergy likewise avoided the capitation; however, sons of clergy and non-ordained churchmen who failed to obtain church appointments could be conscripted by special levy. Nobles, too, starting as early as the mid-sixteenth century, performed obligatory military or civil service. Theoretically, they served for life, or until infirmity, in return for the right to possess land and serfs. Although obligatory service for nobles ended with the emancipation of 1762, Tsar Peter's educational and service reforms had made them the main source of officers for the Russian army. According to the Table of Ranks enacted in 1722, promotion in service became the primary pathway to social advancement, bringing higher rank to nobles and ennoblement to commoners. For these reasons, Russia's hereditary and service nobles, like noble elites across Europe, sought glory, honor, wealth, and status by pursuing military careers.[3]

Observers long have marveled at the Russian government's ability to mobilize human and material resources on a large scale in a peasant society built upon community-based agriculture. As early as 1630/31, well before the Petrine reforms, regular levies of recruits and lifelong terms of service became part of Russian life. During the Thirteen Years' War (1654–67) with Poland, military drafts swept up around 100,000 men, a sizeable number, though one that pales in comparison to the levies of the eighteenth century. Scholarly estimates of recruits into the Petrine army count 205,000 men from 1700 to 1711 and at least 140,000 from 1713 to 1724. At the time of Peter's death in 1725, the army consisted of 130,000 regular troops, 75,000–80,000 garrison troops, and 20,000 Cossack irregulars. By the mid-eighteenth century, the number of men in arms reached 292,000 in a population of 23,230,000, and in 1800, 446,000 in a population of 37,414,000. Stated differently, from 1705 to 1801, the Russian military conscripted roughly 2.25 million men, and from 1796 to 1815, 1,616,199. When combat operations against France ended in 1815, Russian troops numbered 727,414. The empire preserved this capability for the rest of Alexander I's reign, and in the period of relative peace from 1815 to 1853, the army grew even larger. From 1816 to 1822, the number of recruits reached 3,158,199. Compared to the 696,000 troops available at the time of Napoleon's invasion in 1812, the army counted 859,000 troops just prior to the outbreak of the Crimean War.[4]

Russian data are notoriously fragmentary before the late nineteenth century, and in the case of military statistics, it can be unclear which troops historians are counting. In addition to the regular standing army, the Russian military establishment included garrison troops, veterans' units, military colonies, Cossacks, and a variety of irregular hosts manned by ethnic minorities. The absence of precise information is problematic, yet one critical point can be made: the numbers correctly illustrate the organizational effort needed to conscript, train, and maintain Russia's large fighting force. However inefficient and arbitrary this effort sometimes appeared, it effectively sustained costly military victories and imperial expansion over the long duration. Beyond the ability to mobilize resources across a large, sparsely populated territory, Russia's military successes also highlighted the tenacity of the empire's combat troops.[5] As Frederick the Great reportedly commented, opponents found it "easier to kill Russian soldiers than to defeat them."[6] Frederick's words are surely apocryphal, but there is ample evidence and broad scholarly consensus that Emperor Alexander's army performed courageously and honorably in the wars of 1812–14.[7]

Precisely because of Russia's military triumphs, the capabilities of the army aroused distrust among the other great powers of Europe. During the diplomatic negotiations that followed the victory over Napoleon, Russia's allies could not understand why in conditions of peace, Emperor Alexander did not demobilize his soldiers. Preservation of the army on what seemed to be a wartime footing raised questions about the monarch's intentions. In reality, the size and organization of Russia's peacetime forces had less to do with military plans than with the geographic, demographic, economic, social, and legal-administrative conditions of the empire. For economic more than diplomatic reasons, Russia's military commanders understood all too well the need to reduce the number of troops. But within the framework of a society built on serfdom, the problem of how to organize conscription and maintain a reserve ready for call-up in time of war prevented significant reductions.

When not on campaign or assembled in summer camps—where in addition to training, soldiers also performed state works—Russia's semi-standing peasant army quartered primarily in rural villages scattered across vast distances. Equally important, because conscription brought emancipation from serfdom or from the authority of state villages and urban communities, once a recruit became a soldier, his legal status, and that of his wife and future offspring, changed. No longer registered to his place of origin, the soldier belonged to the military command until his release from service. Soldiers could not, therefore, be demobilized or sent home before they became disabled or completed the long term of service (twenty-five years at the time). Due to the great expanse of the empire's borders and the slowness of communications, the monarchy had no choice but to keep large numbers of men in active service. Also because of geographic constraints, the relatively centralized command structure of the Russian army had to be preserved to ensure administrative and fiscal viability.[8] Simply put, in order to understand Russia's military and diplomatic posture after the defeat of Napoleon, it is critical to consider the country's physical vulnerabilities and broad security needs.

The Russian Empire maintained a robust military establishment both to secure extensive landlocked borders and to support imperial expansion into contiguous territories, an ongoing process since the sixteenth century.[9] Prior to the Petrine reforms, the country's enemies included Sweden, the Polish-Lithuanian Commonwealth, the Crimean Khanate, and the Ottoman Empire. Following the Time of Troubles (1598–1613)—a period of government collapse, social rebellion, civil war, and foreign invasion—the reconstituted Muscovite monarchy struggled to protect its borders from opportunistic neighbors. The Treaty of Stolbovo (1617) with Sweden relinquished significant territory along the shores of Lake Ladoga and left Russia completely cut off from the Gulf of Finland. The Deulino armistice (1618) ceded to Poland territory along Muscovy's western border, including the strategically important city of Smolensk. Not surprisingly, Russia's young dynasty spent much of the seventeenth century trying to recover the lands that had been lost. In 1656–58, Tsar Aleksei Mikhailovich (ruled 1645–76), father of Peter I, challenged Swedish control of the Baltic trade, and from the 1620s, when the Orthodox population of Ukraine began to seek protection from Catholic rule, Muscovy again came into conflict with Poland. In 1654, following a rebellion against Poland that had begun in 1648, Ukrainian Cossacks took the oath of allegiance to the Muscovite tsar. That same year Russia also reconquered Smolensk and launched the Thirteen Years' War against Poland. Peace returned in 1667 with the truce of Andrusovo, which left Muscovy in control of Left-Bank (eastern) Ukraine, Kiev, and Smolensk.[10]

Territorial gains in Ukraine also produced a shared frontier with the Ottoman Empire. The Russian-Ottoman War of 1677–81 stemmed from Poland's surrender of a large part of Right-Bank (western) Ukraine to the Ottomans in 1676. The war brought no territorial changes to Russia, and Ottoman policy continued to focus more on southeastern Europe than on thwarting Muscovite acquisitions in Ukraine. But the advances highlighted another ongoing threat from the Crimean Tatars, vassals of the Ottomans, who raided and pillaged Russian settlements in the southern borderland. Because the Crimean Khanate traced its origins back to the empire of Chinggis Khan, Tatar raids not only wrought destruction but also recalled past subjugation to Mongol rule. Although Muscovy tried to confront the Tatars in campaigns of 1687 and 1689, the effort produced little direct combat and did nothing to enhance Russian security. The campaigns did, however, expose Muscovy's limited military capability. Seventeenth-century breakthroughs in military technology, tactics, and operations had not solved the structural problem of endurance—the combined effect of logistics, transport, training, reinforcement, and finance.[11] In other words, Muscovite military effectiveness lacked the capacity to support obvious military needs. It was precisely the problem of endurance, laid bare in the Crimean campaigns, that Peter I's military reforms aimed to address.

Tsar Peter inherited long-standing security challenges in the north, west, and south, yet his early actions also revealed ambitions beyond the protection of borderlands and foreign trade. From the outset, Peter used the military tools at his disposal to project Russian power and pursue aggressive strategic goals. After an unsuccessful campaign in 1695, Peter's troops captured the Ottoman fortress at Azov in 1696, and the monarch ordered the building of a naval fleet in the Sea of Azov. With this move Peter hoped to challenge Ottoman control of the Black Sea—Russia lacked access to a warm water port—and disrupt communications between the Ottomans and Crimean Tatars. Instead, Peter's army suffered a major defeat. In the battle on the Pruth River in Moldavia (9 July 1711), Russian troops succumbed to a much larger Ottoman-Tatar force. Peter was compelled to surrender Azov, dismantle his southern fleet, and destroy fortresses at Taganrog and Kamennyi Zaton. Russia retook Azov in 1739, though only in the reign of Catherine II (ruled 1762–96) did the empire achieve significant victories against the Ottomans.[12]

Developments in Europe told a different story, which hinted at the glorious military history to come. Indeed, the military endeavor that most fully expressed Tsar Peter's ambition and also signaled Russia's emergent power in Europe was the Great Northern War against Sweden. After Charles XII acceded to the Swedish throne in 1697, at the age of fourteen, the surrounding monarchs of Denmark, Poland, and Russia joined in a plot to destroy Sweden's Baltic empire. In the spring of 1700, Frederick IV and Elector Augustus of Saxony initiated military operations, and Peter followed with a declaration of war on 9 August. As is well known, Charles proved to be the most formidable of foes. Even before the Russian mobilization, Sweden threatened Copenhagen by sea, and Denmark sued for peace. Peter began operations with a siege of the Swedish fortress at Narva, and after a few months, on 20 November, the Swedes routed the Russian army. Swedish troops numbering only 9,000 crushed a Russian force of 40,000. Charles quickly seized the advantage and moved on Riga, which had been under siege by Augustus. There he achieved another impressive victory against Russian, Polish, and Saxon troops. This triumph opened the door to an invasion of Poland.

The military failures against Sweden propelled the reforms that over the course of the eighteenth century brought to Russia great power status in Europe and Asia. Alongside mass conscription and the capitation, the translation of human and material resources into effective power resulted from substantial changes in the organization of Russia's armed forces. These included the imposition of military discipline, the creation of centralized sources of supply, the manufacture of armaments and military cloth, the formation of an educated officer corps, the establishment of specialized technical schools, the mastery of strategic planning, and operational practices that emphasized fortification, troop mobility, and naval support.[13] Although Peter's first victory against Charles came in December 1701, before any of the military reforms could have yielded results, the impact of his policies became apparent over the next twenty years. As Russia and Sweden traded victories and defeats, Peter kept up the grueling military effort. A key advance occurred in 1703, when the tsar founded the city of Saint Petersburg, giving to Russia a new capital and a permanent foothold on the Baltic Sea. The following year, a summer campaign led to Russian control of Dorpat, Narva, Swedish Ingria, and the Neva River. Bold as these accomplishments appeared, they quickly faded due to Swedish victories in Poland and Saxony. The abdication of Augustus in 1706 allowed Charles to move against Russia at the beginning of 1708. But instead of marching toward Moscow, Charles led his troops south into Ukraine. There he joined forces with the Cossack hetman Ivan Mazepa, a former ally of Peter.

A more decisive victory over Sweden—one that continues to be celebrated in Russian history and culture—occurred on 28 June 1709 at the fortress of Poltava. Charles fled to the Ottoman Empire, but the threats to Russia did not subside. The Ottomans declared war in 1710, and the battle on the Pruth (1711) resulted in significant territorial losses for Russia. The defeat also forced Peter to grant Charles safe passage back to Sweden. In 1713 the Peace of Adrianople ended hostilities between the Russian and Ottoman empires, and in November 1714, Charles reached Sweden. By that time, Russia also had made gains in Swedish Pomerania and Finland. Still, Charles persevered. In 1716 he attacked Danish possessions in Norway, and only in 1718 did peace talks begin—after Britain, Denmark, Poland, Russia, and Saxony all decided to oppose Sweden. Military operations continued during the negotiations, and even after Charles's death at the end of the year, Russia maintained military pressure by launching destructive raids into Swedish territory. Finally, on 30 August/10 September 1721, Russia and Sweden signed the Treaty of Nystad. Russia acquired Livonia, Estonia, Ingria, part of Karelia, and the Baltic islands of Oesel and Dagoe. Except for Vyborg, Finland was returned to Sweden, which also received an indemnity from Russia. Broadly speaking, Russia replaced Sweden as the dominant Baltic power, a position that would lead to great power status in Europe. What had changed between 1700 and 1721 was the ability to sustain a large-scale military effort over the long duration—to overcome, to a satisfactory degree, the problem of endurance.

Although Russia's early steps toward great power status arose from the need to secure frontiers against dangerous enemies, including the steppe societies of the south and southeast, it quickly became apparent that tsarist military power also would be used to support imperial expansion. The start of the Great Northern War illustrated Peter's aggressive intentions, and as a result of the Persian campaign in 1722, Russia acquired lands along the southwestern and southern shores of the Caspian Sea. Treaties of 1732 and 1735 returned these territories to Persia. But then in 1783, 1787, and 1800, Russia partially occupied, abandoned, and then formally annexed Georgia. Although protracted and uneven, Russia's forward movement into Transcaucasia, Crimea, and Ukraine produced ongoing conflict with the Ottoman Empire. This led to wars in 1695, 1696, 1711, 1735–39, 1768–74, and 1787–91. Peter's initial success against Azov had proven illusory, but in the war of 1735–39, Russia retook the port, briefly occupied part of the Crimean Peninsula, and also gained access to the Black Sea, on condition that the Black Sea trade use Ottoman ships. In short, Russia's ongoing wars (and diplomacy) with the Ottoman Empire encapsulated the crisscrossing of defensive and offensive actions that defined imperial expansion.

Later in the eighteenth century, Catherine II's victories over the Ottoman Empire would produce gains that far surpassed those of her predecessors. In the Russian-Ottoman War of 1768–74, Catherine's army drove the Ottomans from the northern shores of the Black Sea and established a protectorate over the Crimean Khanate. By 1777, the Russian monarch effectively appointed the ruling khan, and in 1783, after a rebellion by Tatar nobles, annexed the peninsula. Henceforth the khanate came under the authority of a Russian governor. Other southern lands incorporated into the empire during Catherine's reign included the territory of the Zaporozhian Cossacks, the Kuban steppe, the Taman Peninsula, and Kabarda in the Caucasus. Of particular importance, Russia gained the right of free navigation in the Black Sea and the Straits of the Bosporus and Dardanelles. Russia also blocked Sweden's effort to reassert power in the Baltic region (war of 1788–90) and ended the independent existence of the Polish-Lithuanian Commonwealth (partitions of 1772, 1793, and 1795). Following the partitions, which also benefited Austria and Prussia, Russia controlled a large swathe of territory stretching from the Baltic to the Black Sea.[14]

Another sphere of empire building, both defensive and offensive, grew out of the porous frontiers separating Russia's sedentary communities from the nomadic peoples of the steppe. The steppe peoples lived in parts of present-day Moldova, Ukraine, Russia, and Kazakhstan.[15] In the imperial period, the steppe's geographical boundaries ran from the Danube River in the west to Lake Balkhash in the east, and from the forest zone of European Russia in the north to the Black and Caspian Seas in the south. Russia's struggle to secure and subjugate the steppe began in the sixteenth century with the conquest of the khanates of Kazan (1552), Astrakhan (1554), and Siberia (1580). The incorporation of these heirs to the Golden Horde then led to struggles against the Nogay Tatars in the north Caucasus, the Bashkirs around the southern Ural Mountains, and from the 1630s, the Kalmyks in the Caspian steppe. The protracted bloodletting took the form of destructive raids, armed rebellions, and brutal suppression. Eventually, the Tatar, steppe, and Volga peoples succumbed to Russian power. The peoples of the Caucasus would submit, and then only sporadically, in the first half of the nineteenth century. The Kazakhs, who during the eighteenth century attained dominance in the steppe, did not become fully integrated into the Russian Empire until the 1860s.

Russia's complicated relations with the steppe and Caucasus lay at the core of empire building but did not deeply impact diplomacy in Europe. Exceptions arose in areas bordering on the steppe such as Crimea and Georgia, where challenges to Ottoman and Persian interests could have consequences for the

European system, especially within the context of nineteenth-century imperialism. On average, however, Russian movement into the steppe, at least during the eighteenth and early nineteenth centuries, remained a domestic affair, much like the westward expansion of the United States. For this reason, policy in the steppe and Caucasus has been characterized as an organic process of colonization driven by geopolitical imperatives such as the need to defend an unstable frontier. But clearly, expansion also aimed to command human and material resources and to impose sovereignty over foreign peoples. Thus, historian John P. LeDonne describes Russia as a Eurasian state in search of hegemony from the Elbe River to eastern Siberia.[16] Although LeDonne's analysis may overstate the intentionality and coherence of Russian imperialism, it recognizes that policymakers and intellectuals viewed territorial expansion as the bringing of civilization to barbarous lands and peoples. In relations with the steppe, the Caucasus, and later Central Asia, Russian elites clearly articulated this colonialist thinking.[17]

Eurasian interests highlighted Russia's global emergence and imperialist reach. Yet in the period of the French Revolutionary and Napoleonic Wars, and subsequently in the Restoration era, the European theater commanded the lion's share of military and diplomatic resources. For decades after the death of Peter I, political instability and struggles over the succession could not be disentangled from diplomatic relations with Europe. The turmoil temporarily abated when Peter's daughter Elizabeth became empress in 1741, roughly one year after Frederick II of Prussia occupied Austrian Silesia (December 1740). During much of Elizabeth's reign (ruled 1741–61), Russia maintained good relations with both Austria and Britain, but grew ever more suspicious of Prussia. According to historians, Prussia's rise to great power status disrupted the equilibrium of the Westphalia state system and caused a realignment in the European balance of power. Prussia abandoned its alliance with France for union with Britain, while Austria left its alliance with Britain for union with France.[18] Eventually, the realignment led to the Seven Years' War (1756–63), in which Austria, France, and Russia faced off against Prussia, whose ally Britain provided subsidies to Frederick and received protection for Hanover. Throughout the conflict, Russia managed to preserve the all-important trade relationship with Britain, and also took an active stand against Prussia. In return for Elizabeth's pledge to support Austria in the recovery of Silesia, Russia received subsidies and the promise of territorial gains in eastern Prussia. The Russian government hoped to use these territories to make border adjustments with Poland that would further secure the Baltic-Black Sea corridor. Elizabeth achieved her war aims in 1758 and continued to honor the commitment to Austria by sending troops on campaign in 1759, 1760, and 1761.[19]

When Elizabeth died in December 1761, her nephew Peter III (ruled 1761–62), a known supporter of Prussia, acceded to the throne.[20] Although Peter ruled for only a few short months before a palace coup brought his wife Catherine to power, he initiated another rebalancing of power relations in Europe. Peter abandoned the war against Prussia, an action that violated treaty obligations to Austria, and handed a key victory to Frederick II. The withdrawal could have benefitted Russia; the empire's finances had become precarious, and the war had become a divisive issue within the governing elite. But Peter, born Prince of Holstein-Gottorp, remained a German ruler. In May 1762, he ordered military commanders to prepare for a summer war against Denmark with the goal of restoring Schleswig to his native Holstein. Although Frederick promised to send 15,000 Prussian troops to assist Peter, the pledge did not convince Russia's elites to support the planned campaign. For this and other reasons, Peter lost his throne on 28 June and his life on 5 July. Russia's military leadership, upper bureaucracy, and guard regiments stationed in Saint Petersburg all supported the accession of Catherine, initially as regent for her son Paul. After Catherine's death, Paul ruled just long enough, from 1796 to 1801, to end the political uncertainty of the eighteenth century by establishing a clear order of succession. Ironically, the promise of security did not save him from a murderous overthrow, tacitly approved by his son and heir, Alexander I, widely known as the tsar who defeated Napoleon and the tsar diplomat who became a key architect of the Vienna settlement.[21]

The decades of war against revolutionary and Napoleonic France, which culminated in the Congress of Vienna, are critically important for historians of European diplomacy and the restorations. Russia's participation in the wars began when Emperor Paul joined the Second Coalition (1798–1802) consisting of Austria, Britain, the Kingdom of Naples, the Ottoman Empire, and Portugal.[22] During the months of negotiation that produced the coalition, Russia sent a naval squadron to support British operations along the Dutch coast (July 1798) and cooperated with the Ottomans to occupy the Ionian Islands (September–November 1798).[23] In February 1799, Russian troops captured Corfu, and Field Marshal Aleksandr V. Suvorov (1729–1800) became commander of a combined Russian-Austrian army. In the spring and summer of 1799, Suvorov scored significant victories in northern Italy, though instead of seizing the opportunity to march on Paris, his superiors sent him across the Alps into Switzerland. There Suvorov was supposed to join forces with General Aleksandr M.

Rimskii-Korsakov (1753–1840), whose corps was advancing from the Rhine valley. In late September, before the Russian armies could be united, Rimskii-Korsakov and the Austrians suffered defeat near Zurich. Faced with unchecked French power, the coalition began to unravel. Suvorov managed to extricate his men from the disastrous situation in Switzerland, and in January 1800, Emperor Paul ordered all Russian troops to return home. Austrian forces fell to the French in the Battle of Marengo in June and again in the Battle of Hohenlinden in December. After Hohenlinden, Austria's military effort collapsed.

The War of the Second Coalition inaugurated one of the most dramatic periods in the history of European warfare. In November 1799, French general Napoleon Bonaparte became First Consul and head of the military dictatorship known as the Consulate. For the next fifteen years, until Emperor Napoleon's final defeat at Waterloo in June 1815, Europe's monarchies faced the threat of military conquest and revolution. France's efforts to dominate Europe led to years of brutal warfare, intermittent peace, and unreliable alliances. Although Britain and Russia remained steady obstacles to French advances, Napoleon's opponents generally failed to unite for collective action. On occasion the need to protect economic interests, freedom of the seas, or established thrones produced a degree of unity. But more often than not, alliances crumbled in the face of French military success. Repeatedly, Napoleon's enemies abandoned allies in hopes of avoiding territorial losses or concluding illusory agreements with France. Thus, the Second Coalition evaporated within a few years, as France reached separate agreements with previously allied states: rapprochement with Russia (1800–1), the Treaty of Lunéville with Austria (February 1801), and the Treaty of Amiens with Britain (March 1802). Thanks to these accords, the defeated powers recouped territorial losses and even made some gains. For the first time in a decade, Europe seemed to enjoy a modicum of peace.

But the respite did not last, as France continued to challenge Britain's control of the seas. By May 1803 the two powers once again went to war, and within two years, in March 1805, Napoleon began to plan an invasion of England. This aggression led in April to the Third Coalition, which joined Austria, Britain, and Russia. The deployment of troops began in late August, and the monumental naval victory of Admiral Horatio Nelson off Cape Trafalgar occurred on 21 October 1805. Britain staved off invasion and preserved naval superiority, while Austria and Russia suffered humiliating losses that paved the way for French domination in the Germanies and Poland. In September Napoleon's Grand Army marched eastward from Boulogne, and Austria invaded Bavaria. A Russian army also moved westward to join up with the Austrians. Before the two armies could be linked, on 20 October, the French defeated the Austrians at Ulm in Bavaria, opening the door to an invasion of Austria. Although Russian forces managed temporarily to delay the French advance, at Dürenstein on 11 November and at Hollabrünn on 15–16 November, they could not prevent the occupation of Vienna. Allied defeats at the hands of Napoleon continued to mount, and on 2 December, Russian and Austrian forces succumbed to French military might at Austerlitz in Moravia. Russia again abandoned its coalition partners and retreated into Poland. Austria surrendered unconditionally and on 26 December signed the Treaty of Pressburg. Prussia already had signed a treaty of alliance with France on 15 December. Roughly six months later, in July 1806, fifteen German states joined the Confederation of the Rhine under French domination, and during the next year, Napoleon consolidated his mastery over Western and Central Europe.

In the aftermath of Austerlitz, Europe's monarchs understood all too well the reality of Napoleon's intentions. But this did not mean that they were ready or able to sustain a unified response. The Fourth Coalition against France began to take shape at the same time that Napoleon formed the Confederation of the Rhine. In July 1806 Prussia and Russia agreed to cooperate in anticipation of further hostilities. The coalition congealed in October with the participation of Britain, Prussia, Russia, and Sweden. On 9 October, in a challenge to France's continued occupation of German lands, Prussian king Frederick William III declared war. But before Emperor Alexander could make good on the commitment to his ally, France defeated Prussia simultaneously at Jena and Auerstadt on 14 October. Frederick William fled to the east, and French troops occupied Berlin. At the end of 1806 Russian forces began to engage the French in limited actions in Poland. Then in February 1807, the Russian and French armies fought the inconclusive Battle of Eylau. Just a few months later, on 14 June, combined Russian-Prussian forces succumbed to the French at Friedland. Alexander I and Frederick William III signed the treaties of Tilsit.

Based on the Treaty of Tilsit (25 June 1807) and the subsequent negotiations in Erfurt (September–October 1808), Russia recognized the French control over Western and Central Europe represented by the Confederation of the Rhine and the Grand Duchy of Warsaw.[24] The Grand Duchy consisted of Prussia's Polish provinces without the district of Belostok, which went to Russia. In addition, Emperor Alexander agreed to break relations with Britain and close the empire's Baltic ports to British trade, unless Britain accepted French demands to respect freedom of the seas and trade among neutral states. Russia also consented to the demand that Britain return Dutch, French, and Spanish colonies taken since

1805. Beyond the direct actions against Britain, the French and Russian emperors pledged to promote the blockade of ports in Denmark, Portugal, and Sweden, and to encourage these powers to declare war on Britain. Finally, Alexander promised to hand over the Ionian Islands to France and withdraw the Russian navy from the Adriatic Sea.

Emperor Alexander's concessions to Napoleon were substantial, but the Russian monarch also seemed to get what he wanted from his would-be ally. The French emperor agreed to mediate in Russia's war with the Ottoman Empire, which had broken out in 1806. If mediation failed, Napoleon promised to support Alexander against the Ottomans. In this scenario, Russia would be required to vacate strongholds in the eastern Mediterranean occupied between 1798 and 1806, while France would accept Russian control over the Ottomans' European provinces of Moldavia and Wallachia. If, however, Russia and the Porte reached an agreement, Alexander would at a future (unspecified) time withdraw his troops from the Danubian Principalities. Finally, the two emperors pledged that France and Russia would fight together as allies in the event of a European war.

Despite the displays of friendship on view in Tilsit and Erfurt, the years of peace from 1807 to 1812 turned out to be an uneasy breathing spell for both empires. "The probability of a new war between Russia and France came into being nearly at the same time as the Peace of Tilsit."[25] This was the judgment in 1812 of Russian statesman Mikhail M. Speranskii (1772–1839), who added that "the peace itself included nearly all the elements of a war." For just as Russia could not "maintain this peace exactly," France could not "believe that the peace would be maintained."[26] Napoleon's hope that he could use the Russian alliance to undermine Britain's economic strength came to naught. The commercial relationship between Britain and Russia had been robust since the sixteenth century. Although in Tilsit Emperor Alexander implicitly adhered to the Continental Blockade, which had been established in 1806 to strangle the British economy, he generally neglected to enforce the ban on trade. In November 1807 Russia broke diplomatic relations with Britain but then never followed up with any military action. As the neglect to act illustrated, the Peace of Tilsit "offered both sides astonishing opportunities to evade unpleasant obligations or to deduce their own claims from the treaty."[27]

Over time, the avoidance of obligations gave way to overtly hostile acts. In 1809 Napoleon challenged Russian interests by incorporating western Galicia, Polish lands taken from Austria, into the Grand Duchy of Warsaw. The Polish question, which during the Congress of Vienna would come close to starting a war among the peacemakers, could not have been more critical for Russia.

Clearly, Emperor Alexander, whose grandmother Catherine II had spearheaded the partitions of the Polish-Lithuanian Commonwealth, did not want to see a strong, independent, or French-dominated Polish state on the western border of his empire.[28] Further French aggressions followed in July 1810 when Napoleon annexed the Kingdom of Holland. Then in December he incorporated the Hanseatic cities of Hamburg, Bremen, and Lübeck, as well as Lauenburg, the territory from Lippe on the lower Rhine to Steckenitz, and the Duchy of Oldenburg. Alexander's sister Catherine was married to the heir apparent of Oldenburg, and the security of the duchy had been explicitly guaranteed by Tilsit.

At the same time that Napoleon displayed increasingly aggressive behavior, Emperor Alexander also violated the spirit of Tilsit. The Russian monarch rejected the Trianon Tariff of August 1810, which heavily taxed British colonial products arriving on neutral ships. In addition, he refrained from closing Russia's ports to the neutral ships that commonly carried British goods. Finally, in December 1810, Alexander openly refused to abide by the rules of the Continental Blockade and even imposed duties on products, primarily of French origin, brought to Russia by land. Napoleon's inability to cripple Britain meant that Alexander's reluctance to act on economic promises carried military implications. Nor did the offenses end there: instead of accepting Napoleon's proposal for the hand of his sister Anna Pavlovna, the Russian monarch suggested postponement due to the girl's young age. Snubbed by Alexander, Napoleon decided to marry Marie Louise of Austria. The marriage negotiations, like the implementation of trade policies, illustrated the Janus-faced nature of the Russian-French alliance. Both parties sidestepped its spirit and concrete provisions. Starting in 1811 and continuing into early 1812, officials in Russia and France talked openly of possible hostilities. The game of chance came to an end, as both countries prepared for war.

The war in Russia started on 24 June 1812, when Napoleon's Grand Army, "one of the largest armies the world had ever seen," crossed the Nieman River. The French forces consisted of 368,000 infantry, 80,000 cavalry, and more than 1,000 guns.[29] From the outset, Russia's military leaders relied on tactics of deep retreat, meaning that they avoided giving battle in order to preserve the fighting capability of their forces.[30] In mid-August, when the French reached Smolensk, the Russians absorbed a two-day assault before setting the city ablaze and leaving it to the enemy. Throughout the war of 1812 Russia's strategic patience and tactics of retreat proved effective against the combat and logistical capabilities of Napoleon's army. French troops carried supplies for just twenty-four days and therefore lacked sufficient shelter and provisions. Napoleon had not prepared for a lengthy campaign, hoping instead to inflict a lethal blow that would force Alexander into speedy accommodation. After the Russians retreated from Smolensk, Napoleon pressed onward to Moscow. Russia's military commanders responded by forcing upon the French a brutal war of attrition.

On 5–7 September, near the village of Borodino, located 120 kilometers west of Moscow, the French and Russian armies met directly on the field of battle. French troops numbering 135,000 faced a Russian force of 125,000 in one of the most vicious contests of the entire Napoleonic era. The dead and wounded on both sides reached harrowing numbers: 58,000 Russian and 50,000 French casualties.[31] Military historians call the Battle of Borodino a draw, though the Russians handed Napoleon a nominal victory by again withdrawing from direct combat. This left the road to Moscow wide open, and on 14 September, Napoleon's army occupied Russia's ancient capital, the site of Romanov coronations since the founding of the dynasty in 1613. Mirroring the tactics of deep retreat, Moscow officials had evacuated most of the city's 300,000 inhabitants. Napoleon's Grand Army entered a ghost town instead of the vibrant second capital of the Russian Empire.

For the French troops, conditions in Moscow quickly deteriorated. Fires broke out almost immediately, destroying the grand and modest homes where Napoleon's men could have quartered, as well as the stores of grain and ammunition that could have supplied their needs. Indeed, by the time the fires were brought under control, one-half to two-thirds of the city had burned down. In mid-October, roughly one month after Napoleon's entry into Moscow, the supply situation became untenable, and the French army began to withdraw. But Russia had not yet won the war. On 24–25 October, at Maloiaroslavets, the two armies again met in battle. Napoleon tried but failed to destroy the main Russian force commanded by General Field Marshal Mikhail I. Kutuzov (1747–1813). Again, in military terms, the battle proved indecisive, as each side suffered casualties of about 7,000 men.[32] Despite the balance of losses, after the Battle of Maloiaroslavets, the French retreat became a catastrophe.

The last major clash between the opposing armies took place at Viazma on 3 November, and for once French losses significantly surpassed those of Russia. Yet even in these circumstances, Russia's commanders did not seek to destroy Napoleon's forces and again pulled back from further military action. In the words of Dominic Lieven, Kutuzov "preferred to leave the job to the winter." Despite milder than normal weather, "Russian Novembers are cold, especially for exhausted men who sleep in the open, without even a tent, with very inadequate clothing, and with little food."[33] The warmer temperatures created the additional problem of thawed ice on the Berezina River. As the French retreated, Russian troops and partisans on both sides of the river kept up attacks on Napoleon's soldiers. When unusually deep cold did come in December, the French army already had been decimated. Of roughly 100,000 men who left Moscow, 60,000 reached Smolensk, and only 40,000 departed the Russian Empire.[34]

To this day, the decision to leave Moscow to Napoleon remains controversial. The occupation and destruction of the city represented a blow to the spirit of the Russian people. Across generations, the experience has been seared into public consciousness by the depiction in Leo Tolstoy's *War and Peace*. But Russia survived the loss, eventually to triumph, and throughout the crisis Emperor Alexander preserved his dignified determination. Repeatedly, the monarch ignored offers of peace put forward by Napoleon. Strengthened by spirituality and Orthodoxy, he weathered the dire circumstances of 1812. Alexander sought solace in daily Bible readings, an activity that in no way indicated a flight into religious mysticism. To the contrary, the monarch's religious experience helps to explain his ability to carry on the war beyond Russia's borders, his subsequent commitment to peace, and the pragmatic flexibility of his foreign policy. Emperor Alexander and his subjects found strength in Christian belief and in the knowledge of their providential role in human history. As the monarch wrote to his friend, ober-procurator of the Synod Prince Aleksandr N. Golitsyn (1773–1844), "in moments such as those in which we find ourselves, I believe that even the most hardened person feels a return toward his creator. . . . I surrender myself to this feeling, which is so habitual for me and I do so with a warmth, an abandon, much greater than in the past! I find there my only consolation, my sole support. It is this sentiment alone that sustains me."[35] After Napoleon's army left Russia, and for virtually the rest of Emperor Alexander's reign, the trauma of the invasion both tested and fueled his resolve.

Following the flight from Russia, more than a year would pass before the allies finally defeated Napoleon and removed him from power. In the spring and summer of 1813, Austria, Britain, Prussia, Russia, and Sweden formed yet another coalition against France. Hostilities began in August, and in mid-October, the Battle of the Nations at Leipzig sent Napoleon's army retreating across the Rhine River. Over the next several months, the French suffered a series of setbacks. The Confederation of the Rhine came apart, the Dutch provinces rebelled, and the Austrians achieved military victories in northern Italy. In Spain, where since the summer of 1808 resistance to Napoleonic domination had been ongoing and supported by British troops, fighting continued, and French losses mounted. At the beginning of 1814 allied forces finally crossed the Rhine, and on 31 March,

Alexander I and Frederick William III rode into Paris. Napoleon abdicated in April and went into exile on the island of Elba. The Bourbon dynasty returned to power when Louis XVIII, brother of the guillotined Louis XVI, ascended the throne as a constitutional monarch. The peacemaking process began immediately in Paris and continued in Vienna later that year, only to be interrupted by Napoleon's return to power in March 1815. Fortunately for the cause of peace, the Hundred Days passed quickly. In June a combined force of Belgian, British, Dutch, and German troops under the command of the Duke of Wellington, who had led successful military operations in Spain, routed Napoleon at Waterloo. On 21 June, Napoleon abdicated for the second time and on 15 July he was sent into remote exile on Saint Helena. There he died on 5 May 1821 at a time when post-Napoleonic peacemaking still demanded constant attention from his opponents.

THE RUSSIAN MONARCHY that helped to forge the European peace had been strengthened, not weakened, by the Napoleonic Wars. Educated in the Enlightenment culture of the Catherinian court, Emperor Alexander I continued the policies of political reform and cultural advancement pursued by his predecessors.[36] Within Russia this meant the improvement of justice and administration, consideration of constitutional projects, the establishment of state schools, the enhancement of educational requirements for advancement in military and civil service, and lavish support for letters, arts, and sciences. Alexander's government also introduced modest reforms to curb the abuses of serfdom, and in the Baltic provinces of Courland, Estonia, and Livonia, carried out an emancipation without guaranteed access to land. Although indicative of humanitarian concerns, none of these measures indicated a serious commitment to the abolition of serfdom, which remained the backbone of Russia's military system. Nor did the political reforms place formal limits on the monarch's absolutist power or even institutionalize consultation with representatives of the nobility and educated service classes. In a word, the authority of the Russian monarchy, legitimized by the Russian Orthodox Church and defended by a peasant army, remained uncontested.

Intellectual dissent had begun to make inroads in the late eighteenth century, and by the time of Alexander's death in December 1825, produced open rebellion. But this development did not prevent the monarchy, church, and educated elites from uniting around the idea that the conditions of human life could be improved through lawful reform, educational progress, and Christian morality. The servicemen who assisted Emperor Alexander in the peacemaking of 1815 to 1823 clearly shared this outlook. Most of the monarch's diplomats originated from the educated Russian, Ukrainian, and Baltic German nobilities who dominated the empire's service classes. A second diplomatic cohort entered Russian service from other European countries, including Poland, at the end of the eighteenth or beginning of the nineteenth century. Finally, the diplomatic corps contained sons of foreigners who long had served the Russian monarchy. As a group, Alexander's high-level diplomats, born primarily in the 1760s, 1770s, and 1780s, were individuals who had grown up in multilingual, multiconfessional, and multiethnic environments and who moved easily in the highest government and social circles of Europe's cosmopolitan capitals and courts.[37]

Emperor Alexander's co-ministers of foreign affairs embodied the worldly qualities of the diplomatic elite. Count Karl V. Nesselrode, minister of foreign affairs under Alexander I and Nicholas I (ruled 1825–55), was born in Lisbon, where his father served as Russia's envoy. Nesselrode was baptized in the Anglican Church and completed gymnasium in Berlin. His Catholic father came from an ancient family of German counts and his Lutheran mother from a family of wealthy merchants. Nesselrode's co-minister, Count Ioannis A. Kapodistrias, originated from the Greek aristocracy of Corfu, received his education at the University of Padua, and served in the government of the Ionian Islands (the Republic of the Seven United Islands) under Russian protection. After the terms of Tilsit transferred the islands to French protection, Kapodistrias entered Russian service. During the European restorations, Nesselrode and Kapodistrias dominated Russia's foreign policy, but other diplomats shared their social profile and cultural orientation. David M. Alopeus, the son of a noble from Finland, received his education in Berlin and Stuttgart. Ivan O. Anstett entered Russian service from French service in 1789. Prince Adam E. Czartoryski originated from a family of Polish magnates but ended his life in exile in Paris. Andrei Ia. Italinskii came from the lesser nobility of Ukraine, graduated from the Kiev Theological Academy, and studied medicine in Saint Petersburg, Edinburgh, and London. Prince Christoph A. Lieven belonged to a renowned family of Baltic German nobles who served the Russian monarchy in numerous military and civil capacities. Peter I. Poletika, also a Ukrainian noble, was born in Kiev province to a Turkish mother captured in the siege of Ochakov. Count Karl O. Pozzo di Borgo represented Corsica in the French Constituent Assembly in 1789–91. A royalist, he emigrated in 1796, entered Russian service in 1805, and became Alexander's minister in Paris in 1814. Not surprisingly, among Emperor Alexander's diplomatic agents, one also finds representatives of Russia's great noble families: Prince Dimitrii I. Dolgorukii, Prince Andrew K. Razumovskii, Baron Grigorii A. Stroganov, and Dmitrii P. Tatishchev.

These are just a few of the men who served Emperor Alexander as professional diplomats. Diverse in their national and religious origins, educational experiences, and career paths, their common language was usually French, and their common loyalty was always to the monarch they served, the personification of Russia's power and greatness. As the foot soldiers of Alexander's foreign policy, they proved capable of putting before the monarch divergent points of view and of taking the initiative in complicated diplomatic negotiations. Yet for as long as they remained in Russian service, they worked faithfully to fulfill the wishes and execute the policies of Emperor Alexander. As the author of Russian foreign policy and as a leading peacemaker in Europe, Alexander expected his diplomatic agents, in their dealings with other powers, to speak his voice collectively and harmoniously. During the years from 1815 to 1823, the diplomats did just that, laboring tirelessly alongside their sovereign to construct and preserve the European peace.

CHAPTER I

Pacification and Peace (1815–17)

T HE HISTORY OF PACIFICATION and peace after the victory over Napoleon in 1814–15 provides unique insight into how Europe's diplomats, socialized and educated in the reformist spirit of the late eighteenth century, responded to changed historical conditions that required imaginative thinking and the recalibration of social and political expectations. The efforts of Europe's post-Napoleonic peacemakers succeeded in some respects and failed in others. Their policies could be progressive and farsighted, but also narrow-minded and self-interested. They left behind a world dominated by great powers in pursuit of empire and riches—a world full of violence, prejudice, cruelty, and exploitation—but they also led their respective societies into a process of accommodation to liberal democratic change. The overarching result of their labors, after more than two decades of excruciating warfare and exhausting diplomacy, was that European society became a little more pluralistic and a little more civilized.

A mélange of ingredients from the so-called old and new regimes, the peace settlement that ended the Revolutionary and Napoleonic Wars has occupied the attention of generations of scholars.[1] Writing in multiple European languages, historians have produced high-quality studies that incorporate a variety of perspectives—national, international, political, diplomatic, military, strategic, and cultural.[2] Recent scholarship stresses the novelty of France's mobilization for revolutionary war and the originality of the peacemakers who brought the wars to an end. From the conduct of total war to the evolution of diplomatic protocol to the chess game of international politics, the impact of new ideas and practices dominates current approaches to study of the era.[3] Consistent with the focus on innovation, scholars argue that the Vienna peace settlement represented not a restoration of the old regime or of the prerevolutionary international order, but rather the codification of new legal principles and procedures for the conduct of European politics and the organization of European society. Eloquently and persuasively set forth in the works of Paul W. Schroeder and others, this interpretation holds that the treaties produced by the Congress of Vienna (1814–15) replaced eighteenth-century balance-of-power politics, which encouraged conflict, greed, and aggression, with a new understanding of European order or the European equilibrium (*l'équilibre européen*) based on mutual restraint, multilateral cooperation (the concert), and respect for treaties, international law, the principle of legitimacy, and the rights of states and nations.[4]

The distinction drawn between the Westphalia state system, which relied on the principle of a balance of power, and the Vienna system, which deployed grouping methods to prevent great power aggression, has in recent years led scholars to see in the diplomacy of the Restoration era a model for world governance in the twentieth and twenty-first centuries. Thus, historians depict the new public law of Europe—elaborated in the treaties of 1814–15 and in the mechanisms of collective security established by regular congresses, conferences, and allied consultations—as the precursor to European integration, the European Parliament, the European Union, the United Nations, and other present-day institutions of world governance. Jennifer Mitzen, for example, highlights the principles of shared European governance enshrined in the Vienna settlement when she characterizes the "Concert of Europe" as "the first international public power." O. V. Orlik's analysis of Russian foreign policy after 1815 describes the Treaty of the Holy Alliance (14/26 September 1815) as Russian emperor Alexander I's European idea, a form of European unity designed to strengthen conservative principles of reaction, legitimism, and restoration. Mark Jarrett similarly claims that Alexander I intended the "Congress System" to function as an "embryonic world government."[5] The effort to achieve an enduring peace based on multilateral treaties, ongoing cooperation, and face-to-face conferences that addressed recalcitrant problems and immediate crises surely required original thinking and enlightened perspectives; however, when historians use anachronistic phrases such as "global governance," "a kind of 'constitutional' order," and "a European legal space," they exaggerate the extent to which systemic integration, behavioral psychology, modern jurisprudence, and even constitutional politics were characteristic of the early nineteenth century.[6]

There is, however, another body of recent scholarship devoted to the Congress of Vienna that provides a more critical and traditional perspective. Adam Zamoyski emphasizes the emergence of great power politics and domination by four or five states in Napoleonic and post-Napoleonic Europe.[7] According to Zamoyski, the Vienna settlement allowed a handful of great powers—in this case Austria, Britain, France, Prussia, and Russia—to impose their will on smaller, relatively vulnerable states.[8] In more nuanced studies that also stress the postwar dominance of the four great powers (Austria, Britain, Prussia, and Russia) or the hegemony of Britain and Russia in deciding territorial arrangements and regulating the peace, there is less emphasis on the Vienna settlement as a security regime or culture and more attention to the mechanisms of strategic restraint that were put into place.[9] In order to make the peace terms palatable to victors, vanquished, bystanders, and secondary players alike, the great powers accepted limits on their own power without, however, giving up their postwar gains. The result was a system of consensus, a "mutually restraining partnership" rather than a "balance against potential aggressors." Based on a belief in eternal principles, a commitment to moderation, the rejection of territorial aggrandizement, and the organization of direct meetings between rulers or their plenipotentiaries, the institutional innovation of the Vienna settlement lay in the ability of the allies to continue into the postwar era the consultations that had led to the defeat of Napoleon.[10] The promise to hold peacetime conferences to address matters of common concern represented the creation of an "ongoing joint management mechanism." Although this mechanism fell short of any specific obligation to provide "mutual protection and enforcement," it repeatedly created opportunities for the great powers to monitor and influence one another's policies and actions.[11]

Also highlighted by recent scholarship is Russia's critical military and diplomatic role in the Restoration era. From the 1790s, Russian policymakers and intellectuals grappled with the question of how to achieve peace and stability in Europe. In the process of conceptualizing European order, they developed ideas about the empire's place in Europe and the larger world. Based on Russian diplomatic communications (usually written in French), this chapter highlights the perspective brought to the Vienna settlement by the empire's historical experience and political practices. The thinking and sentiments of Emperor Alexander I largely defined Russian diplomacy; however, this diplomacy should not be described as the product of a "highly personal and erratic foreign policy."[12] To the contrary, close attention to Russia's understanding of the Vienna settlement reminds scholars that, as Henry Kissinger and his interpreters repeatedly note, the foreign policy of a country or people is rooted in its historical self-awareness, memory, and consciousness.[13] The Russian story also reminds historians that a social science or structural approach to the study of diplomacy—one that focuses on "the question of decisive determinants. . . and their correlations as far as domestic, economic, and international politics are concerned"—cannot effectively account for the messy process of interpreting the terms of the peace and applying them to specific developments on the ground.[14]

The Legal Settlement

Historians date Enlightenment discussions of perpetual peace that envisioned a league of independent European states to the period when the treaties of Utrecht (1713–14) concluded the War of the Spanish Succession (1701–14). By the 1780s the idea of codifying international law to provide the basis for everlasting peace among civilized (read Christian) states appeared in the writings of Jeremy Bentham.[15] Of more immediate significance for this study, the complicated coalition politics that ultimately led to the military defeat of Napoleon and the peace settlement reached at the Congress of Vienna began as early as the summer of 1792 in the wake of the French Revolution and onset of the revolutionary wars. According to historians of Russia, Emperor Paul repeatedly expressed interest in conference diplomacy, and in 1804–5, Emperor Alexander I and his diplomatic agents—for example, assistant foreign minister and Polish patriot Prince Adam E. Czartoryski—developed proposals for an enduring peace in Europe. Communicated in September 1804 to the British government by Nikolai N. Novosil'tsev, one of the monarch's "young friends" and member of the Unofficial Committee, the proposals grew out of negotiations for a military alliance against Napoleon that also articulated general plans for the organization of Europe after France's defeat.[16] The principles presented in the Russian proposals included: (1) recognition of a right to neutrality; (2) the idea that nations should live under political arrangements corresponding to their character; (3) acknowledgment that the world had changed and that the sacred rights of humanity should be respected; (4) acceptance of the need to prevent further revolutions, which could only lead to war; (5) recognition that while principles were universal, their applications varied depending on the locality and people involved; (6) the commitment to administer institutions in a spirit of wisdom and benevolence; (7) the idea of a European federation or league of nations based on respect for nations/peoples, international law (the law of nations), and principles that could serve as the foundation for all European politics; (8) the idea that no government should declare war without first seeking mediation; and finally, (9) the need for an international system to guarantee the peace.[17] Although vague and multifaceted, the principles set forth in the Russian proposals made their way into the peace treaties of 1814–15.

The British response, delivered by William Pitt the Younger in a state paper of 19 January 1805, preferred the language of confederacy or alliance rather than league or federation, but nonetheless accepted the idea of an association of states under Russian and British protection designed to ensure the rights of peoples.

Among the concert of measures presented as acceptable to the British and Russian governments, the state paper envisioned "at the restoration of peace, a general agreement and Guarantee for the mutual protection and security of different Powers, and for re-establishing a general system of public law in Europe." To give solidity and permanence to the peace, the paper proposed "a Treaty to which all the principal Powers of Europe should be parties, by which their respective rights and possessions... shall be fixed and recognized; and they should all bind themselves mutually to protect and support each other, against any attempt to infringe them." The treaty would "re-establish a general and comprehensive system of public law in Europe, and provide, as far as possible, for repressing future attempts to disturb the general tranquility; and above all, for restraining any projects of aggrandizement and ambition similar to those which have produced all the calamities inflicted on Europe since the disastrous era of the French Revolution." The treaty would be placed under the special guarantee of Great Britain and Russia, by which the two powers would commit "jointly to take an active part in preventing its being infringed."

In April 1813, as the alliance that eventually defeated Napoleon took shape, British foreign secretary Robert Stewart, Viscount Castlereagh, forwarded a copy of the state paper of 1805 to the British ambassador in Saint Petersburg, Viscount William Cathcart.[18] According to Castlereagh, even though some of the suggestions made in 1805 no longer applied, the dispatch remained a "masterly outline for the restoration of Europe," which the ambassador was instructed to discuss with Emperor Alexander I.[19] As Pitt's state paper highlighted, the Novosil'tsev mission concerned the formation of a British-Russian alliance to defeat Napoleon, restore the balance of power in Europe, and create a new system of international law.[20] These goals could be pursued and implemented in a variety of ways. For this reason, not all historians are convinced that Alexander's proposals of 1804 actually constituted a plan for perpetual peace. Another decade passed, moreover—a decade filled with volatile coalition politics, failed alliances, broken peace treaties, and bloody military defeats—before the diplomats and statesmen of Europe came together to work out the details of what they hoped would be a stable peace settlement.[21]

Concrete construction of the edifice of pacification and peace began with the Treaty of Chaumont, a military alliance against France concluded on 17 February/1 March 1814. In this treaty, the future peacemakers began to conceptualize the reconstitution of European order, European society, and the European political system—a task they would not complete until the Congress of Aix-la-Chapelle in 1818, when France rejoined the European alliance as one of five great powers. Following Napoleon's final defeat in June 1815, the specific agreements identified as the Vienna settlement included the Treaty of Chaumont, the First Treaty of Paris (18/30 May 1814), the Final Act of the Congress of Vienna (28 May/9 June 1815), the Treaty of the Holy Alliance (14/26 September 1815), the Second Treaty of Paris (8/20 November 1815), the Quadruple Alliance (8/20 November 1815), and the protocols and declaration of the Congress of Aix-la-Chapelle (3/15 November 1818). Taken as a whole, these treaties, conventions, and protocols constituted the public law of Europe and therefore defined the legal framework for European diplomacy, interstate communications, and relations between governments and peoples until the outbreak of World War I, or from the Russian perspective, until the Crimean War of 1853–56.

The Treaty of Chaumont, preceded by Foreign Secretary Castlereagh's project for a "Treaty of Alliance Offensive and Defensive against France" (18 September 1813), was signed separately by each of the four powers—Austria, Britain, Prussia, and Russia—with the other three.[22] At the time, the allies were conducting peace negotiations with France, and in the event that Napoleon rejected the terms offered, the signatories pledged to prosecute a vigorous war to end the misfortunes afflicting Europe and to reestablish a just equilibrium among the powers. Each government agreed to contribute 150,000 soldiers toward the war effort and promised not to sign any separate peace or truce with the enemy, a particularly significant provision in light of the anti-French coalitions that since 1792 repeatedly had collapsed. Britain also promised to pay the allies an annual subsidy of five million pounds sterling for the duration of the war.[23] In addition, at the conclusion of peace with France, the allies would commit to guarantee the rights and liberties of all European nations by acting in concert to prevent France from disturbing the provisions of the settlement. If any of the four powers faced the danger of a French attack, the others promised to intervene to thwart the aggression. Finally, all hostilities, current and future, would be ended by common agreement among the allies united in a defensive alliance against France.

Because the alliance aimed to preserve the equilibrium in Europe, ensure the repose and independence of the powers, and prevent future invasions, the contracting parties accepted the terms for a period of twenty years and agreed to consider a possible extension three years before the date of expiration. More concretely, a separate set of secret articles outlined the specifics of a broader European peace. Germany would be composed of independent sovereign states united in a confederation for purposes of military defense, and Switzerland's independence would be guaranteed by the allies. Italy would be divided into independent states that would serve as intermediary bodies between France and Austria's Italian territories. Spain would be governed by King Ferdinand VII, and Holland would become a free and independent state ruled by the prince of Orange (the future King William II) with augmented territory and suitable borders.[24] Finally, even after the anticipated peace with France became reality, the allies promised to maintain an army on a temporary basis to strengthen the settlement and ensure implementation.

The next step in pacifying Europe and building the peace came after Napoleon's abdication and exile to Elba in April 1814 and the return of the Bourbons to the French throne under King Louis XVIII. By the First Treaty of Paris, the French king and the allies (Austria, Britain, Portugal, Prussia, Russia, Spain, and Sweden) accepted a France confined to the borders of 1792 with the addition of territories in Savoy and the Palatinate. Described by historians as generous and not at all punitive, the peace assigned to France, clearly the aggressor, more than 600,000 inhabitants over its population of January 1792. Nor did the allies impose war reparations, limits on the size of the French army, or border changes along the Pyrenees. The treaty also allowed France to keep art treasures taken during the wars, and most of the French overseas colonies seized by Britain were returned.[25] France reciprocated by renouncing all territorial claims in Belgium, Germany, Holland, Italy, Malta, and Switzerland. Based on additional secret clauses, France ceded Venetia to Austria and Genoa to the Kingdom of Sardinia, the Habsburg-Lorraine dynasty of Ferdinand III was restored in Tuscany, and the Austrian border with Italy was fixed at the Po River and Lake Maggiore. Secret provisions also envisioned an independent German Confederation and recognized the incorporation of Belgium into Holland. The allies agreed that to ensure peace and security in an integrated Europe, France must be strong and stable. For this reason, Britain and Russia favored a constitutional charter for France and a peace of equilibrium. Although significant segments of the French population opposed the final terms of the European settlement, believing that the victors had punished and subjugated their country, historians generally conclude that on average, defense, safety, and the spirt of reconciliation held sway.[26]

The edifice of pacification and peace remained incomplete, however, and so the allies agreed to convene a congress in Vienna to decide outstanding issues: the Polish and Saxon questions, the reorganization of Germany, and territorial adjustments in Germany, Holland, Italy, and Switzerland.[27] For Russia the future of Poland was paramount. The once powerful Polish-Lithuanian state had ceased to exist in the late eighteenth century following three partitions spearheaded by Russia, which also handed over Polish territories to Austria and

Prussia (1772, 1793, and 1795). By the Treaty of Tilsit (25 June/7 July 1807) between France and Russia, Emperor Alexander had accepted the creation of the Duchy of Warsaw, which restored the Polish state and placed it under the king of Saxony.[28] But in 1814–15, Alexander became determined to dissolve the Duchy of Warsaw and replace it with a Polish kingdom tied to Russia by a constitution that granted administrative autonomy, recognized a budgetary role for the diet, and crowned the Russian tsar king of Poland.[29] To reconcile Alexander's plans for Poland with the commitment to return Prussia to its territorial expanse and population of 1805–6, the monarch hoped to compensate Frederick William III with Saxony. Allied discussions began in September 1814, and by October it became clear that Castlereagh and Austrian foreign minister Prince Clemens von Metternich opposed efforts to dispossess or remove the king of Saxony. They instead argued that the king's removal would violate the principle of legitimacy (even though he had been slow to abandon Napoleon).[30]

Negotiations continued into 1815 and throughout the Congress of Vienna, which began in mid-September 1814.[31] Thanks to the personal relationship between the Prussian and Russian monarchs and to Frederick William's loyalty to Alexander, Prussia refused to enter into agreements designed to thwart Russia's plans. Eventually the Russian ruler had his way, though not before his military governor in Saxony handed over provisional administration of the territory to Prussia (8 November 1814) and not before Austria, Britain, and France concluded a secret defensive alliance directed against Prussia and Russia (3 January 1815).[32] Emperor Alexander, a resolute empire builder like his grandmother Catherine II, believed that Russia possessed a moral right to Poland, that the happiness of the Polish people depended on the restoration of a unified national life, and that a united Poland under the Russian crown would help to ensure European security. In December 1814 and January 1815, to achieve this broader goal, Alexander accepted territorial compromises in Poland and recognized that not all of Saxony could go to Prussia. By mid-December, Austria and Britain became reconciled to Russia's position, even though the question of Saxony remained unresolved. Final agreement occurred in February 1815. Austria retained Galicia and made gains in Italy, Cracow became a free city, and Prussia received about half of Saxony's territory and two-fifths of its population, in addition to Swedish Pomerania, the Duchy of Westphalia, and much of the left bank of the Rhine.[33]

The serious tensions among the allies exposed by the Polish-Saxon dispute, France's implicit restoration to great power status as one of "the Five," and the secret defensive alliance directed against Prussia and Russia seemed to evaporate when Napoleon returned to the continent at the end of February, threatening not only the progress of negotiations in Vienna, but also the general peace of Europe. In late March, King Louis XVIII fled to Belgium, and Bonaparte reclaimed the French throne. Throughout the crisis, the Congress of Vienna, which had brought together the representatives of 216 powers (2 emperors, 5 kings, and 209 principalities), continued the work of redrawing territorial boundaries in Europe based on principles of equilibrium and mutual respect among sovereign states.[34] The allies likewise responded to the military danger quickly, effectively, and in unison with a formal renewal of the alliance to overthrow Napoleon (Treaty of 13/25 March 1815).[35] Never mind that war against Napoleon might constitute intervention in France's domestic affairs or that it might violate the right of the French people to choose their ruler and constitution. In this instance, "the Big Eight" (Austria, Bourbon France, Britain, Portugal, Prussia, Russia, Spain, and Sweden) agreed that Napoleon was a criminal who must be defeated.[36] That happened on 18 June at Waterloo, and on 22 June Napoleon abdicated for the second time. On 8 July, Louis XVIII returned to Paris. Despite the dangers, disruptions, and uncertainties of the Hundred Days, the peacemakers signed the Final Act of the Congress of Vienna on 28 May/9 June 1815.[37]

Work at the Congress of Vienna continued over nine months, and by June 1815 the participants had agreed on Europe's territorial boundaries, the form of government to be established in restored and newly independent states, and who would rule in those states.[38] Through land swaps that traded population for population the Final Act of the congress, ratified by all the participants, undid most of the territorial changes imposed by Napoleon. To achieve this outcome, the peacemakers subordinated national sentiments and aspirations to legitimate dynastic claims and the broader geopolitical goals assumed by the four great powers to be in the common interest of all Europe. The Final Act affirmed the First Treaty of Paris and created a German Confederation composed of thirty-nine sovereign states with a federal diet in Frankfurt. The independent states and free cities pledged to join together in a defensive league, the specifics of which would be worked out by the diet.[39] In addition, the Final Act ratified agreements concerning the territorial boundaries and political organization of the United Netherlands (Belgium and Holland), the Ionian Islands, Italy, Scandinavia, and Switzerland.[40] Finally, the proceedings and legislation of the congress established diplomatic regulations and protocols that set the standard for nineteenth-century diplomacy, accepted in principle the abolition of the slave trade, and established international control over the navigation of key rivers.[41] In effect, the Final Act of the Congress of Vienna provided an implicit guarantee of recognition and enforcement by tying together in one package multiple treaties devoted to different situations.

The last components of the legal settlement put into place in 1814–15 consisted of the Second Treaty of Paris and Quadruple Alliance, both of 8/20 November 1815.[42] If the treaties ratified in the Final Act of the congress defined the legal parameters of pacification and peace in Europe, those of November 1815 prescribed how the great powers would regulate and maintain the peace going forward. Not surprisingly, the Second Treaty of Paris imposed harsher terms on France than had the First.[43] Territorial losses returned the country to the borders of 1790: Saarland went to Prussia and part of Savoy to Piedmont. The treaty also levied an indemnity of 700 million francs and a five-year allied military occupation in the north to be funded by France.[44] France agreed to pay for the construction of barrier fortresses in Belgium and Germany as part of the indemnity and to return art works seized during the wars. Most significantly for the future, the allies renewed the Treaty of Chaumont in the form of the Quadruple Alliance and affirmed the twenty-year term. The Quadruple Alliance excluded Bourbon France and established French aggression or the return of Napoleon (or any member of his family) to the French throne as the *casus foederis* or treaty event that would trigger military action by the allies. Based on article 6 of the alliance, the four powers also agreed to call future congresses and conferences to promote peace, prosperity, and the repose of Europe. Described by some historians as an administrative body or a permanent league, the conference of ambassadors established in Paris provided a forum for ongoing diplomatic negotiations to ensure implementation of the Second Treaty of Paris and cooperation on other problems that might arise.[45]

There is a rich historical and juristic literature dating back to the early nineteenth century that depicts the Vienna settlement as a legal system. More recently, Matthias Schulz has referred to instruments of soft and hard power that provided the basis for a collective security mechanism. These included the multilateral guarantee of a territory, the recognized neutrality of a state, the use of mediation to effect compromise, collective dispatches, joint ambassadorial representations, ultimatums, naval demonstrations, naval blockades, and military interventions. Any of these instruments could be deployed collectively or by delegation to individual states, and they could be authorized through diplomatic conferences, congresses, commissions, protocols, and joint communications to the disputing parties.[46] Whether or not these mechanisms rose to the level of a legal system is debatable. It should be noted, moreover, that while Russia invariably claimed to conduct foreign policy based on treaty prescriptions, in Russian governance of the era, justice and strict adherence to the law were not equivalent. Russia was not a rule-of-law state (*Rechtsstaat*), even though the monarchy governed through laws (the rule of laws as opposed to the rule of law). So before declaring the Vienna settlement a coherent legal system, historians must consider how justice was administered and what role law played within specific polities.[47] Different understandings of law and the meaning of legal prescriptions may help to explain the almost immediate disagreements that arose as the powers set out to implement and live by the terms of Chaumont, Paris, and Vienna, and of earlier treaties still in effect.

The Moral Settlement: The Holy Alliance

Emperor Alexander I and his diplomatic agents appreciated the originality of the Vienna settlement; however, their understanding did not give preference to international governance or collective security mechanisms. Nor was their concept of treaty obligations limited to the public law defining territorial arrangements, legitimate political authority, and regular meetings in diplomatic conferences. Of equal significance from the Russian perspective was the Treaty of 14/26 September 1815 (the Holy Alliance), which historians tend to describe either as the cornerstone of a conservative post-Napoleonic foreign policy, designed to prevent revolution by upholding church and monarchy, or as the expression of a proto-Slavophile romantic nationalism inspired by belief in the world historical mission of Orthodox Russia. Although certainly relevant to the history of the Holy Alliance, these interpretations focus more on what the alliance became after the reign of Alexander and less on what it meant at the moment of its inception. In the eyes of Russia's monarch and Ministry of Foreign Affairs, the Holy Alliance functioned as one component in the corpus of European public law that defined territorial arrangements and interstate relations following the victory over Napoleon.[48]

Russian descriptions of the Holy Alliance highlighted the impact of a new moral spirit, visible across Europe, that placed the general interest in peace above the particular interests of territorial states and separate combinations.[49] As the history of Restoration Europe shows, the post-revolutionary need to recalibrate social and political expectations did not require that the peacemakers abandon eighteenth-century principles of enlightened reformism. For this reason, recent biographies consistently make the point that Foreign Secretary Castlereagh, Foreign Minister Metternich, and Emperor Alexander I became successful peacemakers while also remaining men of the moderate mainstream Enlightenment.[50]

Russian efforts to promote the Holy Alliance and explain its relationship to the larger Vienna settlement associated the originality of the peace with lawful political change, Christian morality, and belief in God's providence for His Creation.[51] In other words, the Holy Alliance dovetailed with established eighteenth-century conceptions of good governance and cultural progress.[52]

The Treaty of 14/26 September 1815, signed in Paris by Alexander I, Francis I, and Frederick William III, began by acknowledging the benefactions (*blagodeianiia*) of Divine Providence granted to the monarchs over the past three years.[53] The signatories promised to rule their own states and to organize their relations with other governments in accordance with God's commandments and the divine precepts of love, truth, and peace (*liubov', pravda i mir*), which applied not only to private life but also to political action.[54] More specifically, the three sovereigns pledged to remain united by the bonds of brotherhood, to view one another as countrymen or compatriots (*edinozemtsy*), and to support one another in times of need. Toward their subjects and troops, they would act as fathers, and they would govern in the spirit of brotherhood to preserve faith, peace, and truth (*vera, mir i pravda*).[55] In describing themselves and their peoples as members of a single Christian nation (*narod*), the monarchs vowed to live by God's commandments and to ensure that their subjects did the same. Only through the fulfillment of humanity's duties to God, the treaty proclaimed, could peace be secured. Based on article 3, the signatories agreed to invite the heads of other (European) powers to join the alliance, a step that would obligate them also to govern and order their mutual relations according to the eternal principles of divine law. French King Louis XVIII signed the treaty on 7/19 November 1815, and over the next two years almost every European ruler, great and small, acceded to the alliance. The two exceptions were Pope Pius VII and the prince regent of England (future King George IV). The first rejected the treaty as a violation of Catholic dogma, and the latter, unable to decree the alliance because of the English constitution, nevertheless expressed his support for the Christian principles it professed.[56]

For Emperor Alexander and his diplomats, this act of fraternal Christian alliance embodied the spirit of the European peace, the hand of God in human history, and the role of monarchs as instruments of Divine Providence. In the words of the enlightened Russian statesman Mikhail M. Speranskii, the Holy Alliance emanated not from the self-love or personal actions of the sovereign signatories, but from their having become the organs of a "pure outpouring . . . of Christian goodness."[57] Viewed by Speranskii as "the practical realization of the spiritual function of kingship," the Holy Alliance proclaimed that the purpose of human societies was to lead people to union in Christ, the head of Christian states. The Holy Alliance would endure, moreover, only if sovereigns prayed, read Holy Scripture, and lived as true Christians.[58] Religious teachings about the oneness of church and monarchy, human and providential history, and God's sovereignty over the Christian people had long been pillars of Russian political thought.[59]

From the time of the European Renaissance onward, modern accompaniments to the eternal principles of Christian rulership—ideas about absolutist political authority, the common good, and the social contract—took root across Europe, though in Russia, moral philosophy did not make significant inroads before the late eighteenth century.[60] Even then, as elements of classical and folkloric culture became incorporated into the monarchy's scenarios of power, Orthodox prescriptions dating back to the middle ages held firm. The traumatic experience of 1812 and the military campaigns of 1813–14 further enhanced the Christian foundations of Russian monarchical power. The Treaty of 14/26 September 1815 expressed Alexander I's religious sentiment and sense of God's immediate presence through what today might be called a spiritual experience of existential crisis. Added to the fervor of religious faith were the realities of a Russian government that relied on personalized relationships of authority. In diplomacy, personalized politics translated into bonds of friendship among rulers—friendship that also could be grounded in actual family ties.[61]

Eternal principles, harmonious oneness, and ideals of friendship and family—these aspects of Christian morality, enlightened cosmopolitanism, and sentimentalist empathy all found expression in the lofty abstract language of the Holy Alliance treaty. Consistent with countless legislative acts, official proclamations, and semi-official literary and journalistic compositions, the language of the treaty sounds familiar to historians of eighteenth-and early nineteenth-century Russia. To foreign ears, by contrast, the treaty may seem strange, irrelevant, or even threatening, which is perhaps the reason that modern European historiography so often dismisses or condemns it.[62] That Emperor Alexander was aware of actual and potential criticisms is evident from a rescript of 22 March/3 April 1816 sent to Russia's ambassadors across Europe in which he tried to counter misunderstandings about the purpose of the alliance and provided instructions on how it should be explained to foreign rulers invited to join.[63]

Alexander described the act of alliance as a pledge of unity and harmony brought about by providential action to fight the prevailing spirit of evil. Due to the experiences and struggles of recent years, the monarch and his allies sought to apply to the civic and political relations of states the principles of peace, harmony (*concorde*), and love embodied in Christian morality. Conservative precepts

(*precepts conservateurs*), long relegated to the narrow sphere of individual relationships, would now play a more active and uniform role in political arrangements. After the calamities of recent years, the salutary principles of fraternity and love, the "true source of all civil liberty," needed to be restored. Here, as elsewhere, the peacemakers of 1815 viewed the era of the Revolutionary and Napoleonic Wars as a time of utter moral disaster. The alliance, by contrast, aimed to preserve the peace by rallying the moral interests of peoples that Divine Providence had reassembled under the banner of the cross. In response to persistent fears about Russia's geopolitical intentions, Alexander insisted that the alliance had nothing to do with conquest. Nor could its goals be achieved with the use of military force. Indeed, although the peaceful happiness currently enjoyed by the Christian nations emanated from their religion, the sentiments expressed in the alliance applied to Christians and non-Christians alike. Based on the principles of the Holy Alliance, Emperor Alexander, his brothers in arms, and his allies supported the internal prosperity of individual states and strove to base friendship among rulers on an indissoluble foundation independent of accidental causes.

To address the concerns of non-Christian powers, particularly the Ottoman Porte, and of European states that had not yet acceded to the alliance, Alexander appeared content to rely on diplomatic overtures, carried out in concert with Russia's allies, that proclaimed the peaceful purpose of the alliance. The alliance, Alexander argued, was eminently peaceful because it was religious—a statement that centuries of European history and Russian-Ottoman relations would seem to belie. In 1816, however, the monarch's idealism remained strong. In his view, conservative and immutable principles (*principes conservateurs et immuables*) provided the basis for the act of 14/26 September, which contained nothing contrary to the natural relations of states or to existing treaties. In the old political combinations, which had proven so harmful to the repose and morality of nations, these principles had been forgotten. What made the present alliance unique was precisely the reliance on Christian principles. Explicit recognition of this truth by the allies made the current era a new one for their peoples and for all humanity.

Emperor Alexander ordered that the Treaty of 14/26 September be read out in churches across the empire on 25 December 1815, Christmas day according to the Orthodox calendar in the nineteenth century. As the manifesto explained, the past course of political relations among the European powers had led to tragic consequences for the entire world—consequences that resulted from the absence of political relationships founded upon true principles (*instinnye nachala*) of divine wisdom. Harsh experience had taught Alexander I, Francis I, and Frederick William III that only by means of eternal principles, particularly the divine principle of fraternity, could the peace and flourishing (*pokoi i bla-godenstvie*) of peoples be ensured. To that end, the monarchs had decided to establish a Christian alliance (*soiuz*) and to live as brothers in peace and love.[64]

In the Russian context, the Holy Alliance also carried a deeper politico-religious meaning, signified by the choice of date for the signing. On 14/26 September, Orthodox Christians celebrate the Feast of the Exaltation of the Cross (*Vozdvizhenie*). One of twelve Great Feasts and seven Feasts of the Lord, the Exaltation has longstanding military associations. According to the *Festal Menaion*, the feast highlights the relationship of the cross, rather than the Crucifixion, to the history of the Orthodox Church. The cross is commemorated "in a spirit of triumph" and as a "'weapon of peace and unconquerable ensign of victory' (kontakion of the feast)."[65] Equally significant, the Exaltation is regarded as universal, which is to say that the power of the cross applies to the entire universe, and the salvation it brings affects all creation. In the ceremony of the Exaltation the priest blesses all points on the compass. According to the troparion read at the ceremony, "The four ends of the earth, O Christ our God, are sanctified today."[66] Historical associations also appear in the services for the feast. There are repeated references to the vision of the cross seen by Constantine in 312, shortly before his victory over Maxentius. In addition, the feast recalls the finding of the True Cross by Saint Helen, Constantine's mother, and describes the mass veneration of the cross that occurred in Jerusalem after Helen's discovery. Similarly, the feast commemorates the second great Exaltation of the Cross in Constantinople in 629. In 614 the Persians had captured Jerusalem and taken the cross, which then was recovered by Emperor Heraclius (ruled 610–41), brought to Constantinople, and triumphantly exalted in the Great Church of Hagia Sophia. Finally, the feast alludes to an event commemorated in modern times on 13 September: the dedication of the Church of the Resurrection built by Constantine on the site of the Holy Sepulcher and completed in 335.[67] The reference in the Holy Alliance treaty to the moral interests of peoples being reunited by God under the banner of the cross hints at the Russian association with the Exaltation.

With respect to European politics writ large, the Holy Alliance is best described as the moral component of the Vienna settlement. The edifice of pacification and peace constructed in 1814–15 defined the public law of Europe, and from the perspective of Russian diplomacy, the holy allies placed a moral stamp on the legal arrangements. The text of the Holy Alliance treaty said nothing about acceptable forms of government. The peacemakers recognized that individual states lived under different constitutions, and while it was necessary that governments be legitimate and exercise legal authority, the legitimist principle did not require that they be purely monarchist. Nor were changes to established constitutions illegitimate, as long as these changes occurred by legal means, as opposed to violent or revolutionary action. Alexander's idealism, as expressed in the Treaty of 14/26 September 1815, connected the alliance to a renewed moral spirit based on Christian fraternity that would ensure the peace. Neither the product of religious mysticism nor the cornerstone of a reactionary restoration, the Holy Alliance can be described as the means to implement a large-scale political policy or system grounded in the religious and Enlightenment ideal of a harmonious interlocking universe. Diplomatic communications designed to persuade sovereigns to join the alliance and to counter allegedly erroneous interpretations of the treaty suggest that the Holy Alliance offered more than a statement of moral and political principles, bolstered by pledges of friendship among rulers. In the correspondence of Emperor Alexander and his diplomatic agents, the alliance also established a mechanism for regulating and maintaining the European peace.

Russian Power and Political Relations in Europe

As the process of implementing the peace quickly revealed, it was one thing to agree on principles, however sacrosanct or eternal, and quite another to put them into practice.[68] From the outset Emperor Alexander's role in deciding the Polish-Saxon question and forming the Holy Alliance fueled allied suspicions about Russia's military power and proclaimed rejection of territorial aggrandizement. With hindsight, the principles of Russian policy appear straightforward enough. In defending his own actions and in questioning those of others, Alexander insisted on strict adherence to the treaties of 1814–15. In the larger world of European diplomacy, however, the attention to treaty obligations was not sufficient to allay the allies' distrust.

A clear statement of the Russian effort to address allied fears appeared in a general instruction to diplomatic missions issued by the Ministry of Foreign Affairs on 15/27 May 1815, in the midst of the Hundred Days.[69] The instruction described the basis for political relations among the European powers. States that had joined the European system enjoyed mutual benefits and ties built upon the first causes (*pervonachal'nye prichiny*) found in all civil societies and the new considerations resulting from contemporary conditions. Among the momentous events of the era the instruction identified the origins of the military campaigns of 1812–13; developments leading to the conclusion of peace in Paris; the rules established by the transactions of the Congress of Vienna; the alliance of 13/25 March 1815, which renewed the earlier coalition to defeat Napoleon; and finally, the consequences of the current war, also against Napoleon. After identifying these events with the political foundations of the European system, the instruction highlighted two issues in need of attention: the condition of Europe's political system, including its relationship to the political system of Russia; and the conduct of Emperor Alexander's ministers, who should act consistently to strengthen Russia's peaceful relations with other European powers.

In 1812, the instruction proclaimed, Napoleon had tried to complete the enslavement of the world by invading Russia. Suffering from moral fatigue, the peoples of Europe appeared to accept the inevitability of living under French military despotism. This moral degradation combined with the infamy (*bezslavie*) of governments to fuel Napoleon's power. Although on occasion opposition arose, it lacked sufficient strength to become general or decisive. Eventually, the hope and support needed to overcome Napoleon coalesced, thanks to the firmness (*tverdost'*) of the Russian tsar. Inspired by Russia's military victory in 1812, minds moved to act by revolution and French tyranny took heart. Subjugated governments began to resist and fight for independence. Based on the shared experience of endless hardship, this spirit spread from nation to nation, creating the will to use military force and to introduce representative or constitutional government. Experience, in other words, guided the powers as they worked to rebuild Europe's political system on stable foundations.

Experience likewise showed that no human power could stop the movement of minds or return them to their previous orientation. Thinking had changed. To achieve stability, governments needed to follow wise policies that conformed to the aspirations of peoples. They also needed to maintain the boundaries of authority (*vladenie*), the organization of internal state institutions, and the mutual relations of the powers constituting the great European family. Here the instruction explained how and why the current political system differed from the old political balance (*politicheskoe ravnovesie*), which had relied on the action or effect of weaker states situated between more powerful ones. Because the years of war had sapped moral bonds and mainsprings, and because the influence of military force had increased, states now depended on the possession of sufficient territory to ensure internal stability. In addition, within each state, domestic tranquility required the establishment of wise institutions through constitutional acts. France, for example, possessed ample territory based on the Treaty of 18/30 May 1814 (the First Treaty of Paris); however, Emperor Alexander doubted that the Bourbon dynasty, even when bolstered by other governments, could ensure the stability of Europe or the happiness of the French nation. Only if the people supported the restoration of the monarchy would it succeed.

The instruction of 15/27 May 1815 also addressed concerns about excessive Russian power—concerns that Emperor Alexander hoped to assuage with a policy of moderation. Thus, the Russian monarch had tried to separate diplomatic decisions from the influence of military force, a position illustrated by his interest in assigning to a general congress the task of European restoration. Going forward, diplomatic resolutions should be based on mutual benefit and the sacredness of rights (*sviatost' prav*), as defined by the law of nations (*kodeks narodov*). To ensure stability in Europe, all governments needed effective means to establish legal authority and achieve general trust. At moments when key questions remained undecided—the future of the Belgian provinces, Britain's plans for its colonies and Malta, the borders and political organization of Poland, the constitutional order of the German Confederation, and the assignment of territories to Austria, Italy, and Prussia—Russia had avoided the use of military power to achieve favorable outcomes. While not untrue, this description remained incomplete. In November 1814, in the midst of the Polish-Saxon controversy, Russia's military governor had transferred Saxony to Prussian administration, and Alexander had seemed ready to go to war.[70]

Despite the chronic suspicions and unresolved disputes, the Russian government nonetheless assumed that the allies intended to fulfill the obligations codified in wartime agreements and the [First] Treaty of Paris. Equally important, the Congress of Vienna would enact measures to solidify political equilibrium (*politicheskoe ravnovesie*) among all the states of Europe. To accomplish this goal, the power of each state would be augmented, preferably with contiguous territory, to allow for the preservation of its independence and to prevent any state from violating the independence of others. Clearly, this formulation expressed Russia's understanding of how France could be reintegrated into European society. A state that threatened the peace by infringing the sovereignty of another would meet with a united European response. In other words, any signatory country that broke the rules prescribed by the Final Act of the Congress of Vienna would be considered an enemy in a state of war against other signatories.

When describing political relations in Europe diplomatic communications of Russian provenance invariably presented Emperor Alexander's policies as moderate and his intentions as pure. For example, the monarch always put the law, the well-being of peoples, and the preservation of peace above his own just wishes and even Russia's vital interests. This policy followed from his belief that

Divine Providence governed the fate of states. Changed circumstances came from God, not from human calculations or the efforts of governments. Thus, in connection with the Polish-Saxon question, Alexander had not gone to war over the secret alliance. In addition, he had conceded to Austria and Britain that the Ottoman Empire might be admitted into the Final Act, though only if negotiations with the Porte over disputed provisions in the Treaty of Bucharest continued on a bilateral basis without allied participation.[71]

At the time of writing, the Russian government regarded the alliance of 13/25 March as a success and Napoleon's final dethronement as inevitable. Based on the agreements reached to date, the allies hoped to imbue the new political system with the former respect "for the sacredness of rights, for utility (*pol'za*), and for moral ties." Incrementally, adherence to these principles would make it possible to root out "the pernicious rules introduced by the abuses of military glory." To ensure that all states recognized the advantages of the alliance, Emperor Alexander assumed that the allies always would work toward the common good (*obshchaia pol'za*), whether through military force or legal prescription. Again, the French question represented the key to the Russian formulation. The allied powers would limit their military actions to war with Bonaparte. They would not use violence to compel the French people to accept a political order they did not want, including the return of Louis XVIII. Critical of the Bourbon dynasty, the Russian government insisted that the well-being of France could not be separated from that of Europe. Equally important, governments needed to be in alignment with the wishes of their people. Not at all a plea for democratic politics or a recognition of popular claim making (the will of the people), this principle appeared in numerous Russian documents of the post-war era.[72] In this case, the goal of the great alliance was to establish in France a government that would forever be free of Napoleon and his supporters.

To eliminate the Napoleonic threat to European order, the allies had to do more than remove Bonaparte. The disposition of minds that allowed him to return to power and that encouraged people to accept revolution had to be changed. This could not be achieved by force of arms, but by an enlightened and magnanimous policy that respected freedom (*svoboda/liberale*). Concepts such as freedom or liberal, which should not be read in the modern democratic sense, conveyed a relatively simple message. Effective political authority depended on good governance, which deserved and received the moral support of the people. Indeed, the conceptual novelty of Europe's restored order appeared in the deliberate and explicit attention accorded to the needs and wishes of the people, though without any reference to civil rights, the general will, or popular sovereignty.

Russian worries about the impact of yet another war and the conditions required for a successful outcome extended beyond the problem of political authority in France. The instruction concluded by returning to the theme of unjust and unreasonable distrust of Russia among the allies, despite Alexander I's policies of moderation, discipline, legality, and conservative reform. The visible growth in Russia's military and political power arose from the moral capabilities of the people and therefore represented a natural expansion, not a grab for territory.[73] Russia used its power for the benefit and salvation of other nations. In diplomatic proceedings, the Russian government did not seek primacy, preference, or privilege. Emperor Alexander understood that the favor shown to Russia by Divine Providence and the military brilliance of the Russian people (*narod*) aroused suspicions. Disingenuous or not, the presentation of Russian power as benign and Russian intentions as disinterested would continue over the next two centuries.

The instruction ended with a clear declaration to Russia's ambassadors abroad. They must strive to consolidate the empire's peaceful relations with the European powers and to convince foreign governments of Emperor Alexander's pure motivations. Acceptance of the new political system, based on allied unity, precluded the formation of separate alliances. As Paul Schroeder argues, equilibrium rather than Westphalian balance of power became the order of the day. Yet in May 1815, only Sweden and Prussia appeared convinced of Russia's commitment to peace. To highlight this convergence, Alexander instructed his ambassadors at all the European courts to display sincerity and friendship toward the ministers of these states. To encourage more general trust of Russia, they also should disseminate just information about the progress of the war in the societies where they resided. Finally, Russia's diplomatic representatives should pay close attention to the policies and actions of the governments to which they were accredited and report to Saint Petersburg on how the latest events impacted political conditions in the states where they served.

The Russian experience of distrustful allies persisted throughout 1816 and into the summer of 1817. Diplomatic correspondence involving Emperor Alexander I, co-Minister of Foreign Affairs Karl Nesselrode, co-Minister of Foreign Affairs and State Secretary Ioannis Kapodistrias, Russian ambassador (*posol*) in London Christoph Lieven, Russian envoy (*poslannik*) in Vienna Gustav Stackelberg, and governor-general of the Polish Kingdom Grand Prince Constantine Pavlovich expressed concern about the goals of Austrian and British policy and the need to convince the allies of Russia's peaceful intentions.[74] In a confidential dispatch of 25 January/6 February 1816 addressed to Nesselrode, Lieven reported on tensions between Britain and Russia. Alluding to changes in British policy, he confirmed that the government in London wanted peace, if only because at the moment its primary concerns were domestic.[75] Lord Castlereagh, perhaps encouraged by Austria, feared any action that might disturb the repose of Europe and thus seemed suspicious of Russia. According to Lieven, suspicion arose from the empire's colossal power, the glory attained by its large armies, and the alleged penchant of Emperor Alexander for war. Both Castlereagh and the prince regent affirmed Britain's commitment to the Quadruple Alliance, which obligated the great powers to guarantee the peace and unite against any ally who threatened European order. In addition, the British urged Alexander to handle relations with the Ottoman Empire in a conciliatory manner and promised to facilitate negotiations with Constantinople to prevent further hostilities.

Lieven's dispatch also summarized his reply to Castlereagh, which emphasized Alexander's commitment to the peace he had done so much to achieve. Could the author of such a good deed possibly want to destroy his own work? Castlereagh and the prince regent denied harboring suspicions about Russia's intentions, and both insisted that they had the highest regard for Alexander and his efforts to establish a durable peace. But Lieven characterized the British ruler as a person of weak spirit who appeared jealous of the Russian monarch and of the talents attributed to the Duke of Wellington.[76] Fortunately, according to Lieven, other members of the British government did not share the preference for Austria or the distrust of Russia displayed by Castlereagh and the prince regent, though there was concern about Russia's influence at the courts of France and Spain. Clearly, uncertainties and suspicions persisted; however, Castlereagh also appeared to welcome any proof of Alexander's commitment to peace, including, for example, communications from Poland and the monarch's interest in reforming the internal administration of Russia. Above all, Lieven concluded, the British government continued to appreciate the power of Russia and the advantage of a close and sincere alliance (*union*) with the empire.

In early 1816, tensions among the allies also resulted from Austrian activities in northern Italy, which Russia viewed as a threat to European peace. Through negotiations with the Kingdom of Sardinia, Austria had been trying to gain control of the Simplon Road, which passed through upper Novaria in the region of Piedmont. But the king of Sardinia, supported by Russia, rejected any territorial changes that altered the stipulations of the Vienna treaties. In March, citing the legal obligations enshrined in the Quadruple Alliance, Nesselrode pointed out to the Russian envoy in Vienna, Gustav O. Stackelberg, that the border adjustments proposed by Austria threatened to create new alliances (*combinaisons*) and undermine the restoration of the French monarchy. Such developments would in turn weaken the association of states entrusted with maintaining the European peace.[77]

As the process of implementing European pacification and peace unfolded, the allies struggled to uphold the inviolability of codified principles. To ensure that France did not menace neighboring countries or suffer domestic disturbances, they insisted on the futility of seeking security through alternative alliances. Nesselrode wrote that the moral force of the great alliance had to be preserved, by which he meant that allied courts must subordinate particular interests to the general interest of guaranteeing the tranquility of Europe. In other words, as negotiations continued, no great power (such as Austria) should try to impose its will on a weaker state (such as Sardinia). Nesselrode concluded his dispatch by instructing Stackelberg, in the name of the monarch, to defend the principles of the general system at the court of Vienna. Clearly, Emperor Alexander viewed Austria's negotiations with the king of Sardinia as a violation of the Quadruple Alliance, an opinion he communicated directly in response to an overture from Austrian emperor Francis I. To diminish the force and unity of the alliance constituted a threat to European peace and to Russia's primary goal: consolidation of the order of things established in Europe. Uniformity of action founded on compliance with principles provided the best means to preserve peace. Alexander's appeal to Francis proved effective, and in May 1816 Austria withdrew its claims against the Kingdom of Sardinia.[78]

Strict adherence to treaty stipulations remained a pillar of Russian foreign policy, as diplomats worked to protect the empire's interests and mollify the allies' hostility. On 31 January/12 February 1817, Emperor Alexander approved a personal letter to Stackelberg from Kapodistrias, who was responding to private communications sent by Stackelberg in December 1816.[79] According to Kapodistrias, the Russian government believed that separate alliances such as the secret Treaty of January 1815, directed against Prussia and Russia, originated in the allies' jealousy of the empire's military power and moral influence. In some circumstances, this jealousy might lead to an aggressive policy directed against Russia. But regardless of how other powers of the first order viewed Russia or sought to harm its interests, Alexander remained committed to the immutable principles that provided the basis for Russian foreign policy. This policy aimed to preserve peace through scrupulous execution of established treaty obligations, particularly the Treaty of the Holy Alliance, which Alexander regarded as the cornerstone of the European restoration. Unfortunately, because the pure morality of the Gospel had not penetrated the hearts of allied ministers, as it had the hearts of Alexander's fellow sovereigns, the former pursued a policy at once ambitious and timid.[80]

To highlight Alexander's commitment to the principles of the peace and his desire to consolidate its benefits, Kapodistrias noted that Russia was willing both to accept a degree of isolation and to overlook the intrigues of Austria and Britain. Thus, in matters concerning the German Confederation, Alexander did not want to intervene directly, unless Austrian-Prussian cooperation compelled smaller German states to appeal for assistance. Nor did the emperor see anything alarming in British support for Austrian interests in Italy and the Illyrian provinces (present-day Montenegro and northern Albania) or in Britain's close relationship with Persia, even though this relationship was designed to thwart Russian expansion in the east.[81] Defensive alliances did not threaten allied unity or the eternal principles of the Vienna and Paris treaties, as long as the empire's immediate interests were not affected and the alliances did not become aggressive or hostile toward Russia.

The need to counter allied concerns about Russian power also led Emperor Alexander's diplomats to comment on public discussions. In Kapodistrias's letter to Stackelberg, the co-minister of foreign affairs noted that because the institutions of the old regime had not been fully replaced by new ones, public opinion now played an unprecedented role in mediating social and political order. Kapodistrias's understanding of public opinion had nothing to do with contested politics or unfettered debate. Public opinion was associated with moral authority based on justice and legitimacy (*le bon droit*). In uniting justice and good faith (*la bonne foi*), Divine Providence created an invincible and conservative force (*une force conservatrice*) capable of defeating any power that aspired to universal domination. Thus, the conduct of Emperor Alexander guaranteed the security of his empire, and humanity too learned to avoid political calamities that arose from the vulgar passions of statesmen.

In Stackelberg's response to the instructions from Kapodistrias, the envoy confirmed that Russia's elite stature and military capabilities caused anxiety and jealousy among the great powers.[82] The allies, he wrote, did not understand that Alexander's policy was religious and enlightened or that he was not seeking to expand his empire. Russia's position in Poland represented one source of concern, as did its negotiations with the Ottoman Empire. In addition, Russia's decision to sell warships to Spain had led to rumors about a secret Russian-Spanish alliance. Allegedly, in return for military assistance in the Americas, Spain had agreed to cede to Russia the island of Minorca, so that the empire could moor ships in the Mediterranean. Finally, together with the intrigues of Austria and the phantom fears of Britain about a Russian move against British power in the East Indies (*les grandes Indes*), Stackelberg envisioned the possible development of a German unification or *Germanisme*, including Austria and Prussia, directed against Russia.

The need to address suspicions about Russia's intentions and military power persisted into the spring and summer of 1817. On 1/13 May, Lieven reported to Nesselrode about talks with Castlereagh, during which the ambassador tried to calm British fears.[83] Although the foreign secretary acknowledged the efforts of malicious persons who tirelessly worked to incite agitation, he nonetheless believed that the maintenance of Russia's army on what many considered a wartime footing raised questions about the empire's peaceful intentions. To European states that had reduced the size of their armies, the large number of Russian troops seemed to contradict the government's peaceable declarations. Lieven correctly explained that the distinctive foundations of the Russian army limited the possibility of peacetime cutbacks. But the concerns of Castlereagh went beyond the size of Russia's armed forces. The foreign secretary also believed that Russia's ongoing discussions with the Ottoman Porte about the terms of Bucharest (1812) and earlier treaties allowed these malicious persons to accuse Alexander of harboring plans of conquest. At the same time, Castlereagh recognized that the great and immortal glory attained by the monarch during his last campaigns (against Napoleon in 1813–14) could not be enhanced by additional conquests. Lieven therefore assured Castlereagh that Alexander, whose intentions remained pure and peaceful, was not contemplating military action against the Ottomans. Indeed, the monarch's willingness to publicize discussions with the Porte provided proof of his desire for peace, even though Russia's claims against the Ottoman government were just and moderate. In subsequent decades, at least until the Crimean War of 1853–56, which destroyed the allied unity achieved in 1813–18, Russia would continue to insist that its demands and eventual decisions to go to war resulted from the Porte's violations of recognized treaties.

Another issue discussed in the meetings between Lieven and Castlereagh concerned Russia's ties to Spain, particularly the personal relationship between Dmitrii P. Tatishchev, envoy in Madrid, and the Spanish king, Ferdinand VII. As Stackelberg had reported earlier in the year, suspicions about secret Russian-Spanish accords had spread across Europe. Lieven explained to Castlereagh that Tatishchev exercised no special influence over the king of Spain and that there was nothing unusual about a diplomat enjoying easy access to the court of the sovereign to whom he was accredited. But in the years immediately following the Congress of Vienna, all the allies feared the formation of secret and separate alliances. At the same time, they also understood that European peace depended on maintaining the unity that had made possible the defeat of Napoleon. For this reason, the alliance held, even though ongoing distrust colored the diplomatic thinking of Russia and its allies.

In a dispatch to Lieven sent on 10/22 June 1817, Nesselrode addressed the jealousies and suspicions causing anxiety in the British government.[84] Approved by Emperor Alexander, the dispatch proclaimed the monarch's desire to assuage British fears without, however, harming the legitimacy or dignity of other crowns, including his own. Nesselrode praised Lieven for his explanations to Castlereagh concerning Spain, relations with the Ottoman and Persian empires, and Russia's military posture. Nesselrode admitted that Spain sought to promote its cause in alliance with Russia, though in every situation that had arisen, Alexander had encouraged the king to seek assistance through the great alliance with British mediation. To bolster these arguments and prepare Lieven for his conversations with Castlereagh, the Russian ministry forwarded copies of dispatches sent to Tatishchev. These communications, Nesselrode claimed, showed that Russian policy was based not on private or particular considerations, but on immutable principles.

Interactions with France also led to strong statements of support for the principles and prescriptions of allied agreements. In a dispatch of 21 March/2 April 1817, confirmed by Emperor Alexander, Kapodistrias wrote to Grand Prince Constantine Pavlovich about a formal overture to the allies that affirmed Russia's fixed and immutable viewpoint on all alliances (*combinaisons*) subversive of "the political and social order established by the treaties of Vienna and Paris in the year 1815."[85] Occasioned by the intrigues of French emigres who sought to replace the Bourbon king with a representative of the Russian dynasty or the prince of Orange, Kapodistrias's dispatch identified two republican refugees staying in Warsaw, who were entitled to protection only as long as they did not disturb public order.[86] Kapodistrias asked Constantine to explain the bases of Russian policy to the emigres who sought his support. The edifice of general pacification in Europe rested upon solemn, sacred, and inviolable commitments. In France, "the order of things established in 1815 and cemented by the blood of two generations" was monarchic and constitutional in form. Equally important, all the powers of Europe were bound to respect and ensure adherence to this order, which depended on the principles of religion and justice. No government, moreover, could ignore these principles without attacking its own existence. It was therefore in the interest of France and of every other European state to support the current system and to oppose any new upheaval that undermined the ties already established between governments. In a word, violation of existing social and political agreements could only produce a spirit of conquest and subversion that would threaten peace and the independence of European powers.

Although Emperor Alexander had little confidence in the Bourbons, Kapodistrias's dispatch expressed the view that at last France was on track to reoccupy the honorable position of great power assigned to it by nature. Clearly, the Russian monarch opposed efforts to remove the Bourbons from power. The present government needed to be supported, because its actions represented the best effort to defeat the enemies of peace. National representation, a smaller army of occupation, and the settlement of individual claims (*poursuites*) against the French government illustrated the tendency toward amelioration in France's destiny. Again, Kapodistrias emphasized that the order of things in France had to be respected and that Alexander stood ready "to cooperate with all his power to maintain the rights consecrated by the treaties," whether they be threatened by domestic action or foreign force. The Russian monarch remained absolutely committed to preservation of the just and salutary principles that ensured universal tranquility. Only inviolable adherence to established stipulations could provide the conditions needed for the progress and well-being of peoples. In the eyes of Russia's diplomats, the stipulations contained obligations of a double nature: those between states and those between governments and peoples based on a salutary reciprocity of duties. "The edifice of peace, the dread of factions, and the pitfall of any false policy" rested on these foundations. As long as the relationships of reciprocal duty remained intact, according to Kapodistrias, France had nothing to fear and Europe would enjoy peace. For his part, Alexander would use all the means granted to him by Divine Providence to protect the existing relationships and obligations from anyone who tried to attack them. The treaties of 1814–15 constituted not only the public law of Europe, but also the sacred law of universal peace.

During the years 1816–17, neither political instability in France nor tensions in Russia's relations with Austria and Britain threatened the legal keystones of European order. All the powers believed that the agreed-upon stipulations had to be respected. Suspicions and differences of interpretation arose, but these uncertainties did not weaken the overall commitment to the peace settlement or the political arrangements of any particular country. To ensure that Russia's diplomats understood the principles of tsarist policy and could explain how the government applied them in specific situations, in June 1817 Emperor Alexander sent additional instructions to his missions abroad in the form of an overview (*aperçu*) of Russia's political relations in Europe.[87] The monarch expected his diplomatic agents to approach all issues that might arise from the same point of view and to promote Russian policy with uniform language and conduct. By sending out the overview, the Russian ministry aimed to provide positive directions for the empire's official representatives.

To bolster the confidence of second-order states and to address the suspicions causing anxiety among those of the first order, Emperor Alexander began the instructions by pointing out that he had not created the current policy. To the contrary, the policy or system emanated from "the spirit and the letter of the transactions of Vienna and Paris" concluded in 1815. To preserve the inviolability of these acts, a goal to which all the European powers contributed, remained the sole object of Russian policy. The reasons for the allies' identity of purpose were both moral and political. The moral reasons were carved into the enlightened and pure conscience of every right-thinking person who had witnessed the extraordinary events of the revolutionary period, including the events that had ended that era. The political reasons were consistent with the most essential interests of all the European governments and states, especially those that had been reestablished and reconstructed by the transactions of Vienna and Paris. Emperor Alexander did not yet believe that the European states had succeeded in rebuilding themselves on a solid and natural basis. Those that had emerged from long revolutionary crises continued to search for their line of direction. Others had avoided direct action but still preserved their military posture. All needed, moreover, to undertake, based on different propositions, "the difficult merger of new interests with old habits and of new habits with old interests."

"States have their ages as do men," the overview proclaimed. Governments of the day could not project "the consoling image of a family where order and ease are...inherent in its existence, where domestic peace is not at all a novelty, or an object of discussion, or a problem to resolve." Here Emperor Alexander appeared to acknowledge the turbulence of modern political relations. But contested politics caused him unease, and he insisted that conditions in Russia differed from those in other European countries. All states needed repose in order to survive: Russia enjoyed calm and so did not fear movement. Compared to the power of other states, Russia's was youthful and vigorous. Youthful power needed to act, yet Russia remained peaceful. This led the monarch to conclude that the empire's peaceful policy was voluntary, while that of other states was imposed by circumstances. This difference explained the suspicions caused by Russia's ascendancy in the political order of Europe—suspicions that Alexander hoped to disarm through the example of his conduct. Regardless of the circumstances of one or another power, the Russian Empire's relations with all would be peaceful, amicable, and affectionate in principle, form, and purpose. Not only did Russia proclaim this doctrine, the imperial government put it into practice. Emperor Alexander religiously fulfilled his obligations to all the powers that had acceded to the peace. Equally significant, in excluding from discussion Russia's interests in the Ottoman and Persian empires, the monarch showed the world that neither the force of arms nor that of opinion could add anything to the force of legitimacy (*le bon droit*).

After explaining the principles of tsarist policy, the overview addressed their application and results. Ongoing negotiations between the governments of Austria, Britain, Prussia, and Russia focused on implementation of specific clauses in the treaties of Vienna and Paris. The content of these discussions encompassed the consolidation of thrones, placed under the safeguard of legitimacy; the political and territorial reorganization of Germany; abolition of the slave trade; removal of the Barbary pirates from the Mediterranean; the accession of Spain to the Final Act of the Congress of Vienna; and finally, disagreements that threatened to complicate Spain's relations with the united kingdom of Portugal and Brazil.[88] In the talks devoted to these questions, Alexander ordered Russia's diplomats to refrain from being the first to express an opinion, decision, or vote. In addition, the language they employed needed to be clear, correct, frank, moderate, amicable, benevolent, and true to the text of the treaties. Because of Russia's justice, benevolence, and moderation, the empire exercised a universal ascendancy that jealousy could not undermine. The reason for this was independent of Russia: it resulted from the nature of the current transactions and the spirit of the time.

The treaties of Vienna and Paris had created a universal alliance designed to maintain the current territorial possessions of the signatory states. Participating governments shared a general interest based on the transactions, which meant that they pledged to consult with one another in order to achieve mutual agreement in all relevant matters. This was the primary purpose of the conferences established in Frankfurt, London, and Paris to address issues of common concern to European governments. By taking positions founded on law and directed solely toward the general good, Russia supported parties interested in impartial justice and united the votes of second-order powers and public opinion, which constituted a significant weight in the balance of affairs. The truth, frankness, and precision of Alexander's instructions to his ministers helped to guarantee this result.

The next section of the overview moved beyond general considerations to describe how the principles of Russian policy applied in specific situations.

Austria's efforts to complete its federal policy in Italy by proposing to the king of Sardinia an alliance and territorial changes had blatantly violated existing treaties. Yet after Emperor Alexander explained this to his august ally Emperor Francis, Austria dropped the matter. Based on the intra-German Treaty of Munich (2/14 April 1816), Austria also had requested that Russia agree to guarantee Bavaria's acquisition of the Main-Tauber region. But the treaty neglected to compensate the Grand Duchy of Baden, and so Russia refused to accept the terms. Consequently, the Grand Duke of Baden again controlled the territory, which he remained free to cede in ongoing negotiations. Finally, Austria had proposed that the allies pressure Spain to accept the Final Act of the Congress of Vienna by threatening to deny the infante Marie Louise the territories given to her by the same transaction. The allies resisted the proposal, and in negotiations concerning the installation of Marie Louise and her son, the European powers had returned to a condition of intimate friendship with Spain.[89]

Throughout the diplomatic conversations of 1816–17, Russia did not waver in its commitment to act in concert with the allies to uphold the terms of the Vienna and Paris treaties. As the overview pointed out, relations with Spain highlighted this commitment. Although Spain wanted to place its security under Russian protection, the empire's diplomats consistently urged the Spanish government to work within the parameters of the great alliance and to accept British mediation. Russia's position on abolition of the slave trade revealed the same devotion to legality. Britain, on the other hand, appeared to violate the European legal settlement by going beyond the agreed-upon provisions concerning abolition. Invoking the authority of the united allied powers, Britain wanted to compel Portugal and Spain to accept abolition. In addition, the British government hoped to place the maritime relations of the European states under a central authority to be organized and coordinated in London. At the time of the overview's composition, this proposal was being discussed by the ambassadorial conference in London.

The consolidation of legitimate and constitutional royalty in France represented another goal requiring the solicitude of European governments. But were all the powers equally disinterested? By common accord the allies had ordered a reduction in the size of the army of occupation stationed in France. A problem had arisen, however, that required the attention of all: the conduct of French refugees and exiles, who continued to threaten the French restoration. In response to the large number of refugees gathered in Belgium, the Russian monarch had sent General Alexander I. Chernyshev on special mission to Brussels. In addition, the Paris conference, where all the allies were represented, had been ordered to develop a common approach to bringing the matter before the king of the Netherlands. Based on Alexander's rescript to Chernyshev, dated 21 April/3 May 1817, the purpose of the mission was to dissuade the prince of Orange from supporting French emigres who hoped to engineer the removal of the Bourbon dynasty. According to the rescript, Russia stood ready to use military force to prevent any violation of allied obligations to France.[90]

The overview also accused Austria, Britain, and Prussia of acting in concert against Russia in German affairs and in matters concerning the empire's relations with the Ottoman Porte and Persia, despite Emperor Alexander's commitment to the Vienna and Paris accords. The allies repeatedly had tried to intervene in Russia's eastern relations, and by creating a Germany armed against Russia, they had sought to separate the empire from Europe. Still, the Russian monarch refused to use unauthorized tactics to counter the allies' diplomatic maneuvers. Instead, he expected Russia's diplomats to remain dispassionate spectators in all matters German. The treaties required that Russia refrain from action, and the monarch intended to fulfill this obligation with scrupulous exactitude. At the same time, Russia's relations with the Ottoman and Persian governments, which were regulated by separate bilateral treaties, could not be subject to foreign interference. Like India, these powers lay outside the circle of the European association.

Relations between Portugal and Spain did not, however, fall outside the general interest of Europe. Thus, when the armies of the Portuguese king invaded the territory of the Rio de la Plata, Spain appealed for collective intervention by the European powers. Prospects for allied action in South America and elsewhere remained on the table throughout the years 1815–22. According to the overview, Britain hoped to be the sole mediator between Portugal and Spain, an arrangement that Austria urged Russia to accept. But Russia already had responded directly to Spain, which rendered Austria's overtures irrelevant. Equally significant, according to the Russian government, only concerted action by the ambassadorial conference in Paris could impart to European intervention the character of grandeur and impartiality necessary for success. In other words, intervention in Portuguese-Spanish relations should remain a general European question.

Another situation that raised questions about intervention concerned the Treaty of Kiel, concluded between Sweden and Denmark in January 1814. Austria had invited Emperor Alexander to act in concert to guarantee the treaty by which Denmark had ceded Norway to Sweden in return for Swedish Pomerania and Rügen. In June 1815, as part of the Vienna settlement, Norway had submitted to Swedish rule, and Denmark had accepted the Duchy of Lauenburg in

exchange for Swedish Pomerania, which Prussia then had purchased from Sweden.[91] Alexander acknowledged these terms but argued that the allies were not
authorized to intervene in the Danish-Swedish dispute. Nor was he convinced
that Sweden would fail to meet its obligations under the terms of Kiel.[92] The
monarch therefore concluded that the courts of Copenhagen and Stockholm
should continue their negotiations without collective participation by the allies.

After surveying the disputes that had occupied diplomats since 1815, the overview praised Russian policy for its truth and utility. Going forward Emperor
Alexander instructed his agents at foreign courts to adhere strictly to his policy.
All eyes, the overview warned, looked upon the representatives of Russia, who
were effectively under surveillance. Their action and inaction, speech and silence,
personal liaisons and domestic relations—all were subject to observation. Surveillance was painful; however, it could be neutralized, as soon as those conducting the surveillance understood the uselessness of their work, expenditures, and
anxiety. To that end, the last section of the overview described the principles of
conduct to be followed by Alexander's diplomats. The first rule of behavior was
inertia, which meant that diplomats should not pursue political goals beyond
the fulfillment of existing transactions. Assuming that all states were equally
interested in the inviolable maintenance of the treaties, Russian diplomacy had
to be completely stationary. Any active or anxious attitude toward the general
alliance—which was founded on the Final Act of the Congress of Vienna, sanctioned by the acts of Paris of 8/20 November, and consecrated by the act of 14/26
September—contradicted Russian policy. Any action (*activité*) by tsarist diplomats should signal only the inert and stationary posture of the government.

It was critical, the overview explained, that the empire's diplomats avoid doing
anything, directly or indirectly, to cause suspicion. If suspicions arose, officials
were expected to respond calmly and patiently within the bounds of the legal
stipulations. The goal in these circumstances was to promote trust and to show
European governments seeking to discover the secret of Emperor Alexander's
policy that there was no mystery to uncover. For this reason, the government's
diplomatic correspondence was conducted as conspicuously as possible, so that
the record of Russia's actions contained in its archives could be opened to "the
public in good faith, without regrets, without remorse." Another way to prevent
distrust was to publicize general opinions based on legal transactions, which
then could be applied to specific situations that emerged. In March 1816, in a
confidential note responding to overtures from Bavaria, Emperor Alexander had
addressed a range of questions concerning relations between the German Confederation and non-German powers. In subsequent discussions with Austria,

Britain, and Prussia, the explanations elaborated in the note turned out to be relevant. This was because the Russian government's response to the court of Munich did not articulate an opinion as such. Instead the note affirmed the text of the Final Act of the Congress of Vienna and recounted what had transpired at the congress. In this and other communications, Russian officials tried to approach the subject under discussion from a general point of view that, to the extent possible, directed the gaze and attention of the governments involved.

The conduct of tsarist diplomacy, the overview proclaimed, must be free of pride and independent of personal interests. To prevent any diplomatic mission abroad from becoming a center of convergence for Russia's political alliances, every ambassador, minister, and diplomatic agent was ordered to follow the precepts outlined in the overview for that part of the monarch's service entrusted to him. In observing and reporting on developments in their respective jurisdictions, and in executing the orders they received, Russian missions performed a single task: "to conserve [*conserver*] on the basis of existing transactions, the most amicable relations with the Courts to which they are accredited" and to ensure that these courts did likewise with respect to Russia and other European powers. Through the policy outlined in the overview and through Emperor Alexander's pure intentions and right conduct, the Russian monarch hoped to guarantee long years of peace and prosperity in his states and to contribute to the same across Europe.

In reality, the overview admitted, the treaties and accords making up the Vienna settlement represented particular interests and ran the risk of leading states into the old political relationships and separate combinations that had produced so many disastrous conflicts. It was, therefore, the regenerated moral spirit, based on eternal Christian principles, that would preserve allied unity and ensure European peace. For this reason, the edifice of pacification and peace set forth in the treaties of Paris and Vienna envisioned both a legal and a moral settlement. Although many legal questions remained on the table, to be resolved in ongoing and future negotiations, the moral settlement allowed Russia's diplomats and tsar diplomat to continue their work amid chronic uncertainty and distrust and to believe in the efficacy of their labors and the possibility of achieving a durable peace. Without such hope and a measure of idealism to sustain it, the passage of peoples from destructive war to creative peacemaking would not have been practicable.

CHAPTER 2

Completion of the General Alliance (1817–20)

I N 1818 WHEN THE members of the Quadruple Alliance convened the Congress of Aix-la-Chapelle, they had agreed upon the basic legal principles of European order. The diplomatic accords signed at the congress completed the settlement begun in Vienna and Paris by restoring France to its natural position as a great power in Europe. Since 1814, much had been accomplished, and hopes ran high. Yet even as the French monarchy returned to full membership in European society, political uncertainty persisted in France and the German Confederation.[1] Other unfinished business that demanded the attention of the allies included mechanisms to retire the French debt and settle private claims against the French government, French claims against the supply officers (*commissaires*) of foreign governments, and claims of French citizens against foreign governments. Territorial and financial arrangements between German rulers, particularly the dispute between the Kingdom of Bavaria and the Grand Duchy of Baden, also needed resolution, as did disagreements between Sweden and Denmark arising from the Treaty of Kiel (1814). The prisoner status of Napoleon Bonaparte, still considered a potential military danger, continued to arouse general concern, while the rights of Jews and reform of Jewish life largely affected Britain and Germany. Finally, the slave trade, both legal and illegal, and threats to European peace and commerce from the Barbary states, technically under the suzerainty of the Ottoman Porte but regarded as pirates by the Europeans, remained on the allied agenda. In the protocols of the conferences held in Aix-la-Chapelle in the fall of 1818 (29 September–21 November), the allies addressed all of these issues.[2]

By the time the allies met, differences over the organization and obligations of the codified international order already had arisen, including the legal authority for the congress itself. The British government supported a narrow basis for the meeting, article 5 of the Second Treaty of Paris, which called for a review of allied relations with France after three years. A second source of authorization, reportedly preferred by British foreign secretary Robert Stewart, Viscount

Castlereagh, was article 6 of the Quadruple Alliance, which provided for the convening of conferences and congresses to ensure the general repose of Europe. According to Henry Kissinger, British foreign policy, at least in the European arena, remained defensive and committed to the principle of non-interference in the internal affairs of other countries. Austrian foreign minister Clemens von Metternich, by contrast, opposed any changes to the restored order, and Emperor Alexander I, hoping to include second-order powers in future negotiations, favored a "treaty of guarantee" or *Alliance Solidaire* that would trigger collective action in the event of territorial aggression or internal revolutionary upheaval.[3]

The General Alliance of European States

During the years of active warfare and diplomacy from 1812 to 1823 Emperor Alexander I never lost sight of the hard work and harsh realities of peacemaking in Europe.[4] Despite moments of self-doubt and spiritual abandon, the Russian monarch showed himself to be a determined and pragmatic realist committed to military victory and security. An illustration of these dynamics appears in a report of 24 June/6 July 1818, prepared for Alexander by Ioannis Kapodistrias, the co-minister of foreign affairs, and one of the liberals said to have influenced his diplomacy.[5] After describing the diplomatic principles followed by the Russian government since the treaties of Paris had completed the work of pacification, the report analyzed critical questions to be discussed at the Congress of Aix-la-Chapelle. Russian policy, Kapodistrias wrote, sought to preserve "the political relations of the European association under the conservative [*conservateur*] empire of the law of nations [*le droit des gens*]." Based on principles of truth, benevolence, moderation, and justice, the allied powers acted to enforce established treaties under the auspices, at least publicly, of concord, friendship, and trust. The meetings in Aix-la-Chapelle continued the political process begun in Vienna and Paris, the ultimate results of which could not be doubted. Simply put, the allied governments, enlightened by radiant experience, aimed to ensure the peace and prosperity of the world. In preparing the report, Kapodistrias claimed familiarity with all the official correspondence exchanged among the allies since 1815, including the treaties and acts that preceded and accompanied these communications. In addition, the minister had reviewed the instructions sent to Russia's diplomats and their reports to Saint Petersburg. Based on these sources, the author analyzed the relationship between Russian and allied policies, particularly differences in their understanding of the European system.

Whereas Austria and Britain wanted to conduct negotiations on the authority of the Quadruple Alliance, Emperor Alexander predicated his positions on
the fraternal and Christian alliance (a reference to the Holy Alliance, the general
or European alliance, and the grand alliance).[6] According to Kapodistrias, the
monarch strove for unanimity, while insisting on strict adherence to treaty prescriptions. In order to appear impartial and disinterested, he preferred to hold
diplomatic deliberations in regular and public forums. In other words, although
Austria and Britain sought to limit decision making about general European
policy to the Quadruple Alliance, Alexander envisioned a more inclusive process
with the broad participation of all European states. The tension between Russia's
pursuit of unanimity and the allies' tendency toward exclusivity appeared in
discussions of multiple issues: participation of the Baden court in deciding the
question of the Main-Tauber circle, the matter of Parma, and the accession of
Spain to the Final Act of the Congress of Vienna.[7] Another problem that Russia
wanted to see addressed within the framework of the general alliance was the
abolition of the slave trade. At conferences in London, Portugal and Spain had
reached agreement with Britain on specific measures to limit the trade.[8] Russia
adopted a similar approach by inviting the ministerial conference in Paris to
negotiate liquidation of the French debt and reductions in the size of the occupation force. By contrast, Austria, Britain, and Prussia all preferred that the four allies decide these matters before the opening of the congress in Aix-la-Chapelle.[9]
The consultations illustrated the critical question posed by Kapodistrias: did
the exclusive Quadruple Alliance or the more inclusive general alliance constitute the foundation of the European political system? Kapodistrias believed that
Austria and Britain favored the Quadruple Alliance and that Prussia's policy
remained uncertain. Russia, by contrast, supported a more open system rooted
in legality and publicity.[10]

Why, Kapodistrias continued, did Vienna and London maintain such close
relations? Russia's enormous power and active role in European politics provided
the principal explanation. During earlier negotiations in Vienna and Paris,
the liberal ideas of Emperor Alexander had proven decisive in reconciling the
French population to legitimate royal authority. The monarch's influence also
had helped to solidify the independence and neutrality of Switzerland, restore
the national existence of Poland, and ensure a better future for Europe. These
successes, combined with the Treaty of 14/26 September 1815, had convinced the
Austrian and British governments that Alexander sought and continued to seek
universal domination. Although clearly absurd, this hypothesis encouraged the
allies to separate Russia from France, Germany, Spain, and all the second-order

states. Action in the name of the Quadruple Alliance would make it easier to isolate Russia. For the moment these efforts had failed, and the allies had accepted that France would participate in the meetings of Aix-la-Chapelle. Still, Kapodistrias concluded that while Austria's interpretation of the Quadruple Alliance obligated Russia to accept allied policies, the governments of Berlin, London, and Vienna remained free to contract separate obligations and act independently of the alliance. To bolster this argument, the co-minister described the goals of Austrian and British foreign policy as long-term subordination of France and Spain, dependence of the Netherlands and Portugal on Britain, and subjection of the Italian states to Austrian authority. Other actions designed to block Russian power included arming the German Confederation against Russia's alleged projects of encroachment, the establishment of direct relations between the German Confederation and Ottoman Porte, intervention in the northern states, and finally, interference in Russia's relations with the Persian and Ottoman empires. But, Kapodistrias insisted, despite the allies' policies of distrust and jealousy, Russia's intentions remained pure, its orientation merciful, and the conduct of its government frank and loyal.[11]

Kapodistrias also believed that at least until March 1816 Prussia had avoided the alliances of distrust and seemed committed to the principles of the Holy Alliance. A memorandum written by Prussian state counselor Johann Ancillon depicted the Treaty of 14/26 September as the source of a proposed general alliance.[12] The general alliance would establish a collective guarantee (*garantie solidaire*) of the territorial boundaries sanctioned by the treaties of Vienna and Paris, as well as those recognized in other agreements between European states. The guarantee would secure the inviolability of legitimate sovereignty. Based on the principle of "all for one and one for all," it would require the states of Europe to take up arms against any power that violated the codified territorial boundaries.[13] Force no longer would threaten right, and right would come under the aegis of force. Second-order powers would be protected by the great powers and, therefore, would gain more rights than they would lose. With respect to legitimacy, a treaty of guarantee would prevent violent attacks on constitutional sovereignty, changes imposed from below (*de bas en haut*), and revolution. The internal liberty of each state would be respected, and a government threatened by domestic troubles would be able to appeal to the guarantor states, which in turn would be authorized and obliged to defend the threatened power and social order. A general alliance, as proposed by Ancillon and interpreted by Kapodistrias, would allow each government to work toward the reform and perfection of its own social institutions, while preventing innovations imposed by violence.

The Russian emperor had accepted the Prussian overture and asked that the allies be consulted. But at the time of writing, Kapodistrias could report only that no further communications about the proposal had taken place. The co-minister of foreign affairs took this to mean that Austria and Britain rejected the project. Instead of a "general association founded on development of the Treaty of 14/26 September," they favored the exclusive system of the Quadruple Alliance. For the moment, Kapodistrias also assumed that Prussia's apparent decision to side with Austria and Britain resulted from that power's tendency to support British positions on Portugal and Spain and from the secrecy surrounding Austrian-Prussian negotiations about the German Confederation. Be that as it may, when the allies began to plan the agenda for the meetings in Aix-la-Chapelle, the unity of Austria, Britain, and Prussia seemed unassailable.

In reality, the alliance of the four great powers, the Quadruple Alliance, remained strong. All agreed that the purpose of the congress was to affirm the European system so that the world would be protected from revolution and the right of the strongest (*le droit du plus fort*). Kapodistrias repeatedly distinguished the exclusive Quadruple Alliance from the general alliance based on the Treaty of 14/26 September, as supposedly envisioned by Ancillon, yet he also recognized that since 1815 Russia had followed the policy of general alliance. Precisely because the Treaty of 14/26 September established a Christian fraternity among the sovereigns, it was impossible for any single government to make decisions impacting the interests of the others without their participation. Equally significant, the Quadruple Alliance, which defined the principles for restoration of the French monarchy, had never assigned to the allies the right to intervene in the affairs of other states. Because the Austrians viewed the Quadruple Alliance as confirmation of the Treaty of Chaumont, which they hoped to renew in Aix-la-Chapelle, they wanted to apply the guarantees of Chaumont to the preservation of legitimate authority in France. The distinctions between Chaumont, the Quadruple Alliance, the Holy Alliance, and the general alliance were substantive, yet none threatened allied unity in the months prior to the congress.[14]

Kapodistrias's report repeatedly claimed that the Quadruple Alliance, as a secret alliance limited to the four powers, could not adequately combat revolution or territorial encroachments. Once the alliance decided to act, its actions would become public, and harmful moral consequences would ensue. In such a scenario, governments excluded from the alliance would find themselves under the de facto tutelage of the four great powers, a condition that would undermine their authority, compromise their dignity, and degrade the spirit of their people. This moral impact would in turn fuel the revolutionary tendency of the century. The obligation to combat revolution and invasion would then place an additional military burden on the contracting powers, which would not be able to prevent disturbances and disorders from taking place. Worse still, Europe would be divided into two systems. Decisions by the Quadruple Alliance would appear as an effort to dominate the rest of Europe, an injustice and degradation that other states would resist. Kapodistrias emphatically rejected the Austrian assumption that because the Quadruple Alliance had saved Europe, European peace depended on the Quadruple Alliance. He had a point with respect to the alliance's inability to prevent future revolutions or satisfy the aspirations of second-order states, but it is not at all clear that a more inclusive alliance with numerous active participants could have responded to changing circumstances as effectively as the future grand alliance of the five great powers in consultation with interested parties.

Referencing the ideas attributed to Ancillon, Kapodistrias called for the creation of a general alliance founded on the principles of 14/26 September that would strengthen the European system and affirm legitimate constitutional authority in France. France had fulfilled its obligations as specified in the treaties of 1815. The actions of Louis XVIII and the French government proved that the interests of the nation had become identified with the legitimacy of the throne and the system of representation. Even though the allies needed to take precautions to prevent the return of revolution, conditions in France appeared stable, and the country no longer posed a threat to Europe. Indeed, once the allied occupation ended, a general alliance would offer better protection for France against both internal revolution and external aggression. Among the potential sources of internal revolution, Kapodistrias identified the supporters of Napoleon ("the prisoner of Saint Helena") and his son, or more likely, abuses of royal power. The external threat came from Austria and Britain, for neither wanted a strong France able to challenge Austrian expansion in Italy or British commercial interests and maritime dominance. In the mind of Kapodistrias, one thing was certain: to suppress the potential causes of revolution, both internal and external, measures beyond the existing alliance were needed.

Kapodistrias identified these measures with the idea of a general alliance. How could the legitimate monarchy and constitutional charter governing France, based on the Second Treaty of Paris (8/20 November 1815), be preserved? Equally critical, under what conditions—for example, a new revolution—would France be in violation of treaty obligations, thereby authorizing the allies to expel the country from the European association and use force to bring it back into compliance (the *casus foederis*)? In a strikingly idealistic statement, Kapodistrias argued that combined with a collective guarantee of each state's territorial possessions, the fraternal and Christian alliance would eliminate forever the allure of revolution, conquest, and pillage. A collective guarantee would deny to peoples the hope that they could improve their lot by paying less and gaining more. While revolution was nothing more than the conquest of legitimate property and power, conquering princes were simply revolutionaries assuming the mantle of royal authority. In either case, "the right of the strongest and of the most immoral seeks to triumph." Mutual territorial guarantees would effectively discourage such pretensions. "Providence and time would do the rest."

In the following section of the report, Kapodistrias addressed specific objections to the idea of a collective guarantee or general alliance. These included concerns about French haughtiness and possible weakening of the Quadruple Alliance, the latter seen by some as a more potent means to achieve the goals ascribed to the general alliance. But, Kapodistrias countered, the equality and reciprocity of every power that joined the general alliance would offset any French vanity that might lead the restored power to disturb the harmony of the association. France was obligated by the Treaty of Paris to maintain the Bourbon dynasty and to be governed by a representative system. No other state in Europe had ever assumed obligations of this magnitude; consequently, in a general association France would come under the de facto tutelage of all Europe. The country's own restoration would be strengthened, and possible French aggression in Austria, Belgium, Germany, Italy, or Switzerland would be easier to thwart. Over the previous three years the four powers had decided political questions in union and unanimity, with the participation, not the exclusion, of other interested parties. Here Kapodistrias appeared to contradict his earlier characterization of the Quadruple Alliance as exclusionary. Clearly, its role in ongoing peace negotiations did not preclude participation by other states in discussions touching on their interests. As Kapodistrias himself described the matter, since 1815 European politics had been governed in accordance with the universal benevolence sanctioned by the Treaty of 14/26 September. Still, the co-minister concluded, based on reason and experience, it was the general alliance that would cement the unity of the Quadruple Alliance, not the other way around. It was the general alliance, repeatedly identified with the Holy Alliance, that would allow the union of the four powers to endure independently of immediate circumstances. Not only would the four great powers be discouraged from acting against the alliance; the spirit of insurrection among the peoples also would be opposed by the majority of European states, eager to preserve a system that offered territorial security, civil and political liberty, and substantial recognition.

Relentless in his critique of the Quadruple Alliance, Kapodistrias argued further that an exclusive alliance contained within itself elements of dissolution and discord. The critical question remained how to prevent a return to partial alliances, political egoism, revolution, military despotism, and the right of the strongest. Kapodistrias viewed the Quadruple Alliance and general alliance as separate systems or policies. He underestimated the extent to which they functioned as complementary components in a multifaceted European system policed by the Quadruple Alliance and committed above all else to preserving unity and peace.[15] For Kapodistrias, though perhaps less so for Emperor Alexander, the general alliance offered the best hope for advancing the European system. According to the co-minister's report, two tendencies threatened the peace: (1) the desire of peoples or their leaders (*meneurs*) to establish new relations between nations and sovereigns through revolution from below, and (2) the desire of governments to reproduce or support the old politics of arbitrariness in internal administration and partial alliances in diplomacy. Because revolution had affected every European country, a general alliance based on the Treaty of 14/26 September, which critics erroneously described as a holy league of sovereigns directed against the nations, would obligate all the European states to preserve the existence of their allies on an equal basis. Only this form of alliance, concluded Kapodistrias, could counter revolutionary ambition. The general alliance would be armed not against the progress of social institutions, but against innovations brought about by violence. The system that had brought peace to Europe existed in the treaties of Vienna, Paris, and 14/26 September. There was no need, therefore, to create new political alliances. Established treaties already encompassed all the interests of the European family, and the general alliance already existed in the Treaty of 14/26 September.

If established treaties already constituted the general alliance, why was a new agreement needed? In trying to persuade the allies that a formal collective guarantee or general alliance would not alter the edifice of peace so painstakingly constructed in 1814–15, the Russian government repeatedly undercut the argument for concluding another positive transaction. What did it mean to base decisions on the general alliance, and who specifically would make those decisions? The accords reached in Vienna, Paris, and elsewhere certainly were not formulated by all participating or impacted states. Repeatedly, the four great powers had made decisions among themselves, in consultation with interested parties, and then invited other states to accede to their agreements. Kapodistrias's preference for the general alliance over the Quadruple Alliance was understandable, but from a present-day perspective, one cannot help but hear in his analysis the

pleas of a Greek patriot speaking on behalf of Europe's small peoples.[16] Emperor
Alexander's position on the alliance question seemed less consistent than that of
his advisor, though historians correctly see in the Russian proposals support for
an *Alliance Solidaire*. At the same time, when problems involving second-order
powers appeared to interfere with the primary goal of European peace, Russia's
diplomats did not hesitate to assert great power primacy.[17] The peace process of
1814–15 provided the model for this approach, and Russia's insistence on representing the interests of the Polish nation could not have made the point more
clearly, despite promises of a constitutional relationship.

Emperor Alexander approved Kapodistrias's report of 24 June/6 July 1818 and
asked that a memorandum (*mémoire*) be prepared for submission to the Congress of Aix-la-Chapelle. Dated 12/24 July, the memorandum did not officially
see the light of day. The Russian government had become aware of allied opposition to a formal treaty of general alliance. Consequently, on 26 September/8
October, Russia submitted a modified confidential memorandum to Viscount
Castlereagh, Prince Hardenberg, Prince Metternich, and the Duke of Wellington.[18] During the prior three years, the memorandum proclaimed, the letter and
spirit of the treaties concluded in 1815 had been observed. But once the military occupation of France ended, how would the allied courts ensure the peace,
which depended on the French restoration? How would they protect Europe
from the twin dangers of renewed revolution and the right of the strongest?

In principle, the treaties of 1815 had resolved these questions by creating a new
order in Europe, which contained revolution and protected all interests under
the aegis of justice. The alliance of great powers (*grands États*) had become a general alliance of all the states of Europe. Legitimate government had returned to
France, bolstered by institutions that joined the rights of the dynasty with those
of the people. Principles of equality, friendship, trust, and harmony—the work
of the great powers and of Divine Providence—had overcome past errors that
resulted from human egoism and partial or exclusive alliances (*combinaisons*).
Under "the empire of Christian morality and the law of nations," Europe had
begun to enjoy peace and well-being. As a general association, the European system rested on the legal foundation established by the Final Act of the Congress
of Vienna and the treaties of Paris. Its conservative principle (*principe conservateur*) was the fraternal union of the allied powers, and its primary objective was
to guarantee all recognized rights. As the work of Divine Providence rather than
of any single government, the system favored "the interests most dear to the great
European family and to each particular state." As a policy engraved on the hearts
of men and intended to be eternal, the system ensured the advantages of civil

order for the association of states; the inviolability of persons and things, which consecrated legitimacy *ab antiquo* or legitimacy recognized by treaties; and finally, the territorial boundaries of each power. Situating the Russian overture in the broad context of European restoration, the memorandum noted that like all the communications between allied governments this one addressed present and future interests.

The first question to be addressed in Aix-la-Chapelle was the military occupation of France, described as the material guarantee of the European system based on the treaties of 1815. But to protect the European association from revolution and the right of the strongest, a moral force also was needed, one that went beyond the renewal of existing obligations and temporary material measures. This force could be found in the present European system and in an alliance embodying the cohesion and indissolubility of that system. The components of the moral force included the Quadruple Alliance and the general alliance, the first described as principle and the second as consequence. The Quadruple Alliance, according to the Treaty of 8/20 November 1815, established an armed federation to protect legitimate constitutional monarchy in France. In the eyes of the peacemakers, who understood that restoration of the French monarchy represented the foundation of the European system, this federation performed a critical function. The general alliance, based on the Final Act of the Congress of Vienna and the subsequent treaties of Paris, guaranteed the inviolability of territorial possessions and of the legitimate representative of a given territory (*propriété*). The Quadruple Alliance of great powers, forged by successive accessions in 1814–15, had in practice become the general alliance. Having failed to persuade the allies to accept a treaty of collective guarantee, the Russian government now sought to strengthen the general alliance, which it presented as already in existence.

As Russia's diplomats portrayed the problem, if revolution returned to France, Europe would fall into chaos, and without the general alliance, the effort and sacrifices needed to respond to the crisis would not materialize. Claiming to be in complete agreement with the allies, the Russian monarch hoped that the conferences in Aix-la-Chapelle would illuminate the true relationship between the Quadruple and general alliances. Once this relationship was properly understood, all Europe would accept three key points. First, the sole purpose of the Quadruple Alliance was to maintain legitimate constitutional monarchy in France based on the (Second) Treaty of Paris. To that end, the Quadruple Alliance remained morally and militarily prepared to occupy France should that country violate its treaty obligations. Second, the Final Act of the Congress of Vienna and the treaties of Paris constituted a general alliance among the contracting parties, the purpose of which was collective guarantee (*garantie sol-idaire*) of the territories assigned to each and of legitimate authority *ab antiquo* or as recognized by the treaties. Finally, based on the third point of allied agreement, the original signatories and the powers that later acceded to the treaties of 1815 all belonged to the general association of European states. By presenting these three truths to the world, the powers meeting in Aix-la-Chapelle would fulfill article 5 of the Second Treaty of Paris and article 6 of the Quadruple Alliance. They also would preserve the tutelary and conservative force of the Quadruple Alliance. The very fact of the meeting, and especially the allies' strict adherence to existing treaties, gave to the European system a new guarantee of stability. The organization of the congress and the work to be done likewise represented the fulfilment of treaty obligations, including clauses not yet carried out that required the allies' attention.

As things turned out, and as the Russian memorandum explained, the protocols produced by the congress would extend and further refine the obligations already imposed by the Quadruple Alliance, the Final Act of the Congress of Vienna, and the treaties of Paris. In affirming the Quadruple Alliance, the protocols would define the *casus foederis*; possible military measures to be taken by the allies; and the organization of future meetings, ordinary and extraordinary, of the sovereigns, including precautions designed to ensure that these meetings did not harm the dignity of other crowns or weaken the ties of the general association. Another product of the congress's work would be a declaration of the great powers announcing to Europe the results of the meetings and the allies' commitment to the stipulations of existing treaties. The declaration would explain the basis for the evacuation of French territory and the guarantees that remained in effect, including the responsibilities of all signatories to the treaties of Vienna and Paris. The Russian government accepted the need to preserve the Quadruple Alliance, if only to provide a rapid response to catastrophe in France; however, the real purpose of any action by the alliance would be to maintain the general peace in cooperation with all the states of Europe. Finally, to ensure that the Quadruple Alliance did not become a partial or exclusive alliance, the declaration would direct governments and nations to focus attention on the moral guarantees already enacted and consecrated by reciprocal obligation. If revolution and conquest threatened the general peace, the four powers stood ready to fulfill their obligations. Having clarified their collective responsibilities, they would invite the other states of Europe, France among them, to accede to their declaration. For those fearful of conditions in France, it would become clear that a French revolution would lead to the country's exclusion from the general association.

The conclusion to the memorandum proclaimed that in order to prevent the formation of opposing alliances, the protocols approved in Aix-la-Chapelle should highlight the interconnectedness of the Quadruple and general alliances. The former should not operate in secret, because the conscience of the four contracting powers was insufficient to protect against the vagaries of human nature. In addition, the Quadruple Alliance should be extended to all European states. Otherwise, the second-order states would try to form separate arrangements with one or another of the great powers. Only by invitation to accede to the declaration of Aix-la-Chapelle could the states of Europe be persuaded that the Quadruple and general alliances constituted a single indivisible system, that this system guaranteed all the rights and interests recognized by existing treaties, and that no separate alliance purporting to protect these rights and interests could become part of the public law of nations. Once governments and peoples recognized the value of existing treaties, particularly the territorial guarantee and the principle of legitimacy, they no longer would be attracted to the promises of aggrandizement and pillage associated with revolution and conquest. Once time and experience gave authority to "the moral force of this great association," the law of nations would be placed under a guarantee analogous to that which protected individuals. The security of governments and peoples would be ensured, the spirit of revolution thwarted, and the progressive development of social institutions encouraged. Placed under voluntary obligations rather than dictatorship, governments would be able to give their subjects reformed institutions. As history showed, the enslavement of men and classes diminished in proportion to the improvement of social life. The purpose of the collective association of all the states would be "to regulate application of the principle of mutual defense," a principle elevated from "the sphere of civil society to that of political order" by the interest of humanity. From this state of affairs, the liberties of peoples, wisely regulated, could emerge.

In a supplement to the memorandum, also dated 26 September/8 October 1818, the Russian government evaluated the European political system. In the process of delivering Europe from revolution and conquest, the powers were animated by a spirit of concord and Christian brotherhood, which allowed them to base their mutual relations on principles of law (*droit*). In restoring legitimate monarchies and states, the powers defined territorial boundaries and established mechanisms to preserve peace, the independence of nations, and the progress of peoples toward true civilization. Adherence to the treaties of 1815 obligated all signatories collectively to guarantee their execution, the territorial boundaries defined by the acts, and the legitimate sovereignty representing the territorial possessions of each state. The response of the allies when Napoleon returned to France in March 1815 had proven the effectiveness of the principles followed in 1813–14. The Treaty of 13/25 March 1815 had defined the rules by which the great federation brought France back into compliance with the law. In fall 1818, a time when the temporary military guarantees of French compliance were being dismantled, it was important to reinforce the moral guarantees that the allies also had put into place.

Russia's diplomatic communications repeatedly identified in existing treaties the essential ingredients of the new moral force. Fidelity to the principle of legitimate sovereignty and the inviolability of territorial possessions promised to give the world a long peace. At the same time, the concert of the four powers constituted a precautionary measure, authorized by the past, to protect Europe from the threat of renewed revolution in France.[19] The Russian government assumed that the Quadruple Alliance would be able to count on all the states of Europe to act against an aggressive revolutionary France. To that end, the conferences in Aix-la-Chapelle needed to develop rules to govern the general coalition. This could be accomplished in a protocol or declaration defining the measures to be taken in case of war not only by the Quadruple Alliance, but also by the other states that had acceded to the treaties of Paris and the Final Act of the Congress of Vienna. Critical to the preservation of peace in Europe was an explicit statement of the relationship uniting all states in a general pact—a pact that would prevent the isolation of the four powers from the other governments of Europe and the consequent formation of partial or counter-alliances. In light of Spanish pretensions and French overtures seeking admission to the Quadruple Alliance, it was important to make clear that the Quadruple Alliance was nothing more than "the center of the general alliance of the European system."

Proceedings and Protocols of Aix-la-Chapelle

Despite tensions within the Quadruple Alliance and irrespective of Emperor Alexander's supposed generosity toward France, the proceedings and protocols of Aix-la-Chapelle revealed a flexibility in Russian diplomacy that sought above all to preserve allied unity through concerted action and compromise. The allies departed the conferences in general agreement about a variety of issues and better informed about how the component parts of the European system connected to one another and should work in practice. Of particular significance were the distinctions drawn between the Quadruple Alliance, the grand alliance of "the Five" (the Quadruple Alliance plus France), and the general alliance of European states. Russian hopes for a collective guarantee based on the moral principles of 14/26 September remained on the table but did not play a critical role in the daily meetings of the congress.[20] Taken as a whole, however, the proceedings and protocols of Aix-la-Chapelle did not diverge from the substance of Russia's concerns, arguments, and proposals.

The first item on the congress's agenda concerned the military occupation and financial obligations of France.[21] The French and English kings, who did not attend the congress, were represented by plenipotentiaries, the Duke of Richelieu for France and Viscount Castlereagh and the Duke of Wellington for Great Britain. The three monarchs, Francis I, Frederick William III, and Alexander I, did journey to Aix-la-Chapelle, though in the daily meetings Prince Metternich represented Austria, Prince Hardenberg and Count Bernstorff spoke for Prussia, and Counts Nesselrode and Kapodistrias stood for Russia. General conferences included France and on occasion representatives of Portugal, Spain, and various German states. Other conferences were considered private (*particulière*) and included only the four allies. The distinctions were significant and imparted to the meetings a sense of order, hierarchy, reasoned deliberation, and solemn duty.

The congress opened on 29 September (NS) with discussion of the French question, specifically France's request for a speedy end to the military occupation.[22] The four courts recognized the urgency of the situation, and on 9 October their plenipotentiaries signed a convention ending the occupation and retiring the French debt, which had been under discussion since autumn 1817.[23] By the Convention of 27 September/9 October 1818 the allies agreed to complete the military evacuation of French territory by 18/30 November 1818.[24] Financial terms designed to ensure payment of the 265 million francs owed by France, according to article 4 of the Second Treaty of Paris, made it possible to end the military occupation two years early. Until 18/30 November France would continue to cover the cost of maintaining allied troops. To retire the debt, the French treasury would pay 100 million francs directly as *rentes*, and foreign bankers, Baring Brothers of London and Hope of the Hague, would deliver the remaining sum through bills of exchange to be paid in nine monthly instalments beginning 6 January 1819.[25] Finally, all governments that had signed the Second Treaty of Paris (8/20 November 1815) would be informed about the convention and invited to accede to the agreement.

Closely intertwined with the French question was the European question, usually discussed in the private conferences of the four courts. The European question referred to the application of the Treaty of the Quadruple Alliance, particularly article 6, to the circumstances of 1818. On 19 October, the allied representatives agreed that in light of the current peaceful relations with France, the European powers needed to define new bases for their association.[26] Their first goal was to preserve the power of the Quadruple Alliance for the *casus foederis* defined in the Treaty of 8/20 November 1815. A secret protocol would then define the military measures that the allies planned to implement in case of need. The second goal was to preserve in pure form the moral principle of the Quadruple Alliance, again based on article 6, and to apply this principle in a manner consistent with the general system. Third, the invitation to France to join the allies in maintaining the treaties that ensured the general peace would fall outside the secret protocol affirming the Quadruple Alliance and authorizing the *casus foederis et belli*. France and the four courts would sign a separate protocol explaining the reasons for and the principles of the grand alliance (*la grande union*). In this instance, the five allies would declare their commitment to preserve the general peace based on scrupulous adherence to the treaties of 1815 and the laws (*droits*) regulating relations in the general association. Finally, the five powers would make no decisions concerning the interests of other states without their participation.

At the private conference of 4 November, the allies assigned to the Duke of Wellington the task of communicating to the French prime minister and minister of foreign affairs, Armand Emmanuel du Plessis, Duke of Richelieu, the projects they intended to formalize at the congress: the secret protocol to be signed by the four signatories to the alliance of 1815, a note addressed to Richelieu, and the protocol to be signed by the plenipotentiaries of the five powers as a consequence of Richelieu's response to the allied note. In the exchange of notes (23 October/4 November 1818 and 31 October/12 November 1818), the allies expressed their trust in France, the French king, and his minister, the Duke of Richelieu. The allied note declared that France had fulfilled its obligations based on the Treaty of 8/20 November 1815 and explained that the Convention of 27 September/9 October 1818 constituted a supplement to the general peace.[27] In France's response, Richelieu accepted the allies' invitation to participate in the conferences, adding that no other nation had ever carried out its treaty obligations so scrupulously. Louis XVIII, the note proclaimed, would be pleased to join his counsel to that of his fellow monarchs for the purpose of consolidating the peace, maintaining the treaties, and guaranteeing the mutual rights and relationships recognized by all the states of Europe. Based on the signed convention, the exchange of notes between the French and allied ministers, and the protocol that would be agreed to a few days later, France would be restored to full membership in European society and to great power status in the European political system.

The Protocol of 3/15 November 1818, approved by the plenipotentiaries of Austria, Britain, France, Prussia, and Russia, began with the simple proposition that following ratification of the Convention of 27 September/9 October it had become necessary to define relations between France and signatories to the peace treaty of 8/20 November 1815 (Second Treaty of Paris). The first point of the protocol proclaimed that the monarchs intended to organize their associations with one another and with other states in accordance with the principle of intimate union that heretofore had guided their relations and common interests, a union made "stronger and indissoluble by the bonds of Christian fraternity that the Sovereigns had formed among themselves." Real and durable, their union did not concern an isolated interest or a transitory alliance. Its sole purpose was to maintain the general peace, founded on religious respect for treaty obligations and the totality of rights (*droits*) that derived from them. France too accepted the system that had brought peace to Europe. Going forward, the five powers would hold private meetings to discuss their common interests, and in the event that future meetings touched on the interests of other states, the latter would be invited to participate. The protocol, which the five powers would formally announce to all the courts of Europe, affirmed the moral and religious foundations of the peace.[28] Russia's diplomats could not convince the allies that the Holy Alliance was equivalent to the general alliance, which should supersede the Quadruple Alliance (Kapodistrias's formulation in the report of 24 June/6 July 1818); however, the idea that peace required both moral principles and legal stipulations remained central to diplomatic discussions.

The protocol signed by the five powers expressed the belief that stability in Europe depended on a complete and successful French restoration. At the same time, the four powers understood that lofty aspirations, religious convictions, and good intentions could not guarantee an enduring peace. Consequently, before signing the protocol with France, though also on 15 November, the members of the Quadruple Alliance met in private conference to formalize a secret protocol and a military protocol limited to the four.[29] Unlike the other acts agreed to at the Congress of Aix-la-Chapelle, these protocols remained unpublished. Equally noteworthy, on 21 November, following a trip to Brussels, the Duke of Wellington announced that the king of the Netherlands had sent his minister of foreign affairs to accede to the military protocol.[30]

The Secret Protocol affirmed that because the process of pacification had been completed and allied troops had begun to evacuate French territory, the four powers needed to discuss how the Treaty of the Quadruple Alliance applied to France's new relationship with the allies and the rest of Europe. Unwilling

to remove all the safeguards that had been in place since 1814, the four governments declared that the mutual obligations prescribed in the first articles of the
treaty did not concern current conditions. But then they added that in the event
of war with France, these provisions would again become applicable. Thus, the
allies also decided to preserve the military measures stipulated in the Treaty
of the Quadruple Alliance. These measures appeared to contradict subsequent
provisions of the Secret Protocol describing France as an essential member of
the European system and declaring that military dispositions could not serve as
the basis for permanent peaceful relations. Instead, the intimate union between
the four powers, defined in article 6 of the Quadruple Alliance and reinforced
by the "bonds of Christian fraternity that today unite all the States," provided
the foundation for relations with a France restored to a state of legitimate and
constitutional sovereignty. That said, in yet another attempt to square the circle,
two additional provisions explained the decision to maintain the *casus foederis et
belli* specified in the Quadruple Alliance and the Military Protocol of 3/15 November 1818. Although the obligations set forth in articles 1–4 of the Quadruple
Alliance were reaffirmed, the allies viewed them as potential actions far removed
from present-day circumstances. In addition, France would be included in the
union of the four powers and the general system of Europe, a step that preserved
existing treaties and confirmed the friendly intentions of the allied sovereigns.
The secret nature of the protocol, the allies claimed, actually illustrated their
amicable attitude toward France.

Among themselves the allies represented their decision to preserve the Quadruple Alliance as defensive. They did not want to appear hostile to France or
alarm other European states. Although Emperor Alexander I may have been less
committed to the Quadruple Alliance than Austria or Britain, their differences
paled in comparison with shared concerns about potential troubles in France
and recognition of the need for allied unity in addressing any upheavals that
might occur. The trick was to preserve the mutual defensive obligation without
appearing to isolate France or threaten the second-order powers. Referring to the
grand alliance (*la grande union*) of the five powers, the signatories to the Secret
Protocol agreed to invite France to participate in formulating the protocol that
would define relations between the five courts. This latter protocol, signed by the
four powers and France, would then be announced to all the states that had adhered to the (First) Treaty of Paris of 30 May 1814, the Final Act of the Congress
of Vienna, and the Paris treaties of 1815. With this declaration, the five powers
would show that their alliance aimed only to preserve the general peace, based
on the inviolability of rights assured to every European state by existing treaties

and consolidated by the spirit of mutual goodwill uniting all the members of the European family in the same system of peace.

After repeating familiar statements about friendly intentions, the plenipotentiaries of Austria, Britain, Prussia, and Russia declared that the obligations stipulated in the Treaty of the Quadruple Alliance remained in full force for the *casus foederis et belli*. In case of need the four monarchs or their representatives would meet to discuss appropriate measures. Once again, their goal would be to prevent the deadly consequences of revolutionary upheaval in France. The final statement contained in the Secret Protocol may have been the most revealing, and its theme was one that recurred in Russian documents of the era: "The allies always remember that the progress of the evils that for so long desolated Europe was stopped only by the intimate relations and pure sentiments that unite the four sovereigns for the happiness of the world." Discourses of Christian morality, enlightened harmoniousness, and sentimentalist friendship pervaded the diplomatic discourse of Restoration Europe.

Closely related to the Secret Protocol was the Military Protocol, also secret, unpublished, and dated 3/15 November 1818. The Military Protocol came directly from the Treaty of the Quadruple Alliance (articles 1–4) and the Treaty of Chaumont (articles 7, 8, and 12). According to the protocol, allied agreement on the existence of the *casus foederis* would trigger preparations for a military campaign. Because of the distances involved, Russia would have three months to reach Mainz; however, the British corps in Brussels, the Prussian corps in Cologne, and the Austrian corps in Stuttgart would be assembled within two months. Defensive works already prescribed by the conference protocol of 21 November 1815 would continue in the Netherlands and in other countries bordering France. To man these garrisons, including a second line of fortresses along the old frontier of Holland, troops would be sent from Britain, the Netherlands, and Prussia. Although the Netherlands did not belong to the Quadruple Alliance, the seven ministers (Metternich, Castlereagh, Wellington, Hardenberg, Bernstorff, Kapodistrias, and Nesselrode) agreed that defense of the kingdom was in the interest of all the powers. In their minds, the Military Protocol, to which the Netherlands adhered, constituted a part of the Secret Protocol.

The final act incorporated into the legal settlement completed in Aix-la-Chapelle was the Declaration of 3/15 November 1818 signed by the representatives of the five courts and addressed to all the states of Europe.[31] Like the protocols already discussed, the declaration explained that the pacification of Europe had been achieved. Foreign troops would therefore evacuate French territory, and precautionary measures previously put in place would be dismantled.

The Convention of 27 September/9 October had completed the peace and the political system that preserved it. "The intimate union of the monarchs associated with the system, based on their principles and the interests of their peoples, offers to Europe the most sacred guarantee [*gage*] of future tranquility." The purpose of this union was simple, great, and salutary. It did not constitute a new political alliance or a change in the relations sanctioned by established treaties. To the contrary, the union was calm and constant in its action. Its only goal was to maintain the peace and secure the transactions upon which it rested. Having brought France back into the European fold as one of five great powers, the sovereigns were keen to publicize their commitment to observe in their mutual relations, and in relations with other states, "the principles of the law of nations, principles that in their application to a state of permanent peace alone can guarantee effectively the independence of each government and the stability of the general association." In future meetings to discuss common interests, the sovereigns or their representatives would observe these principles, and they would do likewise when other governments formally asked for their intervention on questions that might arise. Finally, the sovereigns would continue to perfect the work they had begun, in light of their duty before God and their peoples to protect the peace treaties, increase the prosperity of their states, and provide for the world an example of justice, harmony, and moderation.

Although the four allies tried to present their deliberations as consistent with the rights of second-order powers, they rejected a proposal from the Kingdom of Hanover to invite states represented at the Paris conference to accede to the military evacuation of France before the great powers made their decision public. The Hanoverian minister in London had submitted a formal protest to the British government contesting the allies' right to exclude other states from negotiations about the military evacuation and arguing that second-order powers had a right to vote on the question. Keen to assert the rights of every independent state and to preserve the dignity of interested powers without hindering the process of negotiation, the minister warned that great power decisions about European questions aroused jealousy, anxiety, and opposition to "the powerful tribunal of the great States." Clearly, however, the allies viewed the restoration (and sensitivities) of France as more important for European peace than the rights of second-order states. Thus, the five powers meeting in Aix-la-Chapelle informed the states of Europe about France's restoration to its natural position as a great power. Although Austria, Britain, Prussia, and Russia preserved the Quadruple Alliance, in relation to the rest of Europe they treated France as an equal and made sure that its restoration did not appear to follow upon the accession of the second-order states. Despite the decidedly upbeat representations emanating from the Congress of Aix-la-Chapelle, controversy and ambiguity also colored the proceedings.[32]

The ambiguity associated with treating France as an equal power, while preserving the Quadruple Alliance, reappeared as the meetings in Aix-la-Chapelle came to a close, and the Russian government made one last attempt to promote a treaty of guarantee.[33] In a note approved by Emperor Alexander and submitted to the representatives of Austria, Britain, France, and Prussia, Russia's plenipotentiaries returned to questions about the nature of the alliance raised in the months leading up to the congress. The note stated directly that in addition to the protocols of 3/15 November, another more positive transaction was needed, the conservative influence of which would encompass the future. Through such a transaction, states that had acceded to the Final Act of the Congress of Vienna and subsequent treaties of Paris would agree collectively to guarantee "the integrity of their rights and the inviolability of the state of their respective possessions," as defined in the treaties of 1815.[34] Initially proposed by the Prussian government, this collective guarantee already existed in the meaning and literal content of the Treaty of 14/26 September 1815. Thus, Emperor Alexander stood ready, if his allies agreed, to put into more common diplomatic forms the principles consecrated by the Treaty of 14/26 September and "the system of peace and security which is the fruit of these principles."

Russia's plenipotentiaries also prepared a treaty proposal that they hoped would be accepted by Austria, France, the Netherlands, and Prussia.[35] The signatory powers would honor the territorial boundaries established in Europe by the treaties of 1814–15. The only possible changes envisioned by the project were those that resulted from inheritance, marriage, or mutual agreement. The signatory powers also would agree to act together against any state or states that violated the established boundaries. In the event that common action became necessary, the powers would invite Britain to participate on terms of complete reciprocity. Britain also would be invited to accede to the proposed treaty at any time on a temporary or permanent basis. The German Confederation likewise would be invited to join; however, to prevent expectations that might weaken the collective guarantee, no other power would be admitted to the alliance, unless all the contracting parties agreed. In this bid to enact a reciprocal guarantee of defensive action, the Russian government pulled back from earlier formulations suggesting that the general alliance, based on the Holy Alliance, should supersede the Quadruple Alliance. Reduced to a bare minimum, the Russian proposal expressed the desire to offset the vulnerabilities that had led to the

disastrous coalitions, treaties, and military campaigns of the Napoleonic era. If
the Russian project had produced a new agreement, it would have required that
the great powers of the continent, including France, protect one another's territories from war and conquest not by balance of power but by mutual defensive
guarantee. As was the case in 1814–15, the great powers equated peace among
themselves and the protection of their territories and interests with peace for
all Europe.

Organization of the German Confederation

In the afterglow of the Congress of Vienna, another unfinished component
of European order was the reorganization of Germany. The Territorial Commission in Frankfurt completed its work on 8/20 July 1819, bringing to a close
the complicated process of defining borders across Europe.[36] The commission's
General Act (recès général), signed by Austria, Britain, Prussia, and Russia, addressed questions related to territorial swaps, indemnities, rents, maintenance
of garrisons, and rights of inheritance, some of which already possessed legal
standing based on earlier agreements between great and second-order powers.
Technically, the General Act finalized the cessions and reversions initiated in
the treaties of Paris and the Final Act of the Congress of Vienna. In reality,
agreements between individual states on borders, indemnities, property rights,
and family claims continued to be negotiated.[37] Although far less weighty than
the restoration of France or the affirmation of the Quadruple and general alliances, the disputes discussed in Aix-la-Chapelle were noteworthy for what they
revealed about how the great powers understood European order and hoped to
preserve European peace.[38] Several motifs stood out in the decisions concerning
German affairs: the necessity of strict adherence to existing treaties, the commitment to decide territorial questions under the aegis of the Territorial Commission working in Frankfurt, and the critical importance of stability in Germany
to the overall success of the peace settlement.

At the Congress of Vienna it had become strikingly clear that not all of the
legitimate claims of German sovereigns would be satisfied.[39] Nor, given the
localism and diversity of the German states, could all appeals receive equal
consideration. When the Elector of Hessen asked the four powers meeting in
Aix-la-Chapelle to accord him the title of king, they replied with an emphatic
refusal.[40] The allies regarded the elector's request as unjustified, arguing that it
lay outside the authority of the congress. In addition, they and France agreed
to reject any proposed changes to the titles of sovereigns or their own princes

without prior consultation. The protocol of 13 October 1818 affirmed that in making this decision, the powers adhered to established treaties, which is to say, they upheld European public law.

The allies seemed more receptive to overtures from the Grand Duke of Baden, perhaps because the empress of Russia, Elizabeth Alekseevna, was a princess of Baden, but more likely because the military evacuation of France, a matter of general European interest, directly affected the grand duchy.[41] As part of the evacuation Bavarian troops would pass through Baden; consequently, the allies accepted responsibility for limiting the inconveniences this might cause and for facilitating resolution of the ongoing territorial dispute between the two states.[42] Although territorial arrangements between Baden and Bavaria also came under the purview of the commission in Frankfurt, the allies invited the Grand Duke of Baden to send plenipotentiaries to Aix-la-Chapelle to consult (act in concert) with the powers in an effort to restart the stalled negotiations. Through Russia's representatives, the grand duke submitted proposals for an exchange of territory and population between Baden and Bavaria, a military route through Baden for Bavarian troops, and a payment to Baden of more than one million florins to support the troops and defray hospital costs dating from the military campaigns of 1813–14. Because the Bavarian king did not respond to the proposals, the grand duke rejected the territorial cessions requested by the commission in Frankfurt, appealing instead to the Russian government for support. Sensitive as the situation appeared, allied unity held, and the four powers meeting in Aix-la-Chapelle concluded that Baden's demands seemed excessive and not at all conducive to good relations between neighboring states.

Baden's claims dated from 1813 when the grand duke joined the coalition against Napoleon. At the time, he also agreed to give up territory that might be needed in the reconstruction of Germany and received promises from the allies of appropriate compensation for any cessions. The dispute with Bavaria stemmed from the Treaty of Munich, concluded between Austria and Bavaria on 2/14 April 1816, which in return for unfulfilled territorial promises contained in the Treaty of Ried (8 October 1813) assigned to Bavaria the Main-Tauber circle belonging to Baden. Baden received no compensation for this loss, and when Emperor Alexander refused to confirm the agreement, Austria agreed to remove the Main-Tauber provision. The rulers of Baden, Hessen-Darmstadt, Prussia, Russia, and Württemberg all believed that Austria had given too much power and territory to Bavaria, which the Russian monarch characterized as a country with exaggerated pretensions to territorial aggrandizement and great power status.[43] Negotiations dragged on, and during the meetings of 10 November 1818 in Aix-la-Chapelle,

Russia's representatives observed that neither Baden nor Bavaria could be forced to accept the territorial and financial demands being negotiated in Frankfurt. Bavaria already had accepted payment from Austria to concede the Main-Tauber circle, and the Grand Duke of Baden had revised his offer to Bavaria.

According to the modified terms, Baden agreed to exchange upper Wertheim for Geroldseck, give up a monetary claim of 2 million florins against Austria and Bavaria, and allow Bavaria to maintain a military route through Baden's territory in the direction of Frankenthal so that old and new provinces belonging to Bavaria could be connected. Given these concessions, Russia was prepared to insist that Bavaria accept the plan for reconciliation. The territories in question lay within the frontiers of Bavaria, and the Russian government believed that Baden's offer contained more than the Bavarian king had a right to expect. Further postponement of a decision, Emperor Alexander concluded, would be harmful to the internal and external relations of several states within the German Confederation. Allied authority in this matter rested on existing treaties and on the obligation to establish the tranquility of the German states on an immutable foundation.[44] Eager to prevent further trouble and disagreements, the Russian government also proposed that the four courts send a collective communication to the king of Bavaria, urging him to accept Baden's most recent proposals. Prussia agreed that the terms of reconciliation should be accepted and that the repose of Germany superseded all other considerations; however, Frederick William III rejected the idea of sending a joint allied letter.

Discussion of the conflict between Baden and Bavaria concluded when on 20 November 1818 the four powers signed a protocol designed to serve as the basis for a common instruction to allied representatives attached to the Territorial Commission in Frankfurt. In the years after the Congress of Vienna common instructions provided an effective tool for communicating allied agreement on concrete questions without appearing to dictate to the interested parties. Diplomatic pressure in the form of allied consensus did not in itself carry legal standing; however, the common instruction represented a form of concerted action that allowed the great powers to exert influence over second-order states and over one another. Equally significant, the common instruction created a mechanism whereby a government not in agreement with the shared policy could abstain from intervention while remaining fully committed to the alliance and to allied unity. In this instance, France joined the allies in their efforts to persuade the king of Bavaria to agree to Baden's proposals. A Bavarian refusal, the protocol stated, would release the Grand Duke of Baden from the obligations to Bavaria that he had accepted both here and in previous transactions. Bavarian consent would be formalized in separate agreements between the allies and the courts of Baden and Bavaria. Ultimately, Bavaria rejected the indemnity agreed upon in Frankfurt, which meant that Austria continued to pay rent to the kingdom, based on the Treaty of Munich. At the same time, according to the General Act of the Territorial Commission (8/20 July 1819), a treaty of 29 June/10 July 1819 between Austria and Baden, and a second agreement of the same date signed by Austria, Baden, Britain, Prussia, and Russia, Geroldseck went to Baden and upper Wertheim to Austria.[45]

Despite the allied preference for negotiating German territorial disputes within the framework of the commission in Frankfurt, German princes continued to seek great power intervention during the conferences in Aix-la-Chapelle.[46] Among some of the smaller German states there existed a particular tendency to see Russia as their protector.[47] Citing articles 49 and 50 of the Final Act of the Congress of Vienna, the Duke of Oldenburg, the Duke of Sachsen-Coburg, and the landgrave of Hessen-Homburg all solicited support for land swaps and reclamations.[48] The princes hoped to obtain lands closer to their ancient states, exchanges that involved other German states, including Bavaria and Prussia. The Duke of Oldenburg and the count of Bentinck also claimed lands, Elsfleth and Kniphausen respectively, that during the Napoleonic Wars had been incorporated into France, based on treaties between the great powers. Elsfleth had become part of France according to a treaty of 6 April 1803 signed by France and Russia with the mediation of Prussia. Kniphausen had been occupied by Dutch and French armies, mediatized into Oldenburg, incorporated into France, occupied by Russia, and then returned to the Duke of Oldenburg. In 1815 the peacemakers had recognized the independence of Kniphausen, and the count of Bentinck had begun the effort to restore his rights of sovereignty over the seigneury. For his part, the Duke of Oldenburg sought to clarify whether he or the count exercised sovereignty over the territory in question. Although at the session of 7 November Russia's co-minister of foreign affairs, Count Nesselrode, argued that the House of Holstein-Oldenburg possessed the right of succession over Kniphausen, the allies asked Prince Hardenberg of Prussia to investigate and shed further light on the matter. Hardenberg's report addressing the claims of Oldenburg, Sachsen-Coburg, and Hessen-Homburg stated unequivocally that Frederick William III rejected any changes that affected Prussian territory. Based on existing agreements, the princes in question already had received lands on the left bank of the Rhine. The allies therefore concluded that in this case they had no obligation to intervene on behalf of the German princes. The princes remained free to negotiate with Prussia or other powers to obtain

territorial swaps by mutual agreement; however, such negotiations were not the
responsibility of the four allies.

The restoration of Prussia's territory and population had been a cornerstone
of the edifice of pacification and peace constructed in 1814–15, and claims affecting Prussian interests were not likely to produce an affirmative allied response. Count Nesselrode did, however, present demands from the landgrave
of Hessen-Homburg, who sought territory or an indemnity from the Grand
Duchy of Hessen.[49] The allies considered these demands legitimate, and their
ministers in Darmstadt and Frankfurt received orders to urge the grand duke to
reach a just settlement, including a voice for the landgrave in the German Diet.
The four powers repeated this approach in response to the claims of the prince of
Windischgrätz, whose lands had been incorporated into the Kingdom of Württemberg. Based on an agreement of 1811, the prince had given up his sovereign
rights, but only for so long as the Napoleonic Confederation of the Rhine existed. He therefore sought an indemnity or the restoration of his ancient rights.
In response, allied diplomats in Stuttgart received instructions to use friendly
and private means to encourage satisfaction of the prince's claims. The plenipotentiaries meeting in Aix-la-Chapelle agreed that the prince should be paid an
indemnity. Yet another appeal came from the princess of Thurn and Taxis who
was prepared to cede territories to the prince of Hohenzollern-Sigmaringen in
return for recognition by the German Diet as one of the sovereign princes of
Germany. Both Austria and Prussia supported this arrangement.

The claims and counterclaims of German princes, ranging in status from
kings to dukes to free cities to mediatized counts, can seem insignificant and
certainly are difficult to describe based on the legal, archival, and secondary
sources consulted here. The disputes mentioned do not in any sense represent a
complete picture of the complicated process leading to the emergence of modern
Germany.[50] Still, they are noteworthy for the purposes of this study, because
they document the allies' ability to intervene in potentially disruptive situations
without appearing to impose great power decisions on second-order states. In
discussions involving German princes, the allies meeting in Aix-la-Chapelle
appeared willing to support legitimate claims based on treaty obligations and
historic rights, as long as the changes would not significantly alter the settlement codified in the Final Act of the Congress of Vienna. Nor did the allies
rule out future territorial adjustments, land swaps, or indemnities. They insisted,
however, that additional changes should be worked out by mutual agreement
among the princes involved without allied intervention. Mediatized princes and
counts approached the allies gathered in Aix-la-Chapelle, including the Russian

emperor, about their relationship to the German Confederation. But as German states, Austria and Prussia played a more active role and assumed responsibility for ensuring that these princes had a voice in the diet. Precisely because the allies agreed that mediatized princes enjoyed legal and honorific rights based on the Final Act of the Congress of Vienna, they instructed their representatives at German courts to insist that all interested parties adhere to existing treaty obligations.

Discussions about the Kingdom of Westphalia further illustrated the allied preference for negotiations between affected parties based on established treaties. In 1807 Napoleon had created the kingdom for his brother Jerome out of lands taken from Prussia, Hanover, and much of Electoral Hessen. The Congress of Vienna had dissolved the kingdom and restored to Prussia most of old Westphalia, which Napoleon had assigned to the Grand Duchy of Berg.[51] Questions remained, however, about land transactions and obligations incurred within the framework of Napoleonic Westphalia. The Elector of Hessen did not want to recognize any sales or gifts of land concluded under the authority of Jerome's kingdom. The allies held a different view, believing that obligations and rights based on the legislation of Napoleonic Westphalia should be respected. Both article 22 of the First Treaty of Paris (1814) and article 41 of the Final Act of the Congress of Vienna recognized the property rights of French subjects in lands ceded by France. To resolve the outstanding conflicts, Prussia planned to invite interested parties to participate in a commission that would decide questions related to debts, pensions, feudal relations, indemnities, and restitutions in provinces that had belonged to Napoleonic Westphalia. Legitimate claims needed to be satisfied, including those related to the lands of Electoral Hessen. In addition, because the claims in question had arisen from the victory and generosity of the allied powers—from the dissolution of the Kingdom of Westphalia and the reintegration of dispossessed princes—the ministers meeting in Aix-la-Chapelle would ask their sovereigns to send letters to the Elector of Hessen requesting withdrawal of his demands. In situations where similar efforts failed to produce a resolution, the German Diet could refer the dispute to an arbitration commission. The time had come, the four powers agreed, for German authorities to decide German territorial questions.

Russia's general desire to stand aside in German disputes grew as political debates within the confederation intensified. In response to student unrest that erupted during the Wartburg Festival of October 1817, Russia joined Austria and Prussia in denouncing the displays of seditious intent and in criticizing the inaction of the Grand Duke of Saxony-Weimar-Eisenach, Karl August, who presumably could have taken steps to prevent the alarming demonstrations.[52] The Russian government agreed with the allies that the radical proclamations of students and professors from the University of Jena constituted an assault on the German Confederation, the sovereigns of other German states, and an older generation who did not share the nationalist sentiments of liberal youth. Still, Russia's diplomats received instructions to avoid public criticism of Grand Duke Karl August, who nonetheless should be informed of Emperor Alexander's concerns. Consistent with the policy of non-intervention and with the line taken on territorial disputes, the monarch resisted Austrian and Prussian efforts to draw him into concerted (re)action.[53] Alexander recognized the threat posed by unfettered freedom of speech, but he also believed that Russia should remain a spectator in Germany and insisted that the German states must agree on measures to remedy the situation. Despite talk about possible interventions, Alexander ordered his diplomatic agents to avoid any appearance of involvement in the internal affairs of the German Confederation. He did admit, however, that based on the authority of established treaties, intervention to suppress the symptoms of revolution might be warranted, if legitimized by a majority of the federated states or a unanimous decision of the allies.[54]

Emperor Alexander's appraisal of the events in Wartburg illustrated the limits to enlightened reformism (or early liberalism) so characteristic of his reign. As Nesselrode explained the matter, and the monarch confirmed, the constitutional order of Weimar suited both the spirit of the times and the territories governed by Grand Duke Karl August, "the sole dispenser of liberties to his people." Based on their constitution, the subjects of Saxony-Weimar-Eisenach enjoyed freedom of speech and the press, understood as freedom to discuss the public good (*le bien public*) with reference to state, class, and individual interests. In fact, the grand duke could not contest these constitutional liberties without contravening the conservative principle to preserve the German Confederation, the stability of which was critical for European peace. At the same time, the grand duke's federal relations obliged him to repress and prevent abuses of "this same emancipation of discourse and the press" that violated either the constitution of Saxony-Weimar-Eisenach or the jurisdiction of the German Confederation. In other words, no member state should act in a way (or permit actions from within its territory) that prejudiced the federal system or interfered in the internal affairs of a co-state. The Wartburg speeches violated these prescriptions by implicitly condemning all German states and class distinctions and by proclaiming the existence of a pan-German association of youth. Subversive student groups, the Russian government declared, should not be allowed to act as constituent parts of the German Confederation. Universities, in other words, were not diets, and national representation did not mean overt political contestation.

In the summer of 1819, as the Territorial Commission in Frankfurt moved toward conclusion of its work, the foundations for an enduring peace within the German Confederation and between the German states and France appeared to be in place. But events on the ground continued to generate new apprehensions and discussions. As early as March 1819, the assassination by an avowed revolutionary of August von Kotzebue, an agent of the Russian legation in Mannheim, had caused disquiet among Russia's diplomats.[55] More ominous, political unrest and anti-Jewish violence (the Hep! Hep! riots) that began in Würzburg (Kingdom of Bavaria) in August had spread among students, artisans, and farmers across the German lands.[56] These and other signs of radical influence led the federal diet in Frankfurt to enact the Karlsbad Decrees (20 September 1819), which called upon German governments to prevent subversive speech in the universities and forbade universities to employ teachers who had been dismissed for sedition from other institutions. The decrees also created a commission to regulate the press throughout the confederation and established a federal office to investigate the revolutionary agitation that had appeared in several states. Although supportive of strong state action, the Russian government continued to profess a policy of non-intervention in German affairs.[57]

Allied concerns about student unrest in the German states also fueled diplomatic conversations about constitutional politics. Metternich in particular pushed for a concerted response to what he perceived as the revolutionary menace arising from the spread of constitutionalism, though he did not oppose constitutions as a matter of principle. In May 1818, the king of Bavaria decreed a constitution, and three months later the Grand Duke of Baden followed suit. In September 1819 Württemberg received a constitution, based on agreement between the monarch and estates. In Prussia, the efforts of Hardenberg and others to institute national representation continued through the summer of 1819. The Prussian debate ended when Frederick William III ordered Hardenberg to join Metternich in renouncing the idea of universal representation of the people. Austrian-Prussian cooperation then produced the Karlsbad Decrees in September 1819 and the *Schlussakte* the following year. Negotiated at conferences in Vienna, the *Schlussakte* of 1820 replaced the *Bundesakte* of 1815 as the constitutional basis for the German Confederation. The *Schlussakte* strengthened monarchical power and the instruments of political repression but did not eliminate the basic tension, described repeatedly in Russia's diplomatic communications, between the legislative power of the Frankfurt Diet and the independence of individual German states, including constitutionalized states.[58]

Throughout the political debates and social unrest swirling about the German lands in 1817–20, Emperor Alexander refused to join Austria, and eventually also Prussia, in condemning constitutional reforms. In Baden, Bavaria, and Württemberg, legitimate sovereigns had issued the constitutions; in Prussia, after years of social and institutional reform, the monarch finally had decided against constitutional arrangements. In the period since the peacemaking of 1814–15, the Russian government always had insisted that existing treaties be honored, including the Act of Confederation in Germany, and that the sovereignty of all states, large and small, be respected, based on the Final Act of the Congress of Vienna. Both Britain and Russia adhered to the principle of non-intervention in the domestic affairs of sovereign states, as long as revolution did not threaten the general interest of European peace. Repeatedly, Emperor Alexander and his foreign ministry forbade Russia's diplomats to comment on implementation of the Karlsbad Decrees or constitutional reform in German states. Communications with diplomats assigned to German courts made clear that while Alexander supported strong measures to suppress the threat of the revolutionary spirit, he remained legally and morally bound not to take any initiative on German questions or even to offer concrete advice. Only if asked by a fellow monarch, such as his friend the king of Prussia, would Alexander express his opinion on a specific situation.[59]

Emperor Alexander's reluctance to speak in a public or official manner did not indicate indifference to German affairs. Nor did it mean that he and his diplomatic agents had no thoughts or opinions to share. Diplomats' reports from Germany praised the moderate policies of the rulers in Baden and Hessen-Darmstadt who sought to accommodate liberal deputies in the chambers of the Estates.[60] Russia also worked with Britain to coordinate the language their diplomats would employ in the German states and Frankfurt. The Russian government repeatedly expressed fears about the harmful consequences of revolution and of repressive military and police measures. In response to Austria's plans to revise the act of confederation and to evidence that the Karlsbad Decrees had not produced the desired unity in the German Confederation, Alexander and his representatives highlighted the significance of moral influence. This included the moral force represented by the intimate union of allied sovereigns and embodied in the precepts to which they paid homage by the Act of 14/26 September 1815 (the Holy Alliance).[61]

On 21 November/3 December 1819, Emperor Alexander approved an overview of his ideas concerning German affairs in the form of a memorandum issued by the Ministry of Foreign Affairs.[62] Noting that the measures agreed to in Karlsbad had been presented as temporary, the memorandum warned that lack of unity among the German states would make it difficult to prevent anarchy in the future. Alexander expressed support for the Karlsbad Decrees, but on this occasion, he also noted that because they were instituted by the German Diet in Frankfurt, they rested on the principle of the diet's sovereignty. This, however, violated a key provision of the Final Act of the Congress of Vienna, which recognized the equality of rights and sovereignty of all German states. In other words, a contradiction existed between the legislative authority of the diet and the sovereign independence of member states.

Concerned about divisive responses to the Karlsbad Decrees both in Germany and among his own officials, Emperor Alexander insisted that only through persuasion, inspired by moderation and benevolence, could the repressive measures, agreed to in principle, be implemented. In other words, enforcement of the decrees should not violate the 1815 Act of Confederation or the constitutions of second-order states. This meant that individual governments should apply the new decrees based on local conditions. The diet in Frankfurt should not try to impose uniformity in enforcement. Indeed, assignment of supreme legislative power to the diet required either that the diet assume dictatorial authority or that the Act of Confederation be amended. How, the memorandum asked, could the general interest of the German union, upon which peace in Europe depended, be reconciled with the particular interests and institutions, constitutional and non-constitutional, of sovereign member states? In seeking to illuminate a pathway beyond the contradictions of 1819, the memorandum articulated a vision of institutional arrangements that can be described as liberal or constitutional, though not in the sense implied by Enlightenment radicalism or modern politics of contestation.

As things stood, the legislative authority of the German Diet could supersede that of individual states only through dictatorship or changes to the Act of Confederation. Still, Emperor Alexander hoped that within the confederation the unity required for true power could be achieved. In other words, the general interest and legal power of the German Confederation could be realized de facto (*par le fait*). The more powerful states, which were not bound by competing constitutions, could decide the question of legislative authority with the unanimous approval of their co-states, based on visible facts and the development of institutions that responded to legitimate aspirations. A handful of ambitious and malevolent men, the Russian monarch believed, should not be allowed to terrorize German governments. Their ability to do so resulted from the lack of prestige enjoyed by the governments of the day, the power of which depended on the strength of the liberal institutions given to their people. But what did Emperor Alexander and his diplomatic agents mean by liberal institutions? As other foreign policy statements made clear, the Russian government hoped that across Europe public authority would be augmented through the use of moral force, whereby governments would oppose unrest among their peoples by procuring their happiness and well-being.[63] In Russia, from roughly the mid-eighteenth century, enlightened concepts of good governance, embodied in the reforms of monarchs such as Catherine II, defined these legal-administrative policies (or aspirations). In the reign of Alexander I, the prerevolutionary vision of regular government and enlightened monarchy remained predominant.[64]

According to the memorandum of 21 November/3 December 1819, liberal institutions were not pacts wrested from weakness, contracts imposed on sovereigns by the leaders of the people, or "constitutions granted in difficult circumstances. . . to ward off the storm of the moment."[65] Rather, governments, especially those that had emerged from revolutionary crises, were obligated to operate under clearly explained conditions and solidly established forms. In addition, the times demanded that representatives of the nation vouch for and guarantee the inviolability of these conditions and forms. After this nod toward the principle of representation, the memorandum turned to a discussion of liberty, a principle that fit more easily with Russia's legalistic and moralistic understanding of the Vienna settlement. Liberty existed only within just limits, and limits on liberty were "nothing other than the principles of order." These principles in turn corresponded to the practice of Christian morality, so that liberty became a benefit, the fruits of which governments could reap. In recent times, liberty without morality (no doubt a reference to revolution) had produced terrible misfortunes. "Deprived of its natural guide," liberty led to corruption.

Once corruption took root, patriotism turned into passion, honor into immoderate criticism of government, and popularity into the destruction of public power. In these conditions, the fate of the state might hinge on a single election. Corruption also represented the absence of good faith (*bonne foi*), which, as the companion of Christian morality, should be sufficient to guarantee the legitimate supremacy of government. Indeed, benevolent governments that fulfilled their promises had nothing to fear from critics. Their authority rested on the sentiment of happiness. In conditions of happiness, the majority of men, those who knew how to appreciate happiness, would act as an involuntary movement in support of benevolent governments. People would feel connected to official actions, passions would be silenced, and governments would follow victorious, beneficial, and national policies. Assuming that the non-constitutional German states governed in the manner described, uniform principles of administration would emerge as the necessary effect of a happy example. Federal and state interests would meld into one general interest, and the true power of unity would become a reality. Alexander's vision of how the German lands might become united and the German Confederation function alongside the sovereign rights of independent states had much in common with literary idealizations of the patriarchal household. Enlightened harmoniousness and the benevolence of family relationships could be transferred to the political arena.[66]

Notwithstanding the hopes for harmonious development, in early 1820, Britain, France, and Russia continued to express concern about Austrian and Prussian domination in Germany. Second-order German states continued to look to Russia for protection, though Emperor Alexander still insisted that his diplomats appear impartial with respect to German affairs.[67] In response to reports received since August 1819 from Berlin, Frankfurt, Karlsruhe, Munich, Stuttgart, and Vienna, the monarch acknowledged his diplomats' conflicting views on the Karlsbad Decrees and constitutional negotiations in Vienna. To some, Alexander's policy appeared inconsistent and changeable, wavering between support for absolutist monarchy and acceptance of so-called liberal institutions. The monarch noted these criticisms but affirmed that his vote on German matters always resulted from fidelity to established treaties. Finally, while continuing not to take a public position on internal German politics, Alexander did concede that the Karlsbad Decrees and discussions about strengthening the federal German state might give excessive power to Austria, Prussia, and the diet. Development in this direction would be inconsistent with conservation of the political relations defined by established treaties, specifically the Final Act of the Congress of Vienna, the treaties of Paris, and subsequent supplemental and complementary acts. For these reasons, Russia would only support a single federal state if the German states and other European powers agreed to it. Russia now accepted that the transactions of 1814–15 constituted a general guarantee of the territorial possessions of signatory powers. Going forward, European peace depended on sustaining allied unity and opposing a return to the old system of partial alliances and counterforces (the balance of power).[68]

A more emphatic statement of Russia's reaction to the ongoing political debates within Germany appeared in a memorandum dated 4 February 1820 that was sent to the monarchs of Austria and Prussia. Endorsed by the Ministry of

Foreign Affairs, "the Memorandum on the Measures Taken by German Governments with Respect to Freedom of the Press and Public Education" was solicited
by Kapodistrias from Aleksandr S. Sturdza, who also had participated in writing
the Treaty of Alliance of 14/26 September 1815 (the Holy Alliance).[69] Precisely
because signatories to the Treaty of 14/26 September had a duty to speak with
frankness about the political system they had vowed to uphold, Emperor Alexander wanted his allies to receive the memorandum. The document began with
a discussion of press freedom, which recognized the open expression of political
opinions as inherent in representative forms of government. But in the German
Confederation, freedom of the press and all the other rights enjoyed by citizens
needed to be applied differently, depending on local conditions and the laws of
each state. In addition, because human societies remained subject to divine law,
power could not be taken from sovereigns or religion. This meant that governments should not concede to the spirit of the century the authority to define
representative political forms or anything else within the purview of religion,
good morals, and experience. Put another way, legal liberty did not apply to the
religious, moral, scientific, or literary creations of the human spirit. Sovereign
authority rested on divine authority, and concessions in these areas would undermine the work of government.

How did Russia's diplomatic agents understand the spirit of the century? According to the memorandum, the absence of Christian fraternity had caused the
calamities of the last half century. Once a civilization ceased to be religious, it
lost the benefits of civilization. Jealousy and distrustful politics set neighboring
countries against one another, as calculated interest replaced the calming effect
of faith and Christian benevolence. Equally harmful, distrust passed from the
domain of (international) politics into the internal relations of each state. Peoples fell into a state of nature, ceasing to live in the state of society restrained by
the law of nations. Having questioned the power of God, nations easily questioned the power of sovereigns. Having embraced "the phantom of self-interest,
liberty, and vague perfectibility," they silenced the voice of duty. Without faith,
there could be no loyalty. Without the interior peace of conscience, there could
be no public tranquility. Without the principle of harmony (*union*) and submission to God, there could be no durable society. In this section of the memorandum, the voice of Sturdza prevailed. Because the ancient religious and social
values that had created Europe were gone, the best intentions of governments
and the legitimate aspirations of peoples could not be achieved.[70] Prosperity,
material wealth, commerce, discoveries, and gigantic enterprises could not produce tranquility, in contrast to religion, which prepared in silence the happiness

of future generations. Indeed, false science and false virtues thrived in times of crisis, as moral corruption, the extinction of faith, unjustified resentment, and exaggerated pretentions propelled revolution.

Numerous diplomatic documents associated the French Revolutionary and Napoleonic Wars with moral catastrophe. In the Russian ministry's memorandum, Emperor Alexander reminded his fellow monarchs of what this meant. Europe had been rescued from the quagmire of moral collapse by Divine Providence, which had intervened to preserve Creation. This had allowed an unprecedented alliance among the sovereigns of Europe to defeat anarchic military despotism. As a result, through the Treaty of Alliance of 14/26 September 1815, religion and trust had returned to governments. This Holy Alliance recognized God's rights over human societies and guaranteed inviolable rights to sovereigns and peoples by imposing on them the reciprocal duties of conscience and Christian family.

Turning to the restrictions on political speech recently enacted in Germany, the memorandum criticized the Karlsbad Decrees, because they failed to address the interests of religion and public morality. Silent on the rights of God over human societies, the regulations allowed demagogues to use abstract thought and corrupt imagination to fuel radical doctrines. The speech of science and letters, including speech concerning the fundamental truth of the Christian religion and Divine morality, remained unrestricted. Thus, the restrictions on press freedom seemed designed not to protect religion and morality, but to prevent attacks on governments and officials. Because the regulations did not address the convictions of religious men and friends of order, force would be needed to ensure compliance. The effectiveness of legal acts lay in their ability to persuade people that the limits imposed by law were beneficial. But the German regulations failed to do this and therefore missed the opportunity to apply the maxims protective of social order to which all the sovereigns of Europe had adhered in the Treaty of 14/26 September. While one might object that a religiously heterogeneous federation such as the German Confederation could not promulgate a general law of censorship directed at religious works, the law could affirm the truths explained in the Treaty of 14/26 September and already accepted by German rulers. Such restrictions would not impinge on the profession of diverse faiths.

The Russian government's critique of German press regulations also applied to public education. The emancipation of science and abstract thought undermined the surveillance of education. Secret societies might renounce political goals, yet continue to spread impious abstract ideas, a process that would lead to further revolutionary explosions. The solution to this conundrum was Christian regeneration. Christian education, instilled from an early age, inspired voluntary submission and erected insurmountable barriers against revolutionary doctrine. Following the years of revolution and warfare, Divine Providence had given independence to the nations of Europe in return for submission to God's law. So yes, the external enemy was defeated, but the internal enemy remained, and in order to overcome the internal enemy, governments had to do more than apply administrative restrictions. Only through return to the truths consecrated by religion and justified by experience would it be possible to restore the necessary sense of duty and counteract the illusions of the people. Only through proper education could the errors of conscience and understanding that had produced so many calamities be eliminated. If these steps were taken, then once again and for the betterment of all humankind, legitimate authority would be based on the blessings of Divine Providence.

The Politics of Peace and Friendship

When Emperor Alexander and his associates denounced the politics of ideological contestation, this was not because they rejected political reform or even constitutional government.[71] Clearly, they failed to understand modern political pluralism, and they felt uncomfortable with impassioned political debate, whether in the press or in representative bodies; however, they did understand religious and cultural pluralism, and they accepted the reality of competing interests. That said, they also could not conceive of future progress without allied unity—the same allied unity that had made possible the military victory over Napoleon. Only by acting in concert to preserve peace could the repose of Europe and the happiness of the world be achieved. For the Russian monarch, to act in concert also meant that the allies would support each other both materially and morally. Moral influence, no less than military force, represented a critical tool of concerted action. Since the reign of Catherine II, the Russian monarchy had tried to rely more on moral persuasion than overt coercion in the practice of government and the imposition of authority. The attention to moral force may also explain the Russian preference for the general alliance, based on the principles of Christian morality and fraternity contained in the Holy Alliance, over the Quadruple Alliance. Although both Austria and Britain viewed the Quadruple Alliance as more critical to the preservation of peace, Russia's diplomats described it as an alliance of exclusivity rather than inclusiveness.

Despite divergent interpretations of established treaties, both the Russian and Austrian-British perspectives found their way into the protocols of

Aix-la-Chapelle. The difference of opinion (or emphasis) at no point threatened the unity of the alliance or the commitment of the allies to the work they had begun. The personal authority and friendship of the sovereigns remained critical to the process of completing and implementing the peace. The allies strongly believed that recent history and the principle of experience authorized reaffirmation of the Quadruple Alliance in case of revolution in France. In 1818 they expected (or hoped for) stability in France yet continued to see Napoleon and his supporters as a threat.[72] Their understanding of legality and legitimacy, enshrined in the treaties of 1814, 1815 and 1818, also assumed ongoing reform of the social, civic, and political institutions of European states. Laws, treaties, and established political arrangements were needed not only to define constitutional legitimacy and territorial possessions, but also to counter and check the foibles of human nature. It was no accident that post-Vienna diplomatic documents repeatedly presented the moral principles of family and friendship as the model for political relationships and administrative order.[73] The equilibrium so often mentioned in documents of the era referred not only to European politics and international relations, but also to the just equilibrium between governments and the public mood (*l'esprit public*).[74] This was not the balance of power pursued under the old regime. This was a balancing of interests and obligations, domestic and international, designed to preserve tranquility, peace, and order in Europe.

CHAPTER 3

Alliance Unity and Intervention in Naples (1820–21)

G LORIOUS AS THE EDIFICE of peace had appeared at the end of 1818, troubling events continued to unfold. Repeatedly, local circumstances forced the great powers to reexamine the Quadruple and general alliances, including the question of what it meant to act in concert (*concerter*). Simply put, the perils of war and revolution never receded from what the peace-makers saw before them. In the years 1820 and 1821, diplomats faced political uncertainty, the threat of revolutionary upheaval, and the looming prospect of war.[1] Since 1817 German politics had caused concern, and in December 1818, the French government again had shown signs of instability.[2] The departure of the Duke of Richelieu, a moderating influence and trusted interlocutor, fueled nagging suspicions about the viability of the Bourbon restoration.[3] Outright assaults on the Bourbon rulers of Spain and the Kingdom of the Two Sicilies heightened the sense that volatility reigned in French politics, and confirmed the fears of radicalism and revolution.[4] The peace settlement would survive, but the longing for tranquility would not be satisfied.

On 1 January 1820, Spanish troops in Las Cabezas, under the command of Lieutenant Colonel Rafael Riego, disobeyed royal orders to set sail for South America, where colonial insurrections had been underway since 1808–10. The disobedience became more than mutiny when Riego proclaimed restoration of the liberal constitution of 1812. The constitution provided for an independent judiciary, civil liberties for the nation, and an elected Cortes to share power with the king. Initially, the great powers responded to the events in Spain with re-straint, making no commitment to concrete action. Indeed, not until 7 March, when King Ferdinand VII accepted the constitution, did it become clear that a revolution had taken place. Even then, the ambiguity continued. Civil strife erupted in multiple localities, yet the king remained on his throne as a constitu-tional monarch. The allies dared to hope that popular loyalty to the monarchy, which had inspired admiration during the French occupation, would overcome the revolutionary spirit and defeat the forces of disorder.[5] During the summer, however, the situation became more perilous. The constitutional movement spread to Portugal, where on 24 August, liberals proclaimed support for the Spanish constitution. This new political order lasted until May 1823, at which time monarchists emboldened by the French intervention in Spain returned King John VI to absolute power.[6]

Disturbing as conditions in Spanish America, Spain, and Portugal appeared, it was rebellion in the Kingdom of the Two Sicilies that most frightened the allies and led to military intervention.[7] The Neapolitan mutinies began on 2 July 1820 in Nola and quickly spread to Avellino, where General Guglielmo Pepe also declared support for the Spanish constitution. Within a few days, King Ferdinand I and his son Francesco, Duke of Calabria and vicar-general, accepted the Spanish constitution for the kingdom. On 9 July, Ferdinand and Francesco greeted General Pepe as he led royal troops into Naples. Finally, on 13 July, the king swore allegiance to the constitution, while also promising unspecified reforms. As in Spain, where Ferdinand I of the Two Sicilies remained a potential successor to the childless Ferdinand VII, the monarchy in Naples survived liberal revolution by accepting the liberal order. Publication of the constitution on 24 July paved the way for parliamentary elections in September. Once assembled, the parliament elected a Permanent Deputation with seven members to monitor the king's government when the legislative body was not in session.

For the five great powers, developments in Italy transformed abstract condemnations of revolution and discussions about collective intervention into concrete negotiations to address an alarming sequence of events. In the absence of a clear and present danger such as war with Napoleon, talk of an allied response produced public disagreement, which threatened the unity assumed to be so essential to European peace. Beginning with the Spanish Revolution in January 1820 and continuing through the Congress of Verona, which met at the end of 1822, questions of intervention dominated diplomatic discussions and exposed fissures in the European political system. Conflict resulted from divergent interpretations of treaty obligations and from the tension between the legal stipulations defining the alliance and the right of sovereign states to reform their domestic political institutions. As in earlier negotiations concerning the nature of the European alliance and Russia's proposal for a treaty of guarantee, Emperor Alexander I pursued a pragmatic course focused on preserving great power unity. In the end, the overriding commitment to peace held firm, and the allies accepted that an enduring peace required neither complete agreement nor the absence of military action.

Russia Responds to the Revolutionary Spirit

Prior to the allied meetings in Troppau and Laibach that would sanction Austrian intervention in Naples, Russia's diplomats penned a series of surveys assessing political conditions in Europe.[8] The surveys showed that the Russian monarch and his diplomatic agents remained committed to the legal stipulations of 1814, 1815, and 1818, the principles and prescriptions of which they tried to apply to tumultuous events on the ground. Predictably, conditions in France loomed large. Throughout 1819 and into early 1820, Russian officials discussed political instability in France both among themselves and with the other great powers. Their analyses revealed concern about the spirit of party and genie of revolution that had revived in France and threatened to drag the kingdom into political crisis. Revolution, Russia's policymakers believed, easily led to military aggression, which might compel the allies to undertake armed intervention.[9] As early as March 1819, Emperor Alexander had received communications from Austria and Prussia warning of threats to the regime of King Louis XVIII. By September Prince Metternich had proposed convening allied ambassadorial conferences in Paris, where the four powers could monitor developments and coordinate a response.

The British position on possible intervention in France was transmitted by Foreign Secretary Castlereagh to Russia's co-minister of foreign affairs, Ioannis Kapodistrias, and ambassador in London, Christoph Lieven, in a memorandum of 24 September 1819.[10] The British government believed that the political rumbles in France posed no danger to peace or the European system. Equally significant, the creation of a center for allied communication in Paris would violate the protocols of Aix-la-Chapelle, which had brought France into the alliance of great powers. Based on the protocols, if an imminent threat of revolution or military aggression arose, any of the four allies could call for an extraordinary conference to organize a coordinated response.[11] In light of this provision and the need to consider public opinion, the British government refused to commit to any specific action in advance of actual events. Russia's diplomats seemed to understand Britain's constitutional constraints. Moreover, as Castlereagh also pointed out, it was essential that the allies not appear opposed to the current government in France. The French people needed to feel connected to their monarchy, and the perception of foreign opposition could undermine the connection.

On the question of French politics, Russia's monarch and Ministry of Foreign Affairs agreed with Austria and Prussia that France had deviated from the path taken in 1816, which had led to the happy results of Aix-la-Chapelle. Russia's diplomats saw in the allegedly liberal government headed by Élie Decazes, which was formed after elections in the fall of 1819, the potential for military aggression. At the end of 1819, however, before the trajectory of the Spanish insurrection became clear and before the outbreak of revolution in Naples, the Russian commitment to allied unity remained paramount. Emperor Alexander continued to tout the most intimate union of the great powers. This union, which constituted the core of the general alliance of European states, needed to be preserved, so that France could benefit from legitimate and constitutional monarchy. Russia therefore tried to steer a middle course, by which the allies would explain to Louis XVIII the dangers threatening his regime and urge him to change direction.[12] Such action would not alter France's relationship to the general alliance, as defined by the protocols of Aix-la-Chapelle, but it would fulfill an important duty required by both the protocols and the Treaty of 14/26 September 1815 (the Holy Alliance). This was the duty of veracity that obliged the allies to speak truthfully about potential dangers and in this instance to remind France of its obligation to uphold the conservative principles of the social order. Because the allies remained divided, Alexander avoided proclaiming an opinion on French politics. He did, however, instruct his minister in Paris, General Karl O. Pozzo di Borgo, to point out to the French government its responsibility for Europe's present and future tranquility. If France at any moment threatened European peace, Russia stood ready, based on existing treaties, to cross into French territory with an allied army.

One month later, instructions sent to Russia's diplomats abroad affirmed the policy of non-interference in the domestic affairs of France and the German Confederation.[13] If solicited, Russia's opinion could be shared, assuming that any statement conformed "to the principles of law, the dignity of crowns, and the real well-being of the peoples." This well-being would be real, moreover, only insofar as it resulted from the moral force of the governments involved. As things turned out, the Duke of Richelieu returned to power in February 1820, following the assassination of the Duke of Berry, Louis XVIII's nephew.[14] Fears about France had exposed potential rifts in the alliance; however, the decision to stand aside seemed prudent. Spain emerged as the more obvious threat to European peace, and some in the Russian government even expressed an overt pro-France position.

In a memorandum of February 1820, Aleksandr M. Obreskov (1793–1885), counselor (*sovetnik*) at the Russian mission in Vienna, openly called for a Russian-French alliance, based on the idea that the interests of Austria, Britain, and Prussia did not align with those of Russia.[15] Although Obreskov's position

contradicted an important principle of Alexander I's foreign policy, the avoidance of separate alliances in Europe, it is worth reviewing for the discussion of
what constituted a viable political alliance. Writing of the Quadruple Alliance,
Obreskov noted that an effective and sustainable alliance rested on shared interests and provided advantages to all contracting parties. The experience of history
showed that alliances lacking this "principle of existence and conservation" remained illusory, onerous, and unequal. Precisely because nature assigned to each
state a special existence, defined by distinct interests and relationships, alliances
succeeded only where a community of shared interests formed. Not surprisingly,
the greater the number of contracting parties, the more likely it became that particular interests would diverge. Only if all parties agreed could general harmony
be achieved. Complete agreement, moreover, usually required a society of war,
as in the successful coalition to defeat Napoleon, where equality of interests had
existed in the nature of things.

In the current Quadruple Alliance, Obreskov continued, the common purpose lay in maintaining legitimate monarchy in France, if necessary, through
coercive action or war. But despite the shared purpose, members of the alliance
had different interests in its success. England, the natural rival and enemy of
France, sought to weaken the latter by fomenting disorders inside French territory and arming other European states against the kingdom. The vital principle of the Quadruple Alliance, the preservation of the Bourbon dynasty on the
French throne, thus stood in opposition to British interests. A peaceful France
inevitably would grow in power and prosperity, which meant that British participation in efforts to pacify France would never be active or sincere. Nor did
Britain possess the resources needed to take part in a continental war. Because
public opinion and electoral politics played a key role in decisions about taxation and other official actions, the British government could not prosecute an
unpopular war. At the same time, Britain's refusal to participate in a war would
violate both the spirit and letter of the Quadruple Alliance. In other words, in
the event of an allied military intervention in France, the particular and relative
situation of Britain would compel the government to remain on the sidelines as
a benevolent spectator.

The historian can see in Obreskov's appraisal the memory of Russia's wartime
experience in 1812, a moment when the lands and peoples of the empire had
withstood the onslaught of Napoleon's multinational Grand Army. Emperor
Alexander's diplomats had good reason to fear that the burden of a European
war would fall disproportionately on Russian troops. Austria's inability to fight a
war also concerned Obreskov. Another rival of France, Austria too would benefit

from upheaval in the Bourbon kingdom. Moreover, because Austria had reached the apogee of its political power and had exhausted the resources given to it by Divine Providence, fiscal constraints, specifically the discontent fueled by higher taxes, would prevent sincere participation in an armed intervention. For Austria, only peace could secure stability. So once again, the interests of a contracting party stood in opposition to the interests of the Quadruple Alliance, which remained responsible for ensuring tranquility in France. Lacking the earnest involvement of both Austria and Britain, the Quadruple Alliance was doomed to fail. As an alliance of principles, rather than interests, it was illusory. As an alliance that was hostile toward a nonoffending state, it was unequal. France had returned to the rights and great power status of its natural position, and the French government had fulfilled all treaty obligations. Confident that future obligations also would be met, the allies had formally renounced all coercive surveillance of the country's domestic relations and government actions. In other words, the Quadruple Alliance had achieved its legitimate goal of guaranteeing that the French government carry out its legal obligations. In light of this success, the alliance now rested on abstract principles, not positive interests.

Of all the allies, Obreskov continued, Russia had the most interest in preserving the full force of the Quadruple Alliance plus France (sometimes referred to as the grand alliance). Russia was too strong either to need or to wish that other states be weakened. Loyalty had been and remained the supreme regulator, the religion of Emperor Alexander's foreign policy. Loyalty required scrupulous execution of contractual obligations, especially with respect to the *casus foederis et belli*. But could Russia fulfill the purpose of the alliance with its own forces? In the event of an appeal to the Quadruple Alliance, the defection of Austria and Britain would produce a political schism at a time when unity and fraternity among heads of nations would be most needed. Obreskov, like other Russian diplomats since 1815, sensed his country's political separateness. He accepted this as the empire's normal position, but he did not want to isolate France, which an appeal to the Quadruple Alliance would do. In addition, despite Austria's domination in Germany and sovereignty in Italy, Prussia remained independent, though still unable to play an active role. Russia's only useful ally, therefore, was France, which if alienated might ally with Austria.

Obreskov did not conclude that the Quadruple Alliance lacked a purpose or function. The alliance remained beneficial. Peace in Europe depended on good order in France, where the moral force of the Quadruple Alliance strengthened legitimacy and served as an obstacle to rebellion. But if the goals of the Quadruple Alliance began to appear tentative or impossible, Russia should reject appeals for action. Only if France became outwardly aggressive should Russia recognize the *casus foederis et belli*. As long as the conservative treaties of order and peace were respected in Europe, and as long as the form of government adopted in France seemed appropriate and prudent, Russia should remain a passive spectator. Austria's (unspecified) shared interests with other powers, which diminished the influence of Russia, provided proof of the eternal truth that real, useful, and sincere alliances could be based only on the nature of things and on shared positive interests, not on abstractions or individual relationships that invariably changed as circumstances evolved. The nature of things, according to Obreskov, called for an alliance between Russia and France, based on a happy convergence of interests.

Obreskov's realist description of European order did not correspond to the foreign policy of Emperor Alexander I, who upheld the Quadruple Alliance and placed his hopes in personal friendship among the sovereigns. In March 1820 the court of Vienna denied the existence of any separate or secret alliance between Austria and Britain.[16] The Russian monarch had resisted Kapodistrias's earlier critique of the Quadruple Alliance and left Aix-la-Chapelle satisfied, despite the failure to secure a defensive treaty of mutual guarantee. Reasonable concerns persisted, however, as illustrated by Aleksandr S. Sturdza's "Review of the Year 1819," which was prepared by imperial order for anonymous publication abroad.[17] Working from an outline provided by Kapodistrias, Sturdza's composition received Alexander's endorsement. The review's original purpose had been to influence foreign opinion, but circumstances had changed with the outbreak of the Spanish insurrection, and a period of crisis had begun. The review remained unpublished, and the author's reflective voice—said to be inspired by a spirit of concord, peace, and truth—no longer seemed appropriate. Nor did the claim that Sturdza's judgments should not express the viewpoint of a particular party, sect, or government.[18] Although the author's moderate tone conveyed a sense of calm deliberation, he could not disguise his yearning for tranquility or anxiety about the future. The peacemakers may have possessed tools that allowed them to navigate a great deal of turbulence, and the promise of peace seemed real enough, but lofty principles were one thing and harsh realities another.

Despite the tension between principle and reality, an ongoing theme in the review, Sturdza began on an optimistic note. The current historical moment represented a time of calm following years of crisis, an opportunity for impartial reflection, and a period of change in the moral order of the entire world. In writing the review, Sturdza hoped to counter the extremism threatening stability in Europe and preventing recognition of the truth. Truth could be advanced, he argued, through thoughtful, objective appraisal of the political events of 1819. Indeed, even though the spirit of party and the banner of belligerent opinion endangered the fragile peace that Europe had achieved, it remained possible, based on good sense and the examination of past experience, to find the voice of reason. The voice of reason, purportedly embodied in the review, sought to transcend radical positions and illuminate the truth. If we could begin to understand the past, Sturdza explained, it might be possible to achieve a better order of things, a return to moderation, which would allow conscience and religion to be heard and truth to prevail. Progress, in other words, depended on impartial analysis of the past and on the ability of individuals to get hold of and control their passions.

The "Review of the Year 1819" stressed the novelty of the historical moment and rejoiced in the political reunification of Europe—a unity that had not been seen since the "Congress of Westphalia." At the same time, given the difficulty of conducting diplomacy and the enormity of the task undertaken by the peacemakers, Sturdza also concluded that the need to guarantee all the rights, satisfy all the desires, and reconcile all the conflicts of Europe's interested parties created problems without parallel in the annals of the world. It was not surprising that complete reconciliation had not been attained and the germs of disorder persisted. As Sturdza summed up the complications, wishes were not the same as rights, and hopes were not the same as realities. The effort to create a new world had not succeeded in fully reconciling the past with the present or in harmonizing the old and new order of things. Notwithstanding the great and worthy achievements of Vienna, Paris, and Aix-la-Chapelle, critical problems continued to threaten good order. These included political divisions in France, Spain's relations with its American colonies and with Portugal, tensions between Sweden and Denmark, German disquiet, and unilateral British action to suppress the slave trade and Barbary pirates.[19]

Sturdza understood that the peacemakers had not begun their work with a blank slate; past issues and historical claims could not simply be erased. In addition, the desire to restore France to great power status had challenged the idea of a general European alliance in which every state claimed parity and independence. Indeed, as generations of historians have documented, and as Sturdza affirmed, it became clear at the Congress of Vienna that the great powers had become the arbiters of the European system. Second-order states had little choice but to accept decisions made by others that nonetheless affected their interests. According to the review, the diplomatic agents of the great powers shared a deep and sincere desire for good order, yet because of contradictory and ambiguous principles, and more important, because of irreligion and uncontrolled human passions, threats to stability remained.

The next section of the review addressed conditions in critical parts of Europe. For the moment (at the end of 1819), the situation in France had improved, and although deep political divisions remained, the formation of the new government encouraged optimism. Despite the harmful spirit of party, France's recovery from revolutionary upheaval continued and allowed the country to grow stronger.[20] Spain, by contrast, had not been able to restore its position in the European system, a situation that Sturdza attributed to internal political conditions and the government's limited wisdom. Although deserving of a brilliant destiny and loyal to the sacred relationship with its king (this soon would change), the Spanish nation remained vulnerable to insurrection. Dangers loomed throughout Europe, which having been freed of a tyrant, still faced the threat of revolution. Even Britain, which seemed more happily situated than its old rivals, faced the challenges of radicalism and agitation for reform. Like Spain, Britain also possessed a colonial system, which created another source of discontent. If Britain hoped, moreover, to triumph over the threats emanating from attacks on property, religious dissent, indirect taxation, and seditious writings, two conditions were needed: wise government to undertake reform of the colonial system and the continuing strength of the British nation's unwritten laws or *moeurs*, which religiously guarded family life.

In Sturdza's mind, only Russia seemed immune to the pan-European threat of revolution. Deploying some of the proto-Slavophile arguments for which he would become famous, Sturdza did not see in Russia the desire for reform or change that affected social life in the rest of Europe. Russia soon would experience its own jolt of radicalism in the Decembrist Rebellion of 1825, but in 1819 Sturdza still could draw attention to the absence of unrest, and he could attribute what turned out to be a deceptive calm to the continuing influence of religion, which in Russia guided social and political behavior. Characterized by youth, vigor, and savage energy, Russia had been assigned a special destiny embodied in the growth of imperial power. Having reached the apogee of its physical and material grandeur, Russia now was obligated to use those treasures to perfect its own internal condition. Equally noteworthy, unlike the other states of Europe, Russia had not rejected the dictates of religion. Sturdza therefore hoped that in exercising its newly acquired influence, Russia could avoid a mortal blow.

Critical to any understanding of European politics after 1815 were conditions in the reconstituted collective life of Germany, anchored by Austria and Prussia. Here too danger lurked. Germany, in Sturdza's analysis, was a place where the rapid dissemination of ideas, a phenomenon broadly characteristic of contemporary Europe, threatened good order and undermined the national spirit (*esprit national*).[21] The same ideas could affect different places in different ways; in Germany, external influences and irreligion had led to the rejection of reality and attacks on authority. Sturdza did not mention the murder in March 1819 of August von Kotzebue, an agent of the Russian legation in Mannheim, but he did express outrage over assaults on Jews that had begun in August at the University of Würzburg and spread among students, artisans, and farmers in western Germany.[22] Sturdza found it deeply disturbing that this violence could occur in the century of tolerance. Germany needed unity, he concluded, which then compelled him to evaluate the governments of individual German states based on their adherence to the federal system. Critical of the repressive Karlsbad Decrees, which emphasized police measures, and of the Act of Confederation, which created ambiguities and contradictions in the forms of German government and in the relationship between federal power and individual states, Sturdza saw disorder looming in Germany, despite the restoration of Austrian power.[23]

The role of Austrian power in Germany led Sturdza also to consider political conditions in Italy, where the Habsburg Empire's geographic position gave it significant influence. This influence, Sturdza argued, needed to be exercised reasonably within natural limits that did not threaten the general European association. Arguably more dangerous for European order than any abuse of Austrian hegemony was the lack of security and the potential for violence in a territory where individual kingdoms and states had not yet returned to their natural position and where the universal agitation affecting so much of Europe remained visible. Sturdza did not doubt that revolution continued to threaten the European system, even though the tyranny of Napoleon and the decades-long state of war had ended. This was because the state of agitation did not result from social inequity or competing political interests, but from uncontrolled passions that had been stirred up for so long and could not be easily calmed. Religion, reason, wise government, and moral order—these were the ingredients that would guarantee the equilibrium of Europe.

After surveying the fragile stability prevailing (but soon to be overturned) in Europe, the review commented on other parts of the world where specific problems and events affected European politics. Discussion began with America, the New World, though also a world enriched by European civilization. Although Sturdza expected America (North and South) to play a moral and political role commensurate with its physical size and natural endowments, he focused on the more urgent situation in South America, where the descendants of Spanish conquerors and African slaves struggled for liberty and independence. Beginning in January 1820 the Spanish Revolution would force Alexander I to take a more active interest in Latin American affairs. For the moment, however, Sturdza could write that neutrality represented the appropriate course, when geography removed a state from direct participation in events such as the revolts in the Spanish colonies. Nor, while critical of Spain and of the Portuguese court in Rio de Janeiro for their handling of the colonies, did Sturdza see any reason for a European power to support rebellion in the New World. The only possible motive was aggrandizement, and so, given the absence of a viable Spanish plan to reunite the colonies with the metropolis, he expected the troubles to be protracted. The Spanish colonial system lacked the flexibility needed to survive in modern times, and the rebellious Spanish colonies lacked the social maturity of their North American counterparts. Resolution would not come quickly, which did indeed pose a threat to stability in Europe.[24]

Closely related to conditions in the Americas was the question of the slave trade, outlawed in principle by the acts of Vienna and Paris. Sturdza acknowledged that justice cried out for abolition, but he remained suspicious of British intentions. When should the internal policies and principles of a particular nation, in this case Britain, become universal? No doubt aware of the parallels between slavery and serfdom, Sturdza argued that in agreeing to eliminate the slave trade, the European powers had taken a position on a matter in which they had no direct interest. In other words, they had no right (*droit*) or credit (*mérite*) to decide this great and important question. Fortunately, the British initiative to organize a joint military expedition to suppress the slave trade was being replaced with separate negotiated agreements, such as the treaty between Britain and Spain, which as of May 1820 should end Spanish involvement in the trade. Similar negotiations were underway with the court of Rio de Janeiro.[25]

Questions of interest and legitimate authority likewise informed Sturdza's discussion of efforts to suppress the Barbary states, another collective international action being pursued by Britain.[26] Again, the desire to end human suffering—specifically the suffering of European captives—represented a noble idea, as did the implied affinity between the traffic in black Africans and the captivity of white Europeans. But the Ottoman Porte, suzerain of the North African states, refused to reach an agreement on this question. Nor, in Sturdza's opinion, would the effort to protect commerce and other economic interests ever be sufficient to guarantee peaceful navigation of the seas. Of greater consequence were the motives animating the interested parties. To speak and act in the name of suffering humanity represented an appeal for divine intervention, which did

not depend on human actions. Sturdza was reluctant to reject the just principle of eliminating the slave trade and piracy, but he refused to condone joint
European action or ignore the legitimate interests of Spain, Portugal, and the
Ottoman Empire. To reconcile the contradiction, he retreated into a statement
of religious aspiration. Commerce and industry would not bring civilization to
Africa, end the slave trade, or suppress the Barbary pirates. Only the Christian
religion could enlighten Africa and lead the continent to a form of social life
that corresponded to the dignity of the human being and the grandeur of God's
providence. As he did previously in explaining the European powers' generosity
toward France, Sturdza insisted that the work of God be distinguished from
human plans and understandings.

Europe's relations with the Ottoman Empire received more direct attention
in Sturdza's discussion. The author seemed to treat Asia—specifically the Ottoman Empire, Persia, and India—as part of the European political system,
though he also noted that religious differences prevented any fusion of interests and races (*sic*). In civilization, commerce, and enlightenment, peoples competed; only in religion could they be united. This was precisely the reason that
the Muslim states of Turkey and Persia were fundamentally incompatible with
Europe. Although both had forged long-term alliances with European powers
(Austria, Britain, France, and Russia), these alliances were changeable, and as a
result, the Muslim states had not attained a stable position in the European system. Commenting further on conditions within the Ottoman Empire, Sturdza
perceived irreversible decline. He praised Sultan Selim III for his enlightened
views and commitment to reform, proof that he could have been a worthy
Christian, but described the inertia of the empire as both a threat and a form
of resistance to the European association.[27] Unable, moreover, to conceal the
Russian position for which he spoke, Sturdza also claimed that integration of
the Ottoman Empire and of Russia's relations with the Porte into the European
system might lead to disorder. Just as Emperor Alexander did not wish to get
involved in rooting out the transatlantic slave trade, he likewise did not want
his European allies to interfere in Russian-Ottoman relations. The same could
be said of Russia's relations with Persia. Although the principles of Europe's new
political system—equity and Christian fraternity—also should be applied to
the Ottoman and Persian empires, this had to be done in a manner that would
not upset the order of things.[28] The lack of internal change in these societies
was something that human action could not currently overcome. Only God's
providence, his sovereign care in governing his creation, could produce the desired outcome.

Aleksandr Sturdza's "Review of the Year 1819" identified a range of problems
that might impact European peace, and by March 1820, events on the ground,
specifically military rebellion in Spain, had borne out his predictions. Emperor
Alexander had quickly recognized the danger and ordered his diplomats to report on the reactions of allied courts.[29] Once again, the monarch hoped to find
a satisfactory solution in the moral force represented by the intimate union between the first courts. More concretely, he wanted the allies to discuss in confidence three critical questions. What measures would the allies be duty bound to
take: (1) if the Spanish government could not quash the rebellion with wisdom
and proper means; (2) if the Spanish king solicited assistance from the allies;
and (3) if the crisis dragged on in a manner that threatened the peninsula, the
colonies, and the rest of Europe?

In a memorandum written by Kapodistrias and read to Emperor Alexander
on 30 March/11 April 1820, the co-minister of foreign affairs analyzed the ongoing crisis and revolutionary threats, based on reports received from Russia's
missions abroad since the end of 1819.[30] The themes of the memorandum echoed
earlier discussions. Subversive projects threatened the states of the German Confederation. The French government remained weak in its struggle with both the
ultra-royalists and the supporters of Napoleon (*les hommes des Cent jours*), though
steps taken since the assassination of the Duke of Berry—another reorganization
of the government, laws to protect the royal family, and restrictions on civil liberties, especially freedom of the press—represented an effort to return to the administrative course that had proven successful in 1816–18.[31] Schism between the
Belgians and Dutch endangered the Kingdom of the Netherlands, and in Britain,
a host of circumstances fueled disorder and opposition to the government: radicalism and popular unrest; political assassination (a reference to the Cato Street
conspiracy of 23 February 1820 to assassinate the British cabinet); repressive police
measures; and controversy surrounding the accession of George IV and the king's
separation from his wife, who claimed her rights as queen consort. In Spain, the
consequences of the military insurrection had spread: the king had been forced to
accept the constitution of 1812, British and Prussian mediation regarding the Rio
de la Plata appeared ineffective, and the rebellious provinces of Spanish America
continued to move toward emancipation.[32] In the midst of these developments,
Switzerland alone enjoyed tranquility, and Italy's suffering seemed containable.
The northern states (Denmark, Russia, and Sweden) experienced tremors, but not
of the sort to weaken the foundations of social order. In general, and despite some
bright spots, countries across Europe had begun to feel the effects of a conspiracy
secretly organized by men raised in the school of the French Revolution.

How had the revolutionary danger arisen and what had caused the catastrophes menacing the two hemispheres? Could a solution to the problem be found? Revolutionary conspirators persisted in trying to destroy the "old institutions based on principles of morality and religion and to replace them with new [ones] created in the spirit of democracy or in the system of so-called national representations." To that end, they sought to supplant established monarchies with the authority of royal magistrates (*rois magistrats*). The simultaneity of the events described, political conditions in Germany, and the investigations undertaken by the British government all pointed to a growing revolutionary peril. Governments lacked authority in the eyes of their peoples, and the loss of credibility led the inferior classes to demand an active role in lawmaking and public administration. The decisive consequences of these demands could be seen in the independence of North America, the movement to abolish slavery, and the French Revolution. Neither the wars that had ended in 1815, nor the policies of individual governments had effectively stemmed the revolutionary tide. Many governments, moreover, clung to the dangerous illusion that revolution had been imprisoned with Bonaparte on Saint Helena. European governments needed time, wisdom, and moderation to restore their authority. But to expect that five years of political reorganization and legal order could undo the violent action caused by thirty years of military despotism was unrealistic. Kapodistrias did not elaborate on this point, though over the years, Russia's diplomatic communications frequently referred to the need for good governance to prevent revolution.

Broadly speaking, the concept of good governance assumed that people (whether subjects, citizens, or nations) identified with their rulers and that each government had a responsibility to formulate and implement policies designed to reinforce the desired connection. In this instance, Kapodistrias affirmed the critical role of the pact of Christian fraternity (the Holy Alliance) at the center of which stood the alliance of the four great powers (the Quadruple Alliance) plus France. "The intimate union of the sovereigns, founders of the European alliance [had] delivered the world from revolutionary despotism." Only through this union could peace be preserved. Although at the time of writing the allies had not yet agreed to respond collectively to the insurrection in Spain, the Russian government continued to argue for a legal and moral obligation to act in concert, even if only to speak in concert. Revolution in the Kingdom of the Two Sicilies soon would overshadow discussions about Spain, and not until the end of 1822 would the allies finally decide to act on the peninsula. For the moment, Kapodistrias could argue only that the Quadruple Alliance had been cemented through coercive force and that present circumstances required not the passive alliance preferred by Austria and Britain, but an active alliance willing to use military power. Such an alliance inevitably would highlight Russian power, which was exactly what the allies feared.

In the spring and summer of 1820, conditions on the ground continued to worsen.[33] French politics remained inflamed, and Louis XVIII felt increasingly insecure about the monarchy's future. News of the Cato Street conspiracy and the tensions caused by George IV's refusal to recognize his wife as queen likewise rattled the nerves of seasoned peacemakers.[34] Nor did the political crisis in Spain subside. Radicalism and civil strife continued to spread, even though Ferdinand VII appeared to accept the role of constitutional monarch. Most disturbing, however, was the revolutionary eruption in the Kingdom of the Two Sicilies on July 2, even though earlier in the year Italy had been judged containable. Ceding to the will of the people, King Ferdinand I had proclaimed the Spanish constitution of 1812 and turned over the reins of government to his son. Reporting from Paris, Russia's minister plenipotentiary, Count Karl O. Pozzo di Borgo, decried the arrogance of the rebels and the dangerous example being established for the rest of Italy. Nesselrode wondered at how quickly the king of the Two Sicilies had bowed to the alleged wish of the nation by promising to establish a constitutional order.[35] From Prussia, the minister of foreign affairs, Christian Gunther Bernstorff, described his country's political mood and the condition of its military as tranquil, but he nonetheless urged the allies to convene a meeting of the sovereigns. The Prussian government had been countering constitutional demands for two years and wanted the alliance quickly to sanction Austrian action in Italy.[36] In the climate of political uncertainty engulfing the European continent, could the idiom of enduring peace—treaty obligations, legitimate sovereignty, moderate constitutional reform, good governance, and religious morality—sustain allied unity?

The Decision to Intervene in Naples

The revolution in Naples produced a flurry of diplomatic activity, which led to the opening on 11/23 October 1820 of allied conferences in the town of Troppau in Austrian Silesia. Attended by the "holy allies" (the monarchs of Austria, Prussia, and Russia), their most important ministers (Metternich for Francis I, Bernstorff and Hardenberg for Frederick William III, and Kapodistrias and Nesselrode for Alexander I), and observers from Britain and France, the meetings have been described as a congress of the Holy Alliance at which Metternich's policy of social repression to counter revolution got the better of Alexander's willingness to accept liberal constitutional reform.[37] The image of a conservative turn in the Russian monarch's foreign policy downplays both the complexity of the events being addressed and the nuances of his diplomatic posture.[38] Also underestimated is Britain's contribution to critical discussions about the functioning of the alliance. Throughout the conferences in Troppau and subsequently in Laibach, the British government argued that legally established treaty obligations to combat revolution applied only to France. Because France was not threatened by revolution, allied intervention in Spain, Italy, and elsewhere could not be justified. The British insistence on non-intervention did not cause an open breach with the alliance, but it did force policymakers to change their understanding of what it meant to act in concert.

Reports of seditious activities in Naples appeared as early as June 1820, before revolution struck the Kingdom of the Two Sicilies. Earlier in the spring, the Austrian government had suggested a private meeting between Francis and Alexander, which the Russian monarch had declined.[39] Having begun in March to push for joint allied discussion of the events in Spain, Alexander continued to insist that any meeting to discuss Spain or Italy should be constituted as a formal conference of the alliance. The polite back and forth between Austria and Russia dragged on into early September, when the two powers plus France, Prussia, and several Italian governments finally agreed to hold discussions in Troppau.[40] Russian policy remained what it had been since the start of the Spanish insurrection. As important as any concrete decision to address a specific crisis were larger questions about how the alliance should function and on what legal basis the allies possessed the authority to act.

While Russia preferred a broad discussion of the revolutionary crisis, Austria kept the focus on the Kingdom of the Two Sicilies, based on the special relationship between the two countries. By a treaty of 12 June 1815, Francis I and Ferdinand I had promised to honor the territorial integrity of their respective states and protect their subjects from uprisings and innovations that might lead to disorders. In addition, the treaty allowed Francis to station 25,000 troops in Austria's Italian provinces, and if necessary, required Ferdinand to place the Neapolitan army under Austrian command.[41] Consistent with Austria's special interest in the Two Sicilies, a memorandum of 28 August 1820 also informed the governments of Britain, France, Prussia, and Russia that Francis I had sent troops into his Italian territories.[42] Certain of his right to act, the Austrian emperor sought moral support from the allies. He asked them to: (1) declare the Kingdom of the Two Sicilies to be in a state of rebellion against legitimate monarchy; (2) deny recognition to the new Neapolitan government and refuse to negotiate outside the alliance framework; (3) send common instructions explaining the nature and causes of the events in Naples to their diplomatic representatives; and (4) entrust negotiations concerning Naples to an ambassadorial conference in Vienna.

The allies did not question Austria's right to take the initiative in the Kingdom of the Two Sicilies; however, they did hold different views on the nature of the crisis and the appropriate actions to be pursued. Prussia accorded full powers to Austria as the sole guardian and protector of the interests of Italy.[43] Russia continued to press for a unified allied response encompassing Spain and the Two Sicilies. France agreed with Austria that the unrest in Italy represented the more urgent manner. But based on the protocols of Aix-la-Chapelle, the French government also supported a meeting of the sovereigns that would discuss measures to contain the revolutionary spirit. Austria and Britain clearly objected to Russia's call for a common response to the Spanish and Neapolitan crises, arguing that conditions in the two countries were distinct and should be treated separately. In Spain, for example, there were just reasons for discontent, whereas in the Two Sicilies, no justification existed. Britain, moreover, would not participate in any collective response, though in August, Russia's ambassador in London, Christoph Lieven, had reported that Castlereagh supported swift allied action.[44] Repeatedly in August and September, the British government declared neutrality on the Two Sicilies and insisted that both the Spanish and Neapolitan revolutions represented domestic affairs outside the authority of the alliance. In rejecting the Austrian memorandum of 28 August and Russian pressure to attend the meetings in Troppau, Castlereagh explained to Lieven that the allies could not alter the meaning of established treaties. The foreign secretary likewise considered public discussion of abstract questions to be dangerous, and he warned that in addressing the internal crises of independent states, a single allied language could not be found.[45]

The Russian government took a different position on the allies' legal obligations. Based on the treaties of 1814, 1815, and 1818, revolutionary events in Spain and the Kingdom of the Two Sicilies fell under the jurisdiction of the grand alliance (the five great powers) and therefore required a unified allied response.[46] This principle applied to all situations threatening European peace. There existed a single Europe, the unity of which was political, moral, and Christian. At moments when the progress of enlightenment (*le progrès des lumières*) produced disorder, the grand alliance represented the only force, whether moral or coercive, capable of defeating the explosion of evil. Only by speaking with one voice could the allies preserve the Europe of the treaties founded on regular bases of order and truth. In a dispatch of 21 August/2 September 1820, approved by Alexander and sent to Russia's diplomats in Naples, Rome, Turin, Berlin, Frankfurt, London, Paris, and Vienna, Kapodistrias informed Gustav O. Stackelberg, Russia's envoy in Naples, that neither he nor any other Russian diplomat possessed the authority to offer an official opinion on political conditions in the Kingdom of the Two Sicilies.[47] Stackelberg did receive permission to communicate the Russian monarch's disapproval of the criminal revolution, including its origin and means of action. But even though Alexander's condemnation was unambiguous, he still preferred to address the crisis with persuasion. He continued to hope that the Neapolitan government would take effective measures to end the revolution, so that once again it could become "the source of institutions legally adapted to the particular needs of the nation" and capable of rallying "around the throne all moral interests, all affections, and all desires."

Two additional communications produced by Kapodistrias in the weeks prior to the Troppau conferences illustrated the Russian government's preference for moral force. In a letter of 23 September/5 October 1820, Kapodistrias invited Aleksandr Sturdza to communicate his ideas about how to stamp out the dangerous contagion of revolution that had infected Spain, the Two Sicilies, and more recently, Portugal.[48] Because the allied governments would be discussing grave questions central to the fate of the universe and European civilization, Kapodistrias sought advice on how they could extirpate the germs of revolution in the countries affected and how their restorative and conservative policy (*système réparateur et conservateur*) could be implemented so as to receive unanimous consent from the European federation.

In soliciting Sturdza's thoughts, Kapodistrias also summarized Russian policy. The treaties concluded in 1815 and 1818 defined the principles of law governing allied decisions and obliged the allies to deliberate in common on the revolutions disturbing Europe. In the current crisis, the adoption of new principles was unnecessary. The allies could justly apply the principles that had served as the basis for restoring legitimate monarchy in France. The critical problem at stake was how "to pacify the kingdoms of Spain, the Two Sicilies, and Portugal, internally and within the social and political order of Europe, and how to guarantee in a stable manner the territorial integrity and public independence of these States." Clearly, revolution should be suppressed and legitimate monarchy restored, but this had to be done through institutions that allowed each government "to maintain the order, integrity, and independence of the State." In addition, the measures adopted needed to ensure the cohesion of the European association and peace for the world.

The Russian government claimed that countries affected by revolution no longer belonged to the general alliance. Their exclusion not only conformed to established principles of law, but also increased the likelihood of defeating revolution through negotiations wisely combined with obligations. In Naples, therefore, the allies should demand unanimously that the insurrectionary acts be annulled de facto and de jure. In addition, they should expect the king to reestablish his administration and give to his people institutions capable of ensuring their internal well-being and political independence. Finally, the allies should propose reforms, which if rejected by the Neapolitan government, would trigger military intervention. The purpose of the intervention would not be territorial aggrandizement, but the restoration of order. The prospect of military intervention also would protect the royal family and inspire confidence in the kingdom's right-thinking men. Assuming that the measures adopted in the Kingdom of the Two Sicilies were effective, preferably without resort to military force, the allies should then apply the same principles in Spain and Portugal. Kapodistrias asked Sturdza not only to comment on the situation, but also to draft a note that the five allies could address to the Neapolitan government.

A second more opaque statement of Russian policy appeared in a memorandum of 5/17 October 1820, submitted to Emperor Alexander by Kapodistrias.[49] Kapodistrias began by explaining that although the five allies (Austria, Britain, France, Prussia, and Russia) recognized the need to oppose revolution, the enemy of all peoples and governments, they did not agree on how to realize this shared goal. Currently, they pursued two policies: the policy of convenience and the policy of duty. The policy of convenience, advocated by Britain, assumed that existing treaties did not require allied action to combat revolution, except in France. The policy of duty, by contrast, rested on the spirit of the treaties, specifically the Paris treaties of 1815 and the Aix-la-Chapelle protocols of 1818. This policy held that wherever revolution threatened the order established by the general alliance, the five courts must act. The British government continued to insist on the policy of convenience, and France did not want to oppose Britain. Russia's government hoped to persuade the allies to embrace the policy of duty. Once again, Alexander's foreign policy assumed the need for allied unity in crafting an effective response. This meant that even if the British position did not change, the other allies should pursue a common course of action.

The allies might even conclude a new treaty to address the revolutionary crisis. They had done this with the Treaty of 13/25 March 1815, which had affirmed the *casus foederis et belli* against France at the time of Napoleon's escape from Elba. But regardless of the form that the acts of the conference took, they should leave no doubt as to the general course of allied policy or the legal foundations supporting it. Whether justified by established treaties or new agreements, the allies must crush the current revolutions and restore the legitimate authority of sovereigns. Otherwise the victimized states and the larger European association would lose the benefits of internal tranquility and external independence. Again, a precedent existed in the allied restoration of the French monarchy, even though today's statesmen disagreed on how to proceed. Some believed that the principles of 1814–15, particularly the constitutional charter adopted in France, sanctioned the germs of revolution. In their eyes, the original problem had not been solved, and France did not provide a model for action; hence the revolutions afflicting Spain, the Kingdom of the Two Sicilies, and Portugal. Other statesmen focused on the causes and effects of the French Revolution (or any political revolution); however, as historical experience showed, no human power could defeat revolution. In Spain, the Two Sicilies, and Portugal, public authority lacked the means to resist insurrection.

Having acknowledged the differences of opinion among political leaders, Kapodistrias still argued that the principles used to reconcile France with Europe offered a way forward and could be applied on the two peninsulas. Kapodistrias's formulation allowed him to decry as exaggerated and partisan both approaches to the current crisis that were being discussed. The co-minister's preferred solution harkened back to the heady peacemaking represented by the promises of 14/26 September 1815 (the Holy Alliance) and Aix-la-Chapelle. Kapodistrias believed that peace depended on truth (*vérité*), which could be found in the happy medium or middle ground (*le juste milieu*). In other words, the plenipotentiaries meeting in Troppau could find the truth in both responses to the ongoing crisis and agree in principle on measures to restore sovereign authority and deliver the world from revolution. The allies then could apply the agreed-upon measures to the situations in Spain, the Two Sicilies, and Portugal. Here Kapodistrias restated Alexander I's desire for a collective statement of principle, suggested originally in the monarch's response to the Spanish insurrection, but also relevant to the subsequent revolutions. Kapodistrias went beyond his master's proposal, however, by bringing the Treaty of 14/26 September into the conversation, something he previously had tried to do in connection with Russia's proposal for a treaty of guarantee in Aix-la-Chapelle.

Ordinary alliances, Kapodistrias continued, could not rebuild the moral power of a government forced to sign legal acts dictated by a victorious insurrection. Governments in their public relations mirrored individuals in private life. One circumstance or event, happy or unhappy, and one display of courage or weakness could decide the future. It might be difficult for a discredited government to find security without outside help; however, in seeking assistance, such a government risked compromising not only its own interests, but also those of the intervening power. For this reason, extraordinary and unexpected measures were needed—measures promised by the Treaty of 14/26 September. The treaty spelled out great truths that all the courts of Europe accepted, even if for different reasons. But why had these truths not produced the desired extraordinary alliance? Why did sovereigns refuse to recognize that their power was inferior to the authority of divine law? According to Kapodistrias, the Treaty of 14/26 September had established divine law as the basis for political legislation—for a code that would emanate from "the precepts of the supreme legislator of all Christian peoples." This code would consecrate all rights, respect all moral and material attributes, spell out rules of administration, and produce an extraordinary, unexpected system of laws. In addition, it would rally "to the cause of order and legitimate power a great mass of people, friends of the good, convinced that only through religion can empires prosper."

The idea of a code based on the truths of the Treaty of 14/26 September raised another question. How could beneficent laws be protected from the current corruption of morals caused by so many years of crime and immorality? The problem went beyond the moral degradation of the French revolutionary and Napoleonic eras. For three centuries one revolution had followed another across Europe. Impure morals had constituted both cause and effect, as each generation perpetuated the previous immorality. Although good education could effectuate the reform of morals, good education also presupposed good morals. In the context of ongoing political revolution, morals became corrupted and good education impossible. Finally, Kapodistrias declared, only after the elimination of revolution could lawmaking reclaim its conservative power and society reconstitute itself based on the principles of the Christian religion.

The memorandum of 5/17 October was read to Emperor Alexander, but not formally approved. Kapodistrias restated the case for why the revolutions afflicting Europe should be suppressed, which already represented Russian policy, as did the acceptance of Austrian military intervention, assuming moral force failed. Kapodistrias also argued that once revolution was extirpated, the principles of the Treaty of 14/26 September 1815 should become the basis for legislation across Europe. Only then, he implied, would enduring peace be achieved. In the search for solutions to unanticipated challenges Kapodistrias returned to the promise of the Holy Alliance, which in his view had not yet been fulfilled. The co-minister did not say so, but Alexander's diplomacy, while faithful to the presumed truths of 14/26 September, followed a less exalted path: continual application and adaptation of specific treaty obligations to evolving conditions on the ground. Whatever the purpose of Kapodistrias's memorandum or the appeal of his moral vision, neither seemed much in evidence during the Troppau meetings. Russian overtures about the need for an allied statement of principle did not delay or substantially alter the course of decision making. Kapodistrias, moreover, like the monarch he served, revealed the capacity to combine flights of political idealism and religious fervor with the forceful and realistic pursuit of a pragmatic foreign policy.

The daily grind of diplomatic negotiation began formally in Troppau on 11/23 October 1820 and continued until Christmas Eve (12/24 December).[50] Only Austria, Prussia, and Russia participated in the formulation of an official allied policy. British and French diplomats observed the proceedings, and while their governments did not approve the decisions made, they also did not publicly oppose them. Prior to the signing of the infamous Preliminary Protocol, Kapodistrias and Nesselrode held unofficial discussions with Metternich to ascertain Austria's plans for the Kingdom of the Two Sicilies. In reports of 14/26 and 15/27 October submitted to Alexander, Russia's ministers summarized the confidential conversations.[51] The reports affirmed earlier expressions of deference to Austria's special interest in Italy, though clearly, Russia expected the three powers to consider how Austria's plan would be organized and presented not only to the government in Naples, but also to the allies and the rest of Europe. Russia's ministers likewise continued to advocate for the use of moral over military force to achieve the goal of restoration, and they still hoped to bring discussion of Spain into the meetings. Austria, by contrast, continued to insist on keeping the two crises separate. All agreed, moreover, that any armed intervention in the Two Sicilies should be legitimized as a concerted act of the alliance. Russia did not expect allied coordination on the ground, but rather wanted to know in advance what course of action Austria would pursue. In addition, Kapodistrias and Nesselrode tried to impress upon Metternich that the presence of foreign troops in the Two Sicilies might endanger the authority, the credibility, and even the life of King Ferdinand I. Although Metternich acknowledged potential dangers, he insisted that the revolutionary threat to Europe made intervention inescapable. Austria also claimed to have the support of the Neapolitan government and thus to need only moral support from Russia. Nor did Metternich expect the governments of Britain and France to pronounce freely on the question of Naples. "They will speak their constitutional language," he remarked, while also urging that the allied courts remain united in refusing to recognize the new government in Naples.[52]

The moment had arrived, Metternich declared, to support Austria's plan to suppress the revolutionary conspiracy, after which it would be necessary "to reconstruct the monarchy of the Two Sicilies under the auspices of the European alliance." If Russia's ministers hoped that a satisfactory moral solution to the Neapolitan revolution might be possible, they made little effort to convince Metternich to change course. Instead, they seemed to accept Austrian intervention as inevitable and not unjustified, all the while insisting that decisions be made within the framework of the Troppau conferences. The Russian government also assigned great importance to the form and process of the negotiations. Allied governments must coordinate their opinions "in order to present them to the world from a position of moral and political unity." Once again, Alexander's diplomats argued that there could be no victory in the struggle against revolution without a unified alliance. Only by adhering to established treaties could the powers win public support. The revolution in the Kingdom of the Two Sicilies highlighted the potentially divergent views of Austria and Russia on questions concerning the domestic politics of sovereign states. These differences had been apparent since 1814, though only now did they become relevant to concrete policy decisions. If the Russian government was going to offer even moral support for Austrian intervention, it expected the allies to produce a joint statement of principle. Specifically, they must agree on the just milieu (*milieu juste*) and right line (*la ligne droite*) to be followed in deciding such questions, and they should not deviate from the policy both courts had pursued since 1814.

Soon after the private meetings between Kapodistrias, Nesselrode, and Metternich, the allies moved quickly toward public agreement. As Russia's diplomats described the situation, only the three courts meeting in Troppau—Austria, Prussia, and Russia—possessed the freedom to pronounce on the great question of Naples.[53] For the moment, Britain and France supported the Austrian enterprise; however, both governments remained vulnerable to political changes that might result from forthcoming elections, and neither could participate directly in the Troppau deliberations. In another report submitted to Alexander on 15 October, Kapodistrias and Nesselrode described the Austrian government's analysis of the political situation in Europe with reference to the revolution in Naples.[54] Generally speaking, the revolutionary torrent threatened "with total ruin the existence of all the States and all the institutions, old as well as modern." In other words, intervention in the Kingdom of the Two Sicilies was not solely a response to Austrian interests. Nor did action by the three powers represent the realization of a separate Holy Alliance of the absolutist monarchies. The proclaimed basis for allied action was the obligation to support the conservation of society and institutions. Moral solidarity among the great powers, recognition of the duty to act, and uniformity in the point of departure leading to strong action—this was the purpose of the plan for Naples accepted in Troppau. Austria recognized that the condition of strong action could not be fulfilled uniformly by all governments. Governments operated under different regimes, and moral solidarity could not always be maintained. But even though the great powers might not be united in their freedom to act, they still needed to prove to the public that no difference existed "in their fundamental principles or in their real and unanimous wishes."

The importance of public unity among the great powers led to further discussions about a treaty of guarantee. Russia had proposed such a treaty in Aix-la-Chapelle. This time the proposal came from Austria, and again the discussions went nowhere. Kapodistrias and Nesselrode reported on the proposal to Alexander I. Their summary is interesting for what it reveals about Austrian thinking on questions of legitimate sovereignty and intervention.[55] As mentioned previously, the image of a counter-revolutionary alliance of the absolutist monarchies seems overly simplistic. Based on the Austrian proposal, the signatory powers would guarantee legitimate sovereignty and fundamental institutions in the states of Europe. There would be no intervention in an independent state as long as legitimate authority exercised power. The guarantee of fundamental institutions did not rule out political changes, again as long as they occurred by legal means and by the free action of the competent authority. Changes produced by revolt against legitimate authority or by an outside power would not be considered legal. Nor did the de facto existence of a government constitute legitimacy, though legal changes in the forms of government would come under the guarantee. Finally, the signatory powers would consider requests for intervention from a sovereign whose country or institutions had been attacked by an illegal force. In situations where a sovereign had been deprived of his power and could not request intervention, they would discuss measures to restore his rights and reestablish legal order in his country.

On the face of it, the Austrian proposal for a treaty of guarantee (as reported by Kapodistrias and Nesselrode) appeared to be an act of counterrevolution. If a legitimate sovereign later recognized the political changes made by an outside power (as occurred repeatedly during the Napoleonic Wars), these changes could be guaranteed by the proposed agreement, but only if the signatory powers unanimously recognized them as compatible with public order and peace in Europe. Although proponents of political reform accused the allies of seeking to make the state of things immobile, the real goal of the great powers was to reserve the right to make political changes to those who possessed this right. Obviously, this formulation did not accept change brought about by revolution or the will of the people. In addition, because legal changes could produce pernicious results, the allies distinguished imprudent innovations from criminal revolutions. They could not prevent the errors of a legitimate government or function as a supreme tribunal authorized to judge its acts. Nor could they rule on the intrinsic merit of an institution or political change. The allies could, however, stop the enemies of legitimate authority, and they could determine if the origins of a political change were legal or illegal.

The proposed treaty of guarantee focused on political and moral barriers to illegal changes of government but did not exclude material measures. The goal was to establish as principle that the allies would deliberate on the proper means to maintain and restore legitimate power when it was overthrown or threatened by an illegal force. This principle did not prejudge any situation: in each particular case the powers would consider what action might be appropriate. The principle to be agreed concerned the allies' attitude toward illegal changes, a tactic that also could not end the scourge of revolt. The proposed act would not prevent "audacious men, inflamed by chimeric hopes or indifferent to the calamities" of their homelands from embarking on a revolutionary course. Still, the Austrian government hoped that a "moral and political proscription pronounced in advance by a great and respectable part of Europe" would restrain the less decisive and ferocious spirits upon whose support the success of any revolutionary endeavor depended. Perhaps, too, sovereigns who faced these cruel circumstances would be more effective in resisting the factions, knowing that they could rely on the intervention of their allies. The proposed agreement would not represent a definite commitment to act in any set of circumstances. Rather, the agreed-upon principles would serve as the starting point for discussion of possible action.

Although no treaty of guarantee ever materialized, the great powers remained in general agreement concerning political principles and the revolutionary menace to Europe. Two memorandums, presented to Emperor Alexander by Kapodistrias and Nesselrode prior to the signing of formal transactions in Troppau, illustrated this point. The memorandums reviewed allied policy, the decisions reached on Naples, and the plans for implementation.[56] According to the first, the allies had chosen a course of action that applied accepted legal principles to the conditions of the day. Their decisions affected only the Kingdom of the Two Sicilies; however, Russia's ministers hoped that the actions taken would prevent further revolutions and influence developments in Spain and Portugal.

In addition to the formulation of general principles to be applied in the event of revolutionary outbreaks, Kapodistrias and Nesselrode also planned to discuss a new treaty, based on the ideas of Aleksandr Sturdza, that would supplement the fraternal act of 14/26 September 1815. The co-ministers of foreign affairs assumed that the relevant negotiations would be postponed for at least eighteen months. Nor did they anticipate support from Britain or France, where political conditions could change unexpectedly. They also continued to believe that it would be dangerous to conclude any new agreement without the consent of all five great powers. Assuming, moreover, that Britain overcame its domestic difficulties, France recognized and wished to use its power, and allied policy toward the Two Sicilies produced a salutary effect—not only in Italy, but also in Spain and Portugal—it might become possible to achieve "universal peace and complete a system of alliance and solidarity that would embrace all the governments and peoples of Europe."[57]

Alexander I's ministers seemed to expect that the countries joined in the general alliance would accept as codified principle the measures adopted for Naples by Austria, Prussia, and Russia. Based on existing laws, countries that sanctioned revolution stood outside the alliance. Consequently, intervention was appropriate in states that by their revolutionary example, contacts, and influence threatened the repose of others. Using legal and amicable means, the allies always would try to bring excluded states back into the alliance. Only if these measures failed would they resort to military force. In the current crisis, the allies intended to propose to the Neapolitan government measures to restore an internal organization in concert with the king, which would establish the inviolability of legitimate power and lead to the creation of wise institutions consistent with the needs and wishes of the nation. The allies would guarantee Ferdinand I the integrity of his territorial possessions and sovereign authority, and they would work with him to formulate a plan of reparative administration designed to protect his government from insurrection and violence.

The memorandum compared the allied plan, including a temporary military occupation, to the measures implemented in France in 1815. Austrian troops, acting as a European army, would enter the Kingdom of the Two Sicilies, and a conference of allied plenipotentiaries would negotiate specific transactions with the Neapolitan monarchy. Resolution of the crisis in Naples would be followed by similar actions in Spain and Portugal. This would allow the allies to conclude the anticipated pact of true solidarity, which would offer to all European governments the double advantage of political independence and internal security, the latter assured by institutions appropriate for the happiness of their peoples.

Finally, the governments of Austria, Prussia, and Russia would ask Britain and France to accede to the proposed course of action, while acknowledging that particular circumstances might make this impossible.[58]

The second memorandum prepared by Kapodistrias and Nesselrode focused on execution of the allied plan for Naples.[59] Fearing for the safety of the king and his family, the ministers assumed that public knowledge of the plan would intensify the danger. Another problem concerned erroneous opinions about the allies' intentions in Italy. The memorandum affirmed that the allies sought to pacify the Kingdom of the Two Sicilies in its internal relations and to reconcile the country with the European social order. Finally, as earlier Russian communications had emphasized, the allies hoped to achieve their goals through negotiation, though they would use military force, if necessary. Yet another consideration arose from the note of 1 October 1820, sent by the foreign minister of the Neapolitan government, the Duke of Campo Chiaro, to other European states.[60] Directed at Metternich, the note denied that the change of government in Naples represented the work of the Carbonari, a secret society inspired by liberal ideas. Rather, the king, supported by his peoples, had established constitutional government—a form of government that had proven to be no less stable than absolutist government. Indeed, the note proclaimed, "no foreign power has the right to deem as good or bad the Regime that an independent Sovereign thought proper to adopt for his States." The note went on to denounce Austria's hostile reaction to the reforms carried out in the Kingdom of the Two Sicilies and declared that in the event of armed intervention, the Neapolitan people would defend their independence and constitution.

The threat of resistance suggested to Russia's ministers that collective action in response to Campo Chiaro's note might easily be interpreted as a declaration of war, especially if the king appeared to be carrying out the wishes of the allies.[61] It was critical, therefore, to elucidate the legal grounds for the allies' demands. To prevent war and safeguard the king and his family, Kapodistrias and Nesselrode hoped that the Neapolitan nation would abandon the revolution. They argued that rather than respond to the note, the allies should invite the king of the Two Sicilies or his representatives to Troppau to discuss the consequences of the July events.[62] If negotiation succeeded, the allied army would enter Naples with the support of the king and people. In other words, the revolution would end by means of persuasion, backed by the possibility of force, under the auspices of the general alliance. If agreement with the government in Naples did not materialize, the embassy sent to Troppau would remain with the allied army to answer for the safety of the royal family. In addition, regardless of which scenario played out, it would be necessary for the three sovereigns to stay together at least until it became clear whether the peaceful or military path would be required.

The memorandums read to Emperor Alexander by Kapodistrias and Nesselrode outlined Russian policy, expressed the hopes of close advisors, and sometimes went beyond the monarch's generally pragmatic orientation. Alexander may have identified with the ideas of Kapodistrias and Sturdza, and he would have preferred that coercive means be used only with the agreement of all five great powers, but when it came to actual decision making, he consistently compromised to preserve allied unity. Thus, on 26 October/7 November 1820, after Metternich threatened independent action, the monarch accepted the Austrian plan that had been submitted to the allies on 17/29 October.[63] Austria, Prussia, and Russia now formally admitted the possibility of allied intervention in Spain and the Kingdom of the Two Sicilies. Before taking any concrete action, however, they would agree to exclude the offending state from the European alliance. In the Neapolitan case, if the government rejected the peaceful course proposed by the allies, the Austrian army, acting as a European army, would be authorized to invade the kingdom. The authorization would include a commitment to respect the territorial integrity of the country and to strengthen its political and national independence. In addition, if Britain and France remained unable to sign on to the Austrian intervention, they still could become the guarantors of allied promises and take responsibility for determining the duration of the occupation.

A week later, on 2/14 November 1820, Russia's plenipotentiaries submitted to Prince Metternich a memorandum, the content of which closely corresponded to what would become the Preliminary Protocol of 7/19 November 1820.[64] Based on the spirit of established treaties, the memorandum tied allied discussions to the duty to maintain the peace. Collective action had become necessary, because as a revolutionary state, Naples stood outside the alliance and threatened other countries. The allies were obliged, therefore, "to reestablish the king and nation in their independence." Royal power and the order of things in the Kingdom of the Two Sicilies needed to be returned to appropriate foundations that would prevent further revolutionary upheavals. Equally significant, any allied action would be designed to secure tranquility for the nation and integrity for the kingdom. The Russian government preferred the use of amicable measures; however, if these failed, the use of military force would be acceptable. Either way, an army of occupation, composed of Austrian troops but identified as European, would be deployed to benefit the kingdom and the rest of Europe.

The formal Preliminary Protocol, signed on 7/19 November 1820 by the plenipotentiaries of Austria, Prussia, and Russia, elaborated on the points contained in the Russian and other allied memorandums.[65] As noted above, historians tend to associate the protocol with the reactionary goals of a holy league composed of the three absolutist monarchies. Ironically, the text of the protocol made no mention of the Treaty of 14/26 September 1815. The protocol began by characterizing the meetings in Troppau as a response to revolutions that had erupted in multiple states. For that reason, the three powers had come together to consider how the principles of the alliance should be applied to current circumstances. Based on the rights consecrated by the treaties, they hoped to protect their peoples and Europe from the contagion of revolution, which they understood as a criminal act. The allies described their actions as an effort to ensure the happy and peaceful development of civilization and the reign of justice and law under the auspices of Christian morality, order, and enlightened solicitude. Having discussed their respective memorandums, they proclaimed their right and obligation to prevent the progress of the evil that threatened the social body and to remedy its effects in states that experienced revolution.

The protocol went on to explain the principles of allied policy and how they would be implemented. Governments formed out of revolt, which menaced other states, would be excluded from the European alliance. The formulation reinforced the ambiguity of earlier discussions. Did revolutionary governments by definition endanger other countries, or would allied intervention be justified only when these governments threatened others in a concrete manner? Either way, once revolutionary governments provided guarantees of legitimate order and stability, they could return to the alliance (as had happened with France). The protocol insisted that out of respect for the authority of legitimate governments, the allies would refuse to recognize changes effected by illegal means. When a revolutionary state endangered other countries due to geographical proximity, the allies first would try amicable measures to restore the excluded power to the alliance; only if peaceful means failed would they turn to coercive action. Because the conditions authorizing a collective response existed in the Kingdom of the Two Sicilies, the allies had agreed to act. But through their actions they intended to respect the integrity and political existence of the Two Sicilies in order to return liberty to the king and nation. The allies sought to reestablish royal power on foundations capable of withstanding future revolutionary troubles, and they hoped to do this without the use of foreign troops. At the same time, they envisioned a temporary military occupation that would promote the conditions needed for the tranquility and happiness of the nation. As earlier communications already had acknowledged, Austrian troops would carry out the intervention in the name of the European alliance, and a conference of allied plenipotentiaries, working under common instructions and headed by an Austrian representative, then would negotiate with the Neapolitan king.

After signing the Preliminary Protocol, the allies did not immediately move to military action. In a supplement to the protocol, also dated 7/19 November 1820, they agreed to invite the king of the Two Sicilies to meet with them and pledged to send common instructions to their ministers in Naples. The three powers intended to return the king to full liberty of action but still hoped that this goal could be accomplished without the use of force. If the legitimate monarch served as mediator for the nation, it might be possible to reconcile the restoration of order in the Two Sicilies with tranquility in the rest of Italy and Europe. In other words, if the revolutionaries stepped aside, and the king returned to power, he might be able to restore his country to membership in the alliance. Then, depending on what happened in Naples, the allies would adopt concrete measures to implement the plan outlined in the protocol. They hoped, moreover, that Britain and France would participate in their friendly appeals to the king of the Two Sicilies.[66] They also would inform the courts of Rome, Turin (Sardinia-Piedmont), and Tuscany about the agreements reached in Troppau.

Russia Defends the Troppau Protocol

Announcement of the decisions made in Troppau occurred when the representatives of Austria, Prussia, and Russia at foreign courts received a common circular, dated 24 November/6 December 1820, describing the results of the conferences. The circular declared that the allied powers possessed the undeniable right collectively to take measures to ensure the security of states whose governments had been overthrown as a result of revolution. To that end, the three allied monarchs had decided not to recognize the Neapolitan government, which had been created by open rebellion. Because only the legitimate monarch of the Two Sicilies, Ferdinand I, could act as mediator between his people and states threatened by the revolution in Naples, they also had invited the king to meet with them in Laibach (now Liubliana in Slovenia), where they planned to reconvene. In addition, they continued to hope that Britain and France would participate in the proposed course of action.[67] The allies presented their decision as legal, based on the treaties of 1814, 1815, and 1818, and as defensive, based on the assumption that governments created by revolt represented a threat to all legitimate constitutions and governments and especially to their neighbors. The three powers viewed revolution as a crime, though again, it is important to remember that the rejection of revolution did not preclude the acceptance of political change. The allies' judgment stemmed from the experience of the French Revolutionary and Napoleonic Wars, a yoke that Europe had carried for twenty years. Personal experience and the authority of history had taught them that revolution led to military tyranny. Having defeated revolution for a second time during the Hundred Days, it was no surprise that this third time the allies also equated the defeat of revolution with the promise of enduring peace.

Among contemporaries, the Preliminary Protocol signed in Troppau produced a range of critical reactions. Aleksandr Sturdza, whose opinions on diplomatic questions Emperor Alexander I repeatedly solicited, criticized the allies for failing to address the larger revolutionary threat in Europe.[68] The protocol neglected to mention either Spain or the papacy's role in Italy. Given the attacks on sovereign and religious authority, Sturdza argued, the allies had to do more than affirm the policy of cohesion among the great powers. Because governments depended on the support of the people, the popular mood had to be reconciled with legitimate authority. Indeed, if the allies based their political, moral, and material actions on the spirit of the Holy Alliance, they might be able to avoid military measures. In other words, the possibility of religious and social restoration embodied in the Holy Alliance offered the best means for effectively ending the revolutionary crisis visible across Europe. The principles embodied in the Treaty of 14/26 September 1815 not only subordinated sovereigns to divine authority, but also sought to replace the state of nature between independent nations with the state of family.[69]

The Russian government's main defense of the Preliminary Protocol occurred not at home in response to intellectuals such as Sturdza, but in the diplomatic arena where close allies committed to the alliance and to European peace objected to the plan of action. If within the Russian Empire one could not yet speak of legal challenges to the monarch's will, this was not the case within the broader alliance, where sovereign states had to be persuaded of the wisdom and legality of Emperor Alexander's decisions. When trying to explain the measures adopted in Troppau, Russia's diplomats invariably felt compelled also to discuss the meaning of the alliance and the critical importance of allied unity. An early instance of this message occurred when the Kingdom of the Netherlands recognized the new government in Naples. Russia's opposition to this move, conveyed in a verbal note of 10/22 November 1820, rested on the principle that any government or constitution established by violent means could not be accepted as legal.[70] Equally important, alliance unity had to be preserved in order to combat the revolutionary spirit. Only through unity could the moral force of a common policy be effective in preventing the need for military intervention. The deliberations in Troppau aimed to achieve this great goal.

Not surprisingly, despite the disclaimers of the great powers, second-order and especially Italian states expressed concern about allied intentions. In a personal letter from Kapodistrias, dated 11/23 November 1820 and approved by Emperor Alexander, the co-minister of foreign affairs instructed Russia's envoy in Turin to explain to the Sardinian court that the actions agreed upon in Troppau applied only to the Kingdom of the Two Sicilies, which the allies hoped to pacify and reconcile with the European social order.[71] Technically the claim was true, though in light of subsequent events—for example, revolution in Sardinia-Piedmont in March 1821 and the almost immediate Austrian intervention there—the Russian denial of a general policy to suppress revolution seems disingenuous. The allies also repeatedly claimed that the intervention in Naples rested not only on the agreements of 1814, 1815, and 1818, but also on the treaty of 12 June 1815 between Austria and the Kingdom of the Two Sicilies. Thus, the Troppau decisions neither altered existing treaties nor changed the legal bases of peace in central Europe. Despite Russia's lingering concerns about the German Confederation, the officially passive approach to German politics also remained in place.[72]

A memorandum of 19 November/1 December 1820, produced by Russia's Ministry of Foreign Affairs, further detailed the official perspective on the Troppau conferences.[73] The memorandum explained the reasons for the meeting, the questions discussed, the preliminary results of the deliberations, and how the allies proposed to protect the world from the scourge of revolutionary anarchy. As diplomatic pronouncements of the era so often recalled, the intimate union of the great powers had delivered Europe from the military despotism engendered by the French Revolution. Returned to independence, the nations of Europe had begun to enjoy the benefits of general peace under the auspices of the great transactions that guaranteed to all states complete security from the outside and from the inside. Europe's peoples had experienced several years of relief from the hardships of war, yet traces of the revolutionary torment remained, for men (and women) had been "perverted by the errors and calamities of the century." The troubles caused by revolution had returned, embodied in efforts to divide the allied courts, debase the majesty of thrones, and provoke criminal revolt. In Spain, the Kingdom of the Two Sicilies, and Portugal, the foundations of the European edifice—the law of nations (*le droit des gens*), religion, and Christian morality—once again had been undermined. In an epoch when each government strove to address the real needs of its people, gradually and by legal means, the revolutionary onslaught paralyzed the purest intentions, betrayed the most just expectations, and endangered the realization of the most legitimate wishes. Instead of consolidating good order, Europe again faced incalculable horrors.

The Russian government believed that the powers placed at the center of the general alliance (presumably the five great powers) had contracted to combat revolution by the acts of 1814, 1815, and 1818. If they refused to fulfill this obligation, the alliance would fail, and the states of Europe would be subjugated to revolutionary despotism. Out of fidelity to treaty obligations, therefore, the three courts had decided to meet and formulate a common policy. They had taken this step despite uncertainty about allied unity and the effect of the measures adopted. Russia previously had called for a common response to the revolution in Spain, especially after King Ferdinand VII accepted the constitution of 1812, but allied inaction had allowed the revolutionary contagion to spread to Naples. Given that contemporaries judged governments based on the material evidence of facts and events (*faits*), the lack of an allied response had weakened both the authority of governments and their will to battle sectarians seeking to divide and conquer. The ministry's memorandum acknowledged the potential appeal of revolutionaries, but attributed this to allied failings, rather than positive identification with radical goals. In other words, well-intentioned individuals had to be protected from the corruption of revolutionaries, who tried to persuade the people that absolute power (*le pouvoir absolu*) was opposed to the rights of nations (*les droits des nations*). It was essential to demonstrate that the punishment of insurrection did not deny nations their rights. Equally critical, the allies needed to exhibit unity, so that the enemies of governments would not be able to represent the conferences in Troppau as a partial meeting of the three courts or a triple alliance opposed to the constitutional states (Britain, France, the south of Germany, Italy, the Netherlands, Spain, and the two Americas).

The foreign policy statements of Alexander I repeatedly invoked allied unity. Despite different conditions in Austria, Britain, France, Prussia, and Russia, the powers needed to reach agreement on all points for all circumstances. This would move the alliance from the domain of abstract idea to the reality of strong and recuperative action. From the perspective of Alexander's government, only Russia had consistently acted in harmony with treaty obligations. Although Austria had tried to justify intervention in Naples with reference to a partial treaty concluded with the king of the Two Sicilies on 12 June 1815, this approach lacked the authority to reconcile the peoples of Italy with the contracting states. In the effort to bring Naples back into conformity with the laws of society, Russian officials believed, Austria should act as a European power, not as an independent state. Nor had France, which continued to rely on alliance support to restore legitimate government, effectively joined the common cause. For the moment, the allies still had to ensure that France fulfilled its treaty obligations.

Britain also, due to domestic difficulties, could not be counted among the active members of the European alliance. Notwithstanding the power and riches of the British Empire, the three allies could hope only that Britain would avoid the appearance of assisting revolutionaries on the two peninsulas. Finally, Russia's Ministry of Foreign Affairs depicted Prussia as a subordinate or inferior great power lacking the political maturity to think through the urgent questions of the day. Occupied with domestic affairs and still adapting to the German federal system and to new relations with Austria, Prussia remained loyal to the spirit of the general alliance and therefore should accept the solutions proposed by Austria and Russia. In describing the particular circumstances of each country, the Russian government tried to make a simple point: the allies would have to do more, if they wanted to preserve world peace.

In evaluating the decisions of the Troppau conferences, the critical conclusion of the Russian government was that the acts of 7/19 November 1820 (the Preliminary Protocol and supplement) were insufficient to achieve the allies' goals. The conciliatory policy toward the Kingdom of the Two Sicilies would not be successful without British and French participation. Emperor Alexander continued to pressure these countries to join the three monarchs in Laibach, where they planned to complete the deliberations on Naples in consultation with the king of the Two Sicilies and the representatives of other Italian states. If a unified European alliance could restore the reign of justice and law by constituting the Neapolitan king as the legitimate mediator between his subjects and the countries that were threatened by the hostile example of revolution, moral force might be able to defeat insurrection, and peace would be consolidated. Spain too might be delivered from the oppression of insurrection, and thanks to the affirmation of the European system, each state would enjoy the possibility of working calmly on the improvement of its domestic regime. The very act of signing a Preliminary Protocol and reconvening in another location left open the possibility of new beginnings with full British, French, and Neapolitan cooperation. As Russia's diplomats described the allies' dilemma, military intervention, especially after the respite from war enjoyed since 1815, would demonstrate only that peace depended on coercion. It would not solve the broader problem of revolution in Europe. Ultimately the responses from Paris, London, and Naples would decide the question of moral versus military means; however, the Russian government continued to insist that the signatories to the protocol make every effort to rely on persuasion. Through concerted action, the three courts needed to show that they had decided to fight the peoples of the Two Sicilies for the sake of peace and happiness in Europe.

As the Russian memorandum of 19 November/1 December explained, the allies did not view the crisis in Naples as an isolated event. Assuming, therefore, that military intervention proved unavoidable, what could they do to save Europe from new disasters? For answers Russian officials looked to further development of the principles defined in the Preliminary Protocol, an approach that returned the diplomatic conversation to where it had been in the spring and summer of 1820, before the actual meetings in Troppau. Not surprisingly, Emperor Alexander's perspective continued to evolve as events on the ground unfolded. In Aix-la-Chapelle, Russia's diplomats had pushed for a treaty of collective guarantee, beyond the exclusivity and narrow commitments of the Quadruple Alliance, that would require mutual defense of the territorial boundaries and political arrangements defined by the treaties of Vienna and Paris. Prior to the conferences in Troppau, the Russian monarch also had advocated for a collective statement of principle in response to revolutions in Spain, the Kingdom of the Two Sicilies, and Portugal. But in December 1820, Alexander took a more cautious approach to new treaty obligations. A Russian memorandum of 5/17 December 1820, approved by the monarch and addressed to the governments of Austria and Prussia, rejected the recent Austrian proposal for a general guarantee.[74]

According to the Russian memorandum, the governments of Austria, Prussia, and Russia agreed that a treaty of guarantee designed to preserve the domestic legal order of European states could take one of two possible forms: either it would constitute a new alliance (*combinaison*), based on principles of public law not explicitly sanctioned in existing treaties, or it would result from the principles of public law established by the Final Act of the Congress of Vienna and accompanying treaties. In the latter case, it would represent obligations that the European powers previously had contracted. But either way, critical questions would remain. How would the treaty be applied to states that had not signed it? Would contracting governments have the right to intervene to preserve legal order in noncontracting states? Or could the allies assume that all states comprising the general alliance had acceded to the treaty of guarantee? If not, then what would be the relationship of noncontracting states to the others? How would these arrangements impact the general alliance, and how would the measures adopted to prevent revolution affect the noncontracting states? Allied intervention in a state that had not accepted the treaty of guarantee could never be moral, because such an intervention inevitably would require the use of force. In other words, the intervention question could not be addressed without also considering broader questions about the Quadruple and general alliances.

At the end of the Napoleonic Wars all the states of Europe had occupied an analogous position in that all depended on collective guarantee of their territorial reconstruction. Consequently, all had acceded to the treaties and conventions of 1815 and 1818. But in 1820 the security imperative of 1814–15 no longer existed. The Russian government doubted that countries such as Britain, France, the Netherlands, and some German states, where diplomatic transactions had to be justified before a national representative body, would sign a new treaty of guarantee. Without general acceptance, the treaty would cause anxiety, distrust, and isolation in noncontracting states, which would see it as the creation of a new alliance independent of established agreements. The current system of unity and solidarity would therefore be undermined. Was a new treaty really needed, the Russian memorandum asked, to guarantee the legal order of domestic institutions, including the legitimacy of thrones and the powers dependent on them? If so, then was a new treaty also needed to guarantee the inviolability of territorial boundaries? Did not existing treaties guarantee both internal and external security? The Russian government argued that the treaties of 1815 and 1818 already provided the proposed guarantees, at least implicitly. The treaties did not require governments to seek recognition when they reformed domestic institutions; however, based on a virtual convention (*convention virtuelle*), fundamental change did require allied assent. This was why the new governments in Spain, the Kingdom of the Two Sicilies, and Portugal all sought to legitimize their revolutions in the eyes of Europe. If established treaties did not give the allies this right of intervention, then they could not have expressed disapproval of the Spanish Revolution or decided to act in Naples. Precisely because existing treaties contained the guarantee of legal order, to conclude a new treaty would render the decisions that already had been made illegal.

Having dispensed with the legal question of a new treaty, the Russian memorandum turned to future needs, specifically remedies for the ongoing threat to social order. Europe had been enjoying a profound peace, when the catastrophes in Spain, Naples, and Portugal reminded the allies of the presence of a sinister enemy who supposedly had been defeated. In responding to the enemy, they had fulfilled the most important obligation imposed by the treaties of 8/20 November 1815 (the Second Treaty of Paris and Quadruple Alliance) and subsequent protocols of Aix-la-Chapelle. They had acted to defend from revolution the alliance that guaranteed the peace. The decision to intervene in the Kingdom of the Two Sicilies had resulted from the threat to the rest of the peninsula represented by the Neapolitan revolution and from the allies' ability to respond promptly and effectively. The three powers expected that the measures set forth in the Preliminary Protocol would bring Naples back into the alliance without exposing the world to the disasters of war. The return of order in the Two Sicilies would represent the triumph of religion and morality, the victory of law, and the defeat of the odious power of the revolution. This great result would be achieved by the force of allied unity and would demonstrate the value of the treaties and policies previously established to preserve the peace. So rather than conclude a new treaty, the Russian government hoped that the allies would work to perfect the Preliminary Protocol of 7/19 November. This additional protocol would define the principles that the allies intended to apply in all countries experiencing revolution. In each case, the allies would meet to decide on concrete actions, as they had done with respect to Naples. The allies also would agree to communicate with each other regarding the reform of their domestic institutions. Success in the Kingdom of the Two Sicilies would prove to other states the efficacy of the measures adopted, and all the countries of Europe would be invited to adhere to this final protocol.

In the midst of responding to Austria's proposal for a treaty of guarantee, the Russian government also worked to persuade Britain and France to join the allied effort. In 1818 Russia had argued in favor of concluding a new treaty of guarantee, but conditions had changed, and in late 1820, the critical concern had become Britain's relationship to the alliance in light of the Preliminary Protocol.[75] Neither Britain nor France approved the protocol, and for British foreign secretary Castlereagh and the government of King George IV, any codified statement of principle posed a problem.[76] To counter this opposition, Russia's diplomats tried to argue that the Preliminary Protocol did not constitute a new or separate alliance, but rather fulfilled established treaty obligations. They insisted, moreover, that the eternal principles of Emperor Alexander's foreign policy had not changed. Their argument derived from the legal-administrative practices of the Russian Empire, where the spirit of the law invariably superseded the letter of the law.[77] This is why in the Troppau discussions, Russia's diplomats repeatedly pointed to virtual treaties and obligations. As Nesselrode wrote to Lieven, with Alexander's approval, the treaty of 8/20 November 1815 and the protocols of 3/15 November 1818 imposed upon the allies "the virtual obligation" to protect the peace in any country or territory threatened by the ravages of revolution.[78]

The Russian government also accepted that the spirit of a treaty could have multiple interpretations, based on the internal conditions and laws of a given country.[79] On this basis, Russia did not see Britain's rejection of the Preliminary Protocol as a renunciation of the treaties justifying the transaction. Britain remained free to choose its own language in what Russia's diplomats hoped would be a formal pronouncement in support of the measures adopted. Emperor Alexander did not demand allied unanimity in all situations. He did expect, however, that each ally would contribute, according to its power, to the execution of the Troppau plan, the success or failure of which might prove decisive for the destiny of Europe. In the present circumstances, this meant that Britain could remain silent on the question of principles but take a direct or indirect part in their application, according to its judgment of what was appropriate. The Russian response to Britain's stance against intervention wavered between acceptance of divergent policies in concrete situations and insistence that effective action against revolution required British support.

United in a tutelary and holy alliance, the three monarchs meeting in Troppau had pledged to preserve the independence and territorial integrity of revolutionary states, even if military force became unavoidable.[80] The possible use of coercion coexisted with the claim that ambition had been banned from the domain of politics and removed from the counsels of kings. The powers had no intention of acting against the peoples or against "wise liberty, the friend of order." They claimed to respect the rights of nations and of monarchs whose legitimate power should be freely exercised. Nor did the allies forget the needs and interests of the people or the stability that could be guaranteed by concluding a prudent transaction between what would cease to be (the revolutionary regime in Naples) and what should be (the restored monarch and legitimate government). Nesselrode described as bizarre the possibility that Britain, "one of the most civilized states in the world," would not support a doctrine so favorable to the progress of civilization. Emperor Alexander likewise continued to hope that Britain would declare support for the principles and measures agreed to by the three courts or at least give to the allies the sanction of silence.

Charles William Stewart (1778–1854), British ambassador in Vienna and brother of Foreign Secretary Castlereagh, represented his government in Troppau and conveyed to the three courts Britain's rejection of the Preliminary Protocol and supplement of 7/19 November 1820. In a dispatch to Lieven, dated 11/23 November 1820, Nesselrode explained the British opposition on two grounds. First, Lord Stewart had not been consulted during the process of writing the transactions. Second, the form of the Troppau acts could be construed as the formation of an exclusive alliance between the courts of Vienna, Berlin, and Saint Petersburg.[81] According to the British representative, the allies should have sought his input before announcing a general policy to address the current crisis. Lord Stewart agreed that swift action, whether by persuasion or by force, had been necessary, but this could have been done without formalizing in advance the principles of a general policy. From the Russian point of view, Lord Stewart had chosen not to participate in the Troppau conferences. Although Emperor Alexander had urged the British government to send a fully empowered plenipotentiary who would be privy to all the deliberations, this had not been done.

Emperor Alexander also continued to believe that without British support the allies could not be successful in their endeavor. Needed to ensure justice and legality, the participation of Britain would help to show the world that the sole purpose of intervention was to reconcile the rights of legitimate power with the wishes and true needs of peoples. But because Lord Stewart had been instructed to maintain a neutral and passive position, he could not contribute to writing the transactions. Nesselrode's communication hinted at the hope that this particular objection indicated an underlying desire to join the allies in a common course of action. Nesselrode also insisted that the signing of formal acts did not establish a new policy. The spirit of existing transactions, which had been sanctioned by the English Parliament, provided the legal basis for the Troppau agreements. On previous occasions, the British government had been instrumental in defending and helping to perfect the maxims of the alliance. In applying these maxims to the Kingdom of the Two Sicilies, the three monarchs had decided that the statement of their common purpose should be formalized in a legal act. Nesselrode therefore authorized Lieven to read his dispatch to Castlereagh, and if the latter agreed, to communicate the acts of 7/19 November as simple projects without signatures.[82] If Britain's rejection of the transactions rested solely on the form of communication, concerted action might still be possible.

A follow-up dispatch from Nesselrode, issued the next day (12/24 November 1820) and approved by Emperor Alexander, provided Lieven with more detailed instructions about appeals to the British government.[83] Because the allies had an obligation to preserve social order and peace, the Preliminary Protocol represented a just application of principles already consecrated by established treaties. The protocol, in other words, gave a body to the spirit of the treaties. Highlighting the critical importance of allied unity, yet also aware of British objections to the Troppau transactions, Nesselrode acknowledged that allied policy did not result from the letter of existing treaties. It did, however, derive from their essence. Once again, the Russian preference for just outcomes, as opposed to strict adherence to the law, crept into diplomatic negotiations. The measures adopted allowed the allies to fulfill their duty to the European family—a duty defined by the assumption that the well-being of each lay in the well-being of all. Given the current impassioned and agitated mood (*esprit*) of the European public, the planned course of action represented the best means to stop the revolutionary evil that already had affected three states.

To encourage British participation, the Russian government repeatedly made the point that the Preliminary Protocol and supplement required additional development; they were not in their final form. A quick allied response in the Kingdom of the Two Sicilies had been necessary to prevent the consolidation and spread of revolution. For whereas diplomatic negotiations moved slowly, popular identification with sectarians could deepen quickly. Consequently, the three courts had neglected to consult Britain and France before signing the Troppau transactions. The voice of the allies had to be heard as swiftly as possible, and people in the Two Sicilies had to recognize the current regime's incompatibility with world peace. Only the mediation of their king could lead them to reconciliation with the rest of Europe. The Russian desire for full British participation in the upcoming meetings in Laibach could not have been stronger, whether or not the Neapolitan government allowed King Ferdinand I to attend.[84] Again, Nesselrode proclaimed disbelief at the thought that Britain would refuse to help save the world from bloody revolution. Emperor Alexander hoped that British involvement would make it possible to avoid coercion. To preserve peace by moral force required that the great powers act in unison. Resort to military measures could have the dangerous effect of undermining the popular perception of the European alliance as a conservative rather than a conquering association. Britain previously had adhered to the treaties and principles that justified intervention, and at this critical juncture the allies needed British help. Russia's commitment to allied unity was so firm, moreover, that regardless of what the British government decided to do (or not to do), Britain's relationship to the alliance would not change, based on the letter of the transactions of 1814, 1815, and 1818.[85]

Arguments repeated over and over again by Russia's diplomats to justify the Troppau agreements did not alter Britain's opposition to collective allied action. In a state paper of 5 May 1820, Castlereagh made clear that the treaty obligations of 1814–15 applied only to the liberation of Europe from Napoleon and the consequent requirement to ensure the collective security of the continent. The treaties did not concern other countries. Nor did the state paper declare a general principle of non-intervention in foreign lands.[86] The official British response to the Preliminary Protocol came in a note of 4 December 1820, which while condemning the revolution in Naples and acknowledging that the other powers possessed a right to intervene, nonetheless refused to deny recognition to the Neapolitan government.[87] Britain also would not countenance allied interference in Spain and Portugal. Although serious, the crises in those countries did not threaten other states. Finally, the note informed the allies that the British government would reject any declaration designed to establish a policy of mutual guarantees. In subsequent conversations between Lieven and Castlereagh, the foreign secretary acknowledged the goodwill of the three monarchs and even tried to argue that the British position conformed to principles publicly embraced by Emperor Alexander, specifically the rejection of new alliances and of efforts to seek guarantees outside the general alliance.[88] The desire for mutual understanding was palpable, but no amount of politesse or goodwill could change the reality of discord. As Lieven bluntly characterized the situation, the British interpretation of the Troppau agreements was unfortunate and exaggerated.

According to Castlereagh, the Preliminary Protocol constituted a treaty and hence the basis for a new alliance. If the protocol were simply a confidential agreement (*entente*), the result of shared opinions or current circumstances and future possibilities (*futurs contingents*), why would the allies not keep their agreement secret? Instead, they proposed to create a new policy that would invalidate existing agreements and fuel revolutionary discontent. The foreign secretary rejected the Russian argument that the allies had further developed but not replaced old relationships based on established treaties. Worse still, despite the pure motives of the allies, the British government might have no choice but to oppose and even protest the principles set forth in the protocol. The three monarchs had asserted an exclusive privilege to intervene in the domestic affairs of independent states by peaceful or coercive means. This assumed privilege deprived states of rights enshrined in existing treaties. Once again Britain rejected the Russian interpretation, which did not see action against a revolutionary faction that threatened neighboring countries as coercion or interference in the domestic affairs of an independent state. In the Russian view, recourse to coercion would occur only if legitimate power was overthrown, efforts to achieve reconciliation failed, and the repose of Europe was in danger. Although Russia's diplomats believed that Castlereagh, constrained by the perils of British politics, remained sympathetic to the allied cause, the foreign secretary's words to Lieven suggested a more divergent position, one that contemporary liberals and later generations of historians would echo: in Troppau three autocratic sovereigns assumed the authority to judge the appropriateness of intervention.

Castlereagh did not oppose the effort to prevent disorder, revolutionary contagion, and the overthrow of legitimate monarchs. But he did reject the forms and means of action chosen by the allies. The statement of principles contained in the Preliminary Protocol gave the allies a broad mandate to intervene in other countries, and to decide that public unrest or the request of a monarch justified the use of force. In the case of Naples, Castlereagh argued, the application of severe principles that appeared hostile to the independence of nations would exacerbate the revolutionary spirit. Instead of a collective allied proclamation, the Austrian government should explain the reasons and legal grounds for its own decision to intervene, and the other powers should respond in the manner and with the language appropriate to their particular circumstances. Going forward, the allies should act when and where it might be necessary, but without declaring general principles, which then could serve as a rallying cry for revolutionaries. In France, for example, sectarians might be able to use allied pronouncements to accuse the king of relying on a league of monarchs to battle political opposition. This would promote the interests of the revolutionaries and undermine the legitimate government. In Spain, moreover, the Troppau meeting already had caused mistrust and fear among the people. The expectation of an appeal to the three sovereigns by the Spanish king strengthened the perception that royal authority was opposed to the liberties of nations. Even though the allies possessed the ability to act speedily, Castlereagh concluded, they should proceed with caution, and more important, they should not abuse their power.

If the legitimacy of armed intervention by the allies was codified in Troppau, the actual staging of the intervention would take place in Laibach, where the three monarchs planned to meet with Ferdinand I. In the meantime, Britain accepted the practical necessity of intervention, and the allies accepted that Britain would neither sanction nor participate in their collective action. Castlereagh communicated to Lieven that Britain would not disavow the Preliminary Protocol as long as this did not become public.[89] For regardless of how events unfolded, the British government needed to be able to claim before Parliament and people that it had opposed the principles adopted by the allies. Simply put, political conditions in Britain and the constraints imposed on king and cabinet by the English constitution did not permit open support for allied intervention.[90] Lieven claimed that in private conversation both Castlereagh and the Duke of Wellington expressed support and understanding. At no time did the disagreement over Naples seriously threaten the alliance. Castlereagh's biographer tells a different story, one of widening cracks in the alliance from early 1820 and of domestic pressure on the foreign secretary "to extricate himself from any notion of concerted action with the other European courts," as early as December 1819.[91] Contradictory narratives notwithstanding, the Russian interpretation held that unity was preserved, despite differences over the meaning of treaty obligations. France's rejection of the Preliminary Protocol likewise showed that commitment to the alliance did not require unity of action. In a memorandum addressing French objections to the Troppau transactions, the Russian government appeared to walk back the idea of excluding from the European alliance any state whose government was changed by revolution.[92] The five great powers agreed, moreover, to represent the current intervention not as a conquest, but as a reconciliation between the alliance and the Kingdom of the Two Sicilies, mediated by the Neapolitan king.

Legality and Reform

What did the negotiations surrounding the Troppau conferences and the Preliminary Protocol reveal about the foreign policy of Emperor Alexander I? Initially, the Russian government supported a general pronouncement or statement of principle on how the allies, particularly the five great powers, would respond to revolution, not just in France, but throughout Europe. In contrast to the British position, which emphasized the legal specificity of the Quadruple Alliance, Russian policy stressed moral duty; agreement in principle; and the spirit, not just the letter, of treaty obligations. The appeal to moral duty was consistent with Russian diplomatic initiatives since 1815: the Treaty of 14/26 September 1815 (the Holy Alliance), the proposal for a treaty of general alliance to supersede the Quadruple Alliance in the period leading up to the Congress of Aix-la-Chapelle, the proposal for a treaty of guarantee at the congress, and the priority always given to the preservation of allied unity, even if only the appearance of unity. Russia's approach was countered by Britain's refusal to sign on to abstract statements of principle and by Prince Metternich's focus on suppressing the revolutionary threat in central Europe. By the time Austria came around to the idea of a collective guarantee, Russia no longer wanted to present the Preliminary Protocol as a statement of principle or general policy.

Alexander I's foreign policy also illustrated key aspects of Russian political thought, specifically the principle of the monarch's absolutist authority and the elevation of moral outcomes (justice) over strict adherence to the law. In this context, during the critical years from 1815 through 1820, Alexander and his diplomatic agents developed a political message of good governance and religious morality to counter the liberal and radical ideologies emerging in the Restoration era. The period of diplomacy following the Congress of Vienna represented more than restoration, recuperation, and the birth of modern political ideologies. The opposition to political change brought about by revolution and violence was not simply a proclamation of conservative principles or a defense of absolutist monarchy. The sincerity, adaptability, and pragmatism of Alexander's foreign policy shone through in the negotiations concerning Naples. The combination of moderate reformism, historical analysis, and modern nation-or people-based politics—all key components of political culture in the first quarter of the nineteenth century—illustrated both the power of tradition (or social memory) and the capacity for change.

The enlightened institutional reforms of Catherine II—inspired by her reading of Montesquieu, Beccaria, and Bielfeld—could be seen in Emperor Alexander's search for European security within a stable legal framework and in his awareness of political conditions in other countries.[93] The monarch's concern for legality, understood as strict adherence to treaty obligations, continued the reformist trajectory of the eighteenth century, as did his acknowledgment of political realities in second-order states and their legitimate rights within the European system. The lessons of historical experience, particularly the trauma of the Napoleonic Wars, justified Alexander's insistence on the paramount importance of allied unity and inspired the persistent effort to act in concert with the allies. Also based on the authority of history were his determination and assumed obligation to prevent revolution and its consequences, defined as illegality, war, and conquest. Finally, Alexander's recognition of modern political imperatives and his sensitivity to how the world had changed since the French Revolution appeared in the idea that governments and peoples had to be persuaded to accept decisions made by the alliance, even if in the interest of European peace. As an absolutist monarch, Alexander expected obedience, but he also understood that compliance was a two-way street. Governments had an obligation to connect with their people by implementing wise policies and constructing effective institutions that served the nation's needs. Great powers likewise had to convince the less powerful and one another of the benefits their policies could bring by engaging in press debates, applying diplomatic pressure (moral force), encouraging domestic reform, and if necessary, organizing military intervention. In other words, the actions of Emperor Alexander and his allies looked not to the restoration of the old regime, but to the efficacious reconstitution of international order following decades of violent revolution and brutal warfare.

CHAPTER 4

To Act in Concert (1821–22)

I N A MASTERFUL STUDY of the emergence of the modern world, C. A. Bayly describes a world crisis of 1780–1820, which originated in "a growing imbalance between the perceived military needs of states and their financial capacity." Even more consequential than the material crisis, according to Bayly, was the underlying social crisis caused by economic conflict and a culture of opposition that "had made people more skeptical of, and hostile to, established authority." Both the American and French revolutions highlighted the power of popular rebellion and the acceptance of war as a tool of modern progress. Napoleon's empire likewise justified military conquest under the mantle of progressive reform. With this history in mind, the peacemakers of 1814–18 and the European governments established, reestablished, or simply maintained in the aftermath of Napoleon's defeat appear less the harbingers of restoration or recuperation and more the representatives of "a moderating discourse of law, religion, or polity" that held out the hope of enlightened reform and peaceful advancement.[1] Like reform-minded leaders in other countries, Emperor Alexander I and his diplomatic agents saw in the transactions of Paris, Vienna, and Aix-la-Chapelle the political framework and legal foundations for peaceful order in Europe. In the Treaty of 14/26 September 1815 (the Holy Alliance), described by recent Russian scholarship as a form of Christian cosmopolitanism, they also identified the means to end war and unite the peoples of Europe regardless of national and religious affiliations.[2] Their desire for peace and good order could not have been more genuine.

But peace and good order could be understood in myriad ways. Time and again, despite intensive diplomacy and laborious participation in conferences, the process of peacemaking raised questions about the capacity of legal principles and treaty obligations to constrain what Leo Tolstoy called in the second epilogue of *War and Peace* "the movement of peoples" or "the power that moves peoples."[3] From the perspective of Russian diplomacy, the movement of peoples in Spanish America, Spain, Naples, Portugal, and Piedmont threatened

European peace and exposed fissures in the general alliance. In 1821–22 the beginnings of the Greek independence movement and the Russian-Ottoman war scare further underscored the fragility of allied unity, as well as the potential for opposition in Russian society. From the time of the Greek uprisings through the first years of Nicholas I's reign, Russian monarchs and their allies repeatedly chose peace through compromise and the avoidance of confrontation. More than revolution, the peacemakers feared war, and in their experience, war could be prevented only by preserving the European alliance. For several decades, this shared assumption encouraged the concert of great powers to moderate military ambitions on the continent. At the same time, conditions on the ground, among the peoples and their movements, increasingly showed that the accepted framework for peace and order could not contain the larger global dynamics impinging on European realities and relationships. European order did not depend solely on developments in Europe, where it would take more than the actions and commitments of the great powers to preserve peace.

Staging the Alliance in Laibach (1821)

When on 30 December 1820/11 January 1821 the allies resumed deliberations in Laibach, they already had agreed to intervention in the Kingdom of the Two Sicilies. On 4 February, an Austrian army of 35,000 crossed the river Po into Italy. On 13 February, the government in Naples declared war, and King Ferdinand I's son, Francesco, pledged loyalty to the constitution.[4] On 23 March, Austrian troops occupied Naples, and by summer it became clear that their presence would not lead to protracted military conflict. The Neapolitan revolutionaries failed to mount a united resistance, and no broad-based popular uprising in defense of the constitution occurred; consequently, the restoration of the king did not require severe or murderous measures.[5] On 24 June 1821, Austrian foreign minister Metternich could write to Russian co-minister of foreign affairs Nesselrode that the work of the three monarchs (Alexander I, Francis I, and Frederick William III) had produced real and positive results. Nor had the British and French governments raised additional objections to the allies' course of action. France remained a hotbed of revolution, but Metternich believed that for the moment Italy had been pacified.[6]

For the moment, indeed. As Russia's diplomats continued negotiations in Laibach, they paid close attention to how allied actions in Naples would be represented and received. They insisted that the intervention adhere to the legal forms and prescriptions of the Quadruple and general alliances. Equally significant, they did not equate the repression of constitutional government in the Kingdom of the Two Sicilies with outright rejection of liberal political principles. Even the influential foreign policy adviser Aleksandr S. Sturdza, who consistently defended the dignity of sovereigns and religion, feared that intervention might provoke war between Ferdinand I and his son, the heir presumptive.[7] As Sturdza admitted in a report to co-minister of foreign affairs Kapodistrias from 31 December 1820/12 January 1821, the germs of revolution had taken root in Germany, Italy, and Switzerland. Europe had divided into two systems, one old and the other new. Among the states constructed on ancient foundations (*anciennes bases*), Sturdza named the great powers—Austria, Prussia, and Russia—together with second-order powers such as Denmark, Electoral Hessen, Hanover, the Roman (papal) state, Sardinia, and Saxony. States built upon the new constitutional system included Baden, Bavaria, Britain, France, the Netherlands, Portugal, Spain, Sweden, the Two Sicilies, Württemberg, and the two peninsulas (*sic*) of the American continent. The European political system, in other words, had changed forever.

The constitutional party, in Sturdza's analysis, had become preponderant and therefore commanded resources such as the universal language and the universal motor composed of money, commerce, navigation, and science. Religion, by contrast, had become a weak weapon in the struggle against "the unbridled tendency toward general emancipation." Referencing the revolutionary situation in Spain, Sturdza pointed out that entire social classes had lost their property, the press refused to publish opinions favoring the legal regulation of speech, and sectarians of license (*sectateurs de la license*) now controlled the inquisition. In these conditions, defenders of the old system, struggling to counter exalted passions and revolutionary storms, possessed only one means of resistance: the austere voice of experience and duty, grounded in good faith and love of God. Sturdza saw in the pacification of Naples not a solution to, but a respite from, the revolutionary assault on religion and duty, which in its recent manifestations had gone beyond what even the French Jacobins had attempted. Sturdza's recognition of the revolutionary threat seemed at once prescient, reactionary, and potentially reformist. Alongside irreligion, he also cited injustice and fiscal insolvency as vulnerabilities that explained the rebels' success. But while intellectuals and diplomats such as Sturdza believed that only the wholesale defeat of revolution could guarantee peace, the so-called holy allies interpreted their right to intervene in Naples differently.[8]

The intervention in Naples was at once a suppression of revolution and a policy of enlightened reform. As the conferences in Laibach demonstrated, neither at home nor abroad did the Russian monarchy espouse unyielding opposition to political change.[9] Although the holy allies, supported officially by France's representative and unofficially by Britain's, had refused to recognize the revolutionary government in Naples or negotiate with its representative, they nonetheless assumed that King Ferdinand I's restoration would include political reforms.[10] At the start of the meetings, the Russian government once again pushed to conclude a legal act that all the governments of Europe might sanction. Characterizing the Troppau decisions as preparatory and preliminary, Russia's diplomats tried to enhance the solemnity and legality of the final decisions that would be made in Laibach. An official opinion approved by Emperor Alexander on 30 December 1820/11 January 1821 argued for a formal allied statement, based on the recognized legal principles that governed the meetings of the European sovereigns and their plenipotentiaries. According to the Russian government, in matters such as the revolution in Naples, allied deliberations constituted a legal duty unrelated to questions of convenience or suitability. Russia's position did not imply that a new political alliance should be formed; rather it aimed to affirm the system that had given peace to Europe, independence to nations, and the means for governments to promote the happiness of their peoples. In accordance with established treaties, which required allied action on behalf of governments threatened by the events in Naples, the Italian states also had been invited to Laibach. In the end, given Britain's continuing neutrality, the allies expressed appreciation for, but nonetheless rejected, the Russian proposal. As the plenipotentiaries of Austria, France, and Prussia put the matter, the forms followed in Troppau seemed adequate to ensure that the policy of unity and general solidarity would continue to define relations among European states.[11]

During January 1821, the three sovereigns who had accepted the Troppau protocol also reached agreement with King Ferdinand I of the Two Sicilies, who pledged to mediate between his people and the European alliance to eliminate the menace posed by the Neapolitan Revolution. Ferdinand had been allowed to leave Naples on the assumption that he would defend the constitution; however, upon arriving in Laibach, he reversed course and requested allied assistance to restore his authority.[12] With the understanding that the great powers would take no action before all possible means of reconciliation had been attempted, the king accepted the allies' refusal to recognize the current subversive government, including its representative in Laibach. Ferdinand thus appointed his own plenipotentiary, the Duke of Gallo, whom he called to Laibach to hear the explanations of allied policy.[13] The Duke of Gallo would return to Naples with a letter from Ferdinand to his son, the Duke of Calabria, denouncing the political changes implemented since 2 July 1820. The Duke of Gallo also would deliver joint instructions to the diplomatic representatives of Austria, France, Prussia, and Russia who served at the court of Naples. Again, Britain remained neutral, as did the Roman state; however, the plenipotentiaries of the Italian states of Modena, Sardinia, and Tuscany all accepted the plan.[14]

On 18/30 January, the Duke of Gallo met with allied plenipotentiaries to hear the instructions and dispatches that he would deliver to Naples.[15] As the conference pronouncements made clear, the allies expected the king to be restored to power, and they promised not to impose a war levy on the population of the Two Sicilies as long as formal resistance did not materialize. Tellingly, the allocution delivered by Metternich also implied that the great powers possessed the authority to decide what course of action served the true interests of the Two Sicilies and Europe. Peace and well-being, the allies consistently proclaimed, could be ensured only within the general alliance, which the current Neapolitan government had abandoned.[16]

Among the documents presented to the Duke of Gallo, a Russian rescript of 9/21 November 1820 described the transactions of 1814, 1815, and 1818 as a pact of solidarity among all the Christian states of Europe, which aimed to ensure the territorial integrity, political independence, and internal tranquility of each country.[17] Addressed to Count Gustav O. Stackelberg, Alexander I's envoy in Naples, and composed before Ferdinand I of the Two Sicilies agreed to come to Laibach, the rescript included the invitation to the king.[18] Stackelberg was instructed to act in concert with the representatives of Austria and Prussia to persuade Ferdinand that only by meeting with the allied sovereigns in Laibach would he be able to save his country from the disasters of revolution and war. Only by accepting the allied proposal could he lead the Two Sicilies to reconciliation with itself and the world. If the king asked why the British and French monarchs had not signed on to the invitation, the Russian envoy was told to reply that irrespective of the invitation, Britain would never legitimize the revolution in Naples and France would cooperate with the allies to ensure the repose of Europe. Indeed, in 1815 France had accepted allied guarantees (*guaranties concertées*) of its institutions, and in 1818 the country had been admitted into the general alliance. Allied policy toward the Two Sicilies followed exactly this course: the location had changed, but not the system (or policy). In 1815 the powers had embraced the European cause, and in 1820 they intended to defend it.[19]

The Russian version of the common instructions accepted in Laibach also was addressed to Count Stackelberg.[20] The instructions began with a review of key points elucidated in earlier documents. Motivated by duty to their states and the world, the allied sovereigns had negotiated with Ferdinand I of the Two Sicilies, who intended to mediate between his people and the alliance, from which his kingdom had been separated since the July events. Committed to the path of reconciliation, the king hoped to save his country from further misfortunes, while the allies sought to save neighboring states from the threat posed by the revolution. The allies had decided to act during the conferences in Troppau, where they also had recognized that the Neapolitan Revolution could not be treated as an isolated event. Unfortunately, despite the ongoing benefits of the general pacification, the spirit of trouble and disorder, the cause of widespread desolation, had revived. The situation in the Kingdom of the Two Sicilies had become so grave that the current allied action, based on the transactions of Vienna, Paris, and Aix-la-Chapelle, could only be interpreted as favorable to the general interest in the repose and happiness of all Europe.

The sectarians in Naples, by contrast, seeking political reform through revolt and crime, in reality had attacked religion, morality, and social bonds. Equally significant, they had violated their vows to a legitimate sovereign. Having usurped the king's authority, their revolution could lead only to anarchy and military despotism. The allies appreciated Ferdinand I's desire to avoid civil war through compromise; however, they would never accept the current government and so had taken steps to end the disorders, preferably by force of reason. Simply put, the allies expected the king to persuade his peoples to suppress the revolutionary regime, a course that spontaneously would return the Two Sicilies to amicable relations with the states of Europe and to membership in the general alliance. With this goal in mind, the allies had invited Ferdinand to explain how he planned to restore an order of things that could ensure the well-being, true interests, and stability of his subjects and the future security and tranquility of neighboring states. If this outcome could not be achieved, the allies would have no choice but to use armed force to end the disorders.

As the instructions to Stackelberg further recounted, King Ferdinand understood and accepted the allies' terms. To save his peoples from war and coercive measures, he wished to persuade them to disavow the political changes that had occurred. He believed, moreover, that his paternal voice would be heard. The monarch's message would be communicated in a letter to his son, the Duke of Calabria, describing the negotiations in Laibach. Stackelberg and other allied representatives on the ground in Naples would then be responsible for explaining to the duke that his father's letter also corresponded to the decisions of their respective sovereigns. In the process, they would exhort him to recognize the urgency of the situation, repudiate the revolution, and accept his father's advice.

In two additional dispatches, both dated 19/31 January 1821, Stackelberg received further instructions concerning communications with the Duke of Calabria about allied policy, the cooperation of King Ferdinand I, and plans for a
temporary army of occupation that might or might not be used.[21] Again, the
instructions repeated previous admonitions about the unacceptability of the
current government, the isolation of the Two Sicilies from the states of Europe,
the king's desire to serve as mediator in reconciling his country with the alliance,
the need to guarantee peace and repose for all the governments of Italy, and
finally, the inevitability of war, if the kingdom did not reject the revolutionary
regime, which threatened the "happiness, strength, and survival of every political and civil society."[22] Here too Stackelberg's task was to convince the duke
that peace, prosperity, and the exercise of legitimate rights were incompatible
with the existence of a government formed in revolt. For this reason, if military
intervention became necessary to end the crisis and restore the king's authority,
Emperor Alexander stood ready to send Russian troops to assist the allied army.
Again it seems that although the great powers did not intend to compromise the
territorial integrity or independence of Ferdinand's kingdom, they did presume
to define the true interests of a second-order state.

After concluding negotiations with King Ferdinand and explanations with
the Duke of Gallo, the allied plenipotentiaries discussed Austria's plan for the
army of occupation. Presented by Prince Metternich, the Austrian proposals
described the troops poised to cross the river Po and march into the Kingdom
of the Two Sicilies as an allied army operating on the basis of the transactions of
Troppau and Laibach.[23] The army would assist Ferdinand in an auxiliary capacity, and assuming that voluntary submission to the king's authority occurred,
no indemnity or military contribution would be imposed on his peoples. The
Austrian plan also called for an occupation of three years, regulated according
to the forms that had been followed in France after the victory over Napoleon.
The allies then promised to help Ferdinand financially, primarily as loan guarantors, and to meet with him in 1822 to evaluate the kingdom's internal condition
and the duration of the occupation. The conference journal for 21 January/2
February 1821 recorded formal approval of Austria's military proposals, including Alexander's pledge to provide financial assistance to Ferdinand. Prussia's
plenipotentiary also responded positively, though he had not yet received instructions from his government about the financial guarantees. France likewise
accepted that coercive measures might be necessary but refused to participate
in a war against Naples; and the British representatives, who were not authorized to give an opinion, affirmed their king's commitment to the alliance. The

representatives of Modena, the Roman state, Sardinia, and Tuscany likewise lacked the authority to discuss military intervention but deferred to the presumably wise views of the Austrian emperor.[24]

After reviewing Austria's plan for the occupation, the allies considered King Ferdinand's project for political reconstruction.[25] At the conference of 8/20 February 1821, Prince Ruffo, acting as royal plenipotentiary, presented the king's thoughts (*pensées*) on the principles of reform.[26] To enhance the monarch's understanding of the needs and interests of his peoples, the plan envisioned separate administrations for Naples and Sicily, united under one scepter. In both parts of the kingdom, a consultative body would debate legislation and administrative measures prior to enactment, on the assumption that the "interests of the crown, the well-being of the kingdom, and enlightened justice" were of a piece. Provincial councils would allocate taxes, and communal administration would serve the needs of the communes and the preservation of their patrimony (*patrimoine*). Over the next two days, Austria, France, Prussia, Russia, and the participating Italian states (Modena, the Roman state, Sardinia, and Tuscany) approved the proposed principles of reform. In supporting Ferdinand's ideas, Emperor Alexander highlighted the favorable response of the Italian states, which were most impacted by the events of 2 July, and expressed the hope that application of the proposed principles would, in accordance with article 4 of the protocol of 7/19 November 1820, lead to the creation of a stable order of things. Ideally, this order of things would be built upon foundations that would not require foreign assistance to guarantee the tranquility and independence of the Italian states.[27]

The formal closure of the Laibach conferences took place on 14/26 February 1821. Austrian troops had entered the Kingdom of the Two Sicilies on 6 February, and on 7 March the Neapolitan army would be destroyed at Rieti. Satisfied that the principal goal of the Troppau and Laibach meetings had been achieved, the allies agreed to reconvene in Florence in September 1822.[28] The three sovereigns also arranged to stay in Laibach to monitor the intervention.[29] It seemed as if the allies had succeeded in both addressing the revolutionary situation in Naples and preserving the alliance, despite disagreements. But they would enjoy only a brief respite from further crisis. On 9–10 March 1821, insurrection broke out in the Kingdom of Sardinia-Piedmont, where yet another provisional government proclaimed the Spanish constitution of 1812. King Victor Emmanuel I abdicated in favor of his brother, Charles Felix, who then fled to Laibach to appeal for allied support. Austria again intervened and on 8 April defeated the Piedmontese Revolution.[30] To justify this unanticipated action, the plenipotentiaries of the three powers, still in Laibach, issued a declaration, dated 30 April/12 May 1821, which explained the need to repress rebellion in both Naples and Piedmont.[31] Their swift response did not, however, end the revolutionary threat. Greek subjects of the Ottoman Empire, a special Russian interest, also rebelled in March, and within a few months the allies faced the prospect of renewed war. In the midst of the volatile Greek crisis, Emperor Alexander I again worked to preserve allied unity and organize concerted action, based on the agreements of 1814, 1815, and 1818.

The Russian-Ottoman War Scare of 1821–22

Allied decisions in Troppau and Laibach assumed that not only military success but also public perception of the intervention in Naples had broad implications for peace in Europe. The Spanish Revolution continued to be a problem, though before the allies could collectively address that situation, the start of the Greek independence movement created a more immediate crisis. Following the outbreak of the Greek insurrections, the future of the Ottoman Empire, the so-called Eastern Question, emerged as a critical problem for European diplomacy. During the crisis of 1821–22, Russia's diplomats focused on the same issues of rebellion, intervention, and legitimate sovereignty that had occupied the alliance since the revolt in Spain. In the Ottoman sphere, however, the potential consequences of intervention extended beyond the suppression of insurgency into the centuries-old relationship between Christianity and Islam. Russia in particular had a long history of military conflict, political entanglement, and treaty relationships with the Ottoman Empire. From the perspective of Emperor Alexander I, the legal obligations already binding the two empires appeared no less essential to European order than the transactions of 1814, 1815, and 1818. Further complicating the situation, Russian-Ottoman tensions carried broad implications for the interests of other great powers operating in the Balkans, the Mediterranean, and North Africa. Precisely because the allies continued to believe in allied unity and to view European society as a distinct entity, their most immediate goal became the avoidance of war and preservation of the Ottoman Empire. To achieve this goal, they needed to monitor one another's thoughts, actions, and intentions, which they tried to do through the substance and staging of concerted action.

The backdrop to the crisis of 1821–22 lay in the Russian Empire's military and diplomatic successes during the late eighteenth and early nineteenth centuries. Following the military conflicts of 1768–74, 1787–92, and 1806–12, Russia occupied a strong position in the ongoing struggle with the Ottoman and Persian empires to control the Balkans, the Caucasus, and Transcaucasia. Critical Russian interests included internationalization of the Black Sea, free commercial navigation through the Straits of the Bosporus and Dardanelles, protection of the Christian religion and Orthodox coreligionists living under Ottoman rule, support of Balkan aspirations for political autonomy within the framework of Ottoman suzerainty, and finally, in the aftermath of the Napoleonic Wars, use of the European political system to preserve peace and ensure adherence to established treaty obligations. With the Treaty of Bucharest, signed in 1812, the Russian monarchy committed itself to preservation of the Ottoman Empire, enforcement of recognized territorial agreements, the principle of legitimism, and defense of sovereign authority.[32] Still, the reconciliation proved fleeting, for even in the best of times, the potential for conflict between these chronic foes only partially abated.

In the era of European restoration, implementation of the Porte's treaty obligations to Russia did not proceed as Emperor Alexander I had hoped. Tensions quickly arose over delimitation of the Caucasian border, Russia's role as defender of Serbia's recently acquired political autonomy, and guarantees of free navigation in the Black Sea and the straits.[33] Negotiations conducted by Alexander's envoy Baron Grigorii A. Stroganov were ongoing, and as late as June 1817, the Russian government continued to proclaim that the Porte sought friendship and that the diplomatic endeavors in Constantinople would produce results. Russian-Ottoman disputes also had been addressed during the Congress of Vienna, though the Hundred Days had ended the discussions, and going forward Alexander rejected the possibility of European participation in this long-standing bilateral relationship. In the monarch's view, neither the Ottoman nor the Persian Empire belonged to the political association defined by the treaties of Vienna and Paris.[34] This approach prevailed until March 1821, when rebellions erupted among the Ottomans' Greek subjects. Within a few months, the threat of yet another Russian-Ottoman war loomed large.[35]

The immediate crisis in 1821 resulted from multiple uprisings among the Christian subjects of the Ottoman Empire: Greeks in Moldavia, led by Alexandros Ypsilantis (Alexander Ypsilanti), who recently had retired from Russian military service; Greeks in the Morea, in Attica, Thessaly, Macedonia, Epirus, and the Aegean Archipelago; and a peasant revolt in Wallachia, led by Tudor Vladimirescu against the Ottoman-appointed hospodar (governor) and great landowners. Equally ominous, Turkish reprisals against Christian civilians in the Danubian Principalities and Constantinople led to the destruction of churches and the murder on Easter eve (22 April 1821) of Ecumenical Patriarch Grigorios V.[36] Although Baron Stroganov continued to report diplomatic progress, these developments, together with ongoing violations of Russia's economic and other treaty rights, convinced Emperor Alexander that the Porte intended to wage war against the Orthodox religion.[37]

Torn between the obligation to protect Christian subjects of the Ottoman Empire and the post-Napoleonic commitment to legitimist principles, Emperor Alexander consistently opposed the Greek rebellions. By late June, the revolts in the principalities had been suppressed.[38] But Ottoman troops remained, and atrocities, committed by Greeks and Turks, continued.[39] In these circumstances, diplomatic declarations had no effect, and on 6/18 July 1821, Baron Stroganov delivered an ultimatum addressed to the Porte by the Russian government. Russia's demands included: (1) restoration of destroyed and damaged churches; (2) protection of the Christian religion and the rights of Christians; (3) recognition of the distinction between innocent Greeks and those responsible for the troubles; and (4) a role for Russia in the pacification of Moldavia and Wallachia, as established by the spirit of existing treaties. Stroganov's instructions also authorized him to soften the tone of the note, if he thought such a gesture might be useful or justified. But the Porte remained silent, and once the specified eight-day waiting period had passed, the Russian envoy carried out his orders to leave Constantinople with all diplomatic personnel. After this formal break in diplomatic relations, the possibility of war became very real, encouraged in Russia by key foreign policy and military advisers and by pro-Greek sympathies in educated society. A period of dangerous uncertainty and grinding diplomacy ensued. Eventually, the Russian monarch, who had condemned the Greek rebels from the outset, opted for peace in the interest of European unity.[40] How did this happen, and what did it reveal about Russia's relationship to Europe?

When news of the Ypsilantis revolt reached the allies in Laibach, Emperor Alexander immediately disavowed support for both Ypsilantis and Greek rebellion against Ottoman authority. At the same time, the Russian monarch expected a collective response from the allies and therefore wanted to ascertain what their position would be if circumstances forced him to take military action (as Austria had done in Italy). More modestly, he hoped that the allied governments would publish a common declaration on the crisis, in order to mold public opinion and limit unfavorable press coverage. Beginning in the spring of 1821 and continuing into October, Russia's diplomats in Berlin, London, Paris, and Vienna received instructions to pressure allied courts to support Alexander's call for concerted action. The monarch also communicated directly with Francis I, George IV, and

British foreign secretary Castlereagh.[41] Britain already had opposed intervention in Naples, but Russia still hoped to win Austrian, British, and French support in case of war with the Ottoman Empire.[42]

In 1821–22, even though the Ottoman Empire did not belong to European society, Russia's policymakers approached relations with the Porte and insurrection in Moldavia, Wallachia, and Greece from the perspective of the European system. They assumed, therefore, that the maintenance of peace could not be left to any one great power. Because the European alliance had a role to play and a responsibility to fulfill, Russian diplomats, including the tsar diplomat, insisted that both the European allies and the Porte adhere to established treaty obligations and that the Ottoman Empire resume its place in the (European) political order. Thus, when the Russian government informed the allies of the July ultimatum to the Porte, Emperor Alexander also appealed for support and suggested that collective military force might be needed to pacify the East.[43] Convoluted as this thinking sometimes appeared, it had the effect of prioritizing allied unity in the pursuit of international reconciliation.

The note of 6/18 July, delivered to the Porte by Baron Stroganov, began by proclaiming Russia's commitment to the conservation of the Turkish government, considered necessary for the maintenance and consolidation of peace in Europe.[44] After the first signs of insurrection had appeared in Moldavia and Wallachia, the Russian government had encouraged the Divan, the supreme council of the Ottoman government, to take measures to suppress the revolutionary evil. Equally telling, over the previous five years, Russia's diplomats had worked to ensure the "religious fulfilment of the treaties." In other words, through cooperation with the Porte, Russia sought to stamp out rebellion and end the calamities afflicting the people of the principalities, who, despite the insurrection, nonetheless remained innocent and loyal to the Ottoman government. Russia accepted the need to use military force to deliver Moldavia and Wallachia from the foreigners who had undermined internal tranquility; however, such force should be deployed wisely under the protection of a reparative government and in accordance with the public law of the principalities. Unfortunately, rather than following this course, Ottoman policy encouraged sympathy for the very people who attacked the Porte's authority. In this manner, the Porte imparted to insurrection the character of a legitimate defense of the Greek nation and its church.[45]

During past crises, the Russian note continued, the Ottoman government had not encouraged Muslim subjects to persecute Christians. In this instance, however, the conditions of coexistence that for so long had prevailed in the

Porte's European territories had been violated. Four centuries had passed since such vicious attacks on Christianity, exemplified by the murder of the patriarch and the destruction of churches, had been witnessed. The Porte, in other words, appeared to be waging war against the Christian religion. Unable, therefore, to find in the existence of the Ottoman Empire a guarantee of peace, Russia faced the prospect of being forced to defend its "insulted faith, broken treaties, and persecuted coreligionists." At this juncture, the Porte should recognize, based on the representations of the great powers, that Russia's cause constituted a European cause. The Christian monarchs of Europe would not be able to ignore the repressions inflicted both on the people responsible for the troubles and on the Greek nation en masse. Current Ottoman policies clearly threatened European peace, offended the Christian religion, and amounted to the extermination of a Christian people.

Although Russia's immediate actions purportedly aimed only to defend the general interest, the treaties of Kuchuk Kainardji (1774) and Bucharest (1812) also remained in effect. Kuchuk Kainardji stipulated Russia's right to protect the Greek religion in all the states of the Ottoman Empire. Bucharest assigned to the Russian government political rights in Moldavia and Wallachia. Thus, in pressing Russia's claims against the Porte, the note of 6/18 July 1821 subsumed under the mantle of the European alliance the right to protect the Christian religion and Christian subjects of the Ottoman Empire, as prescribed by earlier treaties. Invariably proclaiming the pure and peaceful intentions of the Russian monarch, the language of the note ignored potential distinctions between the Greek church and other Christian denominations, as well as between Greeks, Moldavians, and Wallachians, whose insurrections unfolded as separate movements.[46]

Baron Stroganov's ultimatum to the Porte likewise insisted that Russia's demands remained what they always had been. Furthermore, because the Porte's policies posed a danger to the Ottoman Empire itself, acceptance of the conditions would bring salvation to the Turks. Either the Porte had been operating under the influence of fanatics or its policies had resulted from free will and a well-reasoned plan. In either case, Emperor Alexander demanded an explanation, while also expressing the hope that the current policy could be altered by removing from power a few lost men. By accepting Russia's claims, the Porte would show that it possessed the power to change course and once again engage in negotiations with Christian governments. Pacification in the principalities of Moldavia and Wallachia, to which Russia should contribute based on the spirit of the treaties, could then become a model for the pacification of Greece. If, by contrast, the Porte did not end the repressive and inhuman measures now being applied, the Ottoman Empire would be in a state of open hostility against the Christian world. Russia's government would have no choice but to offer refuge to Greek combatants, whose struggle would be legitimized. In other words, instead of cooperating with the Porte to end the uprisings and restore tranquility to the insurgent provinces, Russia and the Christian world would be duty bound to protect their brothers in religion from blind fanaticism. Russia remained committed to the conservation of the Ottoman Empire and the fulfillment of established treaty obligations. It was the Porte's responsibility, however, to take steps to end the troubles.[47] As Russian diplomats depicted the situation, the Porte refused to accept the very conditions that would ensure its own salvation. Consequently, the break in diplomatic relations had become unavoidable, and the threat of military conflict had intensified.

Because the departure of an entire diplomatic mission usually represented a step toward war, the rift between Constantinople and Saint Petersburg forced the allies to focus on Emperor Alexander's conditions for the restoration of Russian-Ottoman relations. Among the communications generated by the diplomatic crisis, historians have paid particular attention to Britain's role as allied negotiator. In reality, the Russian government did not view allied diplomats as negotiators or mediators. Their accepted role was to pressure the Porte to meet the monarch's legal demands, and in the event of failure, to establish a "concert of views and principles between Russia and the allied powers."[48] Even before the formal break in relations, Russia's diplomats had connected the crisis in the East to European order and the general alliance. In a letter of 22 June/4 July 1821, Kapodistrias had explained to Baron Pavel A. Nikolai, Russian chargé d'affaires in London, that the Porte's actions could only be interpreted as hostile toward Russia.[49] Kapodistrias blamed the British ambassador in Constantinople, Lord Strangford, for the allies' failure to respond to Russian appeals and insisted that they support Baron Stroganov's negotiations.[50] The issues identified by Kapodistrias included Russia's demand that the Porte fulfill established treaty obligations and respect the Christian religion. Equally significant, Kapodistrias reiterated that Emperor Alexander had never supported the Greek insurrections and had even tolerated Ottoman reprisals against rebellious subjects.

From the summer of 1821 until the war scare temporarily abated in the spring of 1822, the Austrian and British governments remained suspicious of Emperor Alexander's objectives and worked collaboratively to prevent a Russian-Ottoman war. Although the issues they identified and the diplomatic arguments they presented did not necessarily correspond, for Russia, the potential dangers of Austrian-British cooperation became painfully evident when Metternich and

Castlereagh met in Hanover from 20 to 29 October 1821 (NS). During the years of arduous diplomacy that followed the Congress of Vienna, the appearance of a unified alliance could be as important as substantive agreement or disagreement. Thus, under the guise of unity, Christoph Lieven, Russia's ambassador in London, traveled to Hanover to convey Emperor Alexander's confidence in his allies.[51]

Lieven arrived in Hanover on 28 October, having learned along the way that Count Bernstorff, Prussia's minister of foreign affairs, had been invited to the meetings, but had declined to attend.[52] Based on conversations with Castlereagh, Lieven then reported to Nesselrode that because the allies feared military conflict, they had not responded to Russia's efforts to ascertain what their positions would be in case of war. Metternich and Castlereagh agreed, however, to instruct their respective diplomats in Constantinople to pressure the Porte to compromise, so that direct communications between the Russian and Ottoman governments could be restored. The ministers seemed to understand that before negotiations could resume, Russia expected to see evidence of military evacuation and just administration in the Danubian Principalities. Both ministers also wrote to Alexander not only to offer moral support, but also to express opposition to military action. For the moment, Britain opposed both Greek independence and the removal of Ottoman power from Europe. Although Lieven generally presented British policy in a positive light, he nonetheless saw in the Hanover meetings the potential for "a separate alliance [*combinaison isolée*], alien to the interests of Russia and contrary to the principles of the general alliance."[53] Russia's envoy in Vienna, Iurii A. Golovkin, stated outright that with respect to the Eastern Question (*la question orientale*), Austrian and British interests stood in opposition to those of Russia.[54]

In Castlereagh's conversations with Lieven (as reported by Lieven), the British foreign secretary highlighted three issues: apprehensions based on Russia's diplomatic communications, particularly the ultimatum to the Porte of 6/18 July 1821; the British government's refusal to consider participation in an armed conflict; and finally, fears about the consequences of a war, including the political alliances that might result. Lieven believed that he had effectively calmed British anxiety about Russia's intentions, and as a result, Britain now accepted the Austrian version of Emperor Alexander's conditions for the restoration of Russian-Ottoman relations. In addition, although both Austria and Britain recognized Russia's demands as legal, just, moderate, and wise, the British government still hoped that Alexander would allow some leeway in the mode and form of Ottoman compliance. Lieven continued to claim that the British government misunderstood

Russian policy, and while in Hanover, he insisted that Alexander's demands could not be altered. Not only did they represent the only way to prevent war; the monarch also had a right to ask his allies to insist that the Porte comply. This did not mean that the desire for allied support and agreement in case of war constituted a call for military action. Emperor Alexander aimed only to preserve peace by means of an allied entente. In other words, it was critical that the enemies of disorder not be able to view Russian-Ottoman hostilities as an isolated war that portended the dissolution or weakening of the European alliance.[55]

Despite Lieven's concerns about a four-power entente (Austria, Britain, France, and Prussia), he did not equate the Hanover meetings with the formation of an allied grouping directed against Russia.[56] To the contrary, Austria and Britain, while eager to prevent war, did not want to offend Alexander. Suspicions among the allies threatened their unity, but in the present circumstances, even if Russia went to war, Lieven did not expect the alliance to be harmed. In fact, he anticipated allied support for Russia, if military conflict erupted. With hindsight, Lieven's appraisal seems overly optimistic. The ambassador assumed that Britain recognized Russia's treaty right to protect the Greek population of the Ottoman Empire, and he characterized Alexander's immediate goal as effective pacification of the Danubian Principalities. The monarch's conservative policy treated the principalities and Greek territories as Ottoman provinces. Equally promising, Russia's position accorded well with Castlereagh's reported belief that European peace would be better served if Christians lived within the Ottoman Empire. This would ensure the presence of a Christian population, as opposed to millions of "fanatical" and "vengeful" Muslims, along Russia's borders. What Lieven did not mention, or perhaps did not understand, was that Alexander's policy of pacification assumed a role for Russia inside the European provinces of the Ottoman Empire, including the archipelago and mainland of Greece. As Nesselrode explained in a confidential expedition to the ambassador, dated 27 November/9 December 1821, Russia had to be associated with any peace proposals directed at the Greeks, based on the empire's treaty right to protect coreligionists.[57] But before this could happen, Russia's diplomatic relations with the Ottoman Empire had to be restored. In other words, pacification of the Porte's rebellious subjects could not begin before Lord Strangford convinced the Ottoman government to implement Russia's requirements for the renewal of diplomatic negotiations.

At the end of December 1821, Austria, Britain, and Russia had not yet found a common path forward that could prevent war between the Russian and Ottoman empires. In a personal letter from Kapodistrias to Lieven, dated 27 November/9

December 1821 and approved by Alexander I, the co-minister of foreign affairs emphatically proclaimed that neither the Austrian nor the British government understood Russia's position vis-à-vis the Porte.[58] Rather, both seemed to interpret the monarch's diplomatic maneuvers as an effort to legitimize war, while drawing the allies into support for Russia—an interpretation that (from the Russian point of view) months of diplomacy contradicted. The focus of Kapodistrias's letter concerned Russia's obligation to protect the Christian subjects of the Ottoman Empire. Before Russia could negotiate, based on established treaties, the Porte needed to take concrete steps to fulfill Alexander's conditions, an intention that could be demonstrated only by implementing "principles of humanity and justice toward the Christians." Instead, the Porte had pursued a policy of vengeance and destruction directed against Greeks in Moldavia, Wallachia, Smyrna, Cyprus, and Crete. It was precisely Turkish persecution of Christians that had caused the rupture in Russian-Ottoman relations. Consequently, Emperor Alexander demanded a return to the conditions of March 1821, including respect for treaty obligations toward Russia's coreligionists.

A second issue identified in Kapodistrias's letter concerned the possibility that together the allies and the Porte might reach an agreement with the Greeks without Russian participation. The co-minister insisted that only through direct and active Russian involvement in the pacification of the principalities would it be possible to rectify the errors and moderate the hopes of the Greeks. But until Russia and the Porte returned to normal diplomatic relations, there could be no Russian participation. For seven months Alexander had asked only that the Ottoman Empire fulfill established treaty obligations. If the monarch had wished to drag the allies into war, he could have marched an army toward the principalities. The allies, having previously recognized the justice of Russia's grievances, would not have been able to condemn the military action. Assuming, Kapodistrias added, that Ottoman troops would have succumbed to Russian forces, Alexander also would have been in a position to dictate the terms of the peace. Yet in contrast to this scenario, the monarch's intentions remained moderate. Throughout the crisis he had kept in view the interests of the European system. For precisely this reason, he sought to engage the allies in a discussion of how, by acting in concert, they could preserve "the tranquility of Europe and the moral character of the European alliance." Once again, Kapodistrias instructed Lieven to try to convince the British government that the Russian monarch continued to seek peace, as he had done since the troubles began in Moldavia and Wallachia. At the same time, notwithstanding Alexander's patience, the monarch still considered war a possibility and hoped to obtain from the allies a commitment to address in concert any consequences that might result. Indeed, in the case of war, Alexander's calculations would concern not the exclusive interests of Russia, but those of the general alliance.

Lieven's conversations with Castlereagh, which had begun in Hanover, continued in London, where once again the ambassador failed to obtain a commitment to support Russia in a war against the Porte.[59] Castlereagh did confirm, however, that Britain had no plans to mediate between the rebellious Greeks and the Ottoman government, a possibility suggested by the British role in negotiations between Spain and the Spanish American colonies. British mediation would require simultaneous invitations from both parties to the conflict, an unlikely development given the sensitivities of the Divan and the lack of local authority among the Greeks. Britain, committed to the survival of the Ottoman Empire, also rejected the idea of an allied guarantee that the Porte would fulfill its obligations to the Greeks. Nor did the British government believe that a general pacification of the Ottoman provinces would succeed or even be consistent with British interests.

Ambassador Lieven accepted that given the uncertainty surrounding the Greek crisis, the British government hesitated to pronounce on a course of action. Even after reports of Greek military success against Ottoman troops and greater unity among rebel leaders reached London, British leaders sought to preserve the Ottoman Empire, though they also expressed little confidence in the Porte's ability to restore order among its Christian subjects. Indeed, Castlereagh associated the Greek insurrections with revolutions in other countries and stated plainly that the Greek cause should not be characterized as a natural defense. The foreign secretary therefore hoped that Emperor Alexander would be able "to draw a line between the legitimate interest that the oppressed Greeks have the right to demand from Russia, based on the treaties, and the guilty men who march today under the banner of revolt."[60]

Serious differences among the allies persisted, but by January 1822, the great powers achieved a measure of consensus on how to approach the Greek question. They agreed that the Porte stood in legal violation of established treaties in relation to both Russia and the Greek/Christian population of the Ottoman Empire. The allies likewise viewed the Greek insurrections as part of the larger revolutionary upheaval spreading across Europe. Agreement on these principles did not, however, satisfy Alexander I's expectations or ease allied pressure on the monarch to soften Russia's demands. In reports from December 1821 and January 1822, Russia's envoy in Vienna, Iurii Golovkin, reported to Nesselrode that Metternich's depiction of the Eastern crisis aimed to make Russia appear responsible if war broke out.[61] The Austrian government believed that a Russian-Ottoman war would represent the triumph of the revolutionary faction in Europe and therefore insisted that Russia drop the three moral demands contained in the ultimatum to the Porte. By contrast, the one legitimate material demand, evacuation of the principalities, should be preserved. Although Metternich viewed the Greek rebellions within the broader framework of stopping the spread of revolution in Europe—a goal that required allied agreement—Golovkin admitted that he had been unable to persuade the Austrian minister of the rightness of Russia's position. Golovkin also remained suspicious of Metternich's intentions, suspected a bilateral Austrian-British effort to intervene in the Greek cause, and expected Austrian neutrality in case of war. Equally concerning, Metternich continued to criticize Russia's acceptance of Greek refugees and to accuse Alexander's government of supporting Greek Etairists, members of a political organization originally based in Odessa who stood behind the Ypsilantis uprising and sought to liberate Greece through armed insurrection.[62]

Emperor Alexander's response to the Austrian claim that a war between the Russian and Ottoman empires would represent the victory of the revolutionary party in Europe appeared in a communication from Nesselrode to Golovkin, dated 31 January/12 February 1822 and approved by the monarch.[63] Nesselrode began by highlighting the shared commitment of the Austrian and Russian courts to preserving the moral force of the European alliance, the intimate union of the allied powers, and the European peace that the powers had enjoyed for the past seven years. In the mind of Alexander, the moral force of the alliance included protection of the peoples from subversive projects. Thus, the Russian government wanted to discuss whether or not war, which seemed inevitable, would advantage the revolutionaries, threaten the alliance, and imperil European peace. According to Nesselrode, the Russian answer to this question implied a need for action, whereas Austria's policy remained one of inaction. As Russia's diplomats repeated over and over again, since June 1821 Emperor Alexander had sought an allied remedy to the crisis based on persuasion. But if the Porte continued the current course, the use of force would be necessary. Consequently, in the event of war, the Russian government stood ready to act in concert with the allies.

If agreed upon in advance, the Russian government believed, war would endanger neither the general alliance nor peace in Christian Europe. Russia had no desire to become the sole arbiter of the Ottoman Empire's destiny, and for this reason, the august friends of Emperor Alexander did not fear his intentions. Nesselrode tried to distinguish between Alexander's fellow monarchs and the allied governments fearful of Russia's aims. Critics of Alexander's foreign policy argued that a war against the Turks would make Russia an effective auxiliary of insurrection. They also expressed concern about the potential for Russia to become bogged down militarily, which could prevent the empire from assisting allies faced with revolution. Such fears were unfounded, Nesselrode insisted, for Russia had never supported the Greek rebels and had been prepared to offer military assistance during the troubles in Italy. Equally important, Emperor Alexander's principles in relation to Greece had always been noble and pure.

Nesselrode went on to identify two problems in need of an allied response. First, the allies must bring to an end the conflict between the Muslims and the Greeks; and second, they must address the obstinance of the Turkish government and the germs of anarchy and dissolution that existed within the Ottoman Empire. Since June, Nesselrode continued, Emperor Alexander had been asking his allies to deliberate on what their common response would be if the current crisis did not subside. Over the course of nine months the allied policy of conciliation had failed to mitigate the evil that ravaged the East. Although the crisis had originated in the Greek insurrections, the Porte's policy had aimed not to suppress the revolutionaries, but to attack the entire Greek nation. From the perspective of the Russian government, the Porte had pursued a war of extermination against Greek merchants, proprietors, and clergy, not just against sectarians. In other words, Muslims had been armed against Greeks in the name of religion. So if the allies hoped to dissuade the entire Greek nation from following the agitators, the Porte had to distinguish the innocent from the culpable. If the Porte hoped to achieve Greek submission to Ottoman authority, the innocent would have to receive guarantees of security, including pardons for those who had supported the revolutionaries in error.

But guarantees for the innocent would be useless, if the Ottomans continued to violate broader treaty obligations to Russia. If this happened, the present misfortunes would go on indefinitely, leading to the total annihilation of the Greek nation. To prevent this, either the Turks had to be persuaded to change course or armed intervention had to be used. Action in the Levant (the islands and coastal areas of the eastern Mediterranean ruled by the Ottomans) might produce unforeseen consequences; however, if the Porte did not cede to the power of reason, they would succumb to force. Russia would make clear that Emperor Alexander wanted to preserve the Ottoman Empire and the peace by cooperating with the Porte "for the reestablishment of tranquility in Greece on solid and durable foundations." This policy would not encourage illegitimate hopes, but by enhancing the Greeks' sense of security, it would allow them to repel agitators and choose a moderate path forward. Inaction, by contrast, would allow the troubles to continue, thereby increasing the revolutionary threat across Europe. In these conditions, Russia would not be responsible for the effects of inaction or the broadening crisis.

Russia Chooses Peace

Although recent scholarship focuses on Austrian-British efforts to block Russian action during the crisis of 1821–22, there can be no question but that Emperor Alexander I sought to avoid war. Clearly, the monarch continued to see the European alliance as the best means to preserve peace. This is why historians of the Greek independence movement are careful to distinguish the rebels' expectations of Russian support from the actual assistance they did or did not receive.[64] Dmitrii P. Tatishchev's 1822 missions to the Austrian court—missions that Alexander hoped would persuade the allies to act in concert (*concerter*) to protect Russia's treaty rights—embodied the commitment to allied unity. The impetus to send Tatishchev to Vienna was Emperor Alexander's ongoing disappointment with efforts to dispel what he considered the Porte's illusions. None of the allies, especially Austria and Britain, had committed to strong support of Russian interests. After close to a year of diplomatic conversation and evasion, Austria had failed to press upon the Porte the legitimacy of Russia's demands. Instead, the threat of war had increased. To rectify this situation, Tatishchev received orders to convince Metternich of the need for (and justice of) forceful concerted action and, once again, to assess what Austria's reaction would be, if the Russian monarch decided to go to war.[65]

Emperor Alexander's instructions to Tatishchev appeared in a rescript dated 5/17 February 1822.[66] From the outset the monarch made clear that Tatishchev's mission concerned the most vital interests—interests that the crisis in the East threatened and that could be protected only through the general alliance, as opposed to the exclusive combinations of the old policy.[67] The substantive instructions began with a summary of Alexander's response to Austria's proposals of 23 December 1821 concerning Russia's claims against the Porte, which was also transmitted to his agents at allied courts.[68] By the time of the mission, Austria had assumed the lead role in allied negotiations with Constantinople, and as the Russian monarch made clear, at the Vienna court Tatishchev spoke for his sovereign. As the instructions emphasized, even though Austria represented the most likely allied participant in the crisis, Alexander expected cooperation from all the great powers. Repeatedly, he insisted that the grave matters at hand needed to be resolved collectively "in the spirit of the alliance and for the common salvation [*salut*] of all the States of Europe." According to the monarch, the current task of the European allies was to protect interests threatened by the crisis in the Levant, if necessary by deploying an armed force that would act for the general good in the name of the alliance.[69] The interests at stake represented one aspect of Russia's relations with the Porte, and to compromise those interests would threaten the order of things enshrined in established treaties.

Having identified Russia's interests with the common European good and desire for peace, Emperor Alexander highlighted the danger posed by allied inaction and by failure to convince the Porte to change course so that diplomatic relations with Russia could be restored. Continuation of the impasse would force Russia to act alone, a step the allies clearly hoped to forestall. As if to counter allied apprehensions that he aimed to expand Russia's economic and territorial interests at Ottoman expense, Alexander warned that in the event of unilateral Russian action, the factions working to disrupt social order in Europe might easily conclude that the alliance was broken.[70] The monarch reiterated his desire to avoid war, a position he believed Russian diplomacy already had established. However, if the Porte remained obstinate and the use of force became necessary, collective allied action would be more effective than any unilateral measures taken by Russia. Alexander rejected the potential claim that to address the Porte in the name of Europe was tantamount to recognizing the Ottoman Empire as a European power. To the contrary, the purpose of collective European action would be to return the Ottoman Empire to the position it had occupied in the political order of March 1821, before the start of the Greek rebellions.

Emperor Alexander's instructions to Tatishchev can be read as a justification of Russian demands and a plea for allied support. Repeatedly the monarch described the policy of the Ottoman government as a threat to the tranquility of Europe. Russia's calls for a formal allied guarantee to specify the actions that would be taken if the Porte refused to accede to Russian demands remained unanswered, though eventually the allies did promise moral support in the event of war. In the meantime, it was the job of Alexander's diplomats to prod the allies into articulating a unified position. Based on the events of the previous nine months, the monarch had concluded that without a change in the allied approach, the Ottomans would continue to violate established treaty obligations. Indeed, if the Porte rejected the modified conditions put forward by Austria, Russia expected to employ coercive measures in the name of the alliance. Alexander understood that any movement of Russian troops into the Danubian Principalities would lead to war, even if Russia did not declare war. But backed

by an allied guarantee, the nature of which was not specified, this war of concert (*guerre concertée*) would quickly produce satisfactory results and would not
compromise peace in other parts of Europe. Again, allied agreement in outlook
and principle represented the best protection against the misfortunes caused by
particular combinations—just the sort of combinations that Napoleon had used
to break up multiple coalitions in the wake of French military victories.

Alexander ended the instructions by comparing the act he currently hoped
to conclude with the Troppau protocol signed by Austria, Prussia, and Russia
in November 1820. Russia's expectations of the allies followed directly from
the actions negotiated in Troppau and Laibach. Never mind that Britain and
France had not formally acceded to the Austrian intervention in Naples. They
had not openly opposed it, and the rift had neither violated nor undermined the
alliance. Similarly, if Russia acted alone to protect its interests in the East, this
would not indicate a lesser commitment to the spirit of the alliance or to the
principles upon which it rested. Ongoing communication, nimble and adaptable
application of eternal principles to practical realities, mutual respect for the vital
interests of the great powers, and an understanding of allied unity that allowed
for unilateral military action—these were the hallmarks of the post-Napoleonic
grand alliance.

Key to Emperor Alexander's eventual decision to opt for peace was the allies'
recognition that Russia possessed a legal right to act. By February 1822, the time
of Tatishchev's first mission, Russia had modified its original ultimatum to the
Porte, based on the Austrian proposals supported by Britain.[71] Henceforth allied
communications concerning the conditions for renewed diplomatic relations
employed Metternich's iteration of Russia's demands: (1) restoration of destroyed
Orthodox churches; (2) protection of the Orthodox religion; (3) recognition of
the distinction between guilty and innocent Greeks; and (4) evacuation of the
Danubian Principalities, accompanied by the appointment of hospodars and the
establishment of a reparative administration.[72] About a month after arriving in
Vienna, Tatishchev could report to Nesselrode (10/22 March) that because the
Porte still refused to evacuate the principalities and even demanded the return
of territories ceded to Russia by the Treaty of Bucharest, Emperor Francis I now
described the Porte's conduct as intolerable and expressed the belief that his fellow sovereign Alexander possessed the right to decide how Russia would obtain
satisfaction. On 28 March/9 April, Tatishchev again wrote from Vienna that
the Austrian government continued to act in a spirit of justice and would accept
the Russian monarch's decision about the use of force. Prussia also promised to
adhere to allied diplomatic measures (2/14 March), and France acknowledged

Russia's rights once the position of the other allies became clear. In early to mid-April, Russian officials still expected war, but they also remained confident that should hostilities become unavoidable, allied support—no mention was made of material support—would be forthcoming.[73]

This appraisal continued into May, when Ambassador Lieven regretfully reported that he had failed to obtain from officials in London the guarantee of support desired by his sovereign. The memorandum of 6/18 February, sent to Alexander I's representatives at the courts of Vienna, London, Paris, and Berlin, had included a proposal for a secret protocol whereby the allies would pledge to break diplomatic relations with the Porte (commercial agents could continue to operate) should the Porte not accept Russia's modified conditions.[74] In keeping with Alexander's demand for proof of action on the fourth condition, the proposal called for complete evacuation of Moldavia and Wallachia, the establishment of a provisional administration under Greek kaimakams (until permanent hospodars could be appointed), and the appointment of Russian and Ottoman plenipotentiaries to regulate jointly the fulfilment of treaty obligations in the principalities. Because recognized treaties placed the Ottoman Empire's Christian provinces under Alexander's protection, the proposal assumed that Russia would participate in ensuring their happy existence. Russia likewise wanted the allies to guarantee to the inhabitants of the insurgent provinces freedom of religion and security of property, person, and communal existence. Perhaps anticipating the refusal to sign on to a formal declaration, the proposal concluded by explaining that Alexander would be content with an allied statement supporting the justice of Russia's demands and a declaration of neutrality in the event of a Russian-Ottoman war.

In a report to Nesselrode from 19 April/1 May 1822, Lieven described ongoing discussions with Castlereagh during which the foreign secretary spelled out Britain's opposition to Russia's proposal for an allied protocol.[75] While Tatishchev appeared to make progress in Vienna, Lieven continued to complain about the cautiousness of the British government and Castlereagh's preference for informal diplomatic communication. According to the foreign secretary, the British government would not be able to justify before the British public the break in diplomatic relations that Emperor Alexander hoped to see. Such a step would endanger the property of British subjects within the Ottoman Empire and invite violent reprisals, which then could lead to war. No responsible ministry could sanction war in pursuit of an interest not directly relevant to the British nation.[76] Britain also opposed Russia's insistence that the Porte respond directly to the original ultimatum, arguing instead for the acceptability of other forms of communication. Finally, Castlereagh forcefully objected to the demand that the Porte act in concert with Russia to restore order in the Christian provinces of the Ottoman Empire. This would constitute an infringement of sovereignty by making Russia a "co-State" inside Ottoman territory. Indeed, the idea of common measures implied the existence of common rights, which further implied shared sovereignty. Britain's understanding of Russia's obligation to protect the Christian subjects of the Ottoman Empire did not envision immediate or direct protection, but rather rested on the Porte's responsibility to protect its Christian subjects. The creation of a continual guarantee on behalf of the insurgent provinces would be equivalent to a Russian assumption of legislative authority inside the Ottoman Empire. Finally, as a noncontracting power, Britain could not guarantee commitments agreed to by the Russian and Ottoman governments.

Lieven countered that given the Muslim atrocities afflicting the Porte's Christian territories—Russia's diplomats invariably neglected to mention Greek atrocities—the Russian government did not see how the insurgent provinces could be pacified or future dissension prevented without Russian-Ottoman agreement on the measures to be adopted. In fact, Russian participation in the pacification process would serve the interests of the Ottoman Empire, for only under the protection of an allied guarantee to ensure a happy existence could the Porte's Greek subjects place their future in the hands of the Turkish government. Despite this telling argument, Emperor Alexander understood, and Lieven accepted, that if the Porte refused to accept Russia's demands, allied declarations of support for the Russian position would necessarily conform to the dignity and interests of each individual government. The collective force of these declarations would then guarantee that the Porte fulfilled the obligations agreed to in negotiations with Russia. Within these limits, moreover, the Divan would be compelled to choose between formal repudiation by the allies and their good offices. To sustain this conclusion in the interest of a united alliance, Russia's diplomats had no choice but to engage in wishful thinking.

The British government remained eager to end the Russian-Ottoman crisis and therefore encouraged Emperor Alexander to treat the four points of the ultimatum as the goal of, rather than the precondition for, negotiations. To suppress the insurrection and to secure Russia's treaty rights and obligations on behalf of the rebellious Greeks, the Russian and Ottoman empires first needed to reestablish diplomatic relations. As things stood, Russia's four demands represented a path to war. Although established treaties supported the Russian conditions, the Porte would never agree to them. Russia, for its part, would not abandon the four points or the Greek people. Before relations with the Porte could be restored, the Russian monarch wanted assurances that the insurrection would end—assurances that required the Porte to change course. Castlereagh applauded Alexander's good intentions, commitment to the general cause of peace, and solicitude for the happy future of the Greek nation, but the British government could not support a formal guarantee for the Christian provinces of the Ottoman Empire. In an official memorandum submitted to Lieven, Britain did agree to support Russia's four demands, if the Russian government pledged to restore diplomatic relations once the Porte accepted them and removed Ottoman troops from the principalities.[77] In the end, Lieven and Castlereagh both recognized that while their governments shared a common goal, they disagreed on how to achieve it. Once again, moreover, as in the case of Naples, Russia did not interpret the disagreements as a threat to a united alliance.

Despite ongoing differences among the great powers, the fruits of the alliance's adaptability became visible by May 1822, when Ottoman troops began to leave the principalities and Russia's diplomats could report evidence of the Porte's willingness to compromise, including the nomination of hospodars. In a letter to Britain's ambassador in Saint Petersburg, Charles Bagot, Nesselrode wrote that evacuation of the principalities would demonstrate the Porte's intention to abide by existing treaties. This would open the door to the first act of peace, the sending of plenipotentiaries to discuss the bases for restoring Russian-Ottoman relations.[78] In a rescript of 14/26 May, Emperor Alexander congratulated Tatishchev on the success of his earlier mission and ordered him back to Vienna as part of the ongoing allied effort to persuade the Porte to fulfill Russia's demands. Alexander had decided against military action, but he retained the right to reconsider. Over the next few months he continued to expect allied diplomacy, now entrusted to the British ambassador in Constantinople, Lord Strangford, to press for humane treatment of the Greeks and the restoration of hospodar administration in the principalities.[79] War had been averted, because both Austria and Britain had committed to pressuring the Porte to satisfy Russia's just demands. But the deeper conflict had not been resolved.[80] Only after complete evacuation of the principalities and the restoration of free navigation in the Black Sea and the straits would Alexander be prepared to reestablish diplomatic relations with the Porte. During conferences of allied plenipotentiaries that began in Vienna at the end of June, the Russian monarch kept open the possibility of war. As the meetings continued in July, he held fast to the idea of joint action should the Porte reject allied demands. The Russian government doubted the Porte's good intentions, which meant that the call for concerted action did not recede.

As early as February 1822, Russian military commanders had begun to develop war plans in case negotiations with the Ottoman Empire failed.[81] By September most Ottoman troops had been withdrawn from Moldavia and Wallachia, and the sultan had nominated new hospodars, or governors. The hospodars came from indigenous boyars and princes rather than Phanariot Greeks; however, the Porte had not consulted the Russian government about the appointments.[82] From Constantinople Lord Strangford also reported that at conferences with the Ottoman minister of foreign affairs (the *reis efendi*) held on 27 August, the Divan, the council of state presided over by the grand vizier, had formally rejected Russia's proposal for a meeting of plenipotentiaries, declaring that there could be no role for the allies in the pacification of Greece.[83] In a letter to Strangford, Prince Metternich confirmed the allies' understanding that all four conditions had to be met before the Russian monarch would restore diplomatic relations with the Porte. The Ottoman government continued to challenge the allies by insisting that it had carried out the first three demands of the Russian ultimatum: the reconstruction of churches, protection of the Orthodox religion, and recognition of the distinction between the innocent and the culpable. In reality, only in Constantinople had protection for the Greek religion been restored. Nor had the military evacuation of the principalities been completed. Lord Strangford's proposal that the Porte communicate directly with Saint Petersburg concerning the appointment of the hospodars also had been ignored. As the reis effendi explained, although in the past Emperor Alexander's minister in Constantinople had been informed of the nominations, such action could not occur in the absence of diplomatic relations.[84]

A clear statement of Russia's position on the restoration of diplomatic relations with the Porte, approved by Alexander on 9/21 September 1822, appeared in the formal record of the allied conferences that opened in Verona on 20 October (NS).[85] With respect to Russian-Ottoman relations, Alexander's decision not to go to war already had been made, and allied negotiations with the Porte were ongoing. The discussions in Verona, like those in Laibach, can therefore be described as a staging of the European alliance. During eighteen months of discussions with the Porte, the Russian statement began, Emperor Alexander had declared his peaceful intentions.[86] Nor had he tried to augment Russian influence. To the contrary, he wanted only to return to the conditions that had existed before the insurrections in Greece, including recognition of Russia's treaty rights and other political and commercial advantages. In actuality, the parameters of Russia's demands had broadened. Before diplomatic relations with the Porte could be restored, three conditions had to be met. First, direct negotiations between plenipotentiaries of the allies, the Porte, and Russia had to be organized to discuss the pacification of Greece (not just Moldavia and Wallachia). The purpose of these negotiations would be to provide guarantees for the Greeks who once again would submit to Ottoman sovereignty. Through concrete action, the Porte would need to demonstrate respect for "the religion that the letter of the treaties placed under the protection of Russia." In other words, the bases for peace in Greece had to satisfy Russia's concern for the fate of its coreligionists by ensuring their happiness and security. Second, with regard to the principalities of Moldavia and Wallachia, Russia expected to receive direct notification of Ottoman plans to complete the military evacuation and nominate hospodars.[87] Once these steps were taken, Russian consuls could return to the principalities as official verifiers (*commissaires vérificateurs*) to confirm that the measures adopted by the Porte and hospodars conformed to the treaties and repaired the damage caused by the military occupation. Finally, free trade in the Black Sea had to be restored. Greek merchants flying the Russian flag handled Russia's grain trade, which for the past year had suffered disruptions.[88] To restore free navigation, the Porte could allow Portuguese, Sardinian, Sicilian, Spanish, and other ships to pass through the straits, or it could respect the flags flown by these vessels. The Russian statement concluded by forcefully proclaiming that the allies had accepted the justice of Emperor Alexander's conditions.

A second statement of Russian policy, contained in a note of 14/26 September 1822, was submitted to the plenipotentiaries of Austria, Britain, France, and Prussia.[89] Included also in the acts of the Verona conferences, this note can be read as a preliminary version of the declaration of 28 October/9 November, which the allies would formally approve and which embodied the success of concert diplomacy in preventing war between the Russian and Ottoman empires. Comparison of these documents illustrates Emperor Alexander's ongoing willingness to modify, moderate, and even obscure Russia's demands in order to give allied diplomacy a chance to work, a tactic he had pursued since the fall of 1821. But the monarch also had reviewed the diplomatic communications produced during eighteen months of negotiations in Constantinople and had come to the painful conclusion that no progress had been made. Not only did the Porte refuse to satisfy Russia's just demands; in recent conferences with the British ambassador, Ottoman officials falsely accused the Russian government of supporting the Greek insurrections, and they claimed that all treaty obligations to Russia had been fulfilled. To counter this characterization, the Russian note described the Greek uprisings as the work of the same sects that had triumphed in Spain and Portugal, achieved temporary victories in Italy, and remained an ongoing threat to other states in Europe. Russia denied any role in fomenting or supporting revolt in Greece and insisted that the Porte, which had not fully evacuated the Danubian Principalities or agreed to send plenipotentiaries to negotiate with the allies, remained in violation of recognized treaty obligations.

The facts set forth in the Russian note aimed to disprove the Porte's accusations. First, Russia had joined the allies to combat revolution in Naples and Piedmont. Second, Russian foreign policy invariably followed the same rules. Third, there existed in Europe a vast conspiracy directed against the security of thrones and the happiness of peoples. If subaltern agents of the Russian Empire supported revolution in Greece, they acted against the monarch's explicit orders. The Russian government had been waiting a year for the Porte to answer Emperor Alexander's demands, and during this period, despite the absence of insurgency in the principalities, Ottoman forces continued to destroy religious sanctuaries and towns. Commerce in the Russian Empire's southern provinces also remained in a state of paralysis. Indeed, the allies recognized the moderation, frankness, and steadfastness of Russian policy, and they likewise understood that Alexander did not seek to expand Russian influence. Rather, he wished only to secure the political rights and commercial advantages already guaranteed by existing treaties. Precisely because the allies acknowledged Russia's just demands, Alexander had entrusted negotiations concerning the restoration of relations with the Ottoman Empire to Austrian and British diplomats.

With one significant exception, the statements of Russia's conditions for restoring relations with the Porte were identical in the note of 14/26 September and the subsequent declaration of 28 October/9 November.[90] The first condition relevant to the pacification of Greece appeared in the same form in both documents. In one scenario, the Porte would negotiate with allied and Russian plenipotentiaries concerning guarantees for Greeks who returned to living under the Ottoman sultan's authority. In an alternative scenario, the Porte would demonstrate through concrete measures respect for the Christian religion, which existing treaties placed under Russian protection. In addition, the Porte's actions should exhibit a desire to restore domestic tranquility to Greece on grounds that ensured peace and satisfied Russia's concerns about the fate of its coreligionists. The second condition, which addressed the situation in Moldavia and Wallachia, contained wording in the September note that did not appear in the November declaration. The Porte would notify Russia about the military evacuation of the principalities and the nomination of hospodars. Russian agents would then return to the territories to exercise the rights granted by the treaties and to verify that the steps taken by the Porte and the new princes met treaty obligations. Removed from the November declaration was the demand to repair damage caused by the Ottoman military occupation, wording that implicitly challenged the sultan's sovereignty in the Danubian Principalities. Finally, the third condition called for the restoration of free commercial navigation in the Black Sea, where the Porte could permit the passage of Portuguese, Sicilian, Spanish, and other vessels, or respect ships flying the flag of navies previously allowed in these waters.

The official declaration of Russia's position on the affairs of the East, read by Dmitrii Tatishchev at the conferences of 28 October/9 November, received approval in individual allied responses of 22 November (NS).[91] In addition to the modified conditions for restoring relations with the Porte, the declaration also contained a full summary of developments since the summer conferences in Vienna, where allied plenipotentiaries had accepted Russia's demands as just, based on a communication from Metternich dated 31 July. At a conference on 26 July in Constantinople, Ottoman ministers had accused Russia of hostile intentions and of trying to interfere in the internal affairs of the Ottoman Empire. But during this time, the Porte continued to violate treaty obligations. Ottoman troops remained in the principalities, and attacks on Christianity persisted, including the destruction of Jassy. For the past year, under the auspices of the allies, Russia had pursued the best means to restore peace in the Christian provinces of the Ottoman Empire. Nor had Russia acted against Ottoman interests. Yet the Porte still refused all reciprocity, including a meeting of plenipotentiaries, and continued to restrict Russian commercial navigation in the Black Sea. Finally, at a conference of 27 August, the Ottoman government again had accused Russia of complicity in the disastrous Greek uprisings, which in reality represented the work of the same revolutionary sects that had infected Spain, Portugal, and Italy. The Porte, it seemed, had forgotten the diplomatic overtures of Baron Stroganov and the fact that Emperor Alexander had ordered his troops to march against revolutionaries in Naples and Piedmont. Despite the mutual recriminations, in November 1822, the Russian monarch stood by his offer to act with the allies to restore peace in Greece.

On 15/27 November, during the conferences in Verona, Tatishchev could declare that his sovereign was satisfied with allied promises to take additional steps through their ambassadors in Constantinople to pressure the Porte to accept Russia's conditions for the restoration of diplomatic relations. The European alliance, directed by the five great powers, once again appeared fully united, as Austria, Britain, France, and Prussia all accepted the Russian declaration of 9 November.[92] Another declaration, approved by Alexander on 16/28 November, acknowledged the allies' response.[93] The allies appreciated the sacrifices Russia had made for peace in Europe and intended to continue their efforts to persuade the Porte to accept Russia's just and moderate conditions. For the moment, Emperor Alexander had decided to act in concert with the great powers to resolve the Greek crisis and to convince the Porte of the need for amicable intervention by the European allies. Through the conferences established in Vienna, the monarch would continue to rely on allied diplomacy to conduct negotiations in Constantinople. Based on the Verona declarations, it appeared that Alexander would not insist on bilateral negotiations between Saint Petersburg and Constantinople to decide matters concerning the principalities or Russia's recognized treaty rights. On 20 November, the allies meeting in Verona agreed not to sign a general protocol, and on 3/15 December, Emperor Alexander departed the conferences.[94]

If the diplomacy surrounding the war scare of 1821–22 revealed an effective European system capable of containing great power competition to ensure peace, this was not the result of shared governance or a collective security regime defined by recognized legal principles and administrative procedures. Between 1814 and the outbreak of the Crimean War in 1853 successful peacemaking evolved from the flexibility of the grand alliance and the ideal of unity that inspired the monarchs and diplomats of Europe.[95] From the Russian perspective, memories of the Napoleonic Wars, particularly the trauma of 1812, reinforced the belief that only through allied unity and the prevention of particular combinations among the great powers could peace be preserved. Emperor Alexander's desire for peace could not have been more powerful. It was so powerful, in fact, that it eclipsed long-standing strategic, economic, and political interests. The realization of Catherine II's plans for territorial aggrandizement and the restoration of a Christian monarchy in Constantinople—as recently as 1812 Russia had acquired Bessarabia from the Ottoman Empire—had been temporarily set aside. Thus, during the war scare of 1821–22, the concert of great powers did not group, contain, or constrain Russia. Alexander I remained committed to allied unity and continued to rely on friendship among the sovereigns to preserve peace. Equally important, he opted for peace only after the European powers recognized the Russian Empire's legitimate demands and right to act.[96] Because of the moral support given to Russia, and the commitment to collective negotiations, represented here by the actions of Austria and Britain, the monarch decided to give diplomacy a chance.

Not surprisingly, the subsequent history of the Greek independence movement exposed fundamental fissures in the much-touted European system. By

February 1824, diplomatic relations between the Russian and Ottoman empires had been partially restored. Still, allied conferences held in Saint Petersburg in June 1824 and March 1825 failed to produce a common policy toward Greece. In a memorandum of 9/21 January 1824, Emperor Alexander had proposed the creation of three semiautonomous principalities under Ottoman suzerainty, an arrangement modeled on political arrangements in the Danubian Principalities and Serbia. The response had been disappointing. Austria and Prussia showed no interest in supporting the claims of Greek rebels against their legitimate sovereign. British officials, the Ottoman sultan, and Greek leaders also refused to discuss the proposal. In the summer of 1825, Russia once again seemed headed toward unilateral action against the Porte. Even the cautious Count Nesselrode adopted a pro-war position, and Alexander, dissatisfied with Strangford's continuing mediation between Russia and the Porte, ended allied negotiations in late July. In December the Russian monarch died, and uncertainties surrounding the succession allowed the empire's first modern political opposition, led by elite military officers, briefly to attempt revolution.

After a temporary pause, diplomatic efforts to address the Greek crisis and Russian-Ottoman disputes resumed in 1826. Britain and Russia signed the Saint Petersburg Protocol, adopting a Greek request for mediation.[97] In October 1826 the Porte accepted the Convention of Akkerman in response to an ultimatum from Emperor Nicholas I, who continued to express disdain for the Greek rebels. The convention affirmed the obligation to implement Russian-Ottoman treaty provisions and to remove the last Ottoman troops from the Danubian Principalities. Parallel to these developments, the European powers continued the effort to negotiate a common policy. Finally, on 6 July 1827, Britain, France, and Russia agreed to the Treaty of London, which called for the establishment of an autonomous Greek state under Ottoman suzerainty. The signatories rejected participation in Greek-Ottoman hostilities, though based on a secret article, they agreed to force the Greeks and Ottomans to accept an armistice. Not surprisingly, the Porte continued to reject allied mediation. On 20 October 1827, following the establishment of a joint British, French, and Russian blockade to prevent Ottoman arms and troops from reaching Greece (already a violation of the Treaty of London), the allied squadron destroyed the Ottoman fleet in the Bay of Navarino. Then on 30 November, Nicholas withdrew from Akkerman. In December the sultan followed suit, vowing also to fight Russia to protect his empire. This step produced a formal break in diplomatic relations with Britain, France, and Russia, based on the Treaty of London. Full-scale war between the Russian and Ottoman empires began in April 1828, with no allied participation or support for Russia. The allies did, however, provide military, naval, and financial assistance to the Greek government. Finally, on 22 March 1829, the Porte agreed to Greek autonomy, and on 3 February 1830, the London Protocol established Greece as an independent monarchy.[98]

Unity amid Divergence

During the years from 1820 through 1822, Europe's peacemakers responded to insurrections in Spanish America, Spain, the Kingdom of the Two Sicilies, Portugal, Piedmont, and Greece by focusing on questions of legality, reform, and revolution. As in earlier discussions about conditions in France and Germany, in the negotiations about possible intervention in Spain and the Two Sicilies, Russian policymakers, instructed by Emperor Alexander I, continued to proclaim the need for good governance and political reform, including even constitutional reform, to prevent rebellion and preserve peace. But although reform could appear both desirable and necessary, the overthrow of legitimate rulers could not be tolerated, even when popular disaffection seemed justified. The allies remained united on this principle, and although Britain and France did not officially participate in the Troppau and Laibach conferences, they did not openly oppose collective action by the other great powers. Perhaps more revealing, when revolutionary situations directly impacted British and French interests, as in Greece and Spain, they actively embraced the commitment to act in concert. Throughout the period from the Congress of Vienna (1814–15) until the French intervention in Spain (1823), all the principals among the great powers viewed revolution as a scourge, and all agreed that the scourge had infected much of Europe.

The Greek crisis and Russian-Ottoman war scare of 1821–22 exposed challenges to the eternal principles of European peace—challenges that arose from developments beyond the confines of Europe. At the same time, events on the ground and ongoing allied negotiations also highlighted the limits to Emperor Alexander's enlightened vision of European unity. Based on documents of Russian provenance, the monarch's moderation and commitment to legality appeared genuine, illustrated by the rift with Kapodistrias and the insistence that Stroganov be prevented from encouraging war and spreading extremist views in Saint Petersburg society.[99] But in relations with the allies, the pressure to address political arrangements and questions of stability within the Ottoman Empire also brought to the fore long-standing suspicions about Russian objectives. Nor did the allies satisfy Alexander's expectations of what it meant to act in concert, based on the legal obligations and moral duties codified in alliance treaties. Even so, despite repeated disappointments embodied in the decisions of Troppau, Laibach, and Verona, allied unity held.

Russia had a long history of diplomatic and military entanglements with the Ottoman Empire. The war scare of 1821–22 at once endangered the peace established by the Treaty of Bucharest (1812) and represented a successful effort to defuse a major crisis within the framework of the European system. Alexander expected the allies to recognize Russia's legal rights, including the right to protect Christians living under Ottoman authority and the right to use military force to compel compliance with treaty obligations. These expectations, according to Russia's policymakers, were consistent with Prussian and Russian support for Austria's intervention in Naples and with Alexander's offer of military assistance to France, if Spanish revolutionaries tried to move into French territory. Finally, the Russian-Ottoman war scare showed that Emperor Alexander's idea of European unity could not be separated from Christian beliefs, which inside and outside of Europe, and certainly within the Russian Empire, undermined ideals of enlightened universalism and religious toleration. Both the Treaty of 14/26 September 1815 (the Holy Alliance) and Baron Stroganov's note to the Porte of 6/18 July 1821 proclaimed the idea of religious coexistence in Europe's relations with the Ottoman Empire. Yet the crisis of 1821–22 exposed ongoing religious and nationalist excesses: anti-Greek, anti-Turk, anti-Christian, and anti-Muslim. As toleration and cosmopolitanism degenerated into religious and national strife, the potential for total war, already evident in the French Revolutionary and Napoleonic Wars, reemerged.[100] Moderate reformism, which embraced legal-administrative (and even constitutional) change without violence against established order, would be tested over and over again.

CHAPTER 5

Spain and the European System (1820–23)

ESTORATION SPAIN'S POSITION IN the European alliance offered a
bird's eye view of the challenges confronting political leaders during the
peacemaking of 1815 to 1823. The Spanish Revolution represented the
first major insurrection of the Restoration era, and in Spain's American colonies, Enlightenment-inspired and popular movements had been ongoing since
1808–10. In other words, the vulnerabilities and limitations of the European
system, as conceived by Russia's monarch and diplomats in the years following
the Congress of Vienna, appeared strikingly evident in Spain's relationship to
the alliance and in the unstable political conditions engulfing the peninsula and
colonies. Well before the great powers (with the exception of Britain) collectively
recognized the Spanish Revolution as a threat justifying intervention, events in
Spain began to disrupt implementation of the peacemakers' vision.

From the perspective of Russian diplomacy, an early challenge to peace in Europe appeared in Spain's refusal to accept the Final Act of the Congress of Vienna
and the Second Treaty of Paris. Based on the treaties of 1815, the duchies of Parma,
Plaisance, and Guastalla belonged to the archduchess of Austria and wife of Napoleon, Marie Louise, and her descendants. Supported by Britain and France,
Spain claimed that following the death of Archduchess Marie Louise, the territories should revert to the infante Marie Louise, daughter of the former Spanish
king, Charles IV; her son, Charles Louis; and his direct male descendants. Despite the legality of Spain's claims and the importance of bringing Spain into the
general alliance, Emperor Alexander hesitated to oppose Austrian interests. In
the end, Austrian emperor Francis I accepted territorial adjustments proposed
by Britain, and in July 1817, Spain acceded to the Final Act of the Congress of Vienna.[1] Two years later, the General Act of the Frankfurt Territorial Commission
(8/20 July 1819) defined the line of succession to the Spanish infante, her son, and
his male descendants. Exceptions included districts on the left bank of the Po,
recognized as Austrian possessions, and the Principality of Lucca, which at the
death of the Austrian archduchess would go to the Grand Duchy of Tuscany.[2]

Although Spain's acceptance of the Vienna settlement represented a crucial step toward securing the peace, a Russian overview of European politics, dated 5/17 June 1817, highlighted additional problems. As happened repeatedly in the history of the alliance, among European governments suspicions about Russia's intentions abounded.[3] In this instance, rumors of a special Russian-Spanish relationship called into question Emperor Alexander's commitment to the European system. The doubts seemed justified when by an agreement of 30 July/11 August 1817 Russia sold warships to Spain. Not surprisingly, Alexander rejected the hostile characterization and even hinted that Britain should act as mediator between Spain and its American colonies.[4] Russia's policy toward Spain, official statements contended, needed to be understood as part of a larger effort to strengthen the integrity (*tselost'*) of Europe's general political system through moral influence. To restore the power of the Spanish crown, a process that had to occur in both hemispheres, Spain required assistance from all the European powers. To that end, Alexander's diplomats in Madrid received orders to communicate Russia's views to the Spanish king and his ministers, who should be urged to reach agreement with Britain about the slave trade and to accept British mediation in reconciling with the colonies.[5] By the time the great powers met in Aix-la-Chapelle in September 1818, both of these suggestions had been accepted.[6]

Another source of concern arose from ongoing competition between Spain and Portuguese Brazil in the territory north of the Rio de la Plata. In 1816 Portuguese troops moved into the disputed territory of Uruguay, and in 1817 they occupied Montevideo, extending Brazil's frontier to the river.[7] The five great powers unanimously condemned the attacks on Spain's American territories, and when the Spanish monarchy requested assistance, accepted the role of mediator in the interest of preserving the general peace.[8] A note sent in February 1817 from the ministerial conference in Paris to the government of Portuguese Brazil stated that refusal to accept mediation would be seen as definite proof of evil intent. The European powers recognized King Ferdinand VII's legal right to the territory but also wanted to make sure that in responding to the dispute Spain did not abandon the rules of moderation. According to the Russian overview of June 1817, the success of the mediation effort remained uncertain, and by the time of the conferences in Aix-la-Chapelle, the conflict had not been resolved.[9] Although the five great powers plus Portuguese Brazil accepted a British proposal for the restitution of Montevideo, in October 1818 Spain had not yet agreed to the plan. Nor did the Spanish monarchy succeed in reestablishing authority over the colonies. By 1825 the independence movements of Central and South America became effectively victorious, though as events unfolded and as the allies faced the harsh realities of revolution on the peninsula, the fate of Spanish America seemed less critical to the preservation of European peace.

Early Responses to the Spanish Revolution

When the revolutionary troubles began on the peninsula, neither rebellion in the colonies nor the conflict with Portuguese Brazil over Montevideo had been resolved.[10] As the crisis deepened, Russian diplomacy focused less on the Spanish monarchy's relations with the colonies and more on the general problem of revolution in Europe. Documents of Russian provenance attributed the revolution in Spain to the government's lack of moral authority and to the persistence of the revolutionary spirit among sectarians and Jacobins. Here as elsewhere, Russia's diplomats called for political reform and good governance to combat disorder. In the mind of Emperor Alexander, support for constitutional reform, and sometimes even liberal principles, could be reconciled with the acceptance of absolutist monarchy.[11] Even when Restoration governments experienced explosive political conflict over the meaning of principles such as constitutionalism and the rights of nations (or peoples), Emperor Alexander clung to a view of European politics based on strict legality (adherence to treaties) and Christian morality. In the monarch's thinking, calls for liberal reform did not assume the acceptance of a specific ideology or political system.

Two weeks after the mutiny led by Lieutenant Colonel Rafael Riego, Count Mark N. Bulgari, Russia's chargé d'affaires in Madrid, wrote to co-minister of foreign affairs Nesselrode about the weakness of the Spanish government and the boldness of the insurrectionists and their sympathizers.[12] In contrast to the good order displayed by the rebel troops, the king's forces appeared demoralized and the monarchy paralyzed. Over the next few weeks, Bulgari's communications became increasingly critical of the Spanish government's inaction, the silence of the monarchy's defenders, and the failure of King Ferdinand VII to fulfill his promises of political reform.[13] While acknowledging that a revolution had occurred, Bulgari also continued to argue that Ferdinand could salvage what had become a dangerous situation for all of Europe by announcing to his nation meaningful reforms. The Russian diplomat even went so far as to urge the king to call the Cortes and grant a constitution. The granting of constitutions by legitimate monarchs remained consistent with Russian policy, though on 7 March, when Ferdinand proclaimed the constitution of 1812, he reportedly did so under duress to avoid the threat of violence. As Bulgari described the situation, the king had become a prisoner in his own palace.[14]

While Europe watched and waited, Russia's monarch and Ministry of Foreign Affairs held to the belief that the great powers acting in concert could preserve the peace. They also hoped to establish extraordinary forms of deliberation that would allow the allied monarchs to respond quickly and effectively to future emergencies.[15] The Russian desire for collective action became more insistent after Ferdinand decided to accept the constitution. Thus, to ascertain what allied cooperation might mean, on 3/15 March 1820 Nesselrode wrote to Count Christoph Lieven, Russia's ambassador in London, seeking information on how the British government viewed the latest developments in Spain.[16] According to Nesselrode, precisely because the spirit of insurrection had assumed diverse forms, the allies had an obligation to discuss confidentially how they would apply the moral force of the alliance to the revolutionary situation. Quoting a communication from Vienna, the co-minister identified several key principles: the intimate union (*union intime*) of the first courts; the spirit of benevolence animating the great monarchs; and the uniformity of their thinking and common experience, which kept at bay all political complications. Given the current crisis, did these principles still represent the cornerstone of the social edifice? To answer this question, Emperor Alexander wanted to know what measures the allies would take if: (1) the wisdom and energy of the Spanish government failed to suppress the volcano simmering under the throne; (2) the king of Spain sought assistance from his allies; or (3) the crisis continued in a manner that appeared more dangerous for the peninsula, the colonies, and the rest of Europe.

Austria's position, communicated to Nesselrode on 13/25 April 1820 by Count Iurii A. Golovkin, recognized the threat of the Spanish insurrection, including the possibility of a massive revolutionary pact that could engulf the peninsula and the colonies.[17] Even so, the Austrian government did not accept any allied responsibility to act. To date the Spanish king had not sought advice or help from the European powers. The Russian government acknowledged this reasoning but continued to press for a collective response. On 19 April/1 May 1820, Nesselrode wrote to Golovkin, Lieven, and Alopeus (Russia's representatives in Austria, Britain, and Prussia) that Emperor Alexander wished to hold a meeting of the allies.[18] Stability in France remained fragile, and now the fall of the Spanish government threatened disaster for all Europe. Again, Russia viewed allied unity, which had saved Europe from the French Revolution and Napoleonic conquest, as the best means to resolve the Spanish crisis.

Significantly, King Louis XVIII also appeared ready to discuss action in Spain, and the Russian government recognized France's right to take the initiative in negotiations concerning the Spanish monarchy. But based on alliance agreements, Alexander and Louis could discuss Spain only after Austria, Britain, and Prussia responded to the overture of 3/15 March.[19] Nesselrode therefore advised the French government to approach the other allies, without referring to Russia's memorandum, also dated 19 April/1 May, which called for allied action, if the Spanish government did not rectify the situation.[20] As things turned out, Britain would consider collective action in Spain only if the royal family or the integrity of Portugal seemed to be in danger.[21] Unable to respond to Russia's proposal with an official statement, due to internal political constraints and opposition to cooperation with France, Foreign Secretary Castlereagh nonetheless communicated to Count Lieven, and to the courts of Vienna and Berlin, that Britain remained committed to the general European system.[22]

Russia's memorandum to the allies arose from a note of 7/19 April 1820 addressed to Nesselrode by Spain's emissary in Saint Petersburg and future foreign minister, Francisco Cea Bermúdez (1779–1850).[23] The note informed Emperor Alexander of Ferdinand VII's decision to accept the 1812 constitution and explained why he had done so. The king wished to provide security, tranquility, and harmony for his people, and he hoped to thwart insurrection by delivering happiness in the form of wise and stable institutions that corresponded to "the spirit and enlightenment of our time." Precisely because the Spanish people strove for freedom and the glory of the monarch, the king's action would unite the Spanish nation with the legal sovereign and therefore deserved the respect of the allies. The constitution of 1812 had been promulgated by the Cortes elected in 1810, and the Treaty of Velikie Luki (8/20 July 1812), which Russia had concluded with the anti-Napoleonic Central Junta of Spain, recognized the exiled King Ferdinand, the Cortes, and the constitution.[24] Based on this treaty, the Spanish note proclaimed, Russian acceptance of the king's recent decision would rest on legal grounds.

Emperor Alexander responded to the Spanish appeal in a note of 18/30 April 1820, addressed to Cea Bermúdez by Nesselrode.[25] The monarch recognized that the prosperity of the Spanish state could not be separated from the glory of the king. In addition, one could argue that the events of March 1820 had become inevitable as early as 1814, the year Ferdinand VII returned to the throne. Regardless, the illegal act that had subjected Spain to the rule of popular passions could not be justified. Russia had accepted the Treaty of 8/20 July 1812 out of respect, admiration, and gratitude for Spain's role in overthrowing the French yoke, sentiments shared by all the European powers. The allies also had shown ongoing concern for the fate of Spain, and Emperor Alexander himself repeatedly had expressed the hope that through legal rules and wise state constitutions the power of the Spanish king in Europe and America would be secured. But in order to strengthen the state, political reform had to be a gift from the government. As history and experience proved, changes arising from disarray and anarchy led to ruin, not happiness. The Spanish government still had time to correct the situation; however, the constitution, established by violence and revolution, could not be accepted. The current danger to Spain affected all the European powers, and Alexander needed to confer with the allies before pronouncing on the events of 7 March.[26] To facilitate deliberations, he asked the Spanish government to address the allies as he had been addressed. In other words, from the moment of Ferdinand VII's initial solicitation, Alexander insisted on responding to the Spanish crisis in concert with allied governments. The Russian government held to this position until the conferences in Verona finally produced agreement on supporting a French intervention.

The memorandum approved by Emperor Alexander on 19 April/1 May 1820, which Austria and Britain later refused to endorse, described the exchange of notes with Cea Bermúdez.[27] Although the Spanish government sought a statement from Alexander on the political changes of 1820, the monarch did not want to act independently of the powers adjacent to Spain and therefore in a better position to judge the threat to that country. Indeed, precisely because the revolution contained seeds of development that might become critically important for all educated peoples, it had attracted the attention of leaders in Europe and the New World. Certain to have a global impact, the revolution demanded a timely response. Otherwise, ill-intentioned men would use the uncertainty as a weapon to further their goals. To prevent this, Alexander wished to make a pronouncement on the unfolding crisis, which he hoped the allies would approve. As the memorandum clearly stated, the monarch wanted his position on Spain to be consistent with "the general principles (*pravila*) of European Policy."

How did Emperor Alexander understand European policy? In 1812 the allied monarchs had taken an interest in the fate of Spain and admired the heroic struggle of the Spanish people against the foreign foe. At the time, they had viewed the constitution as the best way to unite the nation and preserve its political independence. Even after Divine Providence returned Ferdinand VII to the throne, the allies continued to believe that wise and firm institutions were needed to improve the foundations of the old Spanish monarchy. Thus, during discussions related to pacification of the colonies and the conflict with Portuguese Brazil, the allies tried to impress upon Spain's rulers that political reform would lead to prosperity and calm, only if the people perceived the changes as a free gift emanating from the goodwill of the government. If, by contrast, the government appeared to institute change under duress, in an act of self-preservation, the reform would be seen as evidence of weakness.

Following the events of 7 March, the allies generally assumed that the revolution in Spain represented a direct threat to France. Although the protocols of Aix-la-Chapelle (3/15 November 1818) had aimed to eliminate the last traces of the French Revolution, the destructive spirit of the revolutionary evil had survived and now attacked Spain, once again obligating the monarchs to confront political upheaval. Sadly, the allies expected that rebellion in Spain would be no less horrific than it had been in France. Describing 1820 as an unlucky time, Emperor Alexander nonetheless hoped to see the formation of a Spanish government capable of restoring order. But regardless of how conditions in Spain developed, he expressed confidence that the allies would approve Russia's response to Cea Bermúdez and therefore felt compelled publicly to declare opposition to the illegal means employed to introduce the new Spanish institutions. Perhaps, the Russian memorandum suggested, the allies already had sent similar notes to the Madrid court. Indeed, Alexander believed that the unity of wishes and principles defining the alliance inevitably produced likeminded opinions. Thus, the allied monarchs shared the opinion that illegal actions always led to disastrous results, in this case not only for the Spanish nation but also for Europe as a whole.

Because European governments had reacted with sorrow to the new crime imposed on Spain by the rebels, the Russian memorandum suggested a possible solution to the calamity. The best outcome would be for the Spanish nation to offer the peoples of the world an example of repentance. Simply put, Spain could reconcile with the other powers of Europe by rejecting revolution. With respect to the change of government, the interests of Europe and the Spanish Cortes actually coincided. Because the troops protecting the Cortes could rebel at any moment, it was in the interest of the Spanish monarch, fatherland, and legislative assembly to demonstrate that insurrection would not be recognized as legal. The Russian emperor did not expect this to happen, but he did argue that the moral force of unanimous opinion among the great powers, especially concerning the duty of the people's representatives, might bring about the desired result. The diplomats of the five great powers should therefore communicate to Spain's plenipotentiary in Paris their concern for the fate of the Spanish people. Tranquility and prosperity for all Spaniards, the memorandum stated, could be secured by establishing through legal means new institutions in Europe and Spanish America—institutions that corresponded to "the needs of the time and the successes of Civilization (*Grazhdanstvennost'*)."

At this juncture, in both Spain and Spanish America, institutional reform no longer seemed sufficient to counter insurrection. For the salvation of Spain and the benefit of Europe, the Spanish government also needed to repress and denounce insurrection. Significantly, the Russian government viewed the Cortes as part of the solution. Perhaps because King Ferdinand had called the Cortes before taking the oath to the constitution, and because of the assembly's ancient origins, Russian officials distinguished the actions of the revolution from the legitimacy of the Cortes, even though its powers, based on the 1812 constitution, continued to pose a problem.[28] The Cortes possessed the legal authority to establish constitutional forms, as long as this was accompanied by the strictest prohibitions against rebellion. In these circumstances, the allied courts could remain in relations of friendship and trust with the Spanish government, without having to violate their own shared principles. In other words, if the Spanish government heeded the allies' advice, they would be able to declare the revolution at an end. The Cortes in turn would need to pledge obedience to the king in the name of the nation and find a way to establish internal tranquility and order on the peninsula and in the colonies. If these hopes were not answered, however, and Spain remained in the current state of anarchy and riot, at least the allies would have fulfilled their sacred duty and demonstrated "the true principles, purpose, and form of action of the great European alliance."[29]

Russia's diplomats had responded quickly and emphatically to the events of 7 March, yet without advocating intervention or action outside the great European alliance.[30] Aleksandr S. Sturdza's correspondence with co-minister of foreign affairs Ioannis Kapodistrias illustrated the confusion and conflicting impulses that found their way into Alexander I's thoughts on the Spanish Revolution. In a dispatch of 24 April 1820 (NS), which reportedly influenced the memorandum of 19 April/1 May, Sturdza wrote that in Spain the system of liberal ideas had reached its apogee and therefore must either retreat or produce new explosions.[31] Equally disturbing, the Spanish king had become a slave to plebian tyrants. Unable to marry or abdicate without the permission of the Cortes, he had been deprived of his dignity in the eyes of foreign powers. In other words, the liberal furor in Spain had reached the highest degree of absurdity, rendering retreat the only appropriate option.

But how would the retreat of the revolution unfold? Sturdza assigned significant blame for the current crisis to the Spanish monarch. A power restored to its rights after great disturbances needed to legislate in order to revive the old institutions. Sadly, King Ferdinand VII, lacking both a domestic and a foreign policy, had promised reform but not delivered on his pledge. Instead, he had abdicated the right to control the process of reform and become a king who humbly recognized "all the Acts of popular Authority." Sturdza went on to describe his own vision of how Ferdinand should proceed with reform. The restoration of ancient institutions demanded legislation that rested "on a more or less perfect harmony of faith, science, and Authority." Such legislation could guide the government in addressing the primary causes of revolution: irreligion, injustice, and insolvency. Specifically, the Spanish government needed to make public education religious, invigorate police administration, and wisely administer public wealth. None of this had been accomplished, and although Russia had not yet experienced the consequences of revolution, the moral contagion could easily spread, especially in an age of intensified contact between nations. Sturdza did not believe that congresses or repressive alliances could stop the principle of revolution, but he did insist that governments should respond with force and vigilance to the earliest manifestation of this electric jolt.

Despite Sturdza's strong prescriptive rhetoric, his dispatch and other correspondence admitted outright that the crisis in Spain had become difficult to understand. He rejected the fact of revolution as legitimate grounds for intervention in Spain's internal affairs. He did argue for a formal declaration of the allied courts, based on international law (*le droit des gens*). The constitution of 1812 denied the sovereign authority of the king, meaning that it violated rights universally recognized by all European peoples.[32] Nor, Sturdza insisted, could any single policy effectively combat revolution; different policies were needed in different countries.[33] This argument blended with Alexander I's belief (and hope) that allied unity, particularly unity of principle, would ensure the preservation of peace, which revolution inevitably threatened (as shown by history and experience). Sturdza described the Russian monarch's reaction to the Spanish Revolution as profound sorrow.[34] Unfortunately, profound sorrow did not move the allies to act.

Faced with allied inaction, Russia's diplomats continued to argue that domestic reforms could save Spain from the consequences of revolution.[35] Persistent calls for reform suggested that the king might still be able to assert control over the revolution, which then could turn into legal political change. In June and July 1820, diplomatic communications revealed just how complicated, dangerous, and incomprehensible the situation appeared.[36] By July reports of violent resistance to the constitutional system and the government in Madrid reached the Russian Ministry of Foreign Affairs. Writing from Paris, General Karl O. Pozzo di Borgo, Alexander I's minister plenipotentiary, described the intimate union between the Cortes and king as Spain's only hope for peace. By contrast, a royalist reaction that the king did not direct would lead to civil war. Count Bulgari's reports, which previously had described King Ferdinand as a prisoner, seemed to become more optimistic. In communications of 14/26 June and 21 June/3 July 1820, he depicted the preparatory work of the Cortes as orderly and the discussions among the deputies as moderate. Despite hints of opposition from Spanish Americans, the inclusion of thirty substitute deputies to represent America and another three to represent Cuba suggested to Russian officials that the crisis might be headed for resolution.

The Spanish Revolution and the Colonies

Inaction also remained the allied approach to Spanish America. Both before and after insurrection hit the peninsula, political conditions in the Spanish Empire created problems for the European alliance. Rebellion in Spain's American colonies began as early as 1808–10, and the Spanish troops that mutinied on 1 January 1820 were awaiting embarkation to South America. Although Spain's relationship with the colonies did not necessarily represent a European concern, the allies began to discuss possible solutions prior to the conferences in Aix-la-Chapelle. The Russian government accepted the Spanish monarchy's view of the colonies as provinces of the metropolis and hoped that in Spain and Spanish America the establishment of wise institutions, including policies tailored to the specific needs of different territories, would ensure peace, stability, and the preservation of King Ferdinand VII's authority. The allies, particularly Britain, might act as mediators, though in contrast to Russia, which in 1817–18 sold warships to Spain, the British government refused to countenance the possibility of armed intervention. Equally troubling, the diplomatic effort to achieve pacification through mediation failed to win consistent support from the Spanish monarch. In October 1817, Ferdinand rejected Britain's proposal for allied mediation on the grounds that it did not require the rebellious colonies to accept his sovereignty.[37] Russia's envoy in Madrid, Dmitrii P. Tatishchev, agreed that the British proposal did not show sincere interest in the cause of Spain.[38]

Allied discussions about how to pacify Spain's rebellious colonies and resolve the conflict with Portuguese Brazil over the Rio de la Plata continued in 1818 and 1819. At the conferences in Aix-la Chapelle, the five powers, acting as conciliators rather than arbitrators, urged the Spanish and Portuguese monarchs to reconcile.[39] On the question of pacification, the government in Madrid seemed to want allied mediation and to assume that the five great powers would provide moral support for the Spanish position. Although France and Russia did not reject outright the use of force on behalf of Spain, Britain's opposition to military intervention remained firm. Castlereagh, supported by Metternich, pressed for a collective declaration urging Spain to accept mediation and insisting that any allied action be pacific. Kapodistrias, as reported to Emperor Alexander by Nesselrode, criticized the idea of announcing in principle the impossibility of military assistance, arguing that this would only embolden the rebels. Better, the co-minister pleaded, to insist that the Spanish government explain its plans for pacification. Russia's diplomats accepted the reality of allied differences over support for Spain, and Kapodistrias even suggested that uncertainty about the intentions of the great powers could inspire salutary disquiet among the insurgents. But Kapodistrias also admitted that the allies lacked sufficient knowledge of "the real state of America and the circumstances of the insurrection to be able to judge the efficacy of the remedies that they might like to employ to stop the progress of the evil." Russia preferred to act within the alliance and during the negotiations withdrew support for a French-authored memorandum that implied the use of force. Prussia remained silent, a posture that Castlereagh interpreted as support for the British position. Given that Spain was not admitted to the conferences, France also declined to express an opinion on Castlereagh's proposal.[40]

The discussions in Aix-la-Chapelle produced no action on the question of pacification, and as Emperor Alexander made clear to Ferdinand VII in a December communication, military cooperation by the intervening powers to assist Spain in the work of pacification was in fact impracticable.[41] Historians also report that in December Ferdinand again rejected foreign involvement, this time explicitly. Notwithstanding the apparent finality of the monarch's statements, from the end of 1818 through March 1819, Russia's diplomats continued their efforts to persuade the Spanish king to accept British mediation.[42] As noted in a dispatch from Kapodistrias to Tatishchev, dated 13/25 December 1818 and approved by Alexander, in 1815 Spain had placed itself outside the circle of European relations.[43] "Barely restored to its independence, poorly consolidated in its internal relations, damaged in the administration of its colonies, this power . . . wanted to be isolated from all the other States with the intention perhaps to become itself the center of a political system." Indeed, in refusing to accede to the Final Act of the Congress of Vienna, Spain had articulated outdated pretentions incommensurate with the country's "effective weight . . . in the balance of the great interests" of Europe or Spanish America (the other hemisphere).

Although Alexander tried to impress upon King Ferdinand the importance of cooperation with all the powers, based on the conservative principles currently regulating European politics, the Spanish government seemed to assign primacy to relations with Russia. This created tension within the alliance, prompting Kapodistrias to admit that Spain's erroneous ideas about a special relationship with Russia also led to equally false opinions about the influence of the Russian mission in Madrid. These opinions in turn fueled the arrogance of Spanish pretentions in the matter of the Rio de la Plata and in talks concerning the pacification of the colonies. Emperor Alexander hoped to see a prompt and real reconciliation between the courts of Spain and Portuguese Brazil, according to "the principles of an equitable reciprocity," which then could lead to "the most perfect agreement of views and action in the pacification of the other hemisphere." But instead, the Spanish government equivocated in relations with the Portuguese and temporized in dealings with the mediators. With respect to colonial affairs, Spain continued to seek from the allies "the promise or at least the prestige of military cooperation, in order to bring the colonies back to the mother country."

Together with the direct communication sent to King Ferdinand by Emperor Alexander, Tatishchev received instructions to explain to the court of Madrid the conclusions reached in Aix-la-Chapelle on the matter of the colonies. Regardless of the king's desire for armed cooperation, the Spanish government needed to understand that any allied intervention would require a formal invitation from Ferdinand addressed to the five powers. Equally important, cooperation with the allies could not be military, as a matter of principle for Britain and of impracticability for the other courts.[44] Finally, allied cooperation to restore Spain's legitimate power carried conditions. The government in Madrid needed to convince the peoples of the mother country and colonies that reunification would place them "under the permanent safeguard of a liberal policy (*système*)," accorded to them by the Spanish government. The policy of benevolence must be applied quickly to the colonies, so that the paternal voice of their legitimate sovereign could once again exercise a happy empire.

Assuming that King Ferdinand took the steps set forth in Tatishchev's instructions, Spain would be able to embark on the great work of pacification either without foreign cooperation or with friendly assistance from Britain, specifically negotiations led by the Duke of Wellington through the collective intervention of the other four powers. The purpose of this intervention would be to develop a plan for pacification supported by the five great powers and Spain. Indeed, the moral pressure exerted on the insurgents by allied unity would represent a more effective guarantee of promised reform than the actions of any single power.[45] Russian diplomats may have been justified in criticizing Ferdinand (or his subalterns) for a policy based on false ideas and mistaken opinions, but the historian also can understand Spain's refusal to submit to the judgments of the five great powers—powers that in this instance expected deference from the rulers of a centuries-old metropolis and a people repeatedly praised and admired for their resistance to Napoleonic conquest. Not surprisingly, in rejecting mediation Spanish officials deployed the language of friendship among the sovereigns to assert Spain's equal status vis-à-vis the great powers.[46]

Tatishchev's representations to King Ferdinand VII and his minister of foreign affairs, Carlos-Maria-Martinez Casa Irujo (the Marquis of Casa Irujo), continued in January and February 1819. Repeatedly, the Russian envoy reported to Nesselrode, he had attempted to apply to discussion of the colonies "the policy of conciliation introduced into the mutual relations of the European powers."[47] Try as he might, however, the effort to persuade Spain to accept the allies' conditions and begin a process of mediation had failed to elicit the desired response. Equally troubling, Tatishchev's colleagues, the ministers of the other great powers, did not seem to care about engaging the Spanish authorities in a discussion of Europe's general interest or of allied unanimity on this important question. Writing directly to Emperor Alexander on 30 January/11 February 1819, Tatishchev described ongoing frustration at his inability to fulfill the mission entrusted to him.[48] Ferdinand VII refused to accept mediation by Wellington, a course he characterized as "perilous for Spain and humiliating for his person." Tatishchev agreed that British and Spanish interests appeared irreconcilable, primarily because Britain sought only to separate Spain from Europe. Tatishchev also complained of diplomatic intrigue directed against him and even his wife, a situation he attributed to allied suspicions about Russia's ties to Spain and jealousy arising from his close personal relationship with Ferdinand. Feeling isolated and ineffective in the fulfilment of his duties, Tatishchev requested reassignment.

In a report to Nesselrode, dated one day after the appeal to Alexander, Tatishchev elaborated on the reasons for his inability to convince Ferdinand VII to accept Wellington's mediation.[49] Discussions in 1817 and 1818, prior to the conferences in Aix-la-Chapelle, had indicated that the Spanish government hoped to work with Portuguese Brazil to end the insurrection in the colonies. Spain also had seemed willing to make concessions based on earlier British proposals: a general amnesty for all insurgents, the admission of qualified Americans to positions and rewards currently monopolized by European Spaniards, the application of liberal principles to trade between the Spanish American provinces and foreign states, and sincere consideration by the Spanish king of other measures that might be proposed by the allies, as long as they were compatible with the maintenance of his rights and his dignity.[50] Whatever the promises contained in the plan for pacification, Britain eventually concluded that it did not justify formal negotiations. In addition, it became clear that Spain intended to use mediation to secure meaningful cooperation from the allies.

Despite obvious disagreements, in July 1818, Tatishchev still expected King Ferdinand to follow the suggestion that the political and civil regime of the colonies be assimilated into that of the metropolis. Russia hoped that Spain would announce this policy as the basis for administrative reforms in the colonies and present the plan for pacification to the allies meeting in Aix-la-Chapelle. King Ferdinand then would negotiate the plan's implementation. In the summer of 1818, according to Tatishchev, the Spanish government continued to look to Britain for support in achieving its goals. But during the conferences in Aix-la-Chapelle, Ferdinand suspended the discussion of foreign intervention in the affairs of the colonies. Changes in the composition of the Spanish government had led to a reappraisal of British policy and to the realization that British interests were opposed to those of Spain with respect to the Bourbon restoration(s), international trade, and Spanish American independence.

Citing communications from Casa Irujo and Cea Bermúdez, Tatishchev offered a sympathetic description of Spanish policy prior to and during the conferences in Aix-la-Chapelle. In the Restoration era, the Spanish government's primary obligation was "to reconstitute the power of Spain for its internal happiness" and to give the country the forces required to become a truly independent power, "useful in the active system of political equilibrium." To fulfill this destiny in the system of European states, Spain's ministers had surveyed the resources that would be needed to recover the colonies and their availability on the peninsula. Balancing the use of these resources with the losses that the colonies' independence would bring and recognizing the "just value of the moral and material means of resistance" that the insurgents could mobilize, the Spanish government had concluded that sacrifices would be unavoidable if Spain wanted to reestablish relations of patronage with America. Thus, the process of pacification envisioned by Spain, as described by Tatishchev, would need to consolidate the metropolis's power through clemency and moderation. This would require that imperial authority be restored through strength and compromise with the commercial interests of other nations, assuming such compromise did not mean suicide for Spain. In other words, Spain had decided to rely on its own wisdom and energy to pacify the colonies without the complications of foreign involvement. Following the conferences in Aix-la-Chapelle, and despite direct communication between Alexander I and Ferdinand VII, Tatishchev's ongoing effort to encourage pacification within the framework of the alliance had led to naught.

Because both Britain and the United States had interests, opinions, and a public mood that worked against Spain's royal cause, Tatishchev considered British participation in the pacification to be essential. This led to the final effort to persuade Spain to accept mediation headed by the Duke of Wellington and to the announcement that military cooperation between the allies and Spain would not be an option. In responding to Tatishchev, the Spanish government showed a complete lack of confidence in both the efficacy of British mediation and the impact of a morally united alliance. The commercial interests of Britain, King Ferdinand insisted, made it impossible to offer sincere assistance to Spain. Nor did the Spanish government observe any positive results from the ongoing diplomatic negotiations with Portuguese Brazil. Alexander's suggestion that Ferdinand should choose the moral support of all Europe over his own isolated efforts failed to dispel Spanish distrust of allied advice. As Ferdinand remarked to Tatishchev, "I hope that you will never recommend to me an act of weakness."[51]

Tatishchev remained in Madrid, and by the end of March 1819 (NS), he at least could report that the British government now appreciated his efforts to convince Spain to accept the allies' offer of mediation.[52] At the same time, he made clear that it would be pointless to engage in further conversations with the Spanish government concerning pacification of the colonies. The Paris conference of ministers continued to discuss the conflict over the Rio de la Plata, and despite Ferdinand VII's suspicions about the negotiations, Tatishchev still hoped that Spain would accept the agreement with Portuguese Brazil proposed in August 1818.[53] In general, Russia's diplomatic communications held out the possibility of resolution in both the conflict over the Rio de la Plata and the pacification of the colonies. Still, the Ministry of Foreign Affairs also repeatedly seemed to admit defeat. As Nesselrode explained in a circular dispatch of 31 March/12 April 1819—addressed to Russia's ambassador in London (Lieven), envoy in Vienna (Golovkin), envoy in Berlin (Alopeus), and minister plenipotentiary in Paris (Pozzo di Borgo)—in Aix-la-Chapelle the allies had agreed to support mediation between Spain and its American colonies led by the Duke of Wellington, should Spain recognize the inadequacy of the resources at its disposal.[54] In this scenario, Wellington would preside over the formulation of a plan for pacification appropriate to the needs and wishes of Spanish America, while the ministers of the other powers would mediate between Britain and Spain, to ensure Madrid's deference to the intervening courts and to place just limits on cooperation with the British government.

Tasked with explaining to the Spanish government the allied plan, Tatishchev had tried but failed to obtain acceptance of the proposed mode of intervention.

Spain had refused all foreign involvement, preferring instead to rely on its own resources to reconquer its colonies. The Russian government had expected this response and considered it consistent with "the respect that European policy accords to the independence and dignity of all governments." Yet as Tatishchev also pointed out, Spain's wish to rely on its own forces, which would be appropriate for a great power, rested on dangerous illusions rather than positive facts. Emperor Alexander therefore hoped that Spain would evaluate its real resources correctly. In America, for example, Spain could augment these resources through a generous and liberal administrative system, capable of rallying to the cause of legitimacy "all interests and consequently all desires." The Russian monarch wished his fellow sovereign success in the enterprise that lay ahead, though he also could not help but lament Ferdinand's rejection of collective allied assistance.[55]

At a moment when religion and morality supposedly guided European policy, and when unity and peace reigned in the conservative system, Spain's relationship to the great powers, the Portuguese monarchy, and the Spanish American colonies exposed the potentially disruptive dynamics of the post-Napoleonic equilibrium. Delusional, ineffective, and reactionary as the Spanish monarchy appeared, the five great powers, presuming to speak on behalf of all Europe, were equally unrealistic about their ability to mold lesser powers and complicated historical processes into their vision of European peace. Perhaps in the allies' unwillingness to offer military assistance to Spain, they admitted to this inconvenient fact. With respect to Spain and the Spanish Empire, the imagined *juste milieu* of harmony, tranquility, and stability in the Restoration era produced barely a moment of peace.[56]

Following the conferences in Aix-la-Chapelle, preservation of Spanish authority in the Americas ceased to be an allied obligation. Yet throughout 1819 the Russian government continued to hope that political reform emanating from the Spanish government would lead to reconciliation. Just days after the military rebellion that marked the start of the Spanish Revolution, Emperor Alexander again proffered advice to King Ferdinand concerning Spain's relations with Portuguese Brazil and the desirability of administrative reform for all the monarchy's subjects.[57] Speaking for the Russian monarch, Tatishchev conveyed Alexander's feelings of friendship toward Ferdinand and his interest in the prosperity of the king's realm. For the moment—news of the January mutiny had not yet reached the Russian government—the issues at hand remained the conflict over the Rio de la Plata and the reestablishment of durable relations based on unity and reciprocal assistance between Spain and Spanish America.

The first action recommended to King Ferdinand by Emperor Alexander was to restore friendly relations with the court of Portuguese Brazil. Since at least 1815, Alexander I had viewed the concept of Christian brotherhood and friendship among the sovereigns as critical instruments of peacemaking. In this instance, the monarch expected friendship between the Spanish and Portuguese kings to produce a solution to the conflict over the Rio de la Plata. Friendly relations between Spain and Portuguese Brazil also would highlight Ferdinand's good intentions toward the people and therefore exert a favorable influence on his American subjects. More concretely, Alexander advised his fellow sovereign to equalize the rights of all Spaniards in both hemispheres. Uniform administration would guarantee the security of person and property that was needed to undercut the grievances invented by rogue and anarchic spirits.

As time passed, the Russian government's hopes for a Spanish restoration in the Americas receded, especially after the peninsula descended into revolution and civil war. Two detailed memorandums preserved in the papers of co-minister of foreign affairs Kapodistrias illustrated official Russian thinking on the colonies during the early months of the Spanish Revolution. The first document, dated March 1820, began with an account of the insurrection in Spanish America during the years 1808 to 1817.[58] The named causes included recognition of Joseph Bonaparte as king of Spain, the weakness of the Spanish viceroys who administered the colonies, British policy, and enmity among the leaders and judicial officials operating in different territories of Spanish America. Conditions on the peninsula likewise caused problems: the uncertainty surrounding royal authority, resistance to Ferdinand VII and to Napoleon, French military success, the audacity of political factions, and disorder within the Napoleonic government. The memorandum went on to survey the patterns of insurrection in various parts of Spanish America, where loyalists, legislatures, and separate jurisdictions competed for power and legitimacy. Above all, the memorandum highlighted the loss of political resources brought on by the revolutionary explosion in Spain. Absent the crisis on the peninsula, the ordinary causes of disorder would not have been sufficient to fuel rebellion in Spanish America.

The author of the memorandum attributed persistent rebellion to the precarious condition of Spain that had begun with the Napoleonic invasion in 1808 and continued until the return of King Ferdinand VII in 1814. Based on the lessons of history, the maxim that every revolutionary movement invariably produced another explained the simultaneity of the uprisings across Spanish America. As royal authorities tried to maintain neutrality in the struggle between Napoleon and the defenders of Ferdinand, demagogues and factions used the political uncertainty to spread their influence. The memorandum described the Spanish American insurrections as the work of propertied classes and elites of birth engaged in a vast conspiracy. In other words, the revolts did not represent a popular movement or "great political revolution founded on principles." Nor, despite the participation of subalterns, did the American revolutionary scene embody the suffering of a people who demanded change. To the contrary, the troubles in Spanish America arose from an anarchic operation that renounced order and concord.

The second memorandum, dated 30 April/12 May 1820 and attributed by historians to Kapodistrias, offered a more pointed analysis of Spanish America, in light of the reestablishment of the constitutional system in Spain—the same system that had existed in 1814 at the time of Ferdinand VII's restoration to the Spanish throne.[59] Given the events of March 1820, how could the union of Spain with its old American possessions be strengthened? Describing Spanish America as a hybrid society, Kapodistrias highlighted the relationship between Spain's political interests and the future of Spanish America. The revolution in Spain had changed the meaning of political alignments in the colonies and might offer a solution to the problem of pacification. Although freedom of the press in places such as Mexico, Peru, and Cuba deprived Spain of an authority fortified by "the enlightened compression of partial dissent," the Cortes now had the opportunity to enact equitable legislation on the rights and duties (*devoirs*) defining commercial relations between Europe and the colonies. Kapodistrias imagined a relationship between Spain and Spanish America similar to the one that had existed between Britain and the North American colonies in 1775 (before the Declaration of Independence). He also argued that in the current situation the government in Madrid should make sacrifices to achieve reconciliation with the colonies. Although some of Kapodistrias's comments could be interpreted as support for constitutional restoration, his overall analysis adhered to the principles of Russian foreign policy. Throughout the peacemaking of 1814 to 1823, Emperor Alexander's diplomats responded to the upheavals in Spanish America and later to the revolution in Spain with calls for enlightened reform granted by the legitimate monarch, Ferdinand VII.

The vision of reform from above, a product of enlightened monarchy across Europe, made it difficult for peacemakers to adapt the legal stipulations of 1814, 1815, and 1818 to the reality of open political contestation. Simply put, their vision of harmoniousness, stability, and transformation could not contain the social and political changes underway in Europe or the Americas. As the Spanish American independence movements, the Greek insurrections, and the Russian-Ottoman war scare of 1821–22 all illustrated, the suppression of revolution, understood to be essential to the preservation of peace in Europe (and effectively carried out in Italy, Portugal, and eventually Spain) did not depend entirely on developments within the boundaries of Europe. European order had become a transatlantic, transpacific, and transcontinental affair. In March 1822, the United States recognized Spanish American independence in principle, and by December the Russian government admitted that emancipation appeared inevitable, even if it was not yet imminent.[60] Indeed, when emancipation came, Russia did not immediately recognize the newly independent states. In other words, the opaque and contradictory response of Russia's diplomats to the insurrections in Spanish America highlighted the ongoing failure to understand that liberalization had become inevitable. In keeping with eighteenth-century discussions of political dissent and religious toleration, Russia's rulers continued to assume that a handful of instigators—or in post-Napoleonic Europe, a faction of revolutionaries, sectarians, or Jacobins—was responsible for the persistent disorders. As historians document for multiple aspects of Russian political culture, the reliance on personalized relationships of authority meant that disorder and corruption represented individual rather than institutional behavior. Consequently, the solution to inequity and abuse was not systemic reform, but the moral self-reformation of subjects, citizens, and officials.

The Verona Conferences and the Spanish Revolution

During the initial phase of the Spanish Revolution, stretching from the military mutiny of January 1820 until early March, when King Ferdinand VII accepted the 1812 constitution, Emperor Alexander I tried to reach agreement with the allies on a collective European response. The effort failed, though after the conferences in Troppau and Laibach sanctioned Austrian intervention in Italy, Russia's policymakers again dared to hope that Britain and France would join the effort to save Spain. Writing from Laibach to Russia's chargé d'affaires in Madrid, Count Bulgari, co-minister of foreign affairs Kapodistrias expressed the view that restoration in the Kingdom of the Two Sicilies, by illustrating the effectiveness of allied action, could lead to the same result in Spain.[61] Alexander agreed and supported intervention, but only with French participation and British acquiescence. In the meantime, the monarch continued to instruct his diplomatic representatives to maintain a posture of neutrality.[62]

By the time the Verona conferences opened in October 1822, developments within the alliance, especially the three monarchs' accession to the Troppau protocol and successful restorations in the Two Sicilies and Piedmont, combined with events in Spain to produce a new calculus among the allies. Of particular concern, the government in Madrid, still crowned by Ferdinand VII, appeared to take a more radical position on the question of revolution outside Spain's borders. From January 1821, before the Austrian military intervention in Naples, the Spanish government reportedly had come under domestic political pressure to support revolt in other parts of Europe. Notwithstanding proclamations of neutrality from officials in Madrid, it looked as if Spanish diplomats had become involved in revolutions in Italy and Portugal. In addition, although both the Spanish king and government claimed to support implementation of the 1812 constitution, debates in the Cortes revealed that some political leaders viewed allied action in Naples as the precursor to intervention in Spain. Finally, in July 1822, fear of a counter-revolutionary conspiracy inside the king's guard led to disorders that brought Spanish radicals to power.[63] These developments pushed the French government to side with the legitimist alliance and the allies to view King Ferdinand as a prisoner to be saved.[64]

On 20 October 1822 (NS), the day the Verona conferences opened, the French foreign minister, Vicomte Mathieu de Montmorency (1767–1826), delivered a confidential verbal note to the plenipotentiaries of Austria, Britain, Prussia, and Russia. The Russian response to Montmorency's communication, which described an imminent threat to France emanating from Spain, began with an overview of Alexander's position on the Spanish Revolution.[65] Since April 1820 the Russian government had expressed concern about the situation in Spain and had encouraged the allies to show benevolent solicitude for the Spanish nation, which deserved to enjoy happiness after the glorious struggle against foreign rule. Russia had hoped to prevent the misfortunes that inevitably resulted from violent attacks on legitimate authority. But sadly, the fears of Emperor Alexander now seemed justified. Few countries in Europe had suffered as Spain suffered, and few had brought down on Europe comparable disasters.

Among Spain's internal sufferings, the Russian government identified anarchy, destruction, insults to the throne and religion, the loss of rich territories in the New World, the dissipation of public wealth, the open preaching of subversive doctrines, and bans against subjects loyal to the sovereign. Not content with domestic transformation, the artisans of the troubles in Spain had spread revolution to other countries, compelling the allied powers to use military force to restore legitimate authority. In the Kingdom of the Two Sicilies and in Piedmont, beautiful lands desolated by war, sects had conspired against the tranquility of all European states. In other words, by the time the allies met in Verona, the revolution in Spain had become more radical, and so too had the

great powers' understanding of legitimacy and restoration. Russia's condemnation of Spain's revolutionaries bemoaned the obligation of governments—an
obligation imposed by the law of the peoples' salvation (*salut*)—to engage in
rigorous surveillance, which in turn prevented them from pursuing more useful
improvements. In Spain at least—if not also in Italy, Portugal, and Greece—the
enlightened balancing of reform and repression had tilted in favor of repression.
What Russia's monarchy failed to see, and what it would continue to ignore until
the end of the old regime, was the unstoppable advent (or necessity) of vigorously
contested participatory politics. For the moment, the inevitability of further
change could be ignored in France, Germany, Italy, Portugal, and Greece, but
not in Spain or Spanish America.[66]

By the fall of 1822, the insurrection that had begun in Cadiz came to be seen
as a deplorable example of the results of revolution. According to the Russian
government, the events in Naples and Turin had endangered primarily Austria.
The Spanish threat to France, however, affected every European power. Emperor
Alexander accepted Montmorency's claim that the Spanish Revolution exposed
France to imminent peril. He therefore stood ready to act in concert with France
and the other allied courts, based on the proposals of the French foreign minister. Specifically, Russia's plenipotentiary received authorization to reach agreement on breaking diplomatic relations with Spain, defining the moral assistance
that France currently sought, and stipulating within limits the material aid that
France might demand, if compelled to use military force. Simply put, the interests of all Europe required suppression of the Spanish Revolution.

On 19/31 October 1822, the Austrian government responded to this new phase
in the discussion by proposing concerted action in Spain.[67] Approved by Russia,
the Austrian proposal highlighted two questions that the allies needed to address. First was the danger to all Europe represented by the victory of revolution,
and second was the crisis in political relations between France and Spain. The
French government had explained its predicament to the allies, and although
it hoped to maintain peace, the Spanish Revolution had the potential to force
France to repel aggression. For this reason, the French government had asked the
allies whether or not, in case of a just and necessary defense, France could count
on their moral and material support. Austria, Prussia, and Russia had replied
in the affirmative, a response that now required a more precise definition of the
casus foederis and the reciprocal obligations to be assumed. To meet this need,
the allied governments agreed to compose appropriate diplomatic transactions.

The Austrian proposal then turned to Spain's internal situation, where revolutionary anarchy, which also fueled civil war, challenged the efforts of the allied

sovereigns to conserve social order. The language and attitude of the Spanish toward foreign countries had become so provocative that the European powers could no longer remain silent. Thus, the allies had asserted the right to discuss Spain collectively, thereby fulfilling their obligation to deliberate on the means to save Europe from the dangers posed by the triumph of the revolution. Not only France, but also all of Europe would benefit from the elucidation of common commitments that aimed to restore order on the peninsula. Although the great powers continued to hope that the victims and enemies of the revolution in Spain would have the courage to end the troubles, the Austrian proposal openly stated that relations between Spain and the allies depended on restoration of the king's legitimate authority. The king's continued captivity created a new claim or right that allowed the allied powers to decide the basis for future relations with Spain. Austria hoped, and Russia accepted, that any intervention would be pacific and take one of three possible forms. The five powers could adopt a common language by issuing a collective declaration or separate notes that were uniform in their principles and objective. France could rely on the four allies to address the current difficulties, even if they did not agree to participate in a common course of action. Or finally, one of the powers could communicate to the Spanish government the common position of the allies.

Russia's plenipotentiaries formally responded to the Austrian proposals at the conferences of 21 October/2 November 1822.[68] The response conveyed Emperor Alexander's agreement that the allies should pursue a course of action designed to hasten the end of the revolution in Spain by encouraging the Spanish nation to "shake off the yoke of the factions oppressing them." Russia's representatives had received authorization to accede to the Austrian proposals and participate in the development of appropriate resolutions. These resolutions, combined with the commitments arising from France's propositions, would define allied policy toward Spain. Looking beyond broad statements of principle, the Russian government also urged the allies to consider (and specify) how each would proceed, if the representations of their diplomats in Madrid did not yield the desired result. From the start of the Spanish crisis, Alexander had wished to address the situation in concert with his allies. At the meetings in Verona, in light of Austria's reluctance to become materially engaged and Britain's continuing insistence on allied neutrality, Russia accepted the decision to send separate notes of uniform content to the Spanish government.

The Russian response did not explicitly mention the reservations of Austria or the opposition of Britain. By contrast, an unsigned secret memorandum, dated 15 November 1822 (NS) and listed in the Acts of the Conferences, expressed the

Austrian fear that British separateness threatened the alliance, even though Britain remained free in its decisions and actions due to its direct influence over the peninsula (that is, its relations with Portugal).[69] The memorandum also highlighted the agreement among the other great powers to support the Spanish king and end the revolution. The allies currently maintained diplomatic relations with the revolutionary faction in Spain, yet they also functioned as a "league of moral action" united in principle on the acceptability of defensive material action. In other words, the need to define a *casus foederis* in association with France was agreed to in principle, though the actual definition required more specifics. The memorandum also voiced concern about the weakness of the French government and the danger that a new revolutionary shock in France posed for all Europe. Finally, the memorandum reiterated the allies' hope that once they declared their collective readiness to break diplomatic relations with revolutionary Spain, British neutrality would become untenable. Britain would then be compelled to explain its position on preserving political peace between Spain and the allies, restoring order on the peninsula, and maintaining the alliance, "the dissolution of which could be brought about by an unforeseen difference between the course taken by the four continental Courts and that of England."

In conference minutes signed on 7/19 November 1822, the plenipotentiaries of Austria, France, Prussia, and Russia addressed ongoing worries about how the powers should respond, if the Austrian proposal for peaceful intervention in Spain failed.[70] The conference record identified the circumstances that might lead the courts of Austria, Prussia, and Russia to act with the court of France in a declared war or a war provoked by the current government of Spain. Two articles specified the conditions that would make such engagements obligatory. The first focused on three actions by the Spanish government that the allies would treat as the *casus foederis* for war: (1) a military attack by Spain on French territory or an act of the Spanish government that directly provoked rebellion among the subjects of one or another of the powers; (2) the declared downfall (*déchéance prononcée*) of the Spanish king or legal proceedings against him or members of his family; and (3) a formal act by the Spanish government that restricted the royal family's rights of legitimate succession. Article 2 of the minutes left open the possibility that additional unspecified developments might also be treated as the *casus foederis*. Any signatory could present a case to the allied governments, which then would consider whether or not the circumstances belonged to the class of *casus foederis* as foreseen and defined. The understanding reached on the *casus foederis* showed once again that the alliance of the great powers—including the Holy Alliance so often identified with Austria, Prussia, and Russia—did not aim to prevent political change or social reform in Europe. To the contrary, the peacemakers' definition of the *casus foederis* addressed the consequences of violent revolution, based on their experience of the French Revolution and Napoleonic conquests. The allies may have been willfully blind to the realities of emergent democratic politics, but they already had lived through, and now worked assiduously to prevent, the destruction of legitimate rulers and the spread of revolution by military aggression or direct external provocation.

In contrast to the Troppau protocol by which Austria, Prussia, and Russia had declared a common position on resolving the crisis in the Kingdom of the Two Sicilies, at the Verona conferences on 8/20 November 1822, the allies agreed not to issue a general protocol, but to send separate instructions to their ministers in Madrid.[71] These instructions explained mutual concerns and principles of action and ordered diplomats to act in concert with colleagues. On 14/26 November 1822, Emperor Alexander signed instructions to his chargé d'affaires in Madrid, Count Bulgari. Designed to provide a tableau of the Spanish Revolution and its consequences, which Bulgari was directed to propagate in government and elite social circles, the instructions began with a statement of the allies' determination to consolidate peace in Europe and prevent any action that compromised the current state of general tranquility.[72] In March 1820, a military revolt had forced the Spanish king to accept the liberal constitution of 1812—"laws that the public reason of Europe, enlightened by the experience of centuries," greeted with outcries of disapproval. The allied governments had condemned these developments, and the Saint Petersburg government in particular had warned of the misfortunes that would follow. Based not on theories or principles but on the facts, the warnings and fears of 1820 now appeared prescient.

The allies assumed that the Spanish nation shared the wishes of its king and that the Spanish government sought to preserve the integrity of the monarchy. Consequently, the Verona decisions offered to Ferdinand VII an amicable intervention, designed also to restore Spanish authority in the empire's distant provinces, which provided so much wealth and power. According to the instructions, the March events seemed to justify rebellion in America by encouraging loyal provinces that suffered under the weight of revolutionary despotism to separate from the motherland. Regardless of causes and motivations, the anarchy of revolution threatened the prosperity of Spanish America. In conditions of disorder, public and private fortunes were decimated, rights were revoked, heavy contributions were levied, and ruinous loans were needed. Respect for the throne and religion already had been despoiled at the moment when the blind passions of the multitude replaced legitimate authority. For three years the allies had clung

to the hope that the character of the Spanish people, who had stalwartly opposed revolution during the Napoleonic conquest, would prevail over the spirit
of insurrection and allow the king to reclaim the legitimate rights of the throne.

But instead of being restored, the Spanish monarchy had fallen into ruin.
Although Spain's people had endured six years of bloodshed in support of the
monarchy, following the revolt of 7 July 1822, the king and his family became
captives.[73] Civil war ensued, which produced higher levels of violence and larger
numbers of victims. Nor did the conspirators limit their activities to Spain. They
worked openly to spread rebellion, took credit for the revolutions in Italy, and
currently threatened France. Emperor Alexander did not seek conflict with the
Spanish government; however, the revolutionary menace could not be denied,
and the radical doctrines on display could be seductive and fatal. Thus, despite
the allies' desire for friendly relations with Madrid, they feared that the king
lacked the freedom to end the civil war or prevent foreign conflicts. It remained
for the Spanish government to remedy the situation by restoring the country to
the honorable position in the European family that it had occupied in 1814. This
could be done only by defeating the revolution and returning to government
based on ancient virtues and respect for religion.

Emperor Alexander further instructed Count Bulgari to communicate his
good intentions toward the Spanish government. The allies claimed no right of
intervention and did not seek to dictate laws to Spain or attack the country's
independence. They did, however, want to see Spain freed from torment and
bloodshed, and they hoped that the Spanish government would be reestablished
as a wise and national administration. Currently, the revolution endangered the
prosperity of Spain and the security of France. The revolutionary government
in Madrid not only encouraged civil strife, but also prevented reconciliation
with the colonies. Sadly, the allies no longer believed that the king would be
able to reclaim his authority or restore social order. Because Ferdinand and his
family had become virtual prisoners, the Spanish monarch was not free to work
with the allies. As the instructions stated, only the men ruling in Madrid could
accept the means being offered to lead Spain to a tranquil and glorious future.
Thus, although the allies did not insist on any particular form of government,
they clearly rejected the constitution of 1812 and wanted to see the authority of
the king and religion restored.

A second dispatch, also dated 14/26 November 1822, explained to Count
Bulgari how he should proceed in the present grave and perilous situation.[74]
The allies aspired to ameliorate the future of Spain, which implied persuading
the Spanish nation and government to abandon the revolution. This tactic had

proven effective in the Kingdom of the Two Sicilies, where the allies had reached agreement with King Ferdinand I to end the revolution. Yet evil as the consequences of the Spanish Revolution appeared to be, Alexander I and his allies did not expect their efforts to succeed: "In the tumult of the passions, the voice of reason is rarely heard." Assuming that the men who exercised power in Madrid refused to listen to reason, it nonetheless remained critically important to give the Spanish nation the opportunity, based on authentic documents, to hear the views of the allied courts. Diplomats such as Bulgari had therefore received instructions highlighting the losses to Spain caused by the March revolution, the captivity of the king and his family, and the intelligence that exposed how the artisans of the Spanish troubles aimed to incite revolt in France and other countries. Bulgari's assignment was to campaign against the current Spanish government, both among officials and in society, in order to weaken the party oppressing Spain and strengthen the one fighting for the country's deliverance. To that end, he was authorized not only to read to the Spanish foreign minister the allies' chronicle of the revolution and its consequences, but also to provide him with a copy of the document. If the government did not heed the advice of the intervening powers or respond within fifteen days, Bulgari should request the passports of the Russian legation and leave the country. The diplomats of Austria and Prussia received the same instructions, and although all were permitted to negotiate with the Spanish minister of foreign affairs, they could not alter the conditions for preserving diplomatic relations with Spain.[75]

The Verona instructions and the diplomatic maneuvering in Madrid failed to change Spanish policy. In January 1823, Austria, Prussia, and Russia broke diplomatic relations with Spain, and at the opening of the French Chambers, Louis XVIII announced that his troops were ready to march. The actual invasion of Spain began in April, and by September the French army had restored royal rule. In October, King Ferdinand VII rescinded the amnesty he had granted in September, declared that in effect he had been a prisoner since 1820, and renounced the constitution of 1812, together with all laws passed under the revolutionary government. According to historians, after a period of repression in 1823–24, the king pursued more moderate policies, and in 1827 French troops left Spain. The peacemakers of post-Napoleonic Europe won a temporary victory. Still, the Spanish Revolution exposed not only the intractable political schism between liberals and royalists, but also the ease with which political conflict could degenerate into civil strife, guerilla warfare, and atrocities on all sides.[76] Among the peacemakers of 1814, 1815, and 1818, political conditions in Spain caused palpable confusion.

Whither European Peace?

Just one day before Emperor Alexander departed Verona, the courts of Austria, Prussia, and Russia signed a circular on Italian affairs that summed up the decisions taken in response to insurrections in Italy, Greece, and Spain.[77] The three governments viewed the circular of 2/14 December 1822 as a follow-up to instructions issued in May 1821, at the close of the Laibach conferences, and as a common instruction that would be sent to their diplomatic agents abroad. The circular began with the military occupation of Piedmont, which, based on an agreement with the king of Sardinia-Piedmont, would end by 30 September 1823.[78] With respect to the Kingdom of the Two Sicilies, the allies and King Ferdinand I had agreed to reduce the army of occupation to 17,000 troops as quickly as possible.[79] As the circular recalled, in Laibach the three sovereigns also had expressed the hope that the intervention in Italy, which they called a painful duty imposed on them by necessity, would be brief and that another would never be necessary.[80] The monarchs further noted that despite their intentions, allied actions in Italy had produced false alarms, hostile interpretations, and sinister predictions designed to misdirect the opinion of the peoples.[81] The allies had acted not out of secret ambition or calculated interest, but out of the need to resist revolution and prevent the countless disorders, crimes, and calamities that rebellion had inflicted across Italy. In other words, "the sole objective of the thoughts and efforts of the Monarchs" was to restore order and peace and to provide legitimate governments with the assistance they had a right to demand. The sovereigns of Italy remained independent, charged by Divine Providence to ensure the security and tranquility of their peoples, and the three allied monarchs wanted nothing more than to restore power to these princes. Indeed, they characterized their decisions for the relief of Italy as the fulfilment of the alliance's very purpose.

But soon after the allies reached agreement on action in Italy, another complication emerged. The revolutionary genie spread from Spain and Italy to the Ottoman Empire. The allies agreed that all of the recent revolts arose from the same evil (*mal*). The revolutionaries might invoke different pretexts, but the origin, substance, and language of the evil were identical. The men who directed the movement likewise sought to divide the powers and neutralize the forces that could oppose them. In response, the three monarchs had decided "to repel the principle of revolt in whatever place and under whatever form it appeared." During this momentous period for the alliance, the five great powers (Austria, Britain, France, Prussia, and Russia) had exchanged numerous confidential communications, and at the conferences in Verona, they had consecrated and confirmed the supposed unanimity already achieved. In December 1822, the three sovereigns who had signed on to intervention in Italy also still expected to overcome the obstacles preventing the fulfilment of their wishes in relation to the Eastern Question.

The circular then turned to the deplorable situation on the western peninsula of Europe.[82] Spain shared the misfortune of countries that embraced unfortunate means to seek out the good (*le bien*). Thus, a group of disoriented and perverse men presented the evil of revolution as a good deed (*bienfait*), calling it "the triumph of the century of Enlightenment," "the necessary and happy fruit of the progress of civilization," the means to support and bring about civilization, and the motor of a fertile patriotism. If civilization had as its objective the destruction of society, and if military forces could with impunity seize control over empires—the internal and external peace of which they were supposed to guarantee—then, yes, the Spanish Revolution deserved the admiration of the ages, and the military insurrectionists offered a model for reformers. But this was not the reality. Truth demanded its rights, and Spain represented a sad example of the consequences that resulted from violating the eternal laws of the moral world.

Conditions in Spain did indeed look bleak. Legitimate power, currently in chains, was being used to overturn all rights and legal liberties. Arbitrariness and oppression assumed the form of law, all classes of the population appeared agitated, and the kingdom suffered from convulsions and disorders. As civil war consumed the resources of the state, Spain's rich colonies justified their own emancipation with the same maxims proclaimed by the mother country in establishing public law. The misfortunes afflicting a loyal people explained in turn why countries in immediate contact with the peninsula had become worried, troubled, and confused. The current disorganization of Spain threatened the conservative principles that served as the basis for the European alliance. In a situation that became more alarming each day and that posed so many dangers to others, the monarchs could not remain tranquil spectators. Precisely because the presence of allied diplomats in Madrid implied tacit approval for the acts of a faction—a faction that would do anything to preserve its deadly power—the monarchs' missions had received orders to leave Spain.

The decision to break diplomatic relations with Spain would prove to Europe that the allies had not retreated from the "resolve sanctioned by their intimate conviction." The monarchs had agreed to act, based on their friendship toward the Spanish king and their interest in the well-being of the Spanish nation, which more than once in its history had been distinguished by its virtues and grandeur. The allied transactions affecting Spain adhered to the principles that guided the monarchs as they addressed all the great questions of order and stability exposed by recent events. To refute calumnies leveled against them, the monarchs pointed to the evidence of their deeds, the loyalty and benevolence of their intentions, and the force and cohesion of their union. British neutrality and the absence of a general Verona protocol belied the claim of unity, though the acceptance of a possible French intervention in Spain could be seen as proof of a stronger and more broad-based alliance. Still, in the tone of the Verona circular one detects growing frustration and a trace of desperation. Could the moderate reformism of the peacemakers constrain revolutionary war?

The monarchs, the circular continued, wished only for peace. All Europe should therefore recognize that the course pursued by the allies remained fully consistent with the independence of governments and the interests of the peoples. The monarchs viewed as enemies only those who conspired against legitimate authority and misled others to follow them into the common abyss. Indeed, peace among states, even when well established, brought no benefit to society, as long as spirits remained agitated. The circular attributed the current agitation to the perfidious suggestions and criminal endeavors of one faction that wanted only revolution and upheaval. The leaders and instruments of this faction, whether operating in the open or in the shadows to organize sinister plots and to poison public opinion, continued to torment the peoples through the propagation of a somber and mendacious account of current conditions. According to the revolutionaries' tableau, governments did not prosper, improvements did not succeed, and trust among men no longer existed. To render these odious plots powerless, the monarchs had set about the noble task of destroying the weapons that the factions could use to disrupt the tranquility of the world.

The closing section of the circular instructed the diplomats of Austria, Prussia, and Russia to promote its content among the governments to which they were accredited. There could be no true happiness for the nations without calm and stability. Nor could the three signatories to the circular achieve their goals without sincere and constant support from all the governments (of Europe). The monarchs called for this assistance "in the name of their primary interests,... in the name of the conservation of social order, and in the name of future generations." They recognized the great truth that their power rested on a sacred trust, for which they must account not only to their peoples, but also to posterity.

Numerous documents of the era emphasized the obligation to implement the laws and ensure good governance. In this instance, the Verona circular highlighted the monarchs' responsibility to deliver their peoples from the errors and misfortunes for which they as rulers might have prepared the way. The monarchs liked to believe that they would find in all those called to exercise supreme authority, under whatever form (of government), true allies who respected the letter and positive stipulations of the acts constituting the basis of the European system. As important as the spirit and principles of the European system were the legal obligations defined in the treaties. The circular ended with a simple affirmation of the monarchs' determination to use all the means that Divine Providence had put at their disposal for the welfare of Europe.

The revolutionary situations in Piedmont and the Kingdom of the Two Sicilies had been effectively addressed, if not fully resolved. Portugal belonged to the British sphere, and France, the Verona documents implied, would take the lead in Spain. At the same time, the allies expected, though ultimately failed, to define a common position on Greece. With respect to Spain's American colonies, the great powers, except for Britain, also failed to admit the inevitable trajectory toward independence. By 1825 the emancipation of Latin America was all but completed.[83] Emperor Alexander died in December 1825, and Russia experienced its first modern revolt, the Decembrist Rebellion, which aimed to restructure social and political arrangements.[84] In 1830 France returned to the path of revolution, Belgium broke away from Holland, and Poland rebelled against Russian rule. By 1848 revolution again engulfed much of Western and Central Europe: France, Italy, the German states, and the Austrian Empire.[85]

The peace treaties of 1814, 1815, and 1818 remained broadly operative, but the vision of European order embraced by the peacemakers could not contain the movements of peoples or offer satisfactory answers to the radical and ethno-nationalist ideologies of the day. Recent scholarship praises the peacemakers for establishing diplomatic practices that until 1914 prevented pan-European war and that even after the Great War continued to provide a foundation for European unity. Unlike some present-day proponents of the European idea, Jürgen Osterhammel offers an understated and more realistic appraisal of how European unity worked. After the Congress of Vienna, he notes, the European state system no longer produced "fragile balances more or less automatically but required political management structured by a basic set of both manifest and unspoken rules."[86] As the preceding chapters argue, the idealized narrative of European integration does not adequately account for Russia's experience of or contribution to European peace. In the Restoration era, the Russian Empire and its monarch stood at the center of European society, yet in the Crimean War of 1853–56, Britain and France fought on the side of the enemy, and the European alliance ceased to represent the principal pathway to peace.[87] The separate alliances that the Russian government long had claimed to oppose returned to Europe's diplomatic chessboard.

Conclusion

Russia's European Diplomacy

H OW SHOULD HISTORIANS CHARACTERIZE the diplomacy that followed upon a quarter century of pan-European revolution, war, and conquest? Did Russia's conception of European order represent a forward-looking commitment to collective security and international governance? Or was the effort to act in concert a substantive adaptation of enlightened reformism and Christian morality to the realities of European society? What did Russia's peacemakers consider innovative or original about the political system constructed in Vienna, Paris, and Aix-la-Chapelle? How did they define the great European alliance and the obligations of the allies? How did they expect to maintain stability, tranquility, and peace? Clearly, Emperor Alexander I's diplomats saw in the treaties of 1814, 1815, and 1818 not only the end of the French Revolution and Napoleonic Wars, but also the start of a peacemaking process, which, as things turned out, would bring unprecedented challenges.

The congresses of Aix-la-Chapelle, Troppau, Laibach, and Verona highlighted the need for active peacemaking beyond the formal conclusion of treaties and accords. Each of these gatherings had its own personality and concerns, based on the concrete issues at hand, and each commanded the attention of Europe's political leaders. The circumstances and questions in need of discussion, not an impulse toward shared governance, defined the content of the negotiations and the structure of the conferences. The forms of polite intercourse, etiquette, and reasoned argument observed at the congresses already had been established in the public spaces of Enlightenment sociability and the republic of letters.[1] More noteworthy, therefore, than the formalities of diplomatic practice was the hard work required to sustain the peace. One crisis after another challenged the decisions of the allies, who labored incessantly to preserve the unity that had led to peace. The novelty of the political process lay in the conscious commitment of allied leaders to prevent separate alliances and to base decisions on the European public law enshrined in the treaties of Paris, the Final Act of the Congress of Vienna, and the protocols of Aix-la-Chapelle. The treaties defined a system of peaceful relations founded on legitimate sovereignty, the rights of peoples, and the direct governance exercised by each independent state (*puissance*). The role of the alliance—whether the Quadruple Alliance, the grand alliance of the five powers, the general alliance, or the Holy Alliance—was to ensure adherence to the shared treaty obligations.

If the goal of the European political system was to preserve peace and security in Europe (the equilibrium), the mechanism for realizing that goal was the commitment to act in concert (*concerter*). This meant that no great power would conclude a separate agreement with any other or with a second-order power in a situation that affected the general security of Europe. The coalition politics of the French Revolutionary and Napoleonic Wars underscored the necessity of this principle. Repeatedly, alliances had been formed and understandings reached only to evaporate due to military losses and separate agreements with Napoleon. The French emperor's military accomplishments were formidable, but often they resulted from disunity and weakness among his opponents. After the coalition organized in 1813–14 revealed that military effectiveness could be sustained, the allies recognized that in order to keep the peace, they must remain united.[2] This was the primary lesson of the Napoleonic era and the basis for Emperor Alexander I's fidelity to legality and collective action. As events on the ground would prove, preservation of the equilibrium required that diplomats continually reconstruct the peace through negotiation, state building, military mobilization, and above all the obligation to act in concert.

After the Congress of Aix-la-Chapelle restored France to its natural status as a great power in Europe, allied unity appeared fully consolidated. Ironically, however, by completing the edifice of pacification and peace, the allies also exposed one of the primary contradictions in the European system: the distinction between the general alliance of independent states and the grand alliance of the four great powers plus France. In a report of 15/27 March 1818, Russia's envoy in Vienna, Count Iurii A. Golovkin, explained Metternich's justification of domination by the four (the Quadruple Alliance of Austria, Britain, Prussia, and Russia) in light of criticism from lesser powers. According to Metternich, Europe did indeed need a dominant or preponderant power to prevent the political system from becoming democratic. But Napoleonic domination had produced a despotic European system. In the post-war era, by contrast, the concert of the great powers—which eventually also included France and that Divine Providence had given to the peacemakers—tried to address unexpected developments in a manner that served the general good, as opposed to particular interests. Count Golovkin fully embraced Metternich's appraisal when he commented, "I have seen that the republic of Plato already is established."[3]

In another communication prior to the meetings in Aix-la-Chapelle, Golovkin appeared more sensitive to the tension between great and second-order powers that was built into the European system. Based on article 5 of the Second Treaty of Paris, the four sovereigns functioned as plenipotentiaries for all European states that had acceded to the alliance. Based on article 6 of the Quadruple Alliance, which called for future meetings of the sovereigns to deliberate on measures to ensure the peace, the great powers acted as intervening parties and official defenders of common European interests. When Golovkin insisted that voices beyond those of princes and sovereigns needed to be heard, he implicitly acknowledged the problem of an oligarchic tendency in the European system. He also highlighted the question of public opinion or the public mood (*l'esprit public*) that Russia's diplomats had begun to describe. "The moral state of Europe," Golovkin wrote, demanded the "preponderance that the intimate union of the four great courts presents in order to maintain a just equilibrium between governments and public opinion."[4]

Diplomatic discourse touting the advantages of a just equilibrium based on alliance unity blurred the distinction between the grand alliance of great powers and the general alliance of European states. Soon after the conclusion of the meetings in Aix-la-Chapelle, Emperor Alexander reminded his diplomatic agents of the need to speak with one voice in response to misrepresentations of the European system.[5] Hinting at the concerns of second-order powers that had not been invited to participate directly in France's admittance into the alliance, the monarch insisted that neither he nor the allies who had met in Aix-la-Chapelle intended to create a new system or partial combination. To the contrary, the European system was not the work of any single power, but rather was held together by the ties of fraternal friendship that united all the sovereigns of Europe. All the powers contributed equally to its conservation, and all shared the sentiment that identified duty with interest. Because the current system had replaced the separate alliances of the past, every state that adhered to the system enjoyed the same benefits and security. To highlight this message, Alexander repeatedly instructed his diplomats to act with moderation and enlightened benevolence.

As the Russian monarch and his diplomatic agents worked to transform the cacophony of war and revolution into the enlightened harmoniousness of enduring peace, they also articulated a set of concepts and principles that guided their responses to events on the ground. The principle of legality assumed the existence of a body of European public law defined in the treaties of Vienna, Paris, and Aix-la-Chapelle. Legality meant strict adherence to both the letter and spirit of these accords, a formulation that inevitably opened the door to conflicting interpretations. Although consistent with legislative practice in the Russian Empire, the concern for outcomes that embodied the spirit of the law sometimes pushed the expectations of Russia's diplomats beyond what other great powers would accept. Britain's general opposition to military interventions together with repeated allied rejections of Alexander's proposals for joint guarantees and statements of principle countered the Russian tendency to elevate desired outcomes such as morality and justice over strict adherence to legal prescriptions.

Less susceptible to the broadening effect of eternal principles, the concepts of sovereignty and legitimacy played critical and complementary roles in diplomatic discussions. In the restoration and reconstruction of political rights that followed the victory over Napoleon, sovereignty denoted respect for the independence and territorial integrity of all states, large and small, based on the treaties. The great powers may have dominated decision making and imposed solutions on less powerful allies, but this did not mean that they ignored the sovereign rights, including the ancient rights, of minor rulers and second-order states. On this question, principle and interest could coincide. The Russian government repeatedly invoked the claims of lesser powers to prevent a potentially offensive Austrian-Prussian alliance against Russia.[6] Similarly, in dealings with the German Confederation, the great powers cultivated connections with individual client states that relied on their protection. The more powerful states, including Russia, could use the legal rights of weaker allies to counter one another. As ongoing negotiations revealed, the principle of legitimacy did not require the resurrection of prerevolutionary states, but rather the recognition of political power as legally constituted. Nor did the de facto existence of a government make it a legitimate government (de droit).[7]

To repeat, diplomats did not equate legitimacy as legally constituted political authority with the restoration or preservation of old regime governments.[8] Among historians, confusion on this point arises from the peacemakers' absolute rejection of revolution, embodied in both the French Revolution and Napoleonic Empire, as a legitimate means to remove tyrannical rulers or effect political change. Russian efforts to uphold the principle of legitimacy invariably assumed the need for good governance. The concept of good governance called upon rulers and ministers to take account of public opinion and the people's aspirations when formulating policy. Yet unlike Britain, where the cabinet of ministers actually had to navigate a press and public that could influence decision making, in Russia the government viewed public opinion as a force to be guided and a means to affirm, not criticize, official policy. By publicizing allied decisions, Russia's diplomats hoped to counter suspicions about government intentions and mollify the public mood, which, they believed, easily could become democratic and anarchic.[9]

The right to good governance also might require the promulgation of constitutions, though references to the rights of peoples or nations did not imply popular participation in policymaking. Given that the primary purpose of the European alliance was to promote stability and ensure a durable peace, rulers and governments needed to be reconciled with their subjects. Clearly, Russia's diplomats understood the relationship between government and people as something more than simple obedience to church and monarchy. To maintain peace and security, governments had a responsibility to counter the anxiety (*inquiétude*) of peoples, procure their happiness, and augment public authority through moral force. In specific circumstances, based on practical philosophy or experience, as opposed to "beautiful theories," governments could reasonably conclude that popular reconciliation with the legitimate authority of kings and states depended on constitutions or representative bodies. In the midst of discussions about a constitution for Bavaria, which pitted the ancient privileges claimed by the king against the aspirations of recently incorporated Franconia, Count Fedor P. Pahlen, Russia's envoy in Munich, explained to co-minister of foreign affairs Nesselrode that constitutional governments were needed to stabilize Germany and reconcile various states with their new subjects, presumably due to territorial adjustments.[10]

Within the Russian Empire, the Polish Diet could be viewed as a model of moderate constitutionalism sanctioned from above. When in March 1818 Emperor Alexander spoke at the opening of the diet, he declared that liberal institutions were not subversive, as long as they were "created in good faith and steered. . . with pure intentions toward a goal that is conservative and useful for humanity." In the appropriate conditions, liberal institutions were perfectly consistent with order and led to "the true prosperity of the nations."[11] Given the absence of constitutional reform in Russia proper, such comments may seem disingenuous.[12] The Russian government never permitted full implementation of the Polish constitution, and Russia's diplomats operated under strict orders not to become embroiled in the constitutional debates of other powers, irrespective of official or personal opinions. The correct diplomatic posture, as explained in repeated communications, remained one of impartiality. The appearance of impartiality strengthened "the [alliance] system of cohesion and reciprocal trust" upon which European peace depended.[13]

References to cohesion and reciprocal trust hinted at another critical aspect of allied unity: sentiments of friendship and intimate union among the sovereigns.

From the vantage point of the twenty-first century, statements about the political efficacy of personal bonds and feelings can seem contrived and even cyn-
ical. A similar skepticism arises when historians describe social relationships
defined by the duty, obedience, and hierarchies of the patriarchal household or
by paternalistic interactions between persons in positions of authority and their
subordinates—for example, husbands and wives, parents and children, masters
and serfs, commanders and soldiers, or monarchs and subjects.[14] As citizens of
modern bureaucratic states, today's scholars are likely to dismiss the substantive
meaning of sentiment and morality in the exercise of political power.[15] Even for
those inclined to accept official pronouncements as sincere statements of intent,
one cannot help but wonder how the peacemakers imagined that the bonds of
friendship, deemed so necessary for successful diplomacy, would be perpetuated
once they passed from the scene. Perhaps because the coalitions formed to fight
the armies of revolutionary and Napoleonic France had for so long proven ineffective, and equally, because in 1813–15 allied unity finally had made victory over
Napoleon possible, the monarchs and diplomats of the Restoration era could not
imagine a peaceful Europe without direct personal relationships cemented by
the sentiment of friendship.

   The monarchies of old regime Europe all practiced some form of personalized
politics grounded in Christian morality and patriarchal family relations. In the
diplomatic discourse of the Restoration era, where the sentimentalist language of
the late Enlightenment and early Romanticism held sway, affective ties of friendship also provided the means to transcend the reality of great-power domination. The political system of restored Europe relied on the language of friendship
among the sovereigns to sustain the peacemakers' narrative of independent states
participating equally in the benefits and responsibilities of the alliance. Ties
of fraternal friendship united monarchs and promoted unanimity of purpose
among governments. Not surprisingly, policy differences arose, and divergent
interests persisted. But as Emperor Alexander I explained in a rescript of 12/24
January 1818 to Count Golovkin, recently assigned to the court of Francis I, the
count always should keep in mind the affectionate trust between the two monarchs and the unalterable reality of their personal sentiments.[16] According to the
instructions, "the principle of cohesion of the European system resides in the sentiments of fraternal friendship to which the sovereigns devoted themselves, and
in the intimacy of relations that was established between their governments."[17]

   At a moment when the Russian monarch could not help but recall the hostile
Treaty of 3 January 1815 and also suspected that Austria continued to pursue a
defensive system against Russia, the principle of friendship among the sovereigns

helped to preserve alliance unity.[18] Indeed, the general causes that guaranteed the stability of the European system found "a point of reference (*point d'appui*), a central direction in the sentiments of esteem and fraternal friendship, in the relations of intimacy that were established between the principal sovereigns of Europe, [and] between their respective governments during the memorable epoch of the years 1813, 1814, and 1815."[19] The evidence for this truth, the instructions to Golovkin declared, lay in "the experience of all the disastrous coalitions and all the illusory alliances of past times." This same truth characterized the current alliance and defined the assiduous and persistent attention that the Russian monarch brought to maintaining inviolably "the relations of mutual confidence that fortunately exist between H. I. M. and his august brothers in arms, Their Majesties the Emperor of Austria and the king of Prussia, [and] between his government and the governments of these two powers."

During the war against Napoleon, the goal of unity had been easy to achieve. The intimate and personal union of the sovereigns had presided over military operations and over the political arrangements upon which they depended. In 1813–15 there had been a clear enemy, and the universality of the danger had necessitated the fusion of military and moral forces, which alone could vanquish the hydra of revolution. But outside of combat, another "common and general interest... supported and continues to support the existing agreement (*accord*) among the sovereigns." This interest consisted of showing the states of Europe and the world the advantages of "a durable peace founded on the eternal principles of justice and legitimacy (*bon droit*)." Recognizing the egoism and diplomatic habits of some governments, as exemplified by the secret alliance against Russia (and Prussia), Emperor Alexander nonetheless looked to the friendship of the sovereigns to protect and preserve "the edifice of the universal pacification and of the general alliance" that represented its foundation.[20]

In March 1818 preparations for the meetings in Aix-la-Chapelle were underway, and Count Golovkin reported from Vienna to co-minister of foreign affairs Kapodistrias on an audience with Francis I.[21] Like Alexander, the Austrian emperor viewed tender and loyal friendship between the sovereigns as the best guarantee for the happiness of the two empires and for the conservation of the general peace. Precisely because the concert of the allies represented a political phenomenon, direct meetings between the sovereigns, during which they developed the habit of seeing one another and speaking of their common affairs, could ameliorate the consequences of different interests that might arise. The harmony of sentiments and opinions embodied in the concert could not prevent the natural influence of divergent interests or the conflicting views they produced. But the painful results of these differences could be less disruptive and disappointing. Golovkin described the allies' relationships as "a new order of things founded on mutual trust and proven habits between the sovereigns themselves." British foreign secretary Castlereagh likewise emphasized the importance and utility of personal meetings. As reported to Kapodistrias by Christoph Lieven in May 1818, Castlereagh believed that because personal relationships helped to unite the sovereigns, repeated contact would produce happy outcomes for European politics.[22]

Yet just as it appeared that the great powers had solidified alliance unity, events in Europe began to test their conception of how to preserve the peace. Political uncertainty in France and the German Confederation, and later outright revolution in Spain, Italy, Portugal, and Greece—all seemed to emanate from liberal ideas advocating the legitimacy of insurrection and the sovereignty of the people. Throughout the unfolding crises, Russia's monarch and diplomats remained convinced that the union of the powers, as stipulated in Aix-la-Chapelle, remained the only effective means to combat revolutionary agitation.[23] Just as Emperor Alexander felt "united with the sovereigns, his allies, by the ties of personal friendship and truly Christian fraternity," he also expected the same intimacy, trust, and amicable frankness to characterize relations between his representatives at foreign courts and their counterparts from other countries. Regardless of personal habits or motives, and likewise at moments when relations with colleagues became problematic, the cultivation of intimacy and friendship continued to offer the best guarantee for the peacefulness of Europe.

Before dismissing as mere rhetoric the lofty proclamations and sentimentalist language of official sources in early nineteenth-century Russia, and before describing Emperor Alexander's foreign policy as abstract, inconsistent, or utopian, the historian must ask if there could have been an alternative approach—other than through the aspirational language of Christian morality and friendship among the sovereigns—to overcome the distrust and dismay of the Napoleonic era. Was there another mechanism or principle capable of holding together the allies who had ended the war and arrived at the peace? Was there a different way to sustain the seemingly endless effort required of them as they worked to ensure the repose of Europe? In the face-to-face meetings of congresses and semi-permanent ministerial conferences, the proclaimed sentiments of friendship among the monarchs and their diplomats helped to soften the unavoidable disappointments and suspicions that arose from divergent interests, goals, and expectations. In conditions of historic upheaval and unequal power, personal bonds held out the hope of stability.

But how in practice could the friendship of the sovereigns ensure peace? For Emperor Alexander, the answer lay in the moral force codified by the Treaty of Alliance of 14/26 September 1815 (the Holy Alliance), which established the intimate union of the allies on the good faith, love, and humility required of them by the divine savior.[24] During the years of peacemaking from 1815 to 1823, the moral force of allied unity became a key concept in discussions of what it meant to act in concert (*concerter*). Russian sources identified three grounds for collective allied action: legal obligations, the authority of historical experience, and moral principles. In the meetings of Aix-la-Chapelle, Troppau, Laibach, and Verona, and in response to revolutions in Spain, Italy, and Greece, Russia's initial position and proposals invariably stressed the need for a unified allied response. Allied unity constituted the great moral force that could preserve peace, and if necessary, legitimize and guarantee success in war. From this perspective, Britain's reluctance to engage in foreign interventions not directly related to British interests did not pose a serious problem, as long as the lack of engagement did not imply the formation of separate alliances of the old type that had allowed Napoleon to subjugate Europe. As men of European society, Russia's diplomats and above all the tsar diplomat looked beyond the conflicting interests that individual states might have in specific situations to the overarching unity represented by the harmony of sentiments and agreement on eternal principles. Although governments existed under different regimes and could not always be united in their actions, moral solidarity among the great powers could be maintained. To do this, the allies needed always to show the public that there were no differences "in their fundamental principles or in their real and unanimous wishes."[25]

The moral dimension of the Vienna settlement remained critical to the foreign policy of Emperor Alexander I. Close reading of Russia's diplomatic communications reveals a conception of European restoration that implied not a return to the old regime, but rather a Europe restored to peaceful relations, reciprocal obligations, and moral integrity. In Russia proper there was no actual need for restoration—the newly constituted Kingdom of Poland occupied a special and unprecedented position within the Russian Empire. There was, however, a need for economic recovery, institutional recalibration, and moral recuperation. Russia's contribution to the process of European restoration indicated neither nostalgia for the eighteenth-century supremacy of God and monarchy nor progressive movement toward global integration and transnational governance. Rather, Alexander's conservative diplomacy focused on the construction of an enduring peace and a stable political system in Europe. An uncomfortable mélange of principle and pragmatism, the monarch's policies of moderation and moral force helped to define European diplomacy more broadly.

Even after the so-called turn to repressive conservatism in 1820–21, Emperor Alexander preferred to rely on persuasion, sentiment, and morality to combat radicalism. During the conferences in Troppau, the monarch rejected his ministers' proposal to order students from the Baltic provinces to leave German universities where they might be influenced by harmful ideas. Instead, Alexander instructed the governor-general of Riga to use friendly exhortations and moral pressure, applied on an individual basis, to persuade parents and tutors that their children or charges should either return home or transfer to less radicalized German institutions.[26] Although failure to comply might hinder the career prospects of the individuals in question, the monarch did not want to address the danger by issuing a general decree.[27] The hints of potential damage to young careers may sound more like coercion than persuasion. But when historians view political pronouncements through the lens of distinct experiences and cultures, different interpretations inevitably arise.

In early nineteenth-century Russia, the gap between liberal ideas and concrete realities was particularly striking. Emperor Alexander's domestic programs, like his foreign policy, moved uncomfortably between religious idealism, aspirational liberalism, practical possibilities, and the heavy-handed exercise of absolutist political power. The humanistic sentiments, providential beliefs, and cosmopolitan cultural habits that Alexander and his diplomatic agents brought to foreign policy resembled the concerns of enlightened reformers across Europe. Among Russian intellectuals and policymakers, this thinking also coincided with key aspects of the moderate mainstream and religious Enlightenments, particularly the blending of universalistic assumptions with principles such as equality, reason, progress, toleration, and "human flourishing."[28] One need not accept Paul Schroeder's judgments about the originality or efficacy of the Vienna settlement in order to see that like the moderate reformism of the eighteenth century, the congress system of 1815–23 established or gave modern meaning to a set of political principles that allowed change in the present without radical rejection of the past and that to this day define the practical conduct of international relations.[29]

For historians it can be difficult to reconcile Emperor Alexander's moralistic sensibilities with his stubborn and generally effective pursuit of war, peace, and Russian interests.[30] Virtually every account of the Napoleonic Wars and Vienna settlement highlights the monarch's political idealism, religious experience, emotional fervor, and flights of spiritual inspiration. Yet whatever Alexander's psychological qualities, as chronicled by scholars (and described with hints of derision by historians of Europe), they did not prevent him from making tough, intelligent, and unpopular policy choices, and equally important, from sticking to those choices during more than two decades of costly combat and exhausting diplomacy. Whatever the divinely inspired mission assigned by Alexander and others to the Holy Alliance, the idea of a political union cemented by Christian morality represented a reasonable and pragmatic perspective on the European system—one that echoed Russian literary culture, the teachings of enlightened Orthodox prelates, and the established ideology of the Russian monarchy. Put another way, the historiographical categories of modern European politics— categories such as radical, liberal, conservative, constitutional, republican, romantic, and nationalist—do not necessarily fit the Russian case or describe the thinking of the empire's diplomatic agents.

Generations of historians have recognized Russia's European identity during the Napoleonic Wars and the peacemaking that followed. Historians also have highlighted Russia's developmental and political divergence from liberal democratic Europe starting in the second quarter of the nineteenth century and continuing to the present day. Given this trajectory, it is important to focus attention on the intersection of Russian political culture and the European state system during the years of restoration. What were the priorities, characteristics, dynamics, and achievements of Russian foreign policy that made integration into European society and the international order so meaningful? It is clear from Russian sources devoted to war and peace in the first quarter of the nineteenth century that Emperor Alexander and his associates believed in the reality of a European political system and viewed Russia as a full-fledged member of that system. So how and why did Russia end up on the intellectual and psychological periphery of European politics? Is this something that happened later in the nineteenth century, perhaps because of Slavophilism (a form of romantic nationalism), church retrenchment, Eurasianist political thought, or economic development? Or is it simply a conceptual or ideological product of the Bolshevik Revolution and Cold War?

Many unanswered questions remain, and many more will arise, as historians working in the relatively free conditions of post-Soviet Russia rewrite their country's history. At this juncture, study of Alexander I's European diplomacy illuminates a critical dynamic in the political culture of the nineteenth-century Russian Empire. From the perspective of the Russian monarchy and loyal service classes, the French Revolution and Napoleonic Wars had little impact on fundamental religious and political institutions. Notwithstanding the devastation and trauma of 1812 and the subsequent wars of liberation, the Romanov tsardom and Russian Orthodox Church emerged from the period of crisis as strong and legitimate as ever. Not only did Napoleon's invasion fail to unleash popular revolt or widespread support for political change, Russia's conscript army of legally "emancipated" serfs and state peasants, a creation of the Petrine reforms, prevailed over France's dynamic citizen army. The strength and stability of Russia's institutions during a quarter century of revolution and war reinforced, and justified, longstanding practices of enlightened reform combined with moderate censorship and severe punishment of rebellion against legitimate monarchical, hierarchical, and religious authority.

Put another way, the years of peacemaking that followed the victory over Napoleon strengthened the Russian monarchy's legal-administrative approach to social progress and political change. As the great powers and their allies responded to revolutions in Spanish America, Spain, Italy, Portugal, and Greece, they articulated a definite distinction between old and modern institutions. But tellingly, they did not bemoan change by equating modern development with revolution. To the contrary, revolution threatened "with total ruin the existence of all the States and all the institutions, old as well as modern."[31] In other words, political change could be legitimate and might even be encouraged, as long as it did not come about through revolutionary or other violent means.[32] When revolution did occur, Russia's policymakers invariably hoped for reconciliation between legitimate (that is, legal and lawful) governments and their rebellious subjects.

The Decembrist Rebellion of 1825 is usually described as Russia's earliest experience of a modern insurrection that sought to transform social and political arrangements. But like Napoleon, the elite military officers at the center of the rebellion also failed to ignite a popular response. Eighteenth-century practices of reform and repression clearly had begun to falter, yet in the Russian setting, this shift occurred in conjunction with the emergence of romantic nationalism and proto-Slavophilism. In official and societal forms, the nationalist orientation insisted on the special world historical mission of the Russian people and on the nation's unique qualities, all understood in contradistinction to political and socioeconomic development in Western and Central Europe.[33] Despite the realization that revolution could not be totally prevented, the belief in Russian exceptionalism strengthened the old regime commitment to enlightened reform from above.[34] After decades of revolution and war, post-Napoleonic Russian diplomacy helped to perpetuate this powerful eighteenth-century tradition.

The appendix is limited to the diplomats mentioned in this book. Sources: *Ocherki istorii Ministerstva inostrannykh del Rossii. 1802–2002. Volume 3: Biografii ministrov inostrannykh del. 1802–2002* (Moscow: Olma-Press, 2002); *Diplomaticheskii slovar'*, 3 vols. (Moscow: Nauka, 1984–86); Ministerstvo inostrannykh del SSSR, *Vneshniaia politika Rossii XIX i nachala XX veka. Dokumenty Rossiiskogo ministerstva inostrannykh del*, volumes 6–12 (Moscow: Gosudarstvennoe izdatel'stvo politicheskoi literatury, Izdatel'stvo "Nauka," 1960–95); *Russkii biograficheskii slovar'*, 25 vols. (Saint Petersburg: I. N. Skorokhodov, 1896–1918).

Alopeus, Count David Maksimovich (1769–1831)

The son of a diplomat from the nobility of Finland, Alopeus was born in Berlin and educated in the Stuttgart Military School. In 1789 Alopeus began service in the Russian Ministry of Foreign Affairs as a secretary in the Stockholm mission. In 1801 he became chargé d'affaires (*poverennyi v delakh*) in the mission and in 1803 envoy extraordinaire (*chrezvychainyi poslannik*) and minister plenipotentiary (*polnomochnyi ministr*) at the Swedish court. Alopeus's diplomatic service was interrupted by the Russian occupation of Finland in 1808 and by the subsequent replacement of the Swedish king with a regency in 1809. Alopeus participated in the negotiations leading to the Treaty of 5 September 1809 by which Sweden ceded Finland to Russia and joined the Continental System. An appointment as envoy in Naples never materialized, and in 1811 Alopeus became envoy (*poslannik*) in Württemberg. From 1813 he served as envoy extraordinaire and minister plenipotentiary to the king of Prussia, an assignment delayed by the military campaigns of 1813–14. After Napoleon's second defeat Alopeus became envoy in Berlin where he served from 1815 until his death in 1831. In 1820 Alexander I made Alopeus a count of the Polish Kingdom, and in February 1825 the diplomat concluded a trade agreement with Prussia, following years of discussion about trade and borders between Prussia and Poland.

Anstett, Baron Ivan Osipovich (1770–1835)

Anstett entered Russian service from French service in 1789, served in the cavalry with the rank of lieutenant (*poruchik*), and saw action in the war against Sweden (1788–90). In April 1791 he was appointed to the College of Foreign Affairs with the rank of collegial assessor. In 1794 he participated in the negotiations that brought Prussia into the coalition against France. During the Polish campaign, he served in the suite of the Prussian king and then participated in the negotiations leading to the third partition of Poland. In 1801 Anstett served as councilor (*sovetnik*) in the Vienna Embassy and in 1803–4 as chargé d'affaires. In 1809–13 Anstett performed diplomatic duties arising from relations with Austria, dissolution of the Confederation of the Rhine, organization of the coalition against France, and the supply of allied armies. Anstett served in the suite of Alexander I in Paris and in 1815 became envoy extraordinaire and minister plenipotentiary in Frankfurt-on-Main, attached to the Diet of the German Confederation. From 1825/1826, Anstett served simultaneously in Stuttgart and from 1829 also in Hessen-Kassel.

Benkendorff, Major-General Konstantin Khristoforovich (1785–1828)

At age thirteen, Benkendorff became a junker in the College of Foreign Affairs, and from 1803 he served at embassies in Berlin and other German cities, followed by service as secretary in Naples. In 1812 he returned to Russia and entered military service. In 1816 illness temporarily ended Benkendorff's military career, and in 1820–26 he served as envoy extraordinaire at the courts of Württemberg and Baden. Benkendorff returned to active military service in the war with Persia (1826–28); he died in the Russian-Ottoman War that began in 1828.

Bulgari, Count Mark Nikolaevich (1788–1829)

From 1818 Bulgari served as a civil servant (*chinovnik*) and from 1819 as chargé d'affaires at the mission in Madrid.

Czartoryski, Prince Adam Ezhi (1770–1861)

Of Polish princely origins, Czartoryski entered Russian service in 1795 and by 1799 had been appointed envoy to the Kingdom of Sardinia. From 1802 he served as assistant minister of foreign affairs and in 1804–6 as minister of foreign affairs. In 1805 Czartoryski put forward a project to restore the Polish state within the borders of 1772 by means of a dynastic union with Russia. This led in 1815–16 to service in the provisional government of the Polish Kingdom and to support for incorporating Lithuania, Belarus, and Right-Bank Ukraine into the kingdom. During the rebellion of 1830–31, Czartoryski served as minister of foreign affairs in the government established by the diet. After Russia suppressed the rebellion, he emigrated to Paris.

Dolgorukii, Prince Dmitrii Ivanovich (end c. 18–1867)

The grandson of Princess Natali'a Borisovna, Dolgorukii served in the Moscow provincial administration from 1816. After entering diplomatic service, he served as secretary at the Russian missions in Constantinople, Rome, Madrid, London, The Hague, and Naples. In The Hague and Naples, Dolgorukii also served as chargé d'affaires. In 1848–54 Dolgorukii was minister plenipotentiary at the court of Persia and from 1854 a member of the Senate.

Golovkin (Golowkin), Count Iurii Aleksandrovich (1768–1846)

In 1805–6 Golovkin headed an embassy (*posol'stvo*) to China that failed to gain entry into Beijing. In 1813–18 he served as envoy in Stuttgart; in 1818–22 he performed a special mission in Vienna and then became envoy to Austria.

Italinskii, Andrei Iakovlevich (1743–1827)

Born into the lesser (*nebogatyi*) Ukrainian nobility, Italinskii graduated from the Kiev Theological Academy (*Kievskaia dukhovnaia akademiia*) and went on to study medicine in Saint Petersburg, Edinburgh, and London. His diplomatic career began in 1781 as secretary at the mission in Naples, where he also served as chargé d'affaires and envoy. In 1802–6 and 1812–16, Italinskii was envoy in Constantinople, and in 1817–27, envoy in Rome.

Kapodistrias, Count Ioannis Antonovich (1776–1831)

Born into the Greek aristocracy of Corfu, Kapodistrias studied medicine, political science, and philosophy at the University of Padua. In 1802 he was appointed state secretary for foreign affairs in the Republic of the Seven United Islands, then under Russian protection. By the Treaty of Tilsit (1807), the republic became a French protectorate and Kapodistrias entered Russian service. In 1815 he became state secretary of foreign affairs and from 1816 co-headed the Ministry of Foreign Affairs with Count Karl Nesselrode. Kapodistrias repeatedly accompanied Alexander I on trips in Russia and abroad, including the Congresses of Aix-la-Chapelle, Troppau, and Laibach. During the revolutions of 1820–21 Kapodistrias preferred moral action over armed intervention, but he continued to look to Russia to support full independence for Greece, including the possibility of military support independently of the European alliance. In May 1822 Kapodistrias left Russian service on indefinite leave, and in July 1827 he retired. In April 1827 the national assembly of Greece meeting in Trizin elected him president, and on 27 September 1831 he was assassinated.

Khanykov (Canicoff), Vasilii Vasil'evich (1759–1829)

From 1815 to 1829, Khanykov served as envoy in Saxony, Dresden, Hanover, Hessen-Kassel, Weimar, Mecklenburg, Oldenburg, and Saxony-Weimar.

Kozlovskii, Prince Petr Borisovich (1783–1840)

In 1812–18 Kozlovskii served as envoy to the Kingdom of Sardinia and in 1818–20 in Württemberg and Baden. From 1820 he was assigned to the Ministry of Foreign Affairs and from 1827 he was in retirement.

Liven (Lieven), Prince Khristofor (Christoph) Andreeevich (1774–1839)

Lieven began service in the Ministry of Foreign Affairs in 1808, and in 1809–12 served as envoy extraordinaire and minister plenipotentiary in Berlin. In 1822 Lieven represented Russia as a plenipotentiary at the Congress of Verona, and in 1812–34 he served as ambassador (*posol*) in London. From 1834 he served as guardian (*popechitel'*) to the future Alexander II.

Mochenigo (Mocenigo), Count Georgii Dmitrievich (1764–1839)

In January 1811, Mochenigo was appointed envoy in Turin, but he travelled only as far as Vienna, where he remained in 1811–12. In September 1812, he was appointed envoy in Naples, arriving there only in June 1815. In 1815–27, Mochenigo served as envoy in Naples, from 1818 simultaneously in Turin, and from 1823 simultaneously in Parma, Plaisance, and Guastalla. He retired in 1827.

Nesselrode, Count Karl (Karl Robert) Vasil'evich (1780–1862)

Born in Lisbon where his father served as Russian envoy, Nesselrode was the son of a Lutheran mother from a rich merchant family and a Catholic father from an old family of German counts. He himself was baptized in the Anglican Church and completed gymnasium in Berlin. In 1788 Nesselrode's father enrolled him in Russian naval service from which he retired in 1799. After beginning diplomatic service in 1801, Nesselrode worked at the missions in Berlin and Paris. In 1812–14 he was attached to the army where he performed diplomatic tasks such as service in the entourage of Alexander I during the campaigns of 1813–14. In 1814 Nesselrode became a civil servant (*dokladchik*) in the Department of Foreign Affairs, and from 9 August 1816 until 15 April 1856, he directed the Ministry of Foreign Affairs. Nesselrode participated in the Vienna, Aix-la-Chapelle,

Troppau, Laibach, and Verona congresses. He retired soon after the conclusion of the Paris Peace Treaty of 18 March 1856 that ended the Crimean War.

Nikolai (Nicolay), Baron Pavel Andreevich (1777–1866)

Nikolai's father was president of the Academy of Sciences and at age eight he was sent to study at Eton. Subsequently, he completed studies at Erlangen University and in 1796 began service in the chancery of the Ministry of Foreign Affairs. Appointed in January 1800 to the Russian mission in London, Nikolai served there as a civil servant (*chinovnik*), secretary, chargé d'affaires, and councilor. In 1808 he returned to the Ministry of Foreign Affairs, and from February 1810 worked on the survey of the Russian-Swedish border as a commissar plenipotentiary. In 1811 Nikolai became councilor at the embassy in Stockholm, and from August 1812 he served as councilor and then chargé d'affaires at the embassy in London. From May 1816 until April 1847, Nikolai served as minister plenipotentiary in Copenhagen. In 1828 he became a baron of the Grand Duchy of Finland, where he spent his retirement on a family estate.

Novosil'tsev, Nikolai Nikolaevich (1761–1838)

One of Alexander I's "young friends" and member of the Unofficial Committee, Novosil'tsev served as vice president of the Supreme Provisional Council for the Administration of the Grand Duchy of Warsaw in 1813–15, Russian commissar attached to the Governing Council of the Kingdom of Poland in 1815–31, and chairman (*predsedatel'*) of the State Council and Committee of Ministers in 1832–36.

Obreskov (Obrescoff), Aleksandr Mikhailovich (1793–1885)

Obreskov began service in 1804 as a junker in the College of Foreign Affairs. He served at the Stuttgart mission from 1811, followed by service in Constantinople from 1813. In 1815 Obreskov became secretary of the mission in Tuscany, which in 1817 merged with the mission in Rome. In 1817–18 Obreskov served as secretary at the mission in Rome, and in 1818 he was sent to Vienna. In 1820–25 he served as councilor (*sovetnik*) at the mission in Vienna, an assignment that included service as chargé d'affaires at the Austrian court in September–November 1822. In 1825 Obreskov served in Mecklenberg-Schwerin and Anhalt-Zerbst, followed from 1826 by work on Ottoman affairs in Saint Petersburg. In 1827 he became a diplomatic agent attached to troops fighting against Persia, and in 1828, as second plenipotentiary (*upolnomochennyi*), he participated in peace negotiations with Persia culminating in the Treaty of Turkmanchai. This led to appointment as envoy extraordinaire and minister plenipotentiary in Stuttgart in 1828–31, followed by appointment to the same position in Turin from December 1831 to April 1838. Obreskov ended his service career as a senator in 1838–40 and lived for many years in retirement.

Palen (Pahlen), Count Fedor Petrovich (1780–1863)

Palen received a home education and at age fourteen entered service in the Cavalry Guards Regiment. Soon after, he began to prepare for a diplomatic career in Sweden, Paris, and London. In 1810–11 Palen served as envoy in Washington, in 1812–14 as envoy at the Portuguese court in Rio de Janeiro, and in 1815–22 as envoy in Munich. He also served as governor-general of New Russia and helped to negotiate the Peace of Adrianople. From 1832 until his death, Palen was a member of the State Council, where he played an active role in preparing the 1861 emancipation of the serfs.

Pini, Aleksandr Aleksandrovich (1756–?)

In 1812–17 Pini served as general consul in Jassy and in 1817–22 as general consul in Bucharest. From 1822 he was in retirement.

Poletika, Petr Ivanovich (1778–1849)

Born in Kiev province, Poletika was the son of a Ukrainian nobleman and a Turkish mother captured in the siege of Ochakov. From age four Poletika attended the Noble Land Cadet Corps and in November 1796 joined the suite of Emperor Paul with the rank of lieutenant. In February 1798 Poletika became a translator in the College of Foreign Affairs, and from 1799 he worked as a chancery official under vice chancellor Count V. P. Kochubei. In November 1801 Poletika began service in the chancery of the Stockholm mission and in 1803 returned to Saint Petersburg, where he conducted diplomatic correspondence under A. R. Vorontsov. Poletika continued these duties under D. P. Tatishchev in Saint Petersburg and Naples, and then in 1805–8 under various military commanders in the field. He returned to Russia in 1808, an assignment followed by service as councilor at the embassy in Finland (from April 1809), Rio de Janeiro (from June 1811), and Madrid (from February 1812). In 1814 Poletika returned to the work of diplomatic correspondence under Field Marshal Barclay de Tolly. From January 1816 he served as councilor at the embassy in London and from November 1817 as envoy extraordinaire and minister plenipotentiary in Philadelphia. In 1822 he returned to Saint Petersburg, and in 1824–25 he participated in trade negotiations with the United States and Britain. From 1825, as privy councilor and senator, Poletika carried out a range of diplomatic and administrative assignments, retiring in 1842.

Pozzo di Borgo, Count Karl (Charles André) Osipovich (1768–1842)

In 1789–91 Pozzo di Borgo served as Corsican representative to the French Constituent Assembly, and in 1796 he (and other royalists) emigrated from France. In 1805 Pozzo di Borgo entered Russian service and performed diplomatic tasks in Vienna, Naples, and Constantinople. After the Peace of Tilsit, he retired and left Russia. In 1812 Pozzo di Borgo returned to Russian service, and in 1814 became minister plenipotentiary and then from 1821 ambassador in Paris. Pozzo di Borgo also served as a Russian plenipotentiary at the Congresses of Vienna, Aix-la-Chapelle, Troppau, Laibach, and Verona. In 1835–39 he served as Russia's ambassador in Britain, retiring in 1839.

Razumovskii, Prince Andrei Kirillovich (1752–1836)

In 1777 Razumovskii began diplomatic service as envoy extraordinaire and minister plenipotentiary in Venice, followed in 1778–84 by service in Naples. From 1784 he served in Denmark and from 1786 in Sweden. Recalled to Russia in 1799, Razumovskii became ambassador to Austria in 1801. In 1807 Razumovskii retired but continued to undertake diplomatic missions for Alexander I. For example, Razumovskii participated in the Congress of Vienna, and as Russia's first plenipotentiary, he signed the Paris peace treaties of 1814 and 1815.

Stackelberg (Shtakel'berg), Count Gustav Ottonovich (1787–1850)

In 1810–18 (with an interruption in 1812–13), Stackelberg served as envoy in Vienna. In 1818–20 and 1822–35, he served as envoy in Naples, retiring in 1835.

Stroganov, Baron Grigorii Aleksandrovich (1770–1857)

A count from 1826, Stroganov was born into an aristocratic Orthodox family of ennobled merchants from the Urals. He received a liberal education at home and on tour in Europe (1787). Stroganov began diplomatic service in November 1804, and from April 1805 until February 1810, he served as minister plenipotentiary in Spain. In September 1812 he was appointed envoy extraordinaire and minister plenipotentiary in Sweden, and from 1816 he held the same position in the Ottoman Empire. He remained in Constantinople until the break in diplomatic relations in July 1821. In October 1827 Stroganov became a member of the State Council.

Struve, Genrikh Antonovich (1770–1850)

From 1815 Struve served as chargé d'affaires in Hamburg and from 1820 as resident minister in Hamburg. From 1827 he simultaneously served as resident minister in Lübeck and Bremen; from 1829, as resident minister in Oldenburg; and from 1843, as envoy in Oldenburg.

Sturdza (Stourdza), Aleksandr Skarlatovich (1791–1854)

Known for his romantic nationalist and proto-Slavophile ideas, Sturdza served as a civil servant (*chinovnik*) in the Ministry of Foreign Affairs from 1809. He participated in the Congresses of Vienna and Aix-la-Chapelle and in 1816 became a civil servant in the Ministry of Spiritual Affairs and Popular Enlightenment. He retired from service in 1819.

Tatishchev, Dmitrii Pavlovich (1767–1845)

Tatishchev began service in 1782 in the Preobrazhenskii Guards Regiment. In June 1799 he transferred to civil service in the College of Foreign Affairs. In 1802–3 and 1805–8, Tatishchev served as minister plenipotentiary in the Kingdom of the Two Sicilies; in 1804–5 he helped to negotiate and then signed the anti-French coalition agreement between Russia and Austria (Third Coalition). From September 1810 Tatishchev served as a senator, and in 1812 he was appointed envoy extraordinaire and minister plenipotentiary in Spain, arriving in Madrid in 1814. From 1815 until 1821 (de facto 1819) he served as envoy in Madrid. From July 1821 he served as envoy extraordinaire and minister plenipotentiary in the Netherlands, including envoy in The Hague in 1821–22. In February and May 1822 Tatishchev undertook special missions in Vienna; he participated in the Congress of Verona (1822) as Russia's third plenipotentiary; and from August 1823 he returned to special mission at the court of Austria. From August 1826 until September 1841, he served as ambassador extraordinaire and plenipotentiary in Austria.

Introduction: Russia as a Great Power in Europe

1. For English-language coverage of the debates on Peter, see Paul Bushkovitch, *Peter the Great*, 2d ed. (Lanham, MD: Rowman and Littlefield, 2016); James Cracraft, *Revolution of Peter the Great* (Cambridge, MA: Harvard University Press, 2006); Lindsey Hughes, *Russia in the Age of Peter the Great* (New Haven, CT: Yale University Press, 2000).

2. David A. Bell, *The First Total War* (New York: Houghton Mifflin Harcourt, 2007), 1–17.

3. For synthesis of the research on social categories and service obligations, see Elise Kimerling Wirtschafter, *Social Identity in Imperial Russia* (DeKalb: Northern Illinois University Press, 1997).

4. Elise Kimerling Wirtschafter, "Military Service and the Russian Social Order," in *Fighting for a Living: A Comparative History of Military Labour 1500–2000*, ed. Erik-Jan Zürcher (Amsterdam: University of Amsterdam Press, 2013), 394–95; William C. Fuller, Jr., *Strategy and Power in Russia, 1600–1914* (New York: The Free Press, 1992), 45–46; Janet M. Hartley, *Russia, 1762–1825: Military Power, the State, and the People* (Westport, CT: Praeger, 2008), 8–11; Elise Kimerling Wirtschafter, *From Serf to Russian Soldier* (Princeton, NJ: Princeton University Press, 1990), 3.

5. According to information from 1827, in the central Russian province of Tver, a peacetime regiment could march 100 to 110 versts (1 *versta* = 1.06 kilometers) in six to eight days. Wirtschafter, *Russian Soldier*, 81.

6. Quoted in Wirtschafter, *Russian Soldier*, 72.

7. Dominic Lieven, *Russia against Napoleon: The True Story of the Campaigns of* War and Peace (New York: Penguin Books, 2009).

8. On Russia's peacetime army, see Wirtschafter, *Russian Soldier*. For broad treatment, see John L. H. Keep, *Soldiers of the Tsar: Army and Society in Russia, 1462–1874* (New York: Oxford University Press, 1985).

9. The discussion of Russian military history and empire building draws from my earlier works cited above and from Elise Kimerling Wirtschafter, *Russia's Age of Serfdom 1649–1861* (Malden, MA: Blackwell Publishing, 2008).

10. Fuller, *Strategy and Power*, 1–21; J. T. Kotilaine, "Opening a Window on Europe: Foreign Trade and Military Conquest on Russia's Western Border in the Seventeenth Century," *Jahrbücher für Geschichte Osteuropas* 46 (1998): 494–530.

11. Fuller, *Strategy and Power*, 14–34.

12. Fuller, *Strategy and Power*, 37–44; Hughes, *Peter the Great*, 92–98, 174–76.

13. Fuller, *Strategy and Power*, 34, 38–84.

14. Wirtschafter, *Age of Serfdom*, 108–9.

15. On relations with the steppe peoples, see Andreas Kappeler, *The Russian Empire: A Multiethnic History*, trans. Alfred Clayton (Harlow, Eng.: Pearson, 2001); Michael Khodarkovsky, *Russia's Steppe Frontier: The Making of a Colonial Empire, 1500–1800* (Bloomington: Indiana University Press, 2002); Willard Sunderland, *Taming the Wild Field: Colonization and Empire on the Russian Steppe* (Ithaca, NY: Cornell University Press, 2004).

16. John P. LeDonne, *The Grand Strategy of the Russian Empire, 1650–1831* (New York: Oxford University Press, 2004), 9–11; Sunderland, *Wild Field*, 3–5.

17. Wirtschafter, *Age of Serfdom*, 109–13.

18. LeDonne, *Grand Strategy*, 89.

19. Wirtschafter, *Age of Serfdom*, 129–30.

20. The discussion of Russia's internal political situation uses Old Style dating.

21. Wirtschafter, *Age of Serfdom*, 130–32, 200–3.

22. Discussion of the wars against revolutionary and Napoleonic France uses New Style dating. The account of the wars provided here relies on: Fuller, *Strategy and Power*, 177–218; Janet M. Hartley, *Alexander I* (New York: Longman, 1994); Paul W. Schroeder, *The Transformation of European Politics 1763–1848* (New York: Oxford University Press, 1994), 177–582; Lieven, *Russia against Napoleon*; Oleg Airapetov, *Istoriia vneshnei politiki Rossiiskoi imperii. 1801–1914. Vol. 1: Vneshniaia politika Imperatora Aleksandra I, 1802–1825* (Moscow: Kuchkovo pole, 2017).

23. In October 1799, a British-Russian expedition to liberate Holland failed. The French had taken the Ionian Islands in 1797.

24. For recent appraisal of Tilsit from the Russian side, see Claus Scharf, "The Power of the Weak Opponent: The Diplomacy of Alexander I in Tilsit," *Journal of Modern Russian History and Historiography* 12 (2019): 209–23.

25. Quoted in Scharf, "Weak Opponent," 223.

26. Scharf, "Weak Opponent," 223.

27. Scharf, "Weak Opponent," 222.

28. The partitions of Poland are often depicted as the crowning achievement of Catherine II's foreign policy, yet historians past and present question the efficacy of the empress's success. The late Isabel de Madariaga argued that Catherine's conquests not only endangered Russian security in the west but also required that future actions consider the balance of interests among the three partitioning powers (Austria, Prussia, and Russia). More broadly, Alexander Kamenskii concludes that "none of the initial goals of her [Catherine's] foreign policy that she herself had put forward had in fact been accomplished." Alexander Kamenskii, "Catherine the Great's Foreign Policy Reconsidered," *Journal of Modern Russian History and Historiography* 12 (2019): 169–87, quote on 186.

29. Fuller, *Strategy and Power*, 186–90.

30. For detailed treatment, see Lieven, *Russia against Napoleon*, 138–241.

31. Fuller, *Strategy and Power*, 190. Janet Hartley gives similar numbers: 50,000 Russian and 40,000 French casualties. Hartley, *Alexander I*, 115.

32. Lieven, *Russia against Napoleon*, 257–58.

33. Lieven, *Russia against Napoleon*, 264–65.

34. Fuller, *Strategy and Power*, 191–93.

35. Quoted in Lieven, *Russia against Napoleon*, 240.

36. *Imperator Aleksandr I i Frederik-Sezar Lagarp. Pis'ma. Dokumenty*, ed. A. Iu. Andreev and D. Tozato-Rigo, trans. V. A. Mil'china, 3 vols. (Moscow: Politicheskaia entsiklopediia, 2014–17).

37. See the appendix.

Chapter 1: Pacification and Peace (1815–17)

1. The historiographic discussion contained herein is far from exhaustive.

2. The terminology of old regime and new regime is familiar from the historiography of modern France, particularly that of the French Revolution and Napoleonic era. See Isser Woloch, *The New Regime: Transformations of the French Civic Order, 1789–1820s* (New York: Norton, 1994); Eugen Weber, *Peasants into Frenchmen: The Modernization of Rural France, 1870–1914* (Stanford, CA: Stanford University Press, 1976). See also Ambrogio A. Caiani, "Re-inventing the *Ancien Régime* in Post-Napoleonic Europe," *European History Quarterly* 47, no. 3 (2017): 437–60.

3. David A. Bell, *The First Total War: Napoleon's Europe and the Birth of Warfare as We Know It* (Boston: Houghton Mifflin Harcourt, 2007); Paul W. Schroeder, *The Transformation of European Politics 1763–1848* (New York: Oxford University Press, 1994); Marie-Pierre Rey, *Alexander I: The Tsar Who Defeated Napoleon*, trans. Susan Emanuel (DeKalb: Northern Illinois University Press, 2012).

4. Schroeder, *Transformation*. See also Mark Mazower, *Governing the World: The History of an Idea, 1815 to the Present* (New York: Penguin Books, 2012); Jennifer Mitzen, *Power in Concert: The Nineteenth-Century Origins of Global Governance* (Chicago: University of Chicago Press, 2013). For defense of the balance of power concept, see Wolf D. Gruner, "The Vienna System: Reconstruction of Europe beyond Power Politics, 1812–1820: Reflections on New Approaches to the History of International Relations," in *The Transformation of European Politics, 1763–1848: Episode or Model in Modern History?*, ed. Peter Krüger and Paul Schroeder (New York: Palgrave Macmillan, 2002), 165–85.

5. V. M. Bezotosnyi, *Rossiia v napoleonovskikh voinakh 1805–1815* (Moscow: ROSSPEN, 2014), 557–61; Stella Ghervas, "Balance of Power vs. Perpetual Peace: Paradigms of European Order from Utrecht to Vienna, 1713–1815," *The International History Review* (2016), https://doi.org/10.1080/07075332.2016.1214613; O. V. Orlik, *Rossiia v mezhdunarodnykh otnosheniiakh 1815–1829: Ot Venskogo kongressa do Adrianopol'skogo mira* (Moscow: Nauka, 1998), 11–22; Mark Jarrett, *The Congress of Vienna and Its Legacy: War and Great Power Diplomacy after Napoleon* (New York: I. B. Tauris, 2014), chap. 8; Mitzen, *Power in Concert*, 4–5.

6. See the collection of articles titled "'1815': The Power of Balance," *Journal of Modern European History* 13, no. 4 (2015): 427–74, with contributions by Mark Jarrett, Eckart Conze, Beatrice de Graaf, Stella Ghervas, and Matthias Schulz. The phrases quoted here are found on 436–37, 465, 472.

7. Adam Zamoyski, *Rites of Peace: The Fall of Napoleon and the Congress of Vienna* (New York: Harper Perennial, 2007). On the domination of the great powers over small nations, see also Adrian Brisku, "The Holy Alliance as 'An Order of Things Conformable to the Interests of Europe and to the Laws of Religion and Humanity,'" in *Paradoxes of Peace in Nineteenth-Century Europe*, ed. Thomas Hippler and Miloš Vec (New York: Oxford University Press, 2015), 153–69. Referring to the Holy Alliance, Brisku writes: "From a Russian imperial historical perspective, Alexander I was reinvigorating a doctrine in foreign policy established by Peter the Great: namely, dominating through the 'protection' of neighbors." More generally, "the Vienna Congress post-war settlement was for a lasting peace deal between the great powers whose interests took precedence over any smaller nation" (162).

8. On the ability of small states to influence events, see Beatrice de Graaf, "Second-Tier Diplomacy: Hans von Gagern and William I in Their Quest for an Alternative European Order, 1813–1818," *Journal of Modern European History* 12, no. 4 (2014): 546–66.

9. G. John Ikenberry, *After Victory: Institutions, Strategic Restraint, and the Rebuilding of Order after Major Wars* (Princeton, NJ: Princeton University Press, 2001), x–xiii, 80–116. On the Vienna system as a "security regime," see Robert Jervis, "A Political Science Perspective on the Balance of Power and the Concert," *American Historical Review* 97, no. 3 (June 1992): 716–24. On "security culture" as an emotional concept, see Beatrice de Graaf, "Bringing Sense and Sensibility to the Continent: Vienna 1815 Revisited," in "'1815': The Power of Balance," *Journal of Modern European History* 13, no. 4 (2015): 447–57.

10. Ikenberry attributes the idea of continuing the alliance to British diplomacy, strategic constraint, and the commitment to allied unity. For him British foreign secretary Castlereagh is the hero of the Vienna settlement, whereas Alexander is the autocratic author of an inconsistent foreign policy. In reality, the achievements and aspirations that Ikenberry attributes to British policy and constitutionalism belonged equally to Russian diplomacy. Ikenberry's statement: "The autocratic and fickle character of the Russian state, as embodied in its leader, doomed the creation of a stronger institutional settlement" (112), is particularly dismissive and stereotypical. Ikenberry, *After Victory*, 90–98, 109–16. Henry Kissinger's classic study likewise gives center stage to Castlereagh and Austrian foreign minister Clemens von Metternich. See Henry A. Kissinger, *A World Restored: Metternich, Castlereagh and the Problems of Peace, 1812–1822* (Boston: Houghton Mifflin Company, 1957). See also, Henry Kissinger, "The Congress of Vienna: A Reappraisal," *World Politics* 8, no. 2 (1956): 264–80. On the coalition politics of 1813–14, see Dominic Lieven, *Russia against Napoleon: The True Story of the Campaigns of War and Peace* (New York: Penguin Books, 2009).

11. Ikenberry, *After Victory*, 105–8. Paul Schroeder's views have evolved and moderated over time; however, his remains the strongest voice arguing that the concept of balance of power does not apply to the Vienna settlement. Instead, he argues that the

settlement established two hegemonic powers or superpowers, Britain and Russia, and three lesser powers—Austria, France, and Prussia—that potentially could exercise hegemonic power in limited regional contexts. See Schroeder, *Transformation*, 575–82. On the evolution of Schroeder's interpretation, see Gruner, "The Vienna System."

12. Ikenberry, *After Victory*, 83. The best English-language account of Russian foreign policy in this era remains Patricia Grimsted, *The Foreign Ministers of Alexander I: Political Attitudes and the Conduct of Russian Diplomacy, 1801–1825* (Berkeley: University of California Press, 1969).

13. Niall Ferguson, "The Meaning of Kissinger: A Realist Reconsidered," *Foreign Affairs* 94, no. 5 (September/October 2015): 134–43.

14. The structural approach is advocated in Gruner, "The Vienna System."

15. Ghervas, "Balance of Power vs. Perpetual Peace"; Bell, *Total War*, 52–119; Eliana Augusti, "Peace by Code: Milestones and Crossroads in the Codification of International Law," in Hippler and Vec, *Paradoxes of Peace*, 41–43. On the idea of perpetual peace in Russia, see Orlik, *Rossiia v mezhdunarodnykh otnosheniiakh*, 13–15; A. A. Orlov, "Vospriiatie v Rossii nachala XIX veka idei 'vechnogo mira' (na primere 'Rassuzhdeniia o mire i voine' V. F. Malinovskogo," in *Epokha 1812 goda: Issledovaniia. Istochniki. Istoriografiia, XIII. Sbornik materialov. K 200-letiiu Venskogo kongressa*, ed. V. M Bezotosnyi (Moscow: Kuchkovo pole, 2015), 13: 439–54.

16. These negotiations led to the Third Coalition of 1805. Grimsted, *Foreign Ministers*, 104–50. On Emperor Paul, see Hugh Ragsdale, "Russian Foreign Policy, 1763–1815: Does It Exemplify Paul Schroeder's Theses?," in Krüger and Schroeder, *Transformation*, 129–51. Patricia Kennedy Grimsted, "Czartoryski's System for Russian Foreign Policy, 1803: A Memorandum, Edited with Introduction and Analysis," *California Slavic Studies* 5 (1970): 19–91.

17. Philipp Menger, *Die Heilige Allianz: Religion und Politik bei Alexander I. (1801–1825)* (Stuttgart: Steiner, 2014), 118–31; Rey, *Alexander I*, 151–56; Schroeder, *Transformation*, 249–64.

18. Robert Stewart, Second Marquis of Londonderry, Viscount Castlereagh (1769–1822); William Cathcart (1755–1843).

19. C. K. Webster, ed., *British Diplomacy 1813–1815: Select Documents Dealing with the Reconstruction of Europe* (London: G. Bell and Sons, 1921), 1, 389–94.

20. The Novosil'tsev mission led to the British-Russian Convention of 11 April 1805, which called for Russian and Austrian troops, British subsidies and participation in the war with naval and land forces, the return of France to its ancient prerevolutionary frontiers, restoration of the independence of states occupied by France, and territorial compensation for Austria and Prussia. In Schroeder's analysis, the alliance envisioned a blocking coalition against France, a balance of power between the German powers, a barrier system against France for Britain, and protectorates over Germany and Italy for Russia. Schroeder, *Transformation*, 262–76. Orlov, "Vospriiatie," 452. On the Novosil'tsev mission, see also O. V. Orlik, ed., *Istoriia vneshnei politiki Rossii: Pervaia polovina XIX veka (Ot voin Rossii protiv Napoleona do Parizhskogo mira 1856 g.)* (Moscow: Mezhdunarodnye otnosheniia, 1995), 50.

21. For recent studies of the Congress of Vienna, see Brian E. Vick, *The Congress of Vienna: Power and Politics after Napoleon* (Cambridge, MA: Harvard University Press, 2014); Thierry Lentz, *Le congrès de Vienne: Une refondation de l'Europe 1814–1815* (Paris: Perrin, 2013).

22. For Castlereagh's project, see Webster, *British Diplomacy*, 19–33. The treaty was signed on the night of 9–10 March but backdated to 1 March (NS). For the text of the treaty, see Ministerstvo inostrannykh del SSSR, *Vneshniaia politika Rossii XIX i nachala XX veka: Dokumenty Rossiiskogo ministerstva inostrannykh del*, first and second series, vols. 6–12 (Moscow: Gosudarstvennoe izdatel'stvo politicheskoi literatury, Izdatel'stvo "Nauka," 1960–95) (hereafter *VPR*). Here *VPR*, v. 7, doc. 233 (17 February/1 March 1814), pp. 587–95. The treaty published in *VPR* is that between Russia and Austria.

23. In every case where the allies agreed to provide troops, Britain had the option of paying for foreign soldiers instead of providing its own troops. Payments of this sort would be separate from the annual subsidy of 5 million pounds sterling.

24. The Swiss Federation and Spain would be restored to their previous borders. The allies did not carry out the agreed-upon provision to invite the prince of Orange and the monarchies of Portugal, Spain, and Sweden to join the alliance.

25. Exceptions were the Seychelles and Mauritius in the Indian Ocean and Tobago and Santa Lucia in the West Indies. The French part of Santo Domingo went to Spain. The First Treaty of Paris also recognized British control over Malta and the Dutch Cape of Good Hope.

26. Schroeder, *Transformation*, 507–9; Janet M. Hartley, *Alexander I* (New York: Longman Publishing, 1994), 128–36.

27. The day after the signing of the First Treaty of Paris, the Swiss cantons accepted a federal pact that brought Geneva into the Swiss Confederation, returned territories taken by France, and recognized Swiss neutrality. In August, following a Norwegian revolt, Norway accepted autonomy under Sweden. Schroeder, *Transformation*, 513–16.

28. Rey, *Alexander I*, 184–86; Schroeder, *Transformation*, 320–23.

29. The liberal Polish constitution was never fully implemented, and the diet remained a consultative body. Orlik, *Rossiia v mezhdunarodnykh otnosheniiakh*, 24–25.

30. Prince Clemens Wenzel Nepomuk Lothar von Metternich (1773–1859).

31. Preliminary meetings began in September, and Russian scholarship dates the start of the congress to October. Schroeder, *Transformation*, chap. 12; *Ocherki istorii Ministerstva inostrannykh del Rossii. 1802–2002* (Moscow: Olma-Press, 2002), v. 1, pp. 265–66.

32. Bavaria, Hanover, Hessen-Darmstadt, the United Netherlands, and Sardinia also joined the secret alliance against Prussia and Russia. Some historians see in this alliance France's return to great power status. See *VPR*, v. 8, n. 81, pp. 633–36.

33. Austria kept the district of Tarnopol, controlled Northern Italy, and benefited from the establishment of dependent dynasties in Parma and Tuscany. The compromise on Poland was codified in treaties signed separately by Russia with Austria and Prussia (21 April/3 May 1815), and in a supplemental treaty on Cracow signed by all three powers (21 April/3 May 1815). *VPR*, v. 8, annotations (21 April/3 May 1815), pp. 294–95. The summary

of the Polish-Saxon question provided here is based on Schroeder, *Transformation*, 523–38; Rey, *Alexander I*, 288–89; Kissinger, *World Restored*, 149–71; A. V. Torkunov and M. M. Narinskii, eds., *Istoriia mezhdunarodnykh otnoshenii, Tom 1: Ot Vestfal'skogo mira do okonchaniia Pervoi mirovoi voiny* (Moscow: Aspekt Press, 2012), 184–85. A treaty of 1817 delimited the border between Prussia and the Kingdom of Poland; however, uncertainties remained, and negotiations continued until October 1820. On 28 April 1820 Alexander instructed his representative, General d'Ouvray, to adhere to the stipulations of existing treaties and to continue the "line of moderation" in the negotiations. On 5/17 October 1820 the monarch approved the demarcations proposed by the Polish and Prussian commissars and authorized his envoy in Berlin, Baron David M. Alopeus, to begin negotiations with the Prussian government. At the time, points of disagreement between the two governments remained. AVP RI, f. 133, op. 468, d. 2990, Doklady, ll. 24–25, draft dispatch to Baron Alopeus approved by Alexander (24 February 1820); ll. 42–42ob., draft dispatch to General d'Ouvray approved by Alexander (24 February 1820); l. 71, draft office to Count Sobolewski approved by Alexander (3/15 October 1820); ll. 72–72ob., draft dispatch to Baron Alopeus approved by Alexander (3/15 October 1820); ll. 73–75ob., draft note to Count Bernstorff in Berlin approved by Alexander (3/15 October 1820).

34. Schroeder, *Transformation*, chap. 12. Recent Russian scholarship counts 2 emperors, 4 kings, 2 princely heirs (*naslednykh printsa*), 3 grand dukes, 215 heads of princely families, and 450 diplomats and other officials. *Ocherki*, v. 1, pp. 265–66.

35. *VPR*, v. 8, doc. 102 (13/25 March 1815), pp. 240–45, treaty of alliance between Russia and Britain; annotation (13/25 May 1815), p. 347, manifesto of Alexander I to the people of the Kingdom of Poland concerning incorporation into the Russian Empire and the granting of a constitution.

36. Schroeder, *Transformation*, 550–59.

37. Kissinger, *World Restored*, 171–74; Schroeder, *Transformation*, 546–73.

38. Kissinger, *World Restored*, 215–17; Schroeder, *Transformation*, 560–82.

39. "Tableau statistique de la Confédération Germanique," *Le Conservateur impartial*, no. 64 (9/21 August 1818): 284.

40. A four-power Treaty of 5 November 1815 established the United States of the Ionian Islands to be governed by a British high commissioner in accordance with a constitution written by an Ionian assembly. On British rule in the Ionian Islands, see *VPR*, v. 1 (9), doc. 95 (29 October/10 November 1816), pp. 278–84, report from Kapodistrias to Alexander.

41. The Rhine, Neckar, Moselle, Main, Meuse, and Scheldt Rivers.

42. Kissinger, *World Restored*, 179–84, 215–17; Schroeder, *Transformation*, 548–60; Rey, *Alexander I*, 332–33; Hartley, *Alexander I*, 128–36; Tim Blanning, *The Pursuit of Glory: The Five Revolutions That Made Modern Europe: 1648–1815* (New York: Penguin, 2007), 670–75. A regulation of 19 March 1815, further developed in Russian law by the Consular Regulation of 1820, defined diplomatic ranks across Europe: ambassador (*posol*), envoy (*poslannik*), minister plenipotentiary (*polnomochnyi ministr*), resident minister (*ministr-rezident*), and chargé d'affaires (*poverennyi v delakh*). The ambassador personally represented the head of state, the envoy was accredited to the head of the host

state, and the chargé d'affaires was accredited to the foreign ministry of the host country. Diplomatic ranks also included representatives sent on temporary or extraordinary missions. In 1825 the Russian Empire maintained thirty-four general consulates, nineteen of which were in Europe. *Ocherki*, v. 1, pp. 271–73.

43. *VPR*, v. 8, doc. 272 (8/20 November 1815), pp. 600–609, peace treaty between Russia and France.

44. In the end the occupation lasted only three years.

45. Rey, *Alexander I*, 332–33; *VPR*, v. 8, doc. 273 (8/20 November 1815), pp. 609–14, treaty of alliance between Russia and Austria.

46. Matthias Schulz, "Paradoxes of a Great Power Peace: The Case of the Concert of Europe," in Hippler and Vec, *Paradoxes of Peace*, 131–52, here 135–36. See also Matthias Schulz, *Normen und Praxis: Das Europäische Konzert der Großmächte als Sicherheitsrat, 1815–1860* (Munich: De Gruyter Oldenbourg, 2009).

47. Jurists of the early nineteenth century regarded codification of international law as premature. Augusti, "Peace by Code," 41–43.

48. V. M. Bezotosnyi sees the Holy Alliance of the monarchs as the foundation of the Vienna system. In general, Russian scholars assign a more central role to the Holy Alliance than do historians from other European countries. V. M. Bezotosnyi, "Venskii Kongress: Evropa i Rossiia," in Bezotosnyi, *Epokha 1812 goda*, 13: 7–12. Richard Stites describes the Holy Alliance as "the conservative international master document," the product of Alexander I's mystical conversion and Metternich's anti-liberalism. Richard Stites, *The Four Horsemen: Riding to Liberty in Post-Napoleonic Europe* (New York: Oxford University Press, 2014), Kindle edition, 22.

49. See the article by Ioannis Kapodistrias: "Observations sur les véritables intérêts de l'Europe," *Le Conservateur impartial*, no. 18 (2/14 March 1817): 99–101. On Kapodistrias's authorship, see *VPR*, v. 1 (9), annotation (2/14 March 1817), p. 474.

50. Wolfram Siemann, *Metternich: Stratege und Visionär. Eine Biografie* (Munich: C. H. Beck, 2016); John Bew, *Castlereagh: A Life* (New York: Oxford University Press, 2012); Rey, *Alexander I*; Hartley, *Alexander I*. On the moderate mainstream Enlightenment, see Jonathan Israel, *Enlightenment Contested: Philosophy, Modernity, and the Emancipation of Man 1670–1752* (New York: Oxford University Press, 2006).

51. The Holy Alliance has its own substantial historiography, which cannot be fully reviewed here. Suffice it to say that inside and outside of Russian Studies, scholarly treatments often portray the alliance either as a tool of monarchical reaction deployed by Austria, Prussia, and Russia or as the product of Alexander I's religious conversion and mysticism. Neither analysis is fully satisfactory, though the monarch's biography and emergent romantic nationalism in Russia do offer productive lines of inquiry. Modern Russian scholarship, including unpublished works from the 1920s and 1930s, is more sophisticated. This scholarship analyzes the Holy Alliance as an expression of mystical religious spirituality, an aspect of European diplomacy, and a system of internal politics. One of the more interesting claims holds that Alexander sought to transform the language of European diplomacy and politics into a language of religious mysticism. V. K. Nadler, *Imperator Aleksandr i ideia sviashchennogo soiuza*, 5 vols. (Riga: N. Kimmel',

1886–92); Georgii Florovskii, *Puti russkogo bogosloviia* (Minsk: Izdatel'stvo Belorussk-ogo Ekzarkhata, 2006); Francis Ley, *Alexandre Ier et sa Sainte-Alliance (1811–1825) avec des documents inédits* (Paris: Librairie Fischbacher, 1975); Andrei Zorin, *Kormia dvug-lavogo orla. . . Literatura i gosudarstvennaia ideologiia v Rossii v poslednei treti XVIII–pervoi treti XIX veka* (Moscow: Novoe literaturnoe obozrenie, 2001); Rey, *Alexander I*; Menger, *Heilige Allianz*; Brisku, "Holy Alliance." For a clichéd account, see Edward Keene, *International Political Thought: A Historical Introduction* (Malden, MA: Polity Press, 2005), 172–74. On modern Russian scholarship, see Vadim S. Parsamov, "'Apoko-lipsis diplomatii' ('Akt o Sviashchennom soiuze' v interpretatsii K.-V. Metternikha, bar-onessy Kriudner, Zhozefa de Mestra i Aleksandra Sturdzy)," in *Osvoboditel'noe dvizhe-nie v Rossii*, vypusk 20 (Saratov, 2003), 44–66.

52. I began to develop this point in Elise Kimerling Wirtschafter, "Russian Diplomacy as Enlightenment Project: The Holy Alliance and the Vienna Settlement, 1815–1823," in *Vek Prosveshcheniia. Vypusk 6: Chto takoe Prosveshchenie? Novye otvety na staryi vopros* (Moscow: Nauka, 2018), 208–18.

53. *Polnoe sobranie zakonov Rossiiskoi Imperii*, series 1: 1649–1825, 46 vols. (Saint Pe-tersburg: II Otdelenie Sobstvennoi E. I. V. Kantseliarii, 1830) [hereafter *PSZ* (I)] 33: 25943 (14/26 September 1815), pp. 279–81. For the French text, see *VPR*, v. 8, doc. 231 (14/26 September 1815), pp. 516–18. For the history of the treaty text, see *VPR*, v. 8, n. 268, pp. 692–93; n. 276, pp. 695–97.

54. In the French text, "justice, charity, and peace." *VPR*, v. 8, doc. 231 (14/26 Sep-tember 1815), p. 517.

55. In the French text, "religion, peace, and justice." *VPR*, v. 8, doc. 231 (14/26 Sep-tember 1815), p. 517.

56. From 5 February 1811 until George III's death in January 1820, the future King George IV reigned as prince regent and de facto sovereign. On the accession of Denmark and German states such as the free city of Bremen to the Holy Alliance, see *VPR*, v. 1 (9), doc. 192 (11/23 August 1817), pp. 640–42, rescript from Alexander to P. A. Nikolai; doc. 201 (15/27 September 1817), pp. 673–74, Nesselrode to I. O. Anstett.

57. M. M. Speranskii, *Rukovodstvo k poznaniiu zakonov*, ed. I. D. Osipov (Saint Pe-tersburg: Nauka, 2002), 586.

58. Marc Raeff, *Michael Speransky: Statesman of Imperial Russia, 1772–1839* (The Hague: Martinus Nijhoff, 1957), 225–26.

59. Elise Kimerling Wirtschafter, *Religion and Enlightenment in Catherinian Russia: The Teachings of Metropolitan Platon* (DeKalb: Northern Illinois University Press, 2013).

60. Quentin Skinner, *The Foundations of Modern Political Thought*, 2 vols. *Vol. 1: The Renaissance*; *Vol. 2: The Age of Reformation* (New York: Cambridge University Press, 1978); J. B. Schneewind, *The Invention of Autonomy: A History of Moral Philosophy* (New York: Cambridge University Press, 1998); G. M. Hamburg, *Russia's Path toward Enlight-enment: Faith, Politics, and Reason, 1500–1801* (New Haven, CT: Yale University Press, 2016). On kingship in Russia, see Gail Lenhoff and Ann Kleimola, eds., *"The Book of Royal Degrees" and the Genesis of Russian Historical Consciousness* (Bloomington, IN: Slavica, 2010); Cynthia Hyla Whittaker, *Russian Monarchy: Eighteenth-Century Rulers*

and Writers in Political Dialogue (DeKalb: Northern Illinois University Press, 2003); Richard S. Wortman, *Scenarios of Power: Myth and Ceremony in Russian Monarchy from Peter the Great to the Abdication of Nicholas II*, one vol. abridged (Princeton, NJ: Princeton University Press, 2006).

61. Emperor Alexander's wife, Elizabeth Alekseevna, was born Princess Louise of Baden, and his beloved sister Catherine married the Duke of Oldenburg, heir to the duchy. His mother, Maria Fedorovna, was a princess of Württemberg.

62. Alan Sked describes the Holy Alliance as "perhaps the vaguest document ever to trouble European diplomacy." Sked and others repeatedly quote contemporary dismissals of the alliance as a "'loud-sounding nothing'" (Metternich) and a "'piece of sublime mysticism and nonsense'" (Castlereagh). Alan Sked, Introduction to *Europe's Balance of Power 1815–1848*, ed. Alan Sked (New York: Harper and Row, 1979), 3–4. Paul Schroeder, by contrast, recognizes that Metternich, Castlereagh, and Alexander all took seriously "the role and value of moral principles in international politics," and he correctly argues that Alexander's idealistic religious language "should not be dismissed as mystical nonsense or a cover for Russian ambitions." Schroeder, *Transformation*, 558–59. For recent studies that avoid the old stereotypes and highlight the European context, see Anselm Schubert and Wolfram Pyta, eds., *Die Heilige Allianz. Entstehung—Wirkung—Rezeption* (Stuttgart: W. Kohlhammer, 2018).

63. For Alexander's response to foreign criticism, see his correspondence with Castlereagh, Hardenberg, and Pope Pius VII: *VPR*, v. 1 (9), doc. 33 (21 March/2 April 1816), pp. 108–13, Alexander to Castlereagh; doc. 50 (22 April/4 May 1816), pp. 152–56, Alexander to Hardenberg; Grand Duke Nikolai Mikhailovich, *L'Empereur Alexandre Ier: Essai d'étude historique*, 2 vols. (Saint Petersburg: Manufacture des papiers de l'état, 1912), v. 2, pp. 210–14. On papal opposition, see also *VPR* v. 1 (9), doc. 39 (31 March/12 April 1816), pp. 133–34, dispatch from Nesselrode to Major General F. V. Teil'-fan-Seroskerken (Theodor Tuyll van Seroskerken); doc. 81 (23 August/4 September 1816), pp. 244–47, Tuyll to Nesselrode; doc. 127 (15/27 January 1817), pp. 401–7, memorandum of instruction to envoy in Rome A. Ia. Italinskii.

For diplomatic correspondence concerning the Ottoman Empire and the Holy Alliance, see *VPR*, v. 1 (9), doc. 41 (31 March/12 April 1816), pp. 135–37, Nesselrode to envoy in Constantinople A. Ia. Italinskii; doc. 70 (10/22 July 1816), pp. 221–23, supplemental instruction from Nesselrode to envoy in Constantinople G. A. Stroganov. For additional correspondence concerning the Holy Alliance, see also *VPR*, v. 1 (9), doc. 44 (7/19 April 1816), pp. 140–42, Nesselrode to envoy in Naples G. S. Mochenigo; doc. 125 (10/22 January 1817), pp. 398–99, Nesselrode to Anstett; doc. 126 (15/27 January 1817), pp. 400–401, chargé d'affaires in Switzerland Baron Paul de Krudener to Nesselrode. For the rescript, see *VPR*, v. 1 (9), doc. 34 (22 March/3 April 1816), pp. 113–17. A related rescript of 18/30 March 1816 explained the principles motivating the Holy Alliance (peace, harmony, and love) and countered claims that it was directed against non-Christian peoples: see *Sbornik Imperatorskogo Rossiiskogo istoricheskogo obshchestva* (hereafter *SIRIO*), 148 vols. (Saint Petersburg: Imperatorskoe Rossiiskoe istoricheskoe obshchestvo, 1867–1916), v. 112, pp. 455–57; N. K. Shil'der, *Imperator Aleksandr Pervyi: Ego zhizn' i tsarstvovanie*, 4 vols. (Saint Petersburg: Izdanie A. S. Suvorina, 1897–98), v. 3, pp. 532–33; *VPR*, v. 1 (9), annotation (18/30 March 1816), p. 100, rescript from Alexander to Lieven; Rossiiskii gosudarstvennyi arkhiv drevnikh aktov (hereafter RGADA), f. 15, op. 1, d. 279, Documents concerning relations with European powers from the Ministry of Foreign Affairs, ll. 32–42, circular rescript to ministers at the courts of Vienna, London, Berlin, and Paris (18/30 March 1816); d. 284, On the establishment of the Holy Alliance, ll. 1–30ob., rescript from Alexander to Lieven (18 March 1816).

64. *PSZ* (I) 33: 26045 (Manifesto of 25 December 1825), p. 417; *Sobranie Vysochaishikh manifestov, gramot, ukazov, reskriptov, prikazov voiskam i raznykh izveshchenii posledovavshikh v techenii 1812, 1813, 1814, 1815 i 1816 godov* (Saint Petersburg: Morskaia tipografiia, 1816), 187–92.

65. *The Festal Menaion*, trans. Mother Mary and Archimandrite Kallistos Ware (South Canaan, PA: Saint Tikhon's Seminary Press, 1998), 50.

66. *Festal Menaion*, 51.

67. *Festal Menaion*, 41–42, 50–51. On the liturgical symbolism surrounding the Holy Alliance, see also Andrei Iu. Andreev, "Nachalo 'novogo veka': Rozhdestvenskaia simvolika v tsarstvovanii Aleksandra I," *Vestnik PSTGU. II. Istoriia. Istoriia Russkoi Pravslavnoi Tserkvi*, vypusk 1 (44) (2012): 40–48; Andrei Iu. Andreev, "'Liturgika' Sviashchennogo soiuza: K voprosu o religioznykh vzgliadakh Aleksandra I," *Filaretovskii al'manakh*, ed. A. I. Iakovlev, vypusk 12 (Moscow: Izdatel'stvo PSTGU, 2016), 123–54.

68. Territorial disputes and political conflicts did not cease with the signing of the Vienna and Paris treaties. In Germany, Italy, Poland, and Scandinavia, details of internal governance and the broader European settlement still had to be negotiated and codified. As brief perusal of the *Polnoe sobranie zakonov* reveals, there is no full account of the numerous treaties, conventions, and accords signed by Russia with other states during these years. The archival record highlights additional subjects in need of comprehensive research: delimitation of the Prussian-Polish border; economic relations and accords between Prussia and the Kingdom of Poland; and Russia's trade agreements and tariff policies. See the draft dispatches approved by Alexander and cited above. See also AVP RI, f. 133, op. 468, d. 2991, Doklady, ll. 1-30ob., draft dispatch to Count Gur'ev (Gourieff) approved by Alexander (15/27 January 1821); ll. 590b.-63, draft verbal note to British ambassador Sir Charles Bagot approved by Alexander (2 July 1821); ll. 68-68ob., draft dispatch to Baron Nikolai in London approved by Alexander (2 July 1821); ll. 75-80ob., draft note to the minister of Sweden Baron (Nil's-Frederik) Palmstierna approved by Alexander (13 August 1821); ll. 120-31, draft dispatch to Count Alopeus approved by Alexander (13 October 1821); d. 2992, Doklady, ll. 83-87, report presented to Alexander on freedom of trade for the city of Podgorze (3 February 1820).

69. RGADA, f. 15, op. 1, d. 279, ll. 8–310b., general instruction sent to all missions of H. I. M. from Vienna (15/17 May 1815).

70. Ready or not, the potential aggression has to be evaluated with reference to the secret alliance of 3 January 1815 concluded by Austria, Bavaria, Britain, France, Hanover, Hessen-Darmstadt, the United Netherlands, and Sardinia, and directed against Prussia and Russia.

71. In the end the Ottoman Empire remained outside the European system.

72. C. A. Bayley, "The Age of Revolution in Global Context: An Afterword," in *The Age of Revolutions in Global Context, c. 1760–1840*, ed. David Armitage and Sanjay Subrahmanyam (Basingstoke: Palgrave Macmillan, 2010), Kindle edition, location 4851–4943.

73. From the post-colonial perspective, the notion of a moral superiority that justifies expansionist policies is overtly imperialistic, if not also racist.

74. Count Karl von Nesselrode [Karl Vasil'evich Nesselrode (1780–1862)]; Count Ioannis Kapodistrias [John Capo d'Istria; Ivan Antonovich Kapodistrias (1776–1831)]; Count Christoph von Lieven [Khristofor Andreevich Liven (1774–1839)]; Count Gustav Stackelberg [Gustav Ottonovich Shtakel'berg (1787–1850)]; Grand Prince Constantine Pavlovich (1779–1831). Constantine Pavlovich served as governor-general (*namestnik*) of the Polish Kingdom and commander-in-chief of the Polish army from 1815 to 1831.

75. *VPR*, v. 1 (9), doc. 17 (25 January/6 February 1816), pp. 63–68, Lieven to Nesselrode.

76. Arthur Wellesley, first Duke of Wellington (1769–1852).

77. *VPR*, v. 1 (9), doc. 30 (8/20 March 1816), pp. 96–100, Nesselrode to Stackelberg. See also *VPR*, v. 1 (9), doc. 22 (7/19 February 1816), pp. 80–81, Alexander to Victor Emmanuel I (of Sardinia); doc. 23 (13/25 February 1816), pp. 82–85, Nesselrode to envoy in Turin P. B. Kozlovskii.

78. *VPR*, v. 1 (9), n. 20, p. 682; RGADA, f. 15, op. 1, d. 279, ll. 67–680b., appendix to the overview of 5/17 June 1817 on Austria's intention to incorporate Novaria and enter into a separate alliance with Sardinia.

79. *VPR*, v. 1 (9), doc. 136 (31 January/12 February 1817), pp. 450–53, personal letter from Kapodistrias to Stackelberg.

80. Here Alexander distinguished between allied governments and his fellow sovereigns who had imbibed the Gospel's pure morality.

81. Napoleon annexed Austria's Illyrian provinces in 1809. Lieven, *Russia against Napoleon*, 171.

82. *VPR*, v. 1 (9), doc. 146 (9/21 March 1817), pp. 487–90, personal letter of Stackelberg to Kapodistrias; n. 220, pp. 740–41. See also the reports of the French ambassador in Russia, the count of La Ferronnays, in *SIRIO*, v. 127.

83. *VPR*, v. 1 (9), doc. 166 (1/13 May 1817), pp. 537–42, Lieven to Nesselrode.

84. *VPR*, v. 1 (9), doc. 184 (10/22 June 1817), pp. 591–95, Nesselrode to Lieven.

85. *VPR*, v. 1 (9), doc. 151 (21 March/2 April 1817), pp. 502–6, Kapodistrias to Grand Prince Constantine Pavlovich.

86. *VPR*, v. 1 (9), annotation (17/29 March 1817), p. 502, memorandum of the Ministry of Foreign Affairs serving as an instruction to envoys in Vienna, Madrid, Brussels, and Stockholm; to minister plenipotentiary in Paris; and to ambassador in London; n. 230, p. 743.

87. *SIRIO*, v. 119, pp. 239–48; *VPR*, v. 1 (9), annotation (2/14 June 1817), p. 578. For the Russian version, dated 5/17 June 1817, with accompanying documents, see RGADA, f. 15, op. 1, d. 279, ll. 43–1030b.

88. In 1808 the Portuguese royal family relocated to Rio de Janeiro, and in 1822 Brazil declared independence.

89. Based on the Final Act of the Congress of Vienna, the duchies of Parma, Plaisance, and Guastalla belonged to Marie Louise, archduchess of Austria and wife of Napoleon, and her descendants. Britain and France supported the Spanish claim that following the death of Archduchess Marie Louise, these territories should go to the infante Marie Louise, daughter of the former Spanish king, Charles IV; her son Charles Louis; and his direct male descendants. The allies finalized this line of succession in the General Act of the Frankfurt Territorial Commission (8/20 July 1819), except for districts on the left bank of the Po recognized as Austrian territory. In addition, the treaties assigned the Principality of Lucca to the Grand Duchy of Tuscany upon the death of the archduchess. RGADA, f. 15, op. 1, d. 279, ll. 69–730b., appendix to the overview of 5/17 June 1817 on matters concerning the Baden court.

90. Alexander Ivanovich Chernyshev (1785–1857) served as minister of war from 1832 to 1852. *VPR*, v. 1 (9), annotation (21 April/3 May 1817), p. 526, Nesselrode to Alopeus.

91. Brendan Simms, *Europe: The Struggle for Supremacy, from 1453 to the Present* (New York: Basic Books, 2013), 168, 181–88; Schroeder, *Transformation*, 487–88, 572–78, 766–77.

92. Allied involvement resumed in 1818 during negotiations over Swedish responsibility for Norway's debts. The allies agreed that Sweden should honor Norwegian debts based on article 6 of the Treaty of Kiel.

Chapter 2: Completion of the General Alliance (1817–20)

1. Documents of the era are filled with references to France's natural position as a great power in Europe. See, for example, *VPR*, v. 1 (9), annotation (9/21 June 1817), p. 591, Kapodistrias to Richelieu; *SIRIO*, v. 119, no. 119 (9/21 June 1817), pp. 255–57, Kapodistrias to Richelieu. Prior to, during, and after the Congress of Aix-la-Chapelle, the regularization of France's status seemed an urgent matter and also the best means to promote the country's political stability, which remained a serious concern for the allies. *VPR*, v. 2 (10), doc. 113 (6/18 May 1818), pp. 367–70, Lieven to Kapodistrias; doc. 149 (not before 16/28 September 1818), p. 503, memorandum of Alexander to Russia's plenipotentiaries at the Congress of Aix-la-Chapelle; doc. 165 (3/15 November 1818), pp. 570–74, general circular instruction from the Ministry of Foreign Affairs to Russia's diplomatic missions; annotation (9/21 November 1818), p. 584, circular rescript from Alexander to Russia's diplomatic representatives abroad; annotation (13/25 December 1818), p. 611, Kapodistrias to Pozzo di Borgo; doc. 180 (19/31 December 1818), pp. 611–25, memorandum of Kapodistrias; annotation (25 January/6 February 1819), p. 646, Alexander to Richelieu; doc. 187 (25 January/6 February 1819), pp. 647–49, circular dispatch from Nesselrode to Russia's diplomatic representatives abroad; doc. 198 (16/28 February 1819), pp. 691–98, Golovkin to Nesselrode; doc. 199 (17 February/1 March 1819), pp. 698–701, Golovkin to Nesselrode; annotation (25 February/9 March 1819), p. 701, Pozzo di Borgo to Nesselrode; doc. 205 (31 March/12 April 1819), pp. 712–17, Nesselrode to Lieven and Alopeus; *VPR*, v. 3 (11), doc. 56 (22 November/4 December 1819), pp. 166–72, memorial memorandum from the Russian

cabinet to the governments of Austria, Britain, and Prussia; RGADA, f. 15, op. 1, d. 279, Documents concerning diplomatic relations with European powers from the Ministry of Foreign Affairs, ll. 104–270b., on the calculation and payment of France's debts to the subjects of other powers, approved by the emperor (23 October 1817); d. 284, On the establishment of the Holy Alliance, ll. 13–26, general and circular instruction to all missions sent from Aix-la-Chapelle (3/15 November 1818); d. 279, ll. 128–43, Russian version.

2. For detailed treatment, see Heinz Duchhardt, *Der Aachener Kongress 1818: Ein europäisches Gipfeltreffen im Vormärz* (Munich: Piper Verlag, 2018).

3. The "system of conferences" refers to ambassadorial conferences such as those established in Frankfurt, London, and Paris to deal with the implementation of the Paris peace treaties, territorial arrangements in Germany, and the abolition of the slave trade. In the years following the Vienna Congress, ambassadorial conferences functioned as semi-permanent bodies tasked with monitoring or negotiating specific relationships and policies. Ambassadorial conferences remained distinct from the meetings of the great powers (Austria, Britain, France, Prussia, and Russia) that brought together heads of state and/or their representatives to discuss unresolved questions and respond to new crises that arose. Henry Kissinger, *A World Restored: Metternich, Castlereagh and the Problems of Peace, 1812–1822* (Boston: Houghton Mifflin Company, 1957), 221–29. On the idea of a united Europe, see *VPR*, v. 2 (10), doc. 149 (not before 16/28 September 1818), p. 503, memorandum from Alexander to Russia's plenipotentiaries at the Congress of Aix-la-Chapelle. Throughout 1817 Kapodistrias had pushed for a treaty of guarantee. *VPR*, v. 2 (10), n. 215, pp. 770–72.

4. O. V. Orlik, ed. *Rossiia v mezhdunarodnykh otnosheniiakh 1815–1829: Ot Venskogo kongressa do Adrianopol'skogo mira* (Moscow: Nauka, 1998), 29–35; Marie-Pierre Rey, *Alexander I: The Tsar Who Defeated Napoleon*, trans. Susan Emanuel (DeKalb: Northern Illinois University Press, 2012), 335–37; Paul W. Schroeder, *The Transformation of European Politics 1763–1848* (New York: Oxford University Press, 1994), chap. 3; Kissinger, *World Restored*, 225–29.

5. *VPR*, v. 2 (10), doc. 127 (24 June/6 July 1818), pp. 409–33, report from the Ministry of Foreign Affairs to Alexander.

6. According to the report, failed efforts by Austria and Britain to renew the Treaty of Chaumont had led to the Quadruple Alliance of 8/20 November 1815. Historians tend to describe the Quadruple Alliance as the reaffirmation of Chaumont.

7. The "affaire de Parme" resulted from article 99 of the Final Act of the Congress of Vienna, which both assigned the Italian territories of Parma, Plaisance, and Guastalla to Empress Marie Louise, wife of Napoleon, and also allowed for their reversion to Spain. Based on article 99, the Bourbon Spanish king opposed giving the Italian duchies to Archduchess Marie Louise of Austria and her descendants. Russia sought Spanish accession to the Final Act of the Congress of Vienna, and Britain and France supported Spain's claims to the duchies upon the death of Marie Louise. Based on the Treaty of 29 May/10 June 1817, signed by Austria, Britain, France, Prussia, Russia, and Spain, and then finalized in the Final Act of the Territorial Commission of Frankfurt, signed by Austria, Britain, Prussia, and Russia, at the death of Archduchess Marie

Louise of Austria, the duchies would pass to the infante Marie Louise of Spain, her son Charles Louis, and his direct male descendants. Districts on the left bank of the Po would remain under Austrian control, and the Principality of Lucca would pass to the Grand Duchy of Tuscany. Austria also would maintain a garrison in Plaisance. F. F. Martens, ed., *Recueil des traités et conventions, conclus par la Russie avec les puissances étrangères*, 15 vols. (Saint Petersburg: Tipografiia Ministerstva Putei Soobshcheniia, 1874–1909), v. 3, no. 79–96, Final Act of the Congress of Vienna with appendices (28 May/9 June 1815), pp. 207–315; v. 4, no. 107 (29 May/10 June 1817), pp. 55–61; no. 110 (8/20 July 1819), pp. 146–86; no. 111 (4/16 March 1816), pp. 187–204; no. 112-13 (19/30 June 1816), pp. 204–24; no. 114 (27 October/8 November 1816), pp. 224–38; no. 115 (4/16 November 1816), pp. 238–40; no. 116 (28 February/12 March 1817), pp. 241–42; no. 117 (5/17 April 1817, 21 November 1815), pp. 243–46; no. 118 (29 May/10 June 1817), p. 246; no. 119-20 (29 June/10 July 1819), pp. 246–51; no. 121 (2/14 April 1816), pp. 251–64.

8. Kapodistrias argued that Spanish interests in the Americas, which fell outside the separate and exclusive system of the Quadruple Alliance, should be negotiated legally and publicly.

9. The question of ending the military occupation already had been negotiated with France by the Duke of Wellington, acting on behalf of the allies.

10. In earlier communications Kapodistrias and other diplomats developed similar arguments critical of the Quadruple Alliance and of Austrian and British policy. See the response of General Karl O. Pozzo di Borgo, Alexander's representative in Paris, to instructions sent by Kapodistrias in a dispatch of 27 March/8 April 1818: *SIRIO*, v. 119, no. 306 (25 April/7 May 1818), pp. 674–88; *VPR*, v. 2 (10), annotation (25 April/7 May 1818), p. 351. A few months later, Kapodistrias, speaking on behalf of Alexander, reminded Pozzo di Borgo that the emperor did not seek to establish a special relationship with France or Spain, that he continued to see allied unity and adherence to existing treaties as necessary for peace, and that Pozzo di Borgo should moderate his public pronouncements of affection for France. See Kapodistrias's letter of 10/22 July 1818, published in *SIRIO*, v. 119, no. 347, pp. 772–77. On British concerns about Pozzo di Borgo's partiality toward France, see *VPR*, v. 2 (10), doc. 134 (10/22 July 1818), pp. 457–62, secret and confidential letter from Kapodistrias to Lieven.

11. Kapodsitrias's suspicions about Austrian and British efforts to undermine Russia, this time through alliances with the Persian and Ottoman empires, persisted after the Congress of Aix-la-Chapelle. See *VPR*, v. 2 (10), doc. 180 (19/31 December 1818), pp. 611–25, memorandum of Kapodistrias. In 1816 Russia had encouraged Italian states to resist Austrian encroachments and even suggested the possibility of allied intervention (which did not in this context mean military action). Formal intervention by the alliance could be moral or political instead of military. See *VPR*, v. 1 (9), doc. 22 (7/19 February 1816), pp. 80–81, Alexander to Victor Emmanuel I; doc. 23 (13/25 February 1816), pp. 82–85, Nesselrode to envoy in Turin P. B. Kozlovskii; doc. 40 (31 March/12 April 1816), pp. 134–35, Nesselrode to Major General F. V. Teil'-fan-Seroskerken (Theodor Tuyll van Seroskerken); v. 2 (10), doc. 144 (16/28 April 1818); pp. 489–93, Nesselrode to A. V. Sverchkov.

12. Johann Peter Friedrich Ancillon (1767–1837), author of M. F. Ancillon, *Tableau des revolutions du système politique de l'Europe depuis la fin du quinzième siècle,* 7 vols. (Paris: Imprimerie de la Harpe, 1806–1807). Many diplomatic documents of the era did not use the label Holy Alliance but rather Treaty of Alliance of 14/26 September 1815.

13. Territorial disputes would be decided by arbitration at congresses attended by rulers or their representatives.

14. On 2/14 October 1818, Russia's plenipotentiaries to the congress in Aix-la-Chapelle submitted a memorandum to the ministers of Austria, Britain, and Prussia, as well as to Friedrich von Gentz and the Duke of Wellington, in which they analyzed the Treaty of Chaumont in relation to the Quadruple Alliance. In diplomatic negotiations, the memorandum argued, the principle of analysis assumes that a treaty establishes an obligation and that every obligation carries a cause or motivation (*motif*) and a goal (*but*). The legal act of the treaty sets the means to establish the one and expect the other. The motivation of the four signatories to Chaumont was peace with Bonaparte, the goal was an armed defensive system directed against him, and the means were a "pact of solidarity" that guaranteed the mutual security of the four powers and offered the same to other European states seeking to escape domination by the conqueror. Subjecting the Quadruple Alliance to the same principles of analysis, the memorandum identified its motivation as preservation of the general peace founded on the restoration of the French monarchy and the Final Act of the Congress of Vienna. The goal of the alliance was a system armed against France in the sole instance that France violated the pact uniting it, as a legitimate and constitutional kingdom, to the "European family." Finally, the means were the solidarity of the contracting parties on the following points: exclusion of the Bonaparte family from the throne of France, concert with the king of France to resist revolution and combat revolutionary attacks on legitimate and constitutional monarchy, military measures to assist the army of occupation if it was attacked, an armed federation in the event that a France in revolution became a threat to the stability of the European system, and meetings of the sovereigns to ensure execution of the treaties and consolidate the relations that united them for the happiness of the world. *VPR*, v. 2 (10), doc. 154 (2/14 October 1818), pp. 514–17, memorandum from Russia's plenipotentiaries at the Congress of Aix-la-Chapelle to the plenipotentiaries of Austria, Britain, and Prussia.

15. One should add here, the commitment to preserve the ascendancy of the great powers, though only rarely and inadvertently did diplomatic documents of the time admit to this goal.

16. An electrifying and romantic historical figure, Kapodistrias went on to become the first provisional president of modern Greece.

17. For an earlier account of Russia's proposal for a treaty of guarantee, see Elise Kimerling Wirtschafter, "The Congress of Aix-la-Chapelle (1818) and Russia's Proposal for a Treaty of Guarantee," *Journal of Modern Russian History and Historiography* 12 (2019): 245–62. Henry Kissinger describes Alexander's proposal for a treaty of guarantee as "a doctrine of general interference in the domestic concerns of all states superimposed on a system of collective security." Kissinger, *World Restored*, 225–26.

18. *SIRIO*, v. 119, no. 370 (26 September/8 October 1818), pp. 832–44.

19. When revolution returned to France in 1830, the allies did not act to defend legitimate sovereignty or protect Europe from the revolutionary spirit.

20. RGADA, f. 3, op. 1, d. 162. This file (*delo*), titled Précis du Travail des Conférences d'Aix-la-Chapelle, comes from the archives of Kapodistrias and does not represent a full record of the congress proceedings. Although it contains copies of the official protocols, it does not include the supplements (*annexes*) attached to individual sessions.

21. For a pioneering study of the occupation of guarantee as it developed on the ground, see Christine Haynes, *Our Friends the Enemies: The Occupation of France after Napoleon* (Cambridge, MA: Harvard University Press, 2018).

22. The conference protocols used New Style dating, whereas Russian sources generally used double dating, Old Style and New Style.

23. A note from Richelieu dated 10 September 1817 urged the allies to ease the financial burden placed on France by modifying the terms of compensation for private claimants as prescribed in the Treaty of 30 May 1814 and Convention of 8/20 November 1815. Emperor Alexander immediately supported this request, arguing that the Treaty of 8/20 November 1815 aimed to ensure the political existence of France in the interest of European peace. In general, the allies rejected changes to the treaties of 1814–15; however, in this case, citing the seventeenth-century Dutch jurist, Hugo Grotius, diplomats could argue that events on the ground (France's inability to pay an unexpectedly enormous sum) altered the presumed basis for the convention. Thus, the terms of the convention could be changed without violating the principle of legality. At the same time, Alexander tried to make clear that his support for the French position in no way indicated a special interest in France or the pursuit of a partial advantage in Russia's dealings with France or Spain. *SIRIO*, v. 119, no. 211 (27 October/8 November 1817), pp. 438–43; no. 213 (30 October/11 November 1817), pp. 445–46; no. 214–15 (1/13 November 1817), pp. 446–60. Documents elaborating Russia's views on the allied occupation, French exiles, and the French debt can also be found in RGADA, f. 15, op. 1, d. 279, ll. 91–96, 104–270b., appendices to the overview of 5/17 June 1817. Finally, in April 1820, Alexander agreed to pay more than 179,000 francs to compensate France for the cost of Russian troops that had not left the kingdom when the army of occupation departed. AVP RI, f. 133, op. 468, d. 2990, Doklady, ll. 27–270b., draft dispatch to General Pozzo di Borgo approved by Alexander (13 March 1820); d. 2991, Doklady, ll. 49–500b., draft dispatch to Mr. Schröder approved by Alexander (24 April/6 May 1821).

24. *VPR*, v. 2 (10), annotation (27 September/9 October 1818), p. 514, convention between Russia and France; Martens, *Recueil*, v. 7, no. 288, (27 September/9 October 1818), pp. 302–6; RGADA, f. 3, op. 1, d. 162, ll. 40b.–60b., sessions of 9, 11, 12, 13 October; ll. 14–150b., sessions of 3, 4 November.

25. In response to subsequent requests from France, the allies agreed at the sessions of 11 and 19 November to extend the period for payment of the French debt to June 1820. RGADA, f. 3, op. 1, d. 162, ll. 32–330b., session of 11 November; ll. 650b.–68, session of 19 November. On the claims of French subjects against foreign governments, see RGADA, f. 3, op. 1, d. 162, ll. 100b.–11, session of 22 October; ll. 620b.–640b., sessions of 16, 18 November. On private claims against the French government, see Martens, *Recueil*, v.

14, no. 516 (13/25 April 1818), pp. 381–94; *VPR*, v. 2 (10), annotation (13/25 April 1818), p. 317, convention between Russia, Austria, Britain, Prussia, and France on the debts of the French government. On liquidation of the French debt and military contributions, see Martens, *Recueil*, v. 14, no. 517 (20 January/2 February 1819), pp. 395–442; v. 7, no. 288–96 (27 September/9 October 1818, 23 October/4 November 1818, 31 October/12 November 1818, 3/15 November 1818, 4/16 November 1818, 9/21 November 1818), pp. 291–328. For more detailed historical analysis, see Eugene N. White, "Making the French Pay: The Costs and Consequences of the Napoleonic Reparations," *European Review of Economic History* 5, no. 3 (2001): 337–65; Glenda Sluga, "'Who Hold the Balance of the World?' Bankers at the Congress of Vienna, and in International History," *American Historical Review* 122, no. 5 (December 2017): 1403–30; Marion Koschier, "Der Aachener Mächtekongress von 1818 und die Frage der französischen Reparationszahlungen," in *Mächtepolitik und Friedenssicherung. Zur politischen Kultur Europas im Zeichen des Wiener Kongresses*, ed. Reinhard Stauber, Florian Kerschbaumer, and Marion Koschier (Berlin: LIT Verlag, 2014), 135–51.

26. RGADA, f. 3, op. 1, d. 162, ll. 9–100b., session of 19 October.

27. Martens, *Recueil*, v. 7, no. 289 (23 October/4 November 1818), pp. 306–9; no. 290 (31 October/12 November 1818), pp. 309–11.

28. On the exchange of notes with Richelieu and the protocol signed by the five powers, see RGADA, f. 3, op. 1, d. 162, ll. 590b.–62, session of 15 November; ll. 82–820b., note from the plenipotentiaries of the four courts (23 October/4 November 1818); ll. 83–830b., response of Richelieu to the proposal of the allies (31 October/12 November 1818); ll. 84–840b., protocol of 3/15 November 1818.

29. Martens, *Recueil*, v. 7, no. 292 (3/15 November 1818), pp. 314–18; no. 293 (3/15 November 1818), pp. 318–21; RGADA, f. 3, op. 1, d. 162, ll. 540b.–59, sessions of 14, 15 November; ll. 730b.–74, session of 21 November.

30. RGADA, f. 3, op. 1, d. 162, ll. 730b.–74, session of 21 November.

31. Martens, *Recueil*, v. 7, no. 294 (3/15 November 1818), pp. 321–23; RGADA, f. 3, op. 1, d. 162, ll. 590b.–62, session of 15 November; ll. 85–850b., declaration of 15 November.

32. These developments are covered in a communication of 6/18 May 1818 from Russia's ambassador in London, Christoph Lieven, to Kapodistrias. The Hanoverian memorandum expressed distrust of Austria and mentioned Bavaria and the Netherlands as second-order powers eager to arouse opposition to the tribunal of the great powers. As noted, the allies did invite the Netherlands to sign the Military Protocol, which did not include France. *VPR*, v. 2 (10), doc. 112 (6/18 May 1818), pp. 364–67, Lieven to Kapodistrias. The treaties of Westphalia had established a state system based on the principles of sovereignty, territorial integrity, non-intervention, and "great-power restraint and accommodation." Formally equal and independent, states constituted "rightful political units for the establishment of legitimate rule." G. John Ikenberry, "The Logic of Order: Westphalia, Liberalism, and the Evolution of International Order in the Modern Era," in *Power, Order, and Change in World Politics*, ed. G. John Ikenberry (Cambridge: Cambridge University Press, 2014), Kindle edition, location 2264–2322.

33. RGADA, f. 3, op. 1, d. 162, ll. 79–810b., session of 22 November, special conference; *VPR*, v. 2 (10), doc. 174 (11/23 November 1818), pp. 589–91, memorial memorandum from Russia's plenipotentiaries to the plenipotentiaries of Austria, Britain, Prussia, and France. Russian officials did not expect this initiative to produce results. As early as 3/15 November, Alexander approved a general circular instruction addressed to all of the empire's diplomatic missions. The instructions expressed satisfaction with the agreements concluded in Aix-la-Chapelle, emphasized the importance of allied unity in preserving the peace, and ordered strict adherence to all existing treaties, which were beneficial for all European states. *VPR*, v. 2 (10), doc. 165 (3/15 November 1818); pp. 570–74, general circular instruction from the Ministry of Foreign Affairs to Russia's diplomatic missions; *SIRIO*, v. 119, no. 371, pp. 844–50; RGADA, f. 15, op. 1, d. 284, ll. 13–26, general and circular instruction to all missions sent from Aix-la-Chapelle (3/15 November 1818), d. 279, ll. 128–43, Russian version. The instructions were affirmed in early 1819: *VPR*, v. 2 (10), doc. 187 (25 January/6 February 1819), pp. 647–49, circular dispatch from Nesselrode to Russia's diplomatic representatives abroad.

34. The quoted phrase repeated wording found in the Second Treaty of Paris. *VPR*, v. 8, doc. 272 (8/20 November 1815), pp. 600–9.

35. The Russian government already understood that Britain would not agree to the collective guarantee, but still hoped that the other allies could be persuaded. Kissinger, *World Restored*, 226–29; Schroeder, *Transformation*, chap. 13.

36. Martens, *Recueil*, v. 4, no. 110–21, pp. 146–264. For the text of the General Act, see no. 110 (8/20 July 1819), pp. 146–86.

37. Reports from 1820–21 preserved in the archive of the Ministry of Foreign Affairs identify some of the long-term negotiations and disputes. Specific cases include delimitation of the Polish-Prussian border; trade relations between Prussia and the Kingdom of Poland; Russia's trade relations with Sweden (and Norway); Swiss claims against Baden; navigation of the Weser River; freedom of commerce for the city of Podgorze, which Austria's line of tariffs separated from Galicia and therefore put at a disadvantage in relation to merchants from the free city of Cracow; individual claims for financial compensation and land, including the claims of François Borghèse, Prince Aldobrandini, against Hessen-Darmstadt, Bavaria, and Prussia for the saltworks of Kreutznach and Durckeim. AVP RI, f. 133, op. 468, d. 2990, Doklady, ll. 24–240b., 37–370b., 71, 42–420b.; d. 2291, Doklady, ll. 75–800b., 120–31; d. 2992, Doklady, ll. 15–260b., 42–440b., 57–590b., 83–87, 252–550b.; *VPR*, v. 2 (10), annotation (7/19 December 1818), p. 596, trade convention between Russia and Prussia; v. 3 (11), doc. 92 (11/23 February 1820), pp. 264–65, note from Nesselrode to Austria's envoy in Saint Petersburg, Ludwig Joseph Lebzeltern (1774–1854); AVP RI, f. 187, op. 524, d. 37, Various memorandums, projects, plans from 1820-28, ll. 52–630b., memorandum to the great allied powers from Prince Aldobrandini. In October 1820, the Russian government worked steadily to complete the negotiations between Prussia and the Kingdom of Poland. At this stage in the peacemaking process, decisions about the delimitation of borders mostly impacted tariff revenues and other economic interests. AVP RI, f. 133, op. 468, d. 2990, Doklady, ll. 72–720b., draft dispatch to Baron Alopeus approved by Alexander (3/15 October 1820);

73–750b., draft note to [Prussian minister of foreign affairs] Count [Christian Gunther] Bernstorff [1769–1835] in Berlin approved by Alexander (3/15 October 1820).

38. For analysis that places Central Europe at the center of the peace settlement, see Brendan Simms, *Europe: The Struggle for Supremacy, from 1453 to the Present* (New York: Basic Books, 2013).

39. See RGADA, f. 15, op. 1, d. 533, Alexander's instructions of 3/15 February 1815 to Russia's first plenipotentiary at the Congress of Vienna, Count Andrei K. Razumovskii.

40. RGADA, f. 3, op. 1, d. 162, ll. 5–50b., session of 11 October; ll. 60b.–7, sessions of 12, 13, 14 October.

41. According to Kapodistrias, the fragile health of the grand duke also required that a decision be reached. *VPR*, v. 2 (10), doc. 150 (17/29 September 1818), pp. 504–9, report from Kapodistrias to Alexander.

42. RGADA, f. 3, op. 1, d. 162, ll. 50b.–6, session of 12 October; ll. 7–80b., sessions of 13, 14, 17 (?) October; ll. 13–14, sessions of 29 October, 3 November; ll. 27–31, sessions of 9, 10 November; ll. 460b.–48, session of 14 November; ll. 690b.–72, sessions of 20, 21 November.

43. RGADA, f. 15, op. 1, d. 279, ll. 69–730b., affairs of the Baden court; *VPR*, v. 8, doc. 172 (17/29 June 1815), pp. 387–91, secret instruction from Alexander to Pahlen; n. 203–4, p. 681.

44. The treaties mentioned were the Treaty of Frankfurt of 8/20 November 1813 and the Treaty of 15 May 1815.

45. Martens, *Recueil*, v. 4, no. 110 (8/20 July 1819), pp. 146–86; no. 119–20 (29 June/10 July 1819), pp. 246–51; no. 121 (2/14 April 1816), pp. 251–64; *VPR*, v. 2 (10), doc. 200 (5/17 March 1819), pp. 702–3, Nesselrode to Pahlen; n. 309, pp. 841–42; v. 3 (11) doc. 73 (23 December 1819/4 January 1820), pp. 205–10, memorandum of instruction from the Ministry of Foreign Affairs to Russia's diplomatic representatives abroad.

46. RGADA, f. 3, op. 1, d. 162, ll. 21–310b., sessions of 7, 9, 10 November. For basic information about the boundaries and status of German states, I rely on Gerhard Köbler, *Historisches Lexikon der deutschen Länder: Die deutschen Territorien und reichsunmittelbaren Geschlechter vom Mittelalter bis zur Gegenwart* (Darmstadt: Wissenschaftliche Buchgesellschaft; Munich: C. H. Beck, 1988). Except for place names that have recognized Anglophone equivalents, I follow the spelling found in Köbler. For allied pledges to assist German states in obtaining land swaps, see also Martens, *Recueil*, v. 3, no. 79–96 (28 May/9 June 1815), pp. 207–315, especially pp. 272–73 for articles 49–50.

47. *VPR*, v. 2 (10), doc. 150 (17/29 September 1818), pp. 504–9, report from Kapodistrias to Alexander; doc. 169 (9/21 November 1818), pp. 581–82, letter from Alexander to William I of Hessen-Kassel (identical letters were sent Frederick William III and Castlereagh). In spring 1820 individual claims for the restitution of property continued to reach Russia's Ministry of Foreign Affairs. For a claim involving private property that was transferred from French to Russian forces and then from the commander of Russian troops to the city of Hamburg, see AVP RI, f. 133, op. 468, d. 2990, Doklady, ll. 49–51, draft note to the resident minister in Hamburg Struve approved by Alexander (8 May 1820).

48. The relevant articles promised allied assistance for German princes trying to arrange land swaps. Russian interest in the rights of German sovereigns had been evident already at the Congress of Vienna. See RGADA, f. 15, op. 1, d. 533, Alexander's instructions of 3/15 February 1815 to Russia's first plenipotentiary at the Congress of Vienna, Count Andrei K. Razumovskii.

49. During the years 1805–15, Hessen-Homburg was mediatized into Hessen-Darmstadt.

50. On this subject, see Thomas Nipperdey, *Germany from Napoleon to Bismarck, 1800–1866*, trans. Daniel Nolan (Princeton, NJ: Princeton University Press, 1996).

51. In 1815 Berg became a province of Prussia (Rheinprovinz).

52. *VPR*, v. 2 (10), doc. 33 (6/18 December 1817), pp. 104–9, Nesselrode to envoy in Dresden V. V. Khanykov. The Grand Duchy of Saxony-Weimar-Eisenach, known for its liberal government, was established in 1815 and became part of Thuringia in 1920. Köbler, *Historisches Lexikon*, 532.

53. Although the Russian government refrained from public criticism of Karl August, the grand duke responded to pressure from Austria and Prussia by strengthening censorship and initiating judicial proceedings against professors at the University of Jena. *VPR*, v. 2 (10), n. 46, p. 750.

54. *VPR*, v. 2 (10), doc. 20 (17/29 November 1817), pp. 68–69, Nesselrode to Anstett; doc. 31 (3/15 December 1817), pp. 98–100, Nesselrode to Stackelberg; doc. 33 (6/18 December 1817), pp. 104–9, Nesselrode to Khanykov; doc. 39 (21 December 1817/2 January 1818), pp. 123–25, Stackelberg to Nesselrode.

55. The assassin, Karl Sand (1795–1820), viewed the murder as a call to revolutionary action and was executed for his crime. On Sand, the threat of radicalism, and the Karlsbad Decrees, see Wolfram Siemann, *Metternich: Strategist and Visionary*, trans. Daniel Steuer (Cambridge, MA: Harvard University Press, 2019), Kindle edition, 567–601.

56. James J. Sheehan, *German History 1770–1866* (New York: Oxford University Press, 1989), 406–8, 449–50; Stefan Rohrbacher, "Hep-Hep Riots (1819)," in *Antisemitism: A Historical Encyclopedia of Persecution*, ed. Richard S. Levy, 2 vols. (Santa Barbara, CA: ABC-CLIO, 2005), 1: 297–98.

57. For Aleksandr S. Sturdza's analysis of why the German Confederation could not succeed, see RGADA, f. 3, op. 1, d. 78, Reports and correspondence of Sturdza to Kapodistrias, ll. 153–95. Writing to Kapodistrias in February and March 1820, Sturdza highlighted his wish, in light of the conferences in Vienna, to provide the ministry with good ideas that invited reflection.

58. In July 1820 a meeting of German ministers accepted a revised federal constitution that limited discussion of liberal policies (Jewish emancipation, religious toleration, and economic reform), reinforced restrictions on changes to federal and state institutions, allowed the confederation to intervene in the domestic affairs of federated states to preserve order (article 26), and prohibited German sovereigns from accepting constitutions that hampered the fulfilment of obligations to the confederation (article 58). According to James Sheehan, plans of 1821–22 for a federal military policy and wartime army had little practical effect, and from 1819–20 onward, "the German Confederation moved

to the fringes of national life." In 1820 this was not yet apparent to the peacemakers of Europe. Sheehan, *German History*, 391–425. On Metternich's concerns about the spread of revolution, especially if Prussia adopted a constitution, see the report from Russia's ambassador in Berlin, David M. Alopeus, to Nesselrode: *VPR*, v. 3 (11), doc. 23 (19/31 July 1819), pp. 77–80. In July 1820, the Prussian government described the country as politically calm. AVP RI, f. 133, op. 468, d. 2992, Doklady, ll. 284–86. On German constitutionalism, see Markus J. Prutsch, *Making Sense of Constitutional Monarchism in Post-Napoleonic France and Germany* (London: Palgrave Macmillan, 2013); Morten Nordhagen Ottosen, "The Practical Politics of Restoration Constitutionalism: The Cases of Scandinavia and South Germany," in *A History of the European Restorations. Volume I: Governments, States and Monarchy*, ed. Michael Broers and Ambrogio A. Caiani (London: Bloomsbury Academic, 2020), 1: 121–31; Georg Eckert, "Royal Opposition against the *Ancien Régime*: The Case of Württemberg," in Broers and Caiani, *European Restorations*, 1: 133–43.

59. *VPR*, v. 3 (11), doc. 5 (8/20 May 1819), pp. 19–20, Nesselrode to Alopeus; doc. 11 (3/15 June 1819), pp. 35–36, dispatch from Nesselrode to Khanykov (an identical dispatch was sent to Anstett); doc. 23 (19/31 July 1819), pp. 77–80, Alopeus to Nesselrode; doc. 44 (6/18 October 1819), pp. 136–37, Kapodistrias to Alopeus. In a letter of 4/16 October 1819 to Emperor Francis of Austria, Alexander expressed support for the measures adopted in Frankfurt (the Karlsbad Decrees). *VPR*, v. 3 (11), doc. 43, pp. 134–35. Additional documents describing the Russian response to the Karlsbad Decrees can be found in RGADA, f. 15, op. 1, d. 279, ll. 144–840b. These documents, all confirmed in November and early December 1819, include circular letters to Russia's ministers in Germany, a memorandum presenting Emperor Alexander's thoughts on German affairs, and a dispatch to Count Lieven. On the refusal to comment publicly on constitutional debates and reforms inside German states, see *VPR*, v. 3 (11), doc. 67 (30 November/12 December 1819), pp. 190–92, Nesselrode to Pahlen; doc. 89 (4/16 February 1820), pp. 256–57, Nesselrode to envoys Alopeus (Berlin), Anstett (Frankfurt), Golovkin (Vienna), P. B. Kozlovskii (Stuttgart and Karlsruhe), and Pahlen (Munich). On the continuation of moderate policies, despite concern about the impact of harmful ideas on Russian students attending German universities, see Alexander's orders of 11/23 November 1820 sent from Troppau to minister of internal affairs Count Viktor P. Kochubei (1768–1834). AVP RI, f. 133, op. 468, d. 2990, Doklady, ll. 79–82.

60. Genrikh A. Struve's dispatch of 1/13 July 1820 illustrates the ongoing support for moderate constitutional government. Struve wrote this report after the outbreak of revolution in Spain and the Kingdom of the Two Sicilies. AVP RI, f. 133, op. 468, d. 2992, Doklady, ll. 253–540b.

61. See Alexander's letter of 4/16 October 1819 to Francis I and Kapodistrias's dispatch of 6/18 October 1819 to Alopeus. *VPR*, v. 3 (11), doc. 43, pp. 134–35; doc. 44, pp. 136–37. On discussions with Britain, see *VPR*, v. 3 (11), doc. 55 (22 November/4 December 1819), pp. 163–66, Nesselrode to Lieven; doc. 90 (4/16 February 1820), pp. 257–62, Nesselrode to Alopeus; doc. 103 (3/15 March 1820), pp. 318–20, Nesselrode to Lieven; RGADA, f. 15, op. 1, d. 279, ll. 180–840b., dispatch of 22 November/4 December 1819 to

Lieven with a copy of the instruction to ministers in Germany and the thoughts of the emperor on the situation in Germany. On the harmful consequences of the Karlsbad Decrees, see the confidential letter from Kapodistrias to Austria's envoy in Saint Petersburg Ludwig Joseph Lebzeltern: *VPR*, v. 3 (11), doc. 66 (30 November/12 December 1819), pp. 188–90. See also the overview of Alexander's ideas on German affairs: *VPR*, v. 3 (11), doc. 54 (21 November/3 December 1819), pp. 153–62; RGADA, f. 15, op. 1, d. 279, ll. 155–710b. Finally, see the subsequent instructions from the Ministry of Foreign Affairs to Russia's diplomats serving abroad, which reiterated the policy of non-interference in German affairs, including pronouncements on the Karlsbad Decrees, and stressed that only through the use of moral force could governments ensure the well-being of peoples: *VPR*, v. 3 (11), doc. 73 (23 December 1819/4 January 1820), pp. 205–10.

62. *VPR*, v. 3 (11), doc. 54 (21 November/3 December 1819), pp. 153–62; RGADA, f. 15, op. 1, d. 279, ll. 155–710b.

63. *VPR*, v. 3 (11), doc. 67 (30 November/12 December 1819), pp. 190–92, Nesselrode to Pahlen.

64. For a summary treatment and bibliography on this subject, see Elise Kimerling Wirtschafter, *Russia's Age of Serfdom 1649–1861* (Malden, MA: Blackwell Publishing, 2008), chaps. 5, 8. For recent Russian studies, see S. V. Mironenko, *Aleksandr I i dekabristy: Rossiia v pervoi chetverti XIX veka; Vybor puti* (Moscow: Kuchkovo pole, 2017); Mariia Maiofis, *Vozzvanie k Evrope: Literaturnoe obshchestvo "Arzamas" i rossiiskii modernizatsionnyi proekt 1815–1818 godov* (Moscow: Novoe literaturnoe obozrenie, 2008).

65. *VPR*, v. 3 (11), doc. 54 (21 November/3 December 1819), pp. 156–57.

66. On the idealized patriarchal household, see Elise Kimerling Wirtschafter, *The Play of Ideas in Russian Enlightenment Theater* (DeKalb: Northern Illinois University Press, 2003), chap. 3; Carolyn Johnston Pouncy, ed. and trans., *The Domostroi: Rules for Russian Households in the Time of Ivan the Terrible* (Ithaca, NY: Cornell University Press, 1994).

67. *VPR*, v. 3 (11), doc. 88 (4/16 February 1820), pp. 250–56, Nesselrode to Alopeus, Anstett, Golovkin, Kozlovskii, and Pahlen; doc. 90 (4/16 February 1820), pp. 257–62, Nesselrode to Alopeus; doc. 91 (10/22 February 1820), pp. 262–64, Pozzo di Borgo to Nesselrode.

68. *VPR*, v. 3 (11), doc. 90 (4/16 February 1820), pp. 257–62, Nesselrode to Alopeus; doc. 120 (4/16 May 1820), pp. 381–83, Lieven to Nesselrode.

69. RGADA, f. 3, op. 1, d. 78, ll. 104–230b., 3480b.–50. Sturdza, with the assistance of his "collaborateur" Baron Brunness, produced several analyses of German affairs in which he criticized the underlying principles of the German Confederation and the protocols of the Vienna conferences where discussion of constitutional reform (which eventually led to the *Schlussakte*) was ongoing. Sturdza argued that the German Confederation was fundamentally incompatible with the general alliance of European states, suggested that Germany's collective federal existence could only come about through the restoration of imperial power (a reference to the Holy Roman Empire abolished by Napoleon in 1806), and criticized the Karlsbad Decrees for banning subversive political speech but not blasphemy or attacks on religion. The politics of nations, Sturdza insisted,

could not be separated from their morality, by which he meant Christian morality. According to Sturdza, the effort to achieve a united Germany was bound to fail. RGADA, f. 3, op. 1, d. 78, ll. 153–95.

70. Alexander M. Martin, *Romantics, Reformers, Reactionaries: Russian Conservative Thought and Politics in the Reign of Alexander I* (DeKalb: Northern Illinois University Press, 1997); Stella Ghervas, *Réinventer la tradition: Alexandre Stourdza et l'Europe de la Sainte-Alliance* (Paris: Honoré Champion, 2008).

71. Alexander decided not to discuss constitutional principles in Aix-la-Chapelle, because he realized that the mass of Russian nobles opposed both constitutional projects and the abolition of serfdom. Maiofis, *Vozzvanie k Evrope*, 24-26. Equally noteworthy, historians distinguish between old regime and modern constitutions. Modern constitutions such as those of the American and French revolutions of the late eighteenth century represented "the fundamental law of the state from which the legislative, executive and judicial authority of the government derives." Modern constitutions define "the relationship of the government and the governed" and guarantee the "'civil rights' of individuals." Old regime constitutions corresponded to the "body of laws, regulations and customs by which a state is governed." The semantic confusion of the early nineteenth century explains why individual and official attitudes toward constitutions sometimes seemed inconsistent. Janet M. Hartley, "The 'Constitutions' of Finland and Poland in the Reign of Alexander I: Blueprints for Reform in Russia?" In *Finland and Poland in the Russian Empire: A Comparative Study*, ed. M. Branch, J. Hartley, and A. Maczak (London: School of Slavonic and East European Studies, University of London, 1995), 41–59, here 41–42.

72. RGADA, f. 3, op. 1, d. 162, ll. 40–420b., 72–730b., sessions of 13, 20, 21 November.

73. See the Treaty of Alliance of 14/26 September 1815 and the Russian government's memorandum of 26 September/8 October 1818, submitted to the ministers of Austria, Britain, and Prussia.

74. VPR, v. 2 (10), doc. 96 (4/16 April 1818), pp. 297–304, here p. 301, Golovkin to Kapodistrias.

Chapter 3: Alliance Unity and Intervention in Naples (1820–21)

1. *VPR*, v. 3 (11), n. 227, pp. 781–83.

2. On Germany, see *VPR*, v. 3 (11), doc. 196 (26 November/8 December 1820), pp. 635–44, instruction from Nesselrode to Major General Konstantin Khristoforovich Benkendorf. For Russian evaluations of political conditions in France, see *VPR*, v. 3 (11), doc. 7 (8/20 May 1819), pp. 23–27, personal letter from Nesselrode to Kapodistrias; doc. 13 (8/20 June 1819), pp. 38–39, Nesselrode to Lieven; doc. 19 (5/17 July 1819), pp. 53–55, report from Nesselrode to Alexander; doc. 20 (15/22 July 1819), pp. 55–77, report from Kapodistrias to Alexander; doc. 128 (29 May/10 June 1820), pp.408–11, Pozzo di Borgo to Nesselrode. For Russian efforts to organize a common allied communication on French politics addressed to Louis XVIII, see *VPR*, v. 3 (11), doc. 25 (26 July/7 August 1819), pp. 81–84, Nesselrode to Lieven; doc. 32 (12/24 August 1819), pp. 94–104,

memorial memorandum of Kapodistrias; doc. 56 (22 November/4 December 1819), pp. 166–72, memorial memorandum from the Russian cabinet to the governments of Austria, Britain, and Prussia. On French fears about Austria's plans to intervene in Italy and Russia's effort to reassure France that Austria did not seek conquest, see *VPR*, v. 3 (11), doc. 158 (25 August/6 September 1820), p. 496, confidential letter from Kapodistrias to Pozzo di Borgo.

3. The Duke of Richelieu replaced Charles Maurice de Talleyrand as head of the French government in September 1815, following the electoral victory of the ultra-royalists. Richelieu also had been in Russian service, with interruptions, during the years 1790 to 1814 and enjoyed Emperor Alexander's trust. The duke's resignation in December 1818 resulted from the ascendance of Minister of Police Élie Decazes, a centrist known for his efforts to accommodate liberals. Decazes did not formally become head of the government until after elections in the fall of 1819, which increased the power of independents. Following the assassination of Louis XVIII's nephew, the Duke of Berry, on the night of 13–14 February 1820, the king dismissed Decazes and replaced him with Richelieu. But Richelieu again resigned in December 1821, due to radical and ultra-royalist opposition. G. de Bertier de Sauvigny, "French Politics, 1814–47," in *The New Cambridge Modern History. Vol. 9: War and Peace in an Age of Upheaval, 1793–1830*, ed. C. W. Crawley (Cambridge: Cambridge University Press, 1965), 340–49. Allied concern about political stability in France continued into 1822. See *VPR*, v. 4 (12), doc. 149 (23 January/4 February 1822), pp. 414–18, Nesselrode to Pozzo di Borgo; AVP RI, f. 133, op. 468, d. 2992, Doklady, l. 2–110b., summary of reports received from Russia's missions abroad from the end of last year to the present day (30 March 1820).

4. Charles IV of Spain (ruled 1788–1808) was the great-grandson of Louis XIV, brother to Ferdinand I of the Kingdom of the Two Sicilies, and father to Ferdinand VII of Spain. Richard Stites, *The Four Horsemen: Riding to Liberty in Post-Napoleonic Europe* (New York: Oxford University Press, 2014), Kindle edition, chap. 1.

5. Stites, *Four Horsemen*, chap. 2.

6. The king fled to Brazil after France invaded Portugal in November 1807; he returned to Lisbon in 1821 in response to Portuguese and British pressure. Brazil became independent in 1822. Stites, *Four Horsemen*, location 2167–74; R. A. Humphreys, "The Emancipation of Latin America," in Crawley, *New Cambridge Modern History*, 612–38.

7. At the Congress of Vienna, Ferdinand IV of Naples and III of Sicily became Ferdinand I of the Kingdom of the Two Sicilies. Stites, *Four Horsemen*, chap. 3; J. M. Roberts, "Italy, 1793–1830," in Crawley, *New Cambridge Modern History*, 412–38.

8. Nor did ongoing negotiations about allied intervention prevent further revolutionary outbreaks. Following an insurrection in the Kingdom of Sardinia (Sardinia-Piedmont) on 9/10 March 1821, a provisional government proclaimed the Spanish constitution of 1812, and the Sardinian king, Victor Emmanuel I, abdicated in favor of his brother, Charles Felix. Charles Felix then fled to Laibach to appeal to the great powers. Austria intervened, and the revolution ended within a month. Stites, *Four Horsemen*, location 4200–15.

9. *VPR*, v. 3 (11), doc. 56 (22 November/4 December 1819), pp. 166–72, memorial memorandum from the Russian cabinet to the governments of Austria, Britain, and Prussia; doc. 73 (23 December 1819/4 January 1820), pp. 205–10, memorandum of instruction from the Ministry of Foreign Affairs to Russia's diplomatic representatives abroad.

10. The meetings between Castlereagh, Kapodistrias, and Lieven took place in London in August 1819. For the memorandum of 24 September 1819, see *VPR*, v. 3 (11), n. 75, p. 741. On Castlereagh's diplomacy and British policy with respect to Naples, see John Bew, *Castlereagh: A Life* (New York: Oxford University Press, 2012), chap. 16.

11. *VPR*, v. 3 (11), doc. 32 (12/24 August 1819), pp. 94–104, memorial memorandum of Kapodistrias; doc. 56 (22 November/4 December 1819), pp. 166–72, memorial memorandum from the Russian cabinet to the governments of Austria, Britain, and Prussia. See also *VPR*, v. 3 (11), doc. 25 (26 July/7 August 1819), pp. 81–84, Nesselrode to Lieven.

12. *VPR*, v. 3 (11), doc. 56 (22 November/4 December 1819), pp. 166–72, memorial memorandum from the Russian cabinet to the governments of Austria, Britain, and Prussia.

13. *VPR*, v. 3 (11), doc. 73 (23 December 1819/4 January 1820), pp. 205–10, memorandum of instruction from the Ministry of Foreign Affairs to Russia's diplomatic representatives abroad.

14. On the assassination of the Duke of Berry, see also AVP RI, f. 133, op. 468, d. 2992, Doklady, ll. 121–230b.

15. *VPR*, v. 3 (11), doc. 96 (February 1820), pp. 274–85, memorandum of Obreskov.

16. AVP RI, f. 133, op. 468, d. 2992, Doklady, l. 1590b., summary of dispatch from Mr. Anstett submitted to the emperor.

17. RGADA, f. 3, op. 1, d. 78, Reports and correspondence from Sturdza to Kapodistrias, ll. 325–270b., 3450b.–48. Sturdza's role is confirmed by Alexander M. Martin, who discusses the review in *Romantics, Reformers, Reactionaries: Russian Conservative Thought and Politics in the Reign of Alexander I* (DeKalb: Northern Illinois University Press, 1997), 176–79. See also Stella Ghervas, *Réinventer la tradition: Alexandre Stourdza et l'Europe de la Sainte-Alliance* (Paris: Honoré Champion, 2008); Elise Kimerling Wirtschafter, "Russian Perspectives on European Order: 'Review of the Year 1819,'" in *Russia and the Napoleonic Wars*, ed. Janet M. Hartley, Paul Keenan, and Dominic Lieven (New York: Palgrave Macmillian, 2015), 57–69.

18. The review was divided into two parts. The first, dated 12 December 1819, covered the international political events of the year, and the second, dated 14 January 1820, covered political divisions and ideologies in Europe. The document located in RGADA contains only part 1. Martin briefly discusses the contents of part 2 in *Romantics*, 175–79.

19. The Congress of Vienna had outlawed the slave trade in principle, and the British government, which had made the trade illegal in 1807, used its naval power to search suspect vessels at sea. Unilateral British action ended after British courts in the *Le Louis* judgment of 1817 rejected the right of the Royal Navy to stop and search the slaving ships of powers that had not requested assistance. The reference to Sweden and Denmark concerned Sweden's refusal to accept responsibility for Norway's debt. By a treaty of 1815 Denmark had received the Duchy of Lauenburg in return for Swedish Pomerania, which Prussia then purchased from Sweden. According to Schroeder, the territorial settlement

between Denmark and Sweden, mediated by Russia, marked the end of the Northern Question and the beginning of a tradition of Swedish neutrality comparable to that of Switzerland. At this time also, the Norwegians submitted to Swedish rule, and at the Congress of Aix-la-Chapelle, the sovereigns collectively addressed the Swedish monarch concerning Sweden's responsibility for the Norwegian debt. Reportedly, under British mediation, the contracting parties resolved the dispute with a convention concluded in Copenhagen on 1 September 1819. Brendan Simms, *Europe: The Struggle for Supremacy, from 1453 to the Present* (New York: Basic Books, 2013), 168, 181–88; Paul W. Schroeder, *The Transformation of European Politics 1763–1848* (New York: Oxford University Press, 1994), 572, 578, 766–67; *VPR*, v. 3 (11), doc. 73 (23 December 1819/4 January 1820), pp. 205–10, memorandum of instruction from the Ministry of Foreign Affairs to Russia's diplomatic representatives abroad; n. 78, p. 742.

20. Concern about instability in France led in 1818 to a final settlement on reparations and to the early withdrawal of allied occupation forces. In 1817 the Bourbon government had introduced a constitutional charter with a franchise restricted to 100,000 voters. Although Bonapartist and royalist deputies remained critical of the government's willingness to accept allied interference in France's domestic politics, the Bourbons adhered to the terms of the Vienna settlement and resisted popular pressure to pursue a more aggressive foreign policy. Simms, *Europe*, 185–86.

21. For discussion of Sturdza's 1818 *Mémoire sur l'état actuel de l'Allemagne*, see Ghervas, *Réinventer*, 202–17.

22. The attacks on Jews likewise caused Metternich to conclude that Germany lacked security. James J. Sheehan, *German History 1770–1866* (New York: Oxford University Press, 1989), 407–8, 449–50.

23. Instructions of 23 December 1819/4 January 1820, sent to Russia's diplomats abroad, concluded that the German unity represented by the Karlsbad/Frankfurt decrees of 20 September 1819 had proven illusory. The instructions ordered Russia's ministers in Germany not to support a specific policy or participate in German politics. *VPR*, v. 3 (11), doc. 73 (23 December 1819/4 January 1820), pp. 205–10.

24. Another issue being discussed at the time Sturdza wrote the review was the dispute between Spain and Portuguese Brazil over the Rio de la Plata. Related to this was the commercial liberty of the Spanish colonies. A conference in Paris tried to mediate these questions. *VPR*, v. 3 (11), doc. 73 (23 December 1819/4 January 1820), pp. 205–10, memorandum of instruction from the Ministry of Foreign Affairs to Russia's diplomatic representatives abroad.

25. The agreement with Spain ended the legal importation of slaves into Spain proper; however, Spanish involvement in the international slave trade continued. Nor did Portuguese involvement in the transatlantic slave trade end. Simms, *Europe*, 199–200; *VPR*, v. 3 (11), doc. 73 (23 December 1819/4 January 1820), pp. 205–10, memorandum of instruction from the Ministry of Foreign Affairs to Russia's diplomatic representatives abroad.

26. Diplomatic conferences in London addressed the abolition of the slave trade and repression of the Barbary states. In addition, plenipotentiaries meeting in Aix-la-Chapelle authorized Britain and France to organize a mission to resolve the problem of the

Barbary states. Instructions of 23 December 1819/4 January 1820, sent to Russia's diplomats abroad, indicated that to date the efforts had not produced results. *VPR*, v. 3 (11), doc. 73 (23 December 1819/4 January 1820), pp. 205–10, memorandum of instruction from the Ministry of Foreign Affairs to Russia's diplomatic representatives abroad.

27. Selim III (1761–1808) ruled as sultan from 1789 to 1807. He supported European-style military organization and training; the reform of Ottoman administration, taxation, and land tenure; and the development of direct diplomatic contacts with Europe. Selim's reforms triggered rebellion among Janissaries and provincial notables, which led to his imprisonment and assassination.

28. The current order of things referred to Ottoman and Persian relationships with the neighboring Christian powers, Russia and Austria, that had been codified in the treaties of Sistova (1791), Jassy (1792), Bucharest (1812), and Gulistan (1813). Sturdza also expressed concern about the British protectorate over the Ionian Islands, an arrangement that Russia had encouraged (and Kapodistrias supported) in order to prevent Austrian control, which would have represented a significant barrier to Russian policy in the Balkans and to Greek national aspirations. Schroeder, *Transformation*, 86–87, 572–74; Thomas Sanders, Ernest Tucker, and Gary Hamburg, eds., *Russian-Muslim Confrontation in the Caucasus: Alternative Visions of the Conflict between Imam Shamil and the Russians, 1830–1859* (New York: RoutledgeCurzon, 2004).

29. *VPR*, v. 3 (11), doc. 102 (3/15 March 1820), pp. 315–18, Nesselrode to Lieven.

30. *VPR*, v. 3 (11), doc. 108 (30 March/11 April 1820), pp. 337–43, memorandum from Kapodistrias to Alexander; RGADA, f. 3, op. 1, d. 78, ll. 281–990b.; AVP RI, f. 133, op. 468, d. 2992, Doklady, ll. 2–110b., summary of reports received from Russia's missions abroad from the end of last year to the present day (30 March 1820); ll. 12–140b., follow-up to the possible courses of action indicated in the agenda of 30 March (6 April 1820). Emperor Alexander also continued to communicate to the allies the need for collective action. *VPR*, v. 3 (11), doc. 113 (19 April/1 May 1820), pp. 351–53, Nesselrode to Golovkin, Lieven, and Alopeus.

31. Electoral reforms limiting the franchise took place in June 1820. AVP RI, f. 133, op. 468, d. 2992, Doklady, l. 20b., summary of reports received from Russia's missions abroad from the end of last year to the present day (30 March 1820).

32. The Spanish viceroyalty of Rio de la Plata included present-day Argentina, Uruguay, Paraguay, and Bolivia. Rebellion began in the viceroyalty in 1810, and north of the Rio de la Plata, Spain and Portugal competed for territory. In 1815 the Portuguese colony of Brazil became a kingdom, and in 1816 Portuguese Brazil extended its frontier all the way to the river. European efforts to mediate the conflict had not succeeded. Humphreys, "Latin America," 614–21.

33. AVP RI, f. 133, op. 468, d. 2992, Doklady, ll. 236–370b., dispatch from Pozzo di Borgo (27 July 1820). See also the review of events during 1820, up to the month of August, sent by Sturdza to Kapodistrias on 19 September/1 October 1820. RGADA, f. 3, op. 1, d. 78, ll. 281–990b.

34. In modern parlance, George IV sought a divorce. On sedition in Britain and its relationship to economic, social, and political conditions, see Lieven's report to Nesselrode

in *VPR*, v. 3 (11), doc. 87 (2/14 February 1820), pp. 241–50. On the case against the queen, see the report from Nesselrode to Alexander and the dispatches from London (all from July 1820) summarized in AVP RI, f. 133, op. 468, d. 2992, Doklady, ll. 238–45, 247–480b., 252–520b., 265–650b.; Bew, *Castlereagh*, chap. 15.

35. AVP RI, f. 133, op. 468, d. 2992, Doklady, ll. 236–370b., dispatch from Pozzo di Borgo (27 July 1820). From mid-July until late August, Russia's Ministry of Foreign Affairs received a steady stream of reports on the revolution in Naples and revolutionary developments in other parts of Italy. British policy accepted Austria's special interest in the Kingdom of the Two Sicilies but opposed allied intervention. AVP RI, f. 133, op. 468, d. 2992, Doklady, ll. 293–3010b., 303–6, 324–250b., 338–500b., reports from Nesselrode to Alexander summarizing dispatches from Naples and Florence (covering the period from 17 July to 24 August 1820).

36. The Prussian government acknowledged that Britain would not accept Austria's proposals for intervention. AVP RI, f. 133, op. 468, d. 2992, Doklady, ll. 284–86, dispatch of 20 July/1 August 1820 received from Berlin.

37. The Troppau conferences continued until 12/24 December 1820. O. V. Orlik, *Rossiia v mezhdunarodnykh otnosheniiakh 1815–1829: Ot Venskogo kongressa do Adrianopol'skogo mira* (Moscow: Nauka, 1998), 38–45; Schroeder, *Transformation*, 607–14; Henry A. Kissinger, *A World Restored: Metternich, Castlereagh and the Problems of Peace, 1812–1822* (Boston: Houghton Mifflin Company, 1957), 256–66; Jennifer Mitzen, *Power in Concert: The Nineteenth-Century Origins of Global Governance* (Chicago: University of Chicago Press, 2013), 102–23. Christian Gunther Bernstorff (1769–1835) served as Prussian minister of foreign affairs in 1818–31.

38. On Alexander's conservative turn and opposition within Russian society to Austrian intervention in Naples, see M. A. Dodolev, "Russia and the Spanish Revolution of 1820–1823," *Soviet Studies in History* 8, no. 3 (Winter 1970): 252–71. For recent treatment of Alexander's conservatism and continuing interest in constitutional reform, see Patrick O'Meara, *The Russian Nobility in the Age of Alexander I* (London: Bloomsbury Academic, 2019), chap. 8.

39. AVP RI, f. 133, op. 468, d. 2992, Doklady, l. 189, communications about a meeting between Alexander and Francis (May-June 1820).

40. *VPR*, v. 3 (11), doc. 129 (2/14 June 1820), p. 411, Stackelberg to Nesselrode; doc. 131 (2/14 June 1820), pp. 414–15, Nesselrode to Golovkin; doc. 141 (24 June/6 July 1820), pp. 434–36, Stackelberg to Nesselrode; doc. 146 (15/27 July 1820), pp. 450–52, personal letter from Nesselrode to Golovkin; doc. 152 (3/15 August 1820), pp. 475–76, chargé d'affaires in Florence A. V. Sverchkov to Nesselrode; doc. 155 (17/29 August 1820), pp. 482–85, Golovkin to Kapodistrias; doc. 156 (21 August/2 September 1820), pp. 485–91, Kapodistrias to Stackelberg; doc. 171 (26 September/8 October 1820), pp. 532–33, Stackelberg to Kapodistrias. On 3 August 1820 Nesselrode reported to Alexander that Austria continued to seek a private meeting between him and Francis that would not include the Prussian monarch. France had proposed a general meeting of the sovereigns, and Britain had not yet offered a precise response because of preoccupation with the trial of the queen. AVP RI, f. 133, op. 468, d. 2992, Doklady, ll. 303–6, report from Nesselrode to Alexander (3 August 1820).

41. *VPR*, v. 3 (11), n. 260, p. 798.

42. *VPR*, v. 3 (11), n. 212, pp. 776–77. In dispatches of 3/15 and 7/19 August 1820, Count Iurii A. Golovkin, Russia's envoy in Vienna, reported on the deployment of Austrian troops to the Kingdom of Lombardy-Venetia. Golovkin's implied recognition of Austria's special interest in Italy did not prevent him from attributing the poor condition of the Austro-Italian provinces to "the vices" of Austrian administration. AVP RI, f. 133, op. 468, d. 2992, Doklady, ll. 28–320b., summary of dispatches received from Golovkin (3/15 and 7/19 August), Italinskii (28 July/11 August), Alopeus (12 August), and Anstett (no date given) since the departure of H. I. M. from Poltava (17/29 August 1820).

43. AVP RI, f. 133, op. 468, d. 2992, Doklady, ll. 28–320b., summary of dispatches received since 17/29 August 1820.

44. In the dispatches of 3/15 and 7/19 August 1820, Golovkin also reported on British support for swift Austrian action in Naples. On 24 August Nesselrode confirmed that Britain deferred to Austria on the measures to be taken in Naples and therefore communicated directly with the court of Vienna on the matter. See AVP RI, f. 133, op. 468, d. 2992, Doklady, ll. 28–320b., summary of dispatches received since 17/29 August 1820; ll. 339–440b., report from Nesselrode to Alexander (24 August 1820).

45. *VPR*, v. 3 (11), doc. 151 (2/14 August 1820), pp. 468–75, Lieven to Nesselrode; doc. 163 (6/18 September 1820), pp. 504–6, personal letter from Kapodistrias to Lieven; doc. 164 (12/24 September 1820), pp. 506–14, Lieven to Kapodistrias; AVP RI, f. 133, op. 468, d. 2992, Doklady, ll. 28–320b., summary of dispatches received since 17/29 August 1820; ll. 339–440b., report from Nesselrode to Alexander (24 August 1820).

46. *VPR*, v. 3 (11), doc. 156 (21 August/2 September 1820), pp. 485–91, Kapodistrias to Stackelberg.

47. *VPR*, v. 3 (11), doc. 156 (21 August/2 September 1820), pp. 485–91, Kapodistrias to Stackelberg. In a dispatch of 28 July/11 August 1820, Andrei I. Italinksii, Russia's envoy in Rome, reported that due to "national hatred" of Austrians in Italy, fear of an Austrian intervention prevented insurrection in the papal states. AVP RI, f. 133, op. 468, d. 2992, Doklady, ll. 28–320b.

48. *VPR*, v. 3 (11), doc. 170 (23 September/5 October 1820), pp. 527–32, letter from Kapodistrias to Sturdza. The language of contagion appeared in numerous documents: see the report of 19 September/1 October 1820 from Sturdza to Kapodistrias, in RGADA, f. 3, d. 78, ll. 279–800b.

49. *VPR*, v. 3 (11), doc. 175 (5/17 October 1820), pp. 540–47; AVP RI, f. 133, op. 468, d. 2992, Doklady, ll. 374–840b., agenda read to Alexander by Kapodistrias on the works in Troppau.

50. For drafts of agendas, protocols, notes, opinions, observations, and memorandums from the conferences in Troppau, see RGADA, f. 3, op. 1, d. 61, On the political conferences in Troppau (October–December 1820).

51. *VPR*, v. 3 (11), doc. 177 (14/26 October 1820), pp. 555–62, report from Kapodistrias and Nesselrode to Alexander; doc. 178 (15/27 October 1820), pp. 562–66, report from Kapodistrias and Nesselrode to Alexander; AVP RI, f. 133, op. 468, d. 2992, Doklady, ll.

385–930b., 411–24, reports from Kapodistrias and Nesselrode on confidential meetings with Metternich in Troppau (15/27 and 16/28 October 1820).

52. *VPR*, v. 3 (11), doc. 177 (14/26 October 1820), pp. 555–62, report from Kapodistrias and Nesselrode to Alexander; AVP RI, f. 133, op. 468, d. 2992, Doklady, ll. 411–24, report from Kapodistrias and Nesselrode to Alexander.

53. *VPR*, v. 3 (11), doc. 178 (15/27 October 1820), pp. 562–66, report from Kapodistrias and Nesselrode to Alexander.

54. AVP RI, f. 133, op. 468, d. 2992, Doklady, ll. 395–97, report from Kapodistrias and Nesselrode to Alexander on the position of Austria (15 October 1820).

55. AVP RI, f. 133, op. 468, d. 2992, Doklady, ll. 405–10, Austrian proposal for a treaty of guarantee.

56. *VPR*, v. 3 (11), doc. 179 (24 October/5 November 1820), pp. 567–72, memorandum from Kapodistrias and Nesselrode to Alexander; doc. 180 (24 October/5 November 1820), pp. 572–76, memorandum from Kapodistrias and Nesselrode to Alexander; AVP RI, f. 133, op. 468, d. 2992, Doklady, ll. 429–45, reports from Kapodistrias and Nesselrode to Alexander on the execution of the plans for Naples agreed to in Troppau (24 October/5 November 1820).

57. *VPR*, v. 3 (11), doc. 179 (24 October/5 November 1820), pp. 567–72, memorandum from Kapodistrias and Nesselrode to Alexander; AVP RI, f. 133, op. 468, d. 2992, Doklady, ll. 429–37, report from Kapodistrias and Nesselrode to Alexander (24 October/5 November 1820). In August France had supported a declaration of "the five powers placed at the center of the general alliance." The declaration would have denounced the means employed in Naples to change the administration and would have explained that despite the allies' respect for "the independence of governments," they could not recognize the new administration until such time as "the king and the nation" pronounced freely "on the constitutive laws of the Kingdom." AVP RI, f. 133, op. 468, d. 2992, Doklady, ll. 28–32ob., summary of dispatches received since 17/29 August 1820.

58. According to Kapodistrias and Nesselrode, Britain and France had several options. They could become parties to the agreement, postpone their accession, accede only as guarantors of allied obligations to the king of Naples, or participate in negotiations with the king as mediators. *VPR*, v. 3 (11), doc. 179 (24 October/5 November 1820), pp. 567–72, memorandum from Kapodistrias and Nesselrode to Alexander; AVP RI, f. 133, op. 468, d. 2992, Doklady, ll. 429–37, report from Kapodistrias and Nesselrode to Alexander (24 October/5 November 1820).

59. *VPR*, v. 3 (11), doc. 180 (24 October/5 November 1820), pp. 572–76, memorandum from Kapodistrias and Nesselrode to Alexander; AVP RI, f. 133, op. 468, d. 2992, Doklady, ll. 438–45, report from Kapodistrias and Nesselrode to Alexander (24 October/5 November 1820).

60. Kapodistrias read the note to Alexander on 16/28 October 1820. AVP RI, f. 133, op. 468, d. 2992, Doklady, ll. 425–28ob., report of Kapodistrias; *VPR*, v. 3 (11), n. 248, p. 791.

61. *VPR*, v. 3 (11), doc. 180 (24 October/5 November 1820), pp. 572–76, memorandum from Kapodistrias and Nesselrode to Alexander; AVP RI, f. 133, op. 468, d. 2992,

Doklady, ll. 438–45, report from Kapodistrias and Nesselrode to Alexander (24 October/5 November 1820).

62. On 8/20 November 1820, the allies agreed to invite the king of the Two Sicilies to meet with them in Laibach, where they planned to reconvene after leaving Troppau. Ferdinand I received the invitation on 6 December 1820 and arrived in Laibach on 7 January 1821. Stites, *Four Horsemen*, location 3876–4004; *VPR*, v. 3 (11), annotations (8/20 November 1820), p. 594, Alexander I, Francis I, and Frederick William III to Ferdinand I; Alexander I to Frederick William III.

63. *VPR*, v. 3 (11), annotation (21 October/2 November 1820), p. 567, response of the Russian cabinet to the communications of the Austrian and Prussian cabinets presented at the sessions of 11/23 and 17/29 October 1820; doc. 181 (26 October/7 November 1820), pp. 577–78, memorandum of the Russian court concerning Metternich's proposals of 17/29 October; n. 240, p. 787; n. 245, p. 789; n. 253, pp. 794–97.

64. *VPR*, v. 3 (11), doc. 184 (2/14 November 1820), pp. 585–87, memorandum of Russia's plenipotentiaries.

65. *VPR*, v. 3 (11), doc. 186 (7/19 November 1820), pp. 589–93, preliminary protocol signed by the plenipotentiaries of Russia, Austria, and Prussia.

66. For consistency I use "Neapolitan" rather than "Sicilian" when referring to the situation in Naples and the Kingdom of the Two Sicilies. Documents of the era used both terms.

67. *British and Foreign State Papers*. Volume 1820–1821 (London, 1830), 1149–51. The document in *State Papers* is dated 8 December. See also *VPR*, v. 3 (11), annotation (24 November/6 December 1820), p. 628. As indicated above, Ferdinand received the invitation to meet with the allies on 6 December. Concerned about the king's ability to leave Naples, the Russian government argued that if the Neapolitan government did not allow Ferdinand to accept the invitation to Laibach, they should seek the mediation of Pope Pius VII. *VPR*, v. 3 (11), annotations (8/20 November 1820), p. 594, Alexander I, Francis I, and Frederick William III to Ferdinand I; Alexander I to Frederick William III; annotation (24 November/6 December 1820), p. 627, opinion of the Russian cabinet on the means of pacification that the allied courts can apply in Naples if the invitation sent to the king is not accepted.

68. Sturdza conveyed his views to Kapodistrias in a report of 5/17 December 1820. RGADA, f. 3, op. 1, d. 78, ll. 311–170b.

69. RGADA, f. 3, op. 1, d. 78, ll. 357–640b., Sturdza to Kapodistrias, account of Sturdza's official correspondence from 14 November 1819 to 12 December 1820, affairs of Naples. For more on Sturdza's views, see *VPR*, v. 3 (11), n. 247, pp. 790–91.

70. *VPR*, v. 3 (11), doc. 189 (10/22 November 1820), pp. 602–3, verbal note from Russia's envoy in the Netherlands K. L. Ful' (Karl Ludwig August Phull) to the minister of foreign affairs of the Netherlands Nagel' (Ann William Karl Nagell). Phull (1757–1826) was a Prussian general who entered Russian service in 1806 and served as envoy in the Netherlands in 1814–21.

71. *VPR*, v. 3 (11), doc. 191 (11/23 November 1820), pp. 608–10, personal letter from Kapodistrias to Mochenigo. Russia's envoy in Turin was Count G. D. Mochenigo (Mocenigo, 1764–1839).

72. See Nesselrode's instruction to Major General Konstantin Khristoforovich Benkendorff (1783–1828), envoy extraordinaire and minister plenipotentiary to the courts of Württemberg and Baden. *VPR*, v. 3 (11), doc. 196 (26 November/8 December 1820), pp. 635–44.

73. The memorandum was sent to the minister of internal affairs V. P. Kochubei. *VPR*, v. 3 (11), doc. 194 (19 November/1 December 1820), pp. 619–27; n. 262, pp. 798–99.

74. The memorandum, authored by Kapodistrias, refused to equate the Austrian proposal with the Russian project for a treaty of guarantee discussed in Aix-la-Chapelle. *VPR*, v. 3 (11), doc. 198 (5/17 December 1820), pp. 648–55, memorandum from the Russian government to the governments of Austria and Prussia; n. 253, pp. 795–96.

75. *VPR*, v. 3 (11), n. 253, pp. 796–97.

76. The documents consulted here include instructions from Nesselrode to Christoph Lieven, Russia's ambassador in London, and reports from Lieven to Nesselrode containing summaries of Lieven's conversations with Castlereagh. *VPR*, v. 3 (11), doc. 182 (28 October/9 November 1820), pp. 579–82, Nesselrode to Lieven; doc. 192 (11/23 November 1820), pp. 610–13, Nesselrode to Lieven; doc. 193 (12/24 November 1820), pp. 614–19, Nesselrode to Lieven; doc. 195 (26 November/8 December 1820), pp. 628–35, Lieven to Nesselrode; doc. 199 (9/21 December 1820), pp. 655–59, Lieven to Nesselrode. On France's opposition: *VPR*, v. 3 (11), doc. 202 (15/27 December 1820), pp. 665–74, memorandum of the Russian cabinet in response to the comments of France's plenipotentiaries on the preliminary protocol of 7/19 November 1820; doc. 203 (15/27 December 1820), pp. 675–76, Kapodistrias to chargé d'affaires in Paris Andrei Andreevich Schröder (1780–?).

77. I develop this point in Elise Kimerling Wirtschafter, *From Serf to Russian Soldier*. (Princeton, NJ: Princeton University Press, 1990); Elise Kimerling Wirtschafter, *Russia's Age of Serfdom, 1649–1861* (Malden, MA: Blackwell Publishing, 2008).

78. *VPR*, v. 3 (11), doc. 182 (28 October/9 November 1820), pp. 579–82, Nesselrode to Lieven.

79. *VPR*, v. 3 (11), doc. 182.

80. *VPR*, v. 3 (11), doc. 182.

81. *VPR*, v. 3 (11), doc. 192 (11/23 November 1820), pp. 610–13, Nesselrode to Lieven.

82. The representatives of Austria and Prussia in London reportedly received comparable instructions.

83. *VPR*, v. 3 (11), doc. 193 (12/24 November 1820), pp. 614–19, Nesselrode to Lieven.

84. *VPR*, annotations (8/20 November 1820), p. 594, Alexander I, Francis I, and Frederick William III to Ferdinand I; Alexander I to Frederick William III.

85. *VPR*, v. 3 (11), doc. 193 (12/24 November 1820), pp. 614–19, Nesselrode to Lieven.

86. Bew, *Castlereagh*, 480–84.

87. *VPR*, v. 3 (11), n. 264, pp. 799–800.

88. As reported by Lieven, neither he nor Castlereagh doubted the sincerity or good intentions of the other. *VPR*, v. 3 (11), doc. 195 (26 November/8 December 1820), pp. 628–35, Lieven to Nesselrode; doc. 199 (9/21 December 1820), pp. 655–59, Lieven to Nesselrode.

89. *VPR*, v. 3 (11), doc. 199 (9/21 December 1820), pp. 655–59, Lieven to Nesselrode.

90. On the political conditions affecting Castlereagh and the British government, see Bew, *Castlereagh*, 478–517.

91. Bew, *Castlereagh*, 478–79. On 13 March 1821 Castlereagh wrote to his brother, Charles Stewart, questioning the future of the alliance: "We cannot afford to have our Line in any degree Mixed with that of the Three Powers, and their Endeavor to Impute to us an unity of views, which does not exist, only Embarrasses us and drives us in Parliament into more decisive disavowals." The declaration of the three powers "not to admit of any departure from the *Legitimate* State of Things" was, according to Castlereagh, "'so odious and so untenable' as to make future cooperation highly problematic." Bew, *Castlereagh*, 508–9.

92. *VPR*, v. 3 (11), doc. 202 (not later than 15/27 December 1820), pp. 665–74, memorandum of the Russian cabinet in response to the comments of France's plenipotentiaries on the preliminary protocol of 7/19 November 1820; doc. 203 (15/27 December 1820), pp. 675–76, Kapodistrias to Schröder.

93. Charles Louis de Secondat, Baron de Montesquieu, The Spirit of the Laws (1748); Cesare Beccaria, On Crimes and Punishments (1764); Jacob Friedrich Bielfeld, Political Institutions (1765). David M. Griffiths, "Introduction: Of Estates, Charters, and Constitutions," in Catherine II's Charters of 1785 to the Nobility and Towns, ed. and trans. David M. Griffiths and George E. Munro (Bakersfield, CA: Charles Schlacks, Jr., 1991).

Chapter 4: To Act in Concert (1821–22)

1. C. A. Bayly, *The Birth of the Modern World, 1780–1914: Global Connections and Comparisons* (Malden, MA: Blackwell Publishing, 2004), 101–2. On recuperation, see Paul W. Schroeder, *The Transformation of European Politics 1763–1848* (New York: Oxford University Press, 1994), 586–93. On Napoleon, see Alan Forrest, *Napoleon: Life, Legacy, and Image; A Biography* (New York: Saint Martin's Press, 2013).

2. Mariia Maiofis, *Vozzvanie k Evrope: Literaturnoe obshchestvo "Arzamas" i rossiiskii modernizatsionnyi proekt 1815–1818 godov* (Moscow: Novoe literaturnoe obozrenie, 2008), 26–27, 414–15, ch. 8.

3. Leo Tolstoy, *War and Peace*, trans. Louise Maude and Aylmer Maude (New York: Simon and Schuster, 1942), second epilogue.

4. Close to 113,000 Russian troops marched to three locations in the Austrian Empire, where they were held in reserve. By May it became clear that the troops would not be needed in Italy; however, an army of 123,000 troops remained close to the Austrian border. *VPR*, v. 4 (12), annotation (3/15 March 1821), p. 47.

5. Austrian troops remained in the Kingdom of the Two Sicilies until December 1826. Richard Stites, *The Four Horsemen: Riding to Liberty in Post-Napoleonic Europe* (New York: Oxford University Press, 2014), Kindle edition, location 3876–4192; J. M. Roberts, "Italy, 1793–1830," in *The New Cambridge Modern History. Vol. 9: War and Peace in an Age of Upheaval, 1793–1830*, ed. C. W. Crawley (Cambridge: Cambridge University Press, 1965), 428–35.

6. RGADA, f. 15, op. 1, d. 289, Correspondence of Metternich to Nesselrode, ll. 8–11, confidential letter from Metternich to Nesselrode. For defense of the revolution and constitutional government, written by a liberal observer in Naples, see RGADA, f. 15, op. 1, d. 375, Papers of Kapodistrias, ll. 224–41; d. 377, Papers of Kapodistrias, ll. 28–37. The observer warned that in the short term allied intervention could be materially successful, but in the long term it would lead to renewed social revolution. The two *mémoires* are preserved in the papers of Kapodistrias. On the false hope that Italian liberals placed in Emperor Alexander, see *VPR*, v. 3 (11), doc. 210 (6/18 January 1821), pp. 695–701, envoy in Rome A. Ia. Italinskii to Kapodistrias.

7. RGADA, f. 3, op. 1, d. 78, Reports and correspondence from Sturdza to Kapodistrias, ll. 319–240b., report no. 59 to Kapodistrias (31 December 1820/12 January 1821).

8. Nor did Sturdza's rejection of revolution extend to the Greek insurrection against the Ottoman Empire, which erupted during the meetings in Laibach. Like Kapodistrias, Sturdza opposed Emperor Alexander's policy of neutrality, advocating instead for Russian intervention on behalf of the Greeks as a defense of persecuted coreligionists. Theophilus C. Prousis, *Russian Society and the Greek Revolution* (DeKalb: Northern Illinois University Press, 1994), 34–38.

9. The Laibach journals are available in AVP RI, f. 133, op. 468, d. 5938, Journals of the Conferences of Laybach (1821).

10. In a *note verbale* inserted into the Laibach journals, France agreed to send to its representative in Naples the same instructions that the Austrian, Prussian, and Russian diplomats received. Britain, by contrast, denounced the revolution, but refused to abandon the policy of neutrality. AVP RI, f. 133, op. 468, d. 5938, ll. 365–650b., journal of 13 January 1822. On the expectation of political reform, see *VPR*, v. 3 (11), doc. 207 (30 December 1820/11 January 1821), pp. 684–89, report from Kapodistrias to Alexander; doc. 208 (31 December 1820/12 January 1821), pp. 689–91, *promemoria* of Kapodistrias's conversation with plenipotentiary of the Kingdom of the Two Sicilies Ruffo; doc. 209 (2/14 January 1821), pp. 692–94, memorandum of Russia's plenipotentiaries; doc. 210 (6/18 January 1821), pp. 695–701, Italinskii to Kapodistrias. On the allies' posture toward King Ferdinand I, see *VPR*, v. 3 (11), doc. 214 (17/29 January 1821), pp. 707–8, memorandum of Russia's plenipotentiaries.

11. The response of the allies was certified on 25 January. AVP RI, f. 133, op. 468, d. 5938, ll. 5–90b., 355–560b., journals of 30 December 1820 and 31 December 1820/12 January 1821.

12. Roberts, "Italy," 431–33; Stites, *Four Horsemen*, location 3876–4004. The allies assumed that the Neapolitan people supported their king and believed they were obeying his wishes when they accepted the revolution. *VPR*, v. 3 (11), doc. 204 (15/27 December 1820), pp. 677–80, circular dispatch from Kapodistrias to envoys in the states of the German Confederation, the Netherlands, Switzerland, Denmark, and the Swedish-Norwegian kingdom.

13. Martsio Mastrilli, Duke of Gallo (1753–1833).

14. The papal plenipotentiary, Cardinal Spina, did not possess the authority to share the pontiff's views with the allies. The cardinal did note, however, that despite the pope's

neutrality, he wished to see the restoration of order in Naples. AVP RI, f. 133, op. 468, d. 5938, ll. 25–26ob., journal of 1/13 January 1821; ll. 32–38ob., journal of 4/16 January 1821; ll. 52–58, journal of 7/19 January 1821; ll. 63–64, journal of 9/21 January 1821; ll. 77–78, journal of 13/25 January 1821; ll. 84–94, journal of 14/26 January 1821, ll. 99–100, journal of 16/28 January 1821; ll. 356–68ob., journal of 31 December 1820/12 January 1821. See also Stites, *Four Horsemen*, location 3876–4004.

15. On the instructions and dispatches read at the conference and on concerns about the safety of the royal family in Naples, see AVP RI, f. 133, op. 468, d. 5938, ll. 99–100, 368–68ob., journal of 16/28 January 1821.

16. The Duke of Gallo reported that he would return to Naples with the letter from Ferdinand to the Duke of Calabria and that he would request additional orders from the king. AVP RI, f. 133, op. 468, d. 5938, ll. 135–36ob., journal of 18 January 1821); ll. 137–38ob., allocution of Metternich to Gallo (18/30 January 1821); ll. 380–85ob., dispatch to Stackelberg (19/31 January 1821); ll. 386–88, dispatch to Stackelberg (19/31 January 1821); ll. 389–89ob., journal of 18 January 1821.

17. AV PRI, f. 133, op. 468, d. 5938, ll. 117–22, rescript to Stackelberg (9/21 November 1820).

18. Stackelberg, Alexander's envoy in Vienna from 1818 to 1835, served in Naples in 1820–22.

19. AVP RI, f. 133, op. 468, d. 5938, ll. 117–22, rescript to Stackelberg (9/21 November 1820).

20. AVP RI, f. 133, op. 468, d. 5938, ll. 101–8, copy of the Austrian instruction sent to Stackelberg; ll. 369–79, instruction for Austria's ministers and chargés d'affaires (19/31 January 1821).

21. If the disorders ended spontaneously, no war contribution would be levied on the peoples of the Two Sicilies. If military force had to be used and war broke out, a war levy would be imposed. AVP RI, f. 133, op. 468, d. 5938, ll. 111–16, draft dispatch to Stackelberg (19/31 January 1821); ll. 123–25ob., dispatch to Stackelberg (19/31 January 1821); ll. 380–85ob., dispatch to Stackelberg (19/31 January 1821); ll. 386–88, dispatch to Stackelberg (19/31 January 1821).

22. AVP RI, f. 133, op. 468, d. 5938, ll. 111–16, draft dispatch to Stackelberg (19/31 January 1821); ll. 380–85ob., dispatch to Stackelberg (19/31 January 1821).

23. AVP RI, f. 133, op. 468, d. 5938, ll. 144–46ob., Austria's position on the army of occupation (29 January 1821).

24. The conference journal of 8/20 February 1821 recorded formal acceptance of the Austrian military plan by Modena, the Roman (papal) state, and Tuscany. AVP RI, f. 133, op. 468, d. 5938, ll. 141–43ob., journal of 21 January/2 February 1821; ll. 149–50, Russia's opinion on Austria's proposals for the army of occupation (21 January/2 February 1821); ll. 153–55ob., journal containing the thoughts of the "King of Naples" on the principles of political reform (8/20 February 1821); ll. 390–91, journal containing Metternich's presentation of Austria's plan for the army of occupation (21 January 1821); ll. 392–92ob., journal of 8 February 1821.

25. According to Henry Kissinger, the plan for political reconstruction in the Two Sicilies came from Metternich. Henry A. Kissinger, *A World Restored: Metternich, Castlereagh, and the Problems of Peace, 1812–1822* (Boston: Houghton Mifflin Company, 1957), 276–79.

26. AVP RI, f. 133, op. 468, d. 5938, ll. 153–55ob., journal containing the thoughts of the "King of Naples" on the principles of political reform (8/20 February 1821); ll. 392–92ob., journal of 8 February 1821.

27. AVP RI, f. 133, op. 468, d. 5938, ll. 161–69ob., journal containing the responses of the courts of Italy to the principles proposed by the King of Naples (9/21 February 1821); ll. 171–72ob., journal of 10/22 February 1821; ll. 178–79, declaration of Russia's plenipotentiaries approved by the emperor in response to the proposals of Prince Ruffo (20 February) and the responses of the courts of Italy (10/22 February 1821); l. 393, journal containing the responses of the courts of Italy to the principles proposed by the King of Naples (9 February 1821); l. 394, journal of 10 February 1821; *VPR*, v. 3 (11), annotation (10/22 February 1821), p. 717, declaration of Russia's plenipotentiaries in response to the declarations of Prince Ruffo (20 February) and the plenipotentiaries of other Italian courts (21 February); annotation (14/26 February 1821), p. 719, session protocol signed by the plenipotentiaries of Russia, Austria, Britain, Modena, the Kingdom of the Two Sicilies, the Roman (papal) state, Prussia, the Kingdom of Sardinia, Tuscany, and France. At the conferences in Verona in December 1822, the plenipotentiaries of Austria, Britain, France, Prussia, Russia, and the Kingdom of the Two Sicilies approved Ferdinand I's request for allied assistance in hiring Swiss mercenaries to serve in his kingdom. The plenipotentiaries of Austria, Prussia, Russia, and the Two Sicilies also supported Ferdinand I's appeal to Francis I to extend the period of the Austrian occupation, if the king considered this necessary. Nesselrode and Bernstorff accepted Metternich's determination that the occupation remained necessary. *VPR*, v. 4 (12), annotation (8 December 1822), p. 604, session protocol approved by the plenipotentiaries of Russia, Austria, Britain, Prussia, and the Kingdom of the Two Sicilies; annotation (9 December 1822), p. 605, confidential protocol of the meeting of the plenipotentiaries of Russia, Austria, Prussia, and the Kingdom of the Two Sicilies. The original occupation was regulated by the Convention of Naples (6/18 October 1821). *VPR*, v. 4 (12), annotation (6/18 October 1821), p. 319, convention on the occupation of the Kingdom of the Two Sicilies by the Austrian army concluded between Russia, Austria, Prussia, and the Kingdom of the Two Sicilies.

28. AVP RI, f. 133, op. 468, d. 5938, ll. 183–84, journal of 14/26 February 1821; ll. 395–95ob., journal of 14 February 1821; *VPR*, v. 3 (11), annotation (14/26 February 1821), p. 719, session protocol signed by the plenipotentiaries of Russia, Austria, Britain, Modena, the Kingdom of the Two Sicilies, the Roman (papal) state, Prussia, the Kingdom of Sardinia, Tuscany, and France.

29. For reports and bulletins on the military occupation, see AVP RI, f. 133, op. 468, d. 5938, ll. 396–438.

30. Stites, *Four Horsemen*, location 4200–4215; Schroeder, *Transformation*, 612–14; Kissinger, *World Restored*, 279–83.

31. AVP RI, f. 133, op. 468, d. 5938, ll. 189–890b., declaration of Austria, Russia, and Prussia on the decisions made in Laibach (12 May 1821); *VPR*, v. 3 (11), n. 301, pp. 808–10. The declaration appeared in *Conservateur Impartial*, no. 39 (1821), though the copy from the British Library that I consulted did not contain the relevant pages. Alexander left Laibach on 1/13 May 1821. For the text of the declaration, see F. F. Martens, *Recueil des traités et conventions, conclus par la Russie avec les puissances étrangères*, 15 vols. (Saint Petersburg: Tipografiia Ministerstva Putei Soobshcheniia, 1874–1909), v. 4, no. 123, pp. 287–92.

32. After 1815 Russia accepted the return to the Ottoman policy that in peacetime closed the straits to foreign warships. This protected the Black Sea coast from Britain and France. Russian-Ottoman treaties of 1799 and 1805 had allowed the Russian fleet to pass through the straits in wartime. Alexander Bitis, *Russia and the Eastern Question: Army, Government, and Society, 1815–1833* (Oxford: Oxford University Press for the British Academy, 2006), 1–30; E. P. Kudriavtseva, *Russkie na Bosfore: Rossiiskoe posol'stvo v Konstantinopole v pervoi polovine XIX veka* (Moscow: Nauka, 2010), 197–215; Barbara Jelavich, *Russia's Balkan Entanglements, 1806–1914* (New York: Cambridge University Press, 1991), 6–7.

33. I. S. Dostian, "Venskii Kongress (1814–1815) i vostochnyi vopros," in *Balkanskie issledovaniia. Vypusk 18. Aleksandr I, Napoleon i Balkany*, ed. V. N. Vinogradov (Moscow: Nauka, 1997), 248–59.

34. RGADA, f. 15, op. 1, d. 279, Documents concerning diplomatic relations with European powers from the Ministry of Foreign Affairs (1814–21), ll. 99–1010b., relations with Turkey and Persia; Dostian, "Venskii Kongress," 256–58. The Porte (or Sublime Porte) referred to the central government of the Ottoman Empire in Constantinople. The Porte included the sultan, Divan (supreme council of the Ottoman Empire, which advised the sultan and assisted in administration), grand vizier, and other significant ministers. See Theophilus C. Prousis, *Lord Strangford at the Sublime Porte: The Eastern Crisis, Vol. 1: 1821* (Istanbul: Isis Press, 2010), 13.

35. Baron Stroganov's negotiations were ongoing. *VPR*, v. 2 (10), doc. 164 (3/15 November 1818), pp. 567–69, Alexander to Mahmood II; doc. 183 (8/20 November 1819), pp. 630–34, note from Stroganov to the Ottoman government.

36. The Vladimirescu revolt began in January 1821. Starting in the early eighteenth century, the sultan appointed Phanariot Greeks, aristocrats from the Phanar district of Constantinople, rather than local boyars, to serve as hospodars, or governors, in Moldavia and Wallachia. An imperial decree issued by Sultan Selim III in 1802 and the Treaty of Bucharest (1812) allowed Russia to approve these appointments. Revolt in the Morea began on 25 March (OS). Stites, *Four Horsemen*, chap. 4; Bitis, *Russia and the Eastern Question*, 98–115; Jelavich, *Russia's Balkan Entanglements*, 6–8; Prousis, *Greek Revolution*; Prousis, *Lord Strangford (1821)*; Theophilus C. Prousis, *Lord Strangford at the Sublime Porte: The Eastern Crisis, Vol. 2: 1822* (Istanbul: Isis Press, 2012); Victor Taki, "The Russian Protectorate in the Danubian Principalities: Legacies of the Eastern Question in Contemporary Russian-Romanian Relations," in *Russian-Ottoman Borderlands:*

The Eastern Question Reconsidered, ed. Lucien J. Frary and Mara Kozelsky (Madison: University of Wisconsin Press, 2014), 35–72.

37. Attacks on the Orthodox religion violated the Treaty of Kuchuk Kainardji (1774), and starting in May, restrictions on commercial ships flying the Russian flag violated both the treaty of 1774 and the commercial treaty of 1783. Finally, dismissal of the hospodars and tax levies in Moldavia and Wallachia also violated Russia's treaty rights. Bitis, *Russia and the Eastern Question*, 104–15; Jelavich, *Russia's Balkan Entanglements*, 2–5. On Alexander's conclusion that the Porte was waging war not against revolutionaries, but against the Greek population and Christian religion, see *VPR*, v. 4 (12), doc. 43 (11/23 April 1821), pp. 118–19, note from Stroganov to the Ottoman government; annotations (16/28 June 1821), p. 178, Nesselrode to Stroganov. In April, Stroganov still could report progress in discussions about illegal taxation and free trade in the Danubian Principalities: *VPR*, v. 4 (12), annotation (10/22 April 1821), p. 112, Stroganov to Nesselrode.

38. On 24 February/8 March, Ypsilantis wrote to Alexander in Laibach to request retirement from Russian service and assistance for the Greek people. The monarch's reply of 14/26 March called the revolt a criminal act. The patriarch of Constantinople also pronounced an anathema on Ypsilantis, and at the end of March (OS), Nesselrode instructed military commanders in Bessarabia not to accept refugees from the principalities who sought Russian protection. Even so, Ypsilantis may have received support from future Decembrists serving in the Second Army. Among military officers and officials in the south, Alexander's support for Ypsilantis was assumed. In May, moreover, Russia refused to hand over Greek refugees to the Porte. *VPR*, v. 4 (12), annotation (24 February/8 March 1821), p. 39, Ypsilantis to Alexander; annotations (14/26 March 1821), p. 68, Nesselrode to Stroganov, Kapodistrias to Ypsilantis, personal letter from Kapodistrias to R. Edling; Stites, *Four Horsemen*, location 4582–4850; Bitis, *Russia and the Eastern Question*, 98–115. On Russia's role as protector of Balkan Christians and the privileges granted to Moldavia, Wallachia, and Serbia, see Jelavich, *Russia's Balkan Entanglements*, chap. 1. According to Jelavich, there was never a consistent or recognized definition of what it meant to protect the Porte's Orthodox subjects. Russia, however, tended to view political conditions as part of religious protection. Jelavich, *Russia's Balkan Entanglements*, 32–41.

39. A larger Greek crisis and much internal Greek strife continued after the London Protocol of 3 February 1830 established an independent kingdom. The Greek civil war ended in 1834. Jelavich, *Russia's Balkan Entanglements*, 84–89; *VPR*, v. 4 (12), annotation (22 May/3 June 1821), p. 159, note from Stroganov to the Ottoman government; annotation (1/13 July 1821), p. 200, Lebzeltern to Metternich.

40. Bitis, *Russia and the Eastern Question*, 98–115; Prousis, *Greek Revolution*; I. S. Dostian, *Russkaia obshchestvennaia mysl' i balkanskie narody: Ot Radishcheva do dekabristov* (Moscow: Nauka, 1980); Charles and Barbara Jelavich, *The Establishment of the Balkan National States, 1804–1920* (Seattle: University of Washington Press, 1977); Jelavich, *Russia's Balkan Entanglements*; Misha Glenny, *The Balkans: Nationalism, War, and the Great Powers 1804–2011* (New York: Penguin Books, 2012), 16–19, 21–39; Schroeder,

Transformation, chap. 13. For the text of the Russian ultimatum and the Porte's failure to respond, see *VPR*, v. 4 (12), annotation (16/28 June 1821), p. 178, Nesselrode to Stroganov; doc. 78 (6/18 July 1821), pp. 203–10, note from Stroganov to the Ottoman government; annotation (14/26 July 1821), p. 224, note from Stroganov to the Ottoman government; doc. 83 (15/27 July 1821), pp. 224–25, Stroganov to Nesselrode; doc. 84 (17/29 July 1821), pp. 227–28, Nesselrode to Alopeus, chargé d'affaires in London P. A. Nikolai, and Pozzo di Borgo; AVP RI, f. 133, op. 468, d. 11853, Vienna and Verona (1822), t. 1, ll. 348–510b., summary of note from Stroganov to the Porte (16/28 July 1821); letter from the Russian government to the grand vizier (13/25 September 1821); memorandum to Russia's representatives in Vienna, Berlin, Paris, and London to serve as an instruction (13/25 September 1821); note from the British ambassador to Nesselrode (10/22 May 1822); response from Nesselrode to Chevalier Bagot (13 May 1822); rescript to Tatishchev of 14 May 1822 (14/26 May 1822). In a letter of 13/25 September 1821 to the grand vizier of the Ottoman Porte, the Russian government affirmed the ultimatum of 6/18 July and the actions taken by Baron Stroganov. *VPR*, v. 4 (12), annotation (13/25 September 1821), p. 289, memorandum of the Russian government to the grand vizier of the Ottoman Porte. On support for the Greek cause in Russian society, see also *VPR*, v. 4 (12), annotation (24 July/5 August 1821), p. 238, appeal of the minister of spiritual affairs and popular enlightenment A. N. Golitsyn to the population of Russia; doc. 141 (16/28 December 1821), pp. 400–1, Nesselrode to the main commander of the southern provinces of Russia A. F. Langeron; doc. 145 (31 December 1821/12 January 1822), pp. 408–9, Langeron to Nesselrode.

41. *VPR*, v. 4 (12), annotation (11/23 July 1821), p. 215, Alexander to Francis I; annotations (29 August/10 September 1821), p. 279, letter from Alexander to Castlereagh; circular dispatch from Nesselrode to Alopeus, Golovkin, Nikolai, and Pozzo di Borgo; doc. 100 (29 August/10 September 1821), pp. 279–81, circular dispatch from Nesselrode to Alopeus, Golovkin, Nikolai, and Pozzo di Borgo; doc. 103 (3/15 September 1821), pp. 283–86, envoy in Turin G. D. Mochenigo to Nesselrode; doc. 106 (13/25 September 1821), pp. 290–92, Nesselrode to Golovkin; annotation (13/25 September 1821), p. 292, Nesselrode to Golovkin; doc. 107 (13/25 September 1821), pp. 292–94, personal letter from Nesselrode to Metternich; annotation (26 September/8 October 1821), p. 310, Pozzo di Borgo to Nesselrode.

42. *VPR*, v. 4 (12), annotation (10 July 1821), p. 197, French ambassador in Saint Petersburg Pierre-Louis-August La Ferronnays (1777–1842) to French minister of foreign affairs Pasquier; annotation (3/15 July 1821), p. 200, Lebzeltern to Metternich; annotation (7/19 September 1821), p. 286, La Ferronnays to Pasquier; annotations (13/25 September 1821), pp. 289–90, memorandum from the Russian government to the grand vizier of the Ottoman Porte; Nesselrode to Golovkin; doc. 122 (21 October/2 November 1821), pp. 330–40, Lieven to Nesselrode.

43. *VPR*, v. 4 (12), annotations (22 June/4 July 1821), pp. 191–92, confidential circular dispatch from Nesselrode to Golovkin, Alopeus, Pozzo di Porgo, and Nikolai; Nesselrode to Golovkin; Nesselrode to Golovkin.

44. *VPR*, v. 4 (12), doc. 78 (6/18 July 1821), pp. 203–10, note from Stroganov to the Ottoman government. For a statement of Russia's position, including Alexander's expectations

of the allies, see the communication from Nesselrode to the monarch's envoys in Berlin, London, and Paris: *VPR*, v. 4 (12), doc. 72 (22 June/4 July 1821), pp. 189–91, Nesselrode to Alopeus, Nikolai, and Pozzo di Borgo. See also Alexander's letter to Austrian emperor Francis I, in which he compared the principles being applied in the Levant to those that had been successful in Italy. *VPR*, v. 4 (12), annotation (11/23 July 1821), p. 215.

45. *VPR*, v. 4 (12), doc. 78 (6/18 July 1821), pp. 203–10, note from Stroganov to the Ottoman government.

46. *VPR*, v. 4 (12), doc. 78 (6/18 July 1821), pp. 203–10.

47. *VPR*, v. 4 (12), doc. 78 (6/18 July 1821), pp. 203–10.

48. *VPR*, v. 4 (12), doc. 100 (29 August/10 September 1821), pp. 279–81, circular dispatch from Nesselrode to Alopeus, Golovkin, Nikolai, and Pozzo di Borgo; annotation (7/19 October 1821), p. 320, Nesselrode to Lieven. Russia accepted allied participation in resolving the crisis but did not accept allied mediation between the empire and the Porte. According to Nesselrode, the allies recognized Russia's right to protect the Christian population of the Ottoman Empire, a claim that some sources dispute. As noted above, the right to protect Christians living under Ottoman suzerainty could be interpreted in myriad ways. Prousis, *Lord Strangford*, vols. 1–2; *VPR*, v. 4 (12), annotation (13/25 September 1821), pp. 289–90, Nesselrode to Golovkin; doc. 106 (13/25 September 1821), pp. 290–92, Nesselrode to Golovkin.

49. In 1821 Nikolai served as chargé d'affaires (*poverennyi v delakh*) in London. *VPR*, v. 4 (12), doc. 73 (22 June/4 July 1821), pp. 192–96, personal letter from Kapodistrias to Nikolai.

50. Percy Smythe, Sixth Viscount Strangford (1780–1855).

51. *VPR*, v. 4 (12), doc. 122 (21 October/2 November 1821), pp. 330–40, Lieven to Nesselrode; n. 153, p. 666.

52. Count Christian Gunther Bernstorff (1769–1835) served as Prussia's minister of foreign affairs from 1818 to 1832. Before entering Prussian service, he was Denmark's ambassador in Berlin (1816–18).

53. *VPR*, v. 4 (12), doc. 122 (21 October/2 November 1821), pp. 330–40, Lieven to Nesselrode.

54. *VPR*, v. 4 (12), doc. 115 (2/14 October 1821), pp. 310–14, personal letter from Golovkin to Kapodistrias.

55. *VPR*, v. 4 (12), doc. 122 (21 October/2 November 1821), pp. 330–40, Lieven to Nesselrode.

56. *VPR*, v. 4 (12), doc. 122, pp. 330–40.

57. *VPR*, v. 4 (12), doc. 132 (27 November/9 December 1821), pp. 369–71, Nesselrode to Lieven.

58. *VPR*, v. 4 (12), doc. 133 (27 November/9 December 1821), pp. 371–79, personal letter from Kapodistrias to Lieven.

59. *VPR*, v. 4 (12), doc. 134 (27 November/9 December 1821), pp. 379–82, Lieven to Nesselrode; doc. 136 (27 November/9 December 1821), pp. 384–86, Lieven to Nesselrode.

60. *VPR*, v. 4 (12), doc. 136 (27 November/9 December 1821), pp. 384–86, Lieven to Nesselrode.

61. *VPR*, v. 4 (12), doc. 140 (16/28 December 1821), pp. 396–400, Golovkin to Nesselrode; doc. 148 (20 January/1 February 1822), pp. 411–14, Golovkin to Nesselrode.

62. Prousis, *Greek Revolution*, 18–24. In 1818 *Philiki Etaireia* (Friendly Society), the nationalist society working to create an independent Greek state, moved its headquarters from Odessa to Constantinople. Lucien J. Frary, "The Russian Consulate in the Morea and the Outbreak of the Greek Revolution, 1816–21," in *Diplomacy and Intelligence in the Nineteenth-Century Mediterranean World*, ed. Mika Suonpää and Owain Wright (London: Bloomsbury Academic Publishing, 2019), 57–77. Since June 1821, the Austrian government had promoted the idea that Greek rebels in Moldavia and Wallachia maintained ties to revolutionaries and Freemasons in other parts of Europe. Police reports from Vienna also tried to connect Kapodistrias to individuals suspected of involvement in the Greek rebellions. AVP RI, f. 133, op. 468, d. 2993, Doklady, ll. 1–5, Nesselrode to Alexander (11 June 1821); ll. 5–70b., translation of police report from Vienna (5 May 1821); ll. 8–100b., interrogation of Colonel Lisgara in Vienna (4–5 May 1821); ll. 11–13, interrogation of Antoine Zuni in Vienna (4 May 1821).

63. *VPR*, v. 4 (12), doc. 152 (31 January/12 February 1822), pp. 421–26, Nesselrode to Golovkin.

64. Frary, "Russian Consulate," 57–77.

65. *VPR*, v. 4 (12), annotations (27 November/9 December 1821), p. 369, Nesselrode to Lieven, Nesselrode to Golovkin, Nesselrode to Lieven; doc. 150 (25 January/6 February 1822), pp. 418–19, Alexander to Metternich; annotation (31 January/12 February 1822), p. 421, Nesselrode to Golovkin; doc. 152 (31 January/12 February 1822), pp. 421–26, Nesselrode to Golovkin. Ongoing conversations between Golovkin and Metternich in Vienna did not produce satisfactory results. *VPR*, v. 4 (12), doc. 140 (16/28 December 1821), pp. 396–400, Golovkin to Nesselrode; doc. 148 (20 January/1 February 1822), pp. 411–14, Golovkin to Nesselrode.

66. *VPR*, v. 4 (12), doc. 153 (5/17 February 1822), pp. 426–30, rescript from Alexander to Tatishchev.

67. Alexander's policy, according to the rescript, had been developed over the past nine months in communications between his government and the allies; in a personal letter of 17/29 July 1821 addressed to Austrian emperor Francis I; and in another letter to British foreign secretary Castlereagh, dated 29 August/10 September 1821. See *VPR*, v. 4 (12), annotation (11/23 July 1821), p. 215; annotations (29 August/10 September 1821), p. 279.

68. The Austrian proposals were summarized in a memorandum sent to Alexander's representatives at the courts of Berlin, London, Paris, and Vienna. See *VPR*, v. 4 (12), doc. 154 (6/18 February 1822), pp. 430–43.

69. The term "Levant" referred to the islands and coastal areas of the eastern Mediterranean ruled by the Ottomans. See Prousis, *Lord Strangford (1821)*, 13. Although historians of Europe tend to use the term "Eastern Question," the documents of the era referred to "the crisis in the East."

70. At this time, all the diplomatic principals among the allies believed in the existence of a revolutionary directorate operating from Paris that sought to foment rebellion

across Europe. *VPR*, v. 4 (12), annotation (13/25 September 1821), pp. 289–90, Nesselrode to Golovkin.

71. *VPR*, v. 4 (12), doc. 154 (6/18 February1822), pp. 430–43, instruction from the Ministry of Foreign Affairs to Golovkin, Alopeus, Lieven, and Pozzo di Borgo; doc. 155 (8/20 February 1822), pp. 443–45, Nesselrode to Alopeus, Lieven, and Pozzo di Borgo; annotation (27 February/11 March 1822), p. 447, personal letter from Tatishchev to Nesselrode. Metternich and Castlereagh met in Hanover in October 1821 to discuss the crisis, and in December, Austria communicated to Russia proposals for modification of the ultimatum. On the Hanover meetings, see Lieven's report to Nesselrode in *VPR*, v. 4 (12), doc. 122 (21 October/2 November 1821), pp. 330–40. According to Jelavich, Austria and Britain assumed that Russia sought domination in the East and therefore agreed to refuse or block Alexander's requests for allied cooperation. Jelavich, *Russia's Balkan Entanglements*, 52–75.

72. Alexander also agreed to accept a statement of Ottoman intentions regarding the first three points along with proof of action on the fourth. Previously, the emperor had demanded proof of action on all four points. AVP RI, f. 133, op. 468, d. 11853, t. l, ll. 348–510b., summary of note from Stroganov to the Porte (16/28 July 1821); letter from the Russian government to the grand vizier (13/25 September 1821); memorandum to Russia's representatives in Vienna, Berlin, Paris, and London to serve as an instruction (13/25 September 1821); note from the British ambassador to Nesselrode (10/22 May 1822); response from Nesselrode to Chevalier Bagot (13 May 1822); rescript to Tatishchev of 14 May 1822 (14/26 May 1822).

73. *VPR*, v. 4 (12), annotation (26 September/8 October 1821), p. 310, Pozzo di Borgo to Nesselrode; doc. 154 (6/18 February 1822), pp. 430–43, instruction from the Ministry of Foreign Affairs to Golovkin, Alopeus, Lieven, and Pozzo di Borgo; doc. 157 (28 February/12 March 1822), pp. 447–53, Tatishchev to Nesselrode; annotation (2/14 March 1822), p. 454, verbal note from Tatishchev to Metternich; doc. 159 (10/22 March 1822), pp. 454–57, Tatishchev to Nesselrode; doc. 164 (28 March/9 April 1822), pp. 470–71, Tatishchev to Alexander; doc. 165 (3/15 April 1822), pp. 471–74, Nesselrode to Tatishchev; doc. 166 (3/15 April 1822), pp. 474–75, Nesselrode to Tatishchev, Lieven, and Pozzo di Borgo.

74. *VPR*, v. 4 (12), doc. 154 (6/18 February1822), pp. 430–43, instruction from the Ministry of Foreign Affairs to Golovkin, Alopeus, Lieven, and Pozzo di Borgo.

75. *VPR*, v. 4 (12), doc. 171 (19 April/1 May 1822), pp. 482–96, Lieven to Nesselrode.

76. To break diplomatic relations implied that war was in the offing.

77. *VPR*, v. 4 (12), n. 233–36, p. 702.

78. Russia proposed the city of Kamenets-Podolsk in Ukraine as the site for the meeting. *VPR*, v. 4 (12), doc. 174 (13/25 May 1822), pp. 506–7, letter from Nesselrode to Britain's ambassador in Saint Petersburg Bagot; AVP RI, f. 133, op. 468, d. 11853, t. l, ll. 348–510b., note from Stroganov to the Porte (16/28 July 1821); letter from the Russian government to the grand vizier (13/25 September 1821); memorandum to Russia's representatives in Vienna, Berlin, Paris, and London to serve as an instruction (13/25 September 1821); note from the British ambassador to Nesselrode (10/22 May 1822); response from Nesselrode to Chevalier Bagot (13 May 1822); rescript to Tatishchev of 14 May 1822 (14/26 May 1822).

79. *VPR*, v. 4 (12), doc. 175 (14/26 May 1822), pp. 507–13, rescript from Alexander to Tatishchev; doc. 176 (16/28 May 1822), p. 513, Nesselrode to Tatishchev; doc. 178 (17/29 May 1822), p. 515, Nesselrode to Pozzo di Borgo; doc. 182 (9/21 June 1822), pp. 526–29, Tatishchev to Alexander; annotation (28 June 1822), p. 536, session journal from the Vienna conference of the plenipotentiaries of Russia, Austria, Britain, and France; annotation (27 July 1822), p. 547, session journal from the Vienna conference of the plenipotentiaries of Russia, Austria, Britain, Prussia, and France. Although Alexander preferred to see the return of hospodar rule, based on the regulations stipulated in previous treaties, he also expressed a willingness to entertain changes in the organization of local government. *VPR*, v. 4 (12), annotation (13/25 September 1821), pp. 289–90, Nesselrode to Golovkin; annotation (24 February/8 March 1822), p. 446, verbal note from Tatishchev to Metternich.

80. AVP RI, f. 133, op. 468, d. 11853, t. l, ll. 348–510b., note from Stroganov to the Porte (16/28 July 1821), letter from the Russian government to the grand vizier (13/25 September 1821); *VPR*, v. 4 (12), doc. 189 (13/25 July 1822), pp. 543–46, Nesselrode to Tatishchev.

81. RGADA, f. 3, op. 1, d. 82, Papers of Kapodistrias (1822), plan for military action against Turkey presented by Colonel Buturlin; Bitis, *Russia and the Eastern Question*, 149–60.

82. By the end of the year a new ecumenical patriarch had been selected, but the Porte still had not consulted with Russia about the appointment of the hospodars. Prousis, *Lord Strangford (1822)*, 11–12.

83. The Porte interpreted the sending of envoys as acceptance of allied intervention in the Ottoman Empire's internal administration, in this case, represented by the pacification of Greece. AVP RI, f. 133, op. 468, d. 11853, t. l, ll. 352–75, summary of the conference of 27 August 1822 with the reis effendi in Constantinople.

84. AVP RI, f. 133, op. 468, d. 11853, t. l, ll. 348–510b., memorandum to Russia's representatives in Vienna, Berlin, Paris, and London to serve as an instruction (13/25 September 1821); note from the British ambassador to Nesselrode (10/22 May 1822); response from Nesselrode to Chevalier Bagot (13 May 1822); rescript to Tatishchev of 14 May 1822 (14/26 May 1822).

85. The conferences in Verona focused on Spain, but also addressed the situation in Italy and the crisis in the East. The full record is preserved in two volumes as AVP RI, f. 133, op. 468, d. 11853. In May 1822, after opposing the decision to address the Greek question at allied conferences scheduled for September, Kapodistrias went on indefinite leave from Russian service. In general, Kapodistrias supported the independence of Greece and the use of Russian military force on behalf of the Greeks. He also opposed European involvement in Russian-Ottoman conflicts. Because of Castlereagh's suicide on 12 August, the allied conferences were delayed. Bitis, *Russia and the Eastern Question*, 112–15; *Ocherki istorii Ministerstva inostrannykh del Rossii. 1802–2002. Vol. 3: Biografii ministrov inostrannykh del. 1802–2002* (Moscow: Olma-Press, 2002), 88–99.

86. AVP RI, f. 133, op. 468, d. 11853, t. l, ll. 376–780b., Russian statement approved by Alexander (9/21 September 1822).

87. Although by September 1822 most Ottoman troops had left, the last units remained until 1826.

88. Reports of restrictions on Russian commercial shipping began to appear in May 1821. *VPR*, v. 4 (12), doc. 58 (4/16 May 1821), pp. 154–55, note from Stroganov to the Ottoman government; annotation (12/24 May 1821), p. 156, note from Stroganov to the Ottoman government; doc. 61 (17/29 May 1821), pp. 158–59, circular dispatch from Stroganov to Russia's consular representatives in Alexandria, Aleppo, Athens, Dardanelles, Patras, Salonica, Saint Jean d'Acre (Akko), Skalanova (Izmir), Sinop, Smyrna, Enos, Jaffa, and on the islands Keia, Kipr, Mitilini, Naksos, Rodos, Samos, Santorini, Tinos, Khios.

89. AVP RI, f. 133, op. 468, d. 11853, t. l, ll. 379–85ob., Russian note to the plenipotentiaries of Austria, France, Britain, and Prussia (14/26 September 1822); *VPR*, v. 4 (12), doc. 202 (14/26 September 1822), pp. 581–85, note from Nesselrode to Metternich, Montmorency, Wellington, and Bernstorff.

90. AVP RI, f. 133, op. 468, d. 11853, t. l, ll. 379–85ob., Russian note to the plenipotentiaries of Austria, France, Britain, and Prussia (14/26 September 1822); t. l, ll. 424–28, Russia's declaration on the "Affairs of the East" (9 November 1822).

91. AVP RI, f. 133, op. 468, d. 11853, t. l, ll. 424–55ob., Russia's declaration on the "Affairs of the East" (9 November 1822); *VPR*, v. 4 (12), annotation (28 October/9 November 1822), p. 589, declaration of Tatishchev.

92. AVP RI, f. 133, op. 468, d. 11853, t. l, ll. 436–55ob., responses of Austria, France, Prussia, and Britain to Russia's declaration of 9 November; Alexander's response to the allies' responses; insertion of the declaration into the protocol of the conference (16/28 November 1822). According to Bitis, in 1822 Austria and Britain worked to prevent Russian action. To that end, Metternich manipulated Alexander to allow time for the Ottomans to suppress the revolt, and during three years of conferences, Austria and Britain blocked Russian efforts to conclude an allied agreement on action in Greece. Bitis, *Russia and the Eastern Question*, 112–15, 161–67.

93. AVP RI, f. 133, op. 468, d. 11853, t. l, ll. 440–44, 450–55, discussion of Russia's declaration (26-27 November 1822).

94. AVP RI, f. 133, op. 468, d. 11853, t. l, ll. 47–48ob., conferences of 18, 19, 20 November 1822.

95. The impact of public opinion is also relevant but must be studied in local/national context.

96. In instructions to diplomatic appointees, Alexander repeatedly stated his commitment to allied unity. See, for example, *VPR*, v. 4 (12), doc. 172 (27 April/9 May 1822), pp. 496–500, rescript from Alexander to Ivan Illarionovich Vorontsov-Dashkov (1790–1854).

97. From March 1823 Britain recognized the Greeks as legal belligerents entitled in wartime to the same rights as sovereign states, though without acknowledging Greek sovereignty.

98. Will Smiley, "War without War: The Battle of Navarino, the Ottoman Empire, and the Pacific Blockade," *Journal of the History of International Law* 18 (2016): 42–69; Schroeder, *Transformation*, chap. 14; Jelavich, *Balkan National States*, 38–52;

Jelavich, *Russia's Balkan Entanglements*, 65–89; Bitis, *Russia and the Eastern Question*, 161–76, 426–29; Glenny, *The Balkans*, 30–39; Prousis, *Greek Revolution*, 52–54; Prousis, *Lord Strangford (1822)*, 356; Kissinger, *World Restored*, 260–97; Patricia Grimsted, *The Foreign Ministers of Alexander I: Political Attitudes and the Conduct of Russian Diplomacy, 1801–1825* (Berkeley: University of California Press, 1969), 259–63; Jennifer Mitzen, *Power in Concert: The Nineteenth-Century Origins of Global Governance* (Chicago: University of Chicago Press, 2013), 102–41; O. V. Orlik, *Rossiia v mezhdunarodnykh otnosheniiakh 1815–1829: Ot Venskogo kongressa do Adrianopol'skogo mira* (Moscow: Nauka, 1998), 40–48. See also *VPR*, v. 4 (12), doc. 175 (14/26 May 1822), pp. 507–13, rescript from Alexander to Tatishchev; doc. 176 (16/28 May 1822), p. 513, Nesselrode to Tatishchev; doc. 182 (9/21 June 1822), pp. 526–29, Tatishchev to Alexander; annotation (28 June 1822 NS), p. 536, session journal signed by the plenipotentiaries of Russia, Austria, Britain, and France at the Vienna conference convened at Russia's request; doc. 189 (13/25 July 1822), pp. 543–46, Nesselrode to Tatishchev; annotation (13/25 November 1822), p. 593, Nesselrode to Metternich; annotation (15/27 November 1822), p. 599, declaration of Tatishchev. In April 1827 Kapodistrias was elected president by the national assembly of Greece in Trizin, in July he formally retired from Russian service, and on 27 September 1831, he was assassinated. *Ocherki*, v. 3, pp. 88–99.

99. Ironically, Alexander's insistence that news of military and popular uprisings not be published in the *Vedomosti* and that the Russian press not be allowed to discuss official policy on the Eastern Question also highlighted his moderation. *VPR*, v. 4 (12), doc. 9 (1/13 March 1821), p. 47, Interim Minister of Foreign Affairs P. G. Divov to Golitsyn; annotation (13/25 September 1821), p. 292, Nesselrode to Golovkin. On Alexander's orders to constrain Stroganov, see *VPR*, v. 4 (12), annotation (12/24 September 1821), p. 288, Alexander to Nesselrode. On the rift with Kapodistrias, long encouraged by Metternich, see *VPR*, v. 4 (12), annotation (28 December 1821/9 January 1822), p. 405, Lebzeltern to Metternich; doc. 143 (29 December 1821/10 January 1822), pp. 405–6, Alexander to Metternich; annotations (29 December 1821/10 January 1822), p. 406, letter from Kapodistrias to Nesselrode, letter from Nesselrode to Kapodistrias; annotation (31 December 1821/12 January 1822), p. 406, letter from Kapodistrias to Alexander; annotation (not before 31 December 1821/12 January 1822), p. 406, letter from Alexander to Kapodistrias; doc. 179 (17/29 May 1822), pp. 515–16, personal letter from Kapodistrias to Lieven. For Kapodistrias's views on the crisis, see *VPR*, v. 4 (12), doc. 73 (22 June/4 July 1821), pp. 192–96, personal letter from Kapodistrias to Nikolai; doc. 95 (9/21 August 1821), pp. 256–65, memorandum from Kapodistrias to Alexander; doc. 121 (11/23 October 1821), pp. 327–30, memorandum of Kapodistrias; doc. 173 (1/13 May 1822), pp. 500–506, report from Kapodistrias to Alexander.

100. David A. Bell, *The First Total War: Napoleon's Europe and the Birth of Warfare as We Know It* (New York: Houghton Mifflin Harcourt, 2007).

Chapter 5: Spain and the European System (1820–23)

1. Spain's accession resulted from the Treaty of Paris of 10 June 1817. AVP RI, f. 133, op. 468, d. 2992, Doklady, ll. 204–40b.

2. RGADA, f. 15, op. 1, d. 279, Documents concerning relations with European powers from the Ministry of Foreign Affairs, ll. 74–76ob., appendix to the overview of 5/17 June 1817 on the accession of Spain to the acts of the Congress of Vienna; M. A. Dodolev, *Rossiia i Ispaniia, 1808–1823: voina i revoliutsiia v Ispanii i russko-ispanskie otnosheniia* (Moscow: Nauka, 1984), 116–23.

3. RGADA, f. 15, op. 1, d. 279, ll. 88–90ob., appendix to the overview of 5/17 June 1817 on the political system in Spain.

4. On the sale of the warships, see *VPR*, v. 1 (9), doc. 190 (30 July/11 August 1817), pp. 626–30, act on the sale of warships to Spain by Russia; v. 2 (10), doc. 8 (17/29 October 1817), pp. 24–27, Nesselrode to Tatishchev; doc. 10 (26 October/7 November 1817), pp. 30–35, Lieven to Nesselrode; v. 3 (11), doc. 39 (15/27 September 1819), pp. 118–21, supplemental convention between Russia and Spain to the act on the sale of warships to Spain by Russia; doc. 63 (26 November/8 December 1819), pp. 184–85, Nesselrode to Tatishchev; doc. 135 (10/22 June 1820), pp. 424–25, Nesselrode to Pozzo di Borgo; Dodolev, *Rossiia i Ispaniia*, 128–35.

5. Russia's envoy in Rio de Janeiro also received instructions to encourage Portuguese Brazil to cooperate with the European powers to end the slave trade. *VPR*, v. 2 (10), doc. 170 (9/21 November 1818), p. 583, Alexander to Ferdinand VII; doc. 172 (9/21 November 1818), pp. 585–88, instruction from Nesselrode to envoy in Rio de Janeiro F. V. Teil'-fan-Seroskerken (Theodor Tuyll van Seroskerken). By April 1818, British foreign secretary Castlereagh had concluded treaties on the slave trade with Portugal, Spain, and the Netherlands. Portugal agreed to abolish the trade, except along the African coast south of the equator. Spain agreed to abolition north of the equator and everywhere else after May 1820. In addition, both Portugal and Spain received 700,000 pounds in compensation. The Netherlands accepted complete abolition without compensation. John Bew, *Castlereagh: A Life* (New York: Oxford University Press, 2012), 446–47.

6. RGADA, f. 3, op. 1, d. 162, Précis of the work of the conferences of Aix-la-Chapelle (1818), ll. 11-12, sessions of 23, 24 October on the Spanish colonies and abolition of the slave trade; ll. 16–17ob., session of 4 November on abolition of the slave trade; ll. 18ob.–21, session of 7 November, memorandum from the Russian government on the measures proposed by Britain to ensure abolition of the slave trade; ll. 33ob.–36ob., session of 11 November on the French, Austrian, and Prussian responses to Britain's proposals concerning abolition of the slave trade, and on threats to trade and navigation from piracy.

7. The Spanish viceroyalty of Rio de la Plata (present-day Argentina, Bolivia, Paraguay, and Uruguay) began to break up and proclaim independence in 1810. Montevideo remained loyal to the Spanish regency; however, in addition to combating independence movements, Spain competed with Portuguese Brazil for the territory north of the Rio de la Plata. Brazil became independent of Portugal in 1822–23. R. A. Humphreys, "The Emancipation of Latin America," in *The New Cambridge Modern History. Vol. 9: War*

and Peace in an Age of Upheaval, 1793–1830, ed. C. W. Crawley (Cambridge: Cambridge University Press, 1965), 618–21, 630–32.

8. RGADA, f. 15, op. 1, d. 279, ll. 102–1030b., appendix to the overview of 5/17 June 1817 on disputes between Spain and Portugal. Russia initially pushed for allied intervention, if Portuguese Brazil did not rectify the aggression against Spain. Austria, Britain, and Prussia rejected the possibility of military action. Nor did the Spanish monarchy seek such assistance. Russell H. Bartley, *Imperial Russia and the Struggle for Latin American Independence, 1808–1828* (Austin: University of Texas Press, 1978), Kindle edition, location 2363–2495.

9. RGADA, f. 3, op. 1, d. 162, ll.70b.–80b., sessions of 15, 17 October on the question of Spain; ll. 78–79, session of 22 November on the question of Spain.

10. *VPR*, v. 3 (11), doc. 75 (not later than 31 December 1819/12 January 1820), pp. 215–18, Tatishchev to Ferdinand VII.

11. One recent popular biography identifies Alexander as a "sovereign" or "autocratic republican." Leonid Mikhailovich Liashenko, *Aleksandr I. Samoderzhavnyi respublikanets* (Moscow: Molodaia gvardiia, 2014). For illuminating and balanced discussion of Alexander's domestic policies and understanding of constitutions, see Patrick O'Meara, *The Russian Nobility in the Age of Alexander I* (London: Bloomsbury Academic, 2019), chap. 8.

12. *VPR*, v. 3 (11), doc. 83 (15/27 January 1820), pp. 232–34, Bulgari to Nesselrode.

13. Ferdinand VII returned to power in 1814. *VPR*, v. 3 (11), doc. 99 (24 February/7 March 1820), pp. 300–6, Bulgari to Nesselrode; doc. 100 (24 February/7 March 1820), pp. 306–12, Bulgari to Nesselrode.

14. *VPR*, v. 3 (11), doc. 101 (24 February/7 March 1820), pp. 312–14, Bulgari to Nesselrode. On 19 April/1 May 1820, Nesselrode conveyed a reprimand from Alexander to Count Bulgari, who had exceeded his authority and instructions by trying to counsel Ferdinand VII on how to respond to the revolutionary crisis. See *VPR*, v. 3 (11), doc. 115 (19 April/1 May 1820), pp. 356–57, Nesselrode to Bulgari. Russian diplomatic documents repeatedly referred to the revolution of 8 March; however, historians identify 7 March as the day that Ferdinand accepted the constitution, after summoning the Cortes. On 8 March the king ordered the release of political prisoners, and on 9 March, celebrated as the day of the revolution, he took the oath to the 1812 constitution. Richard Stites, *The Four Horsemen: Riding to Liberty in Post-Napoleonic Europe* (New York: Oxford University Press, 2014), Kindle edition, location 1485–1638; Dodolev, *Rossiia i Ispaniia*, 166–68. Reports that reached Saint Petersburg in March described support for the Spanish insurrection in the provinces and the capital, King Ferdinand's acceptance of the 1812 constitution, the failure of allied mediation in the dispute over the Rio de la Plata, and the encouragement to Spanish American insurgents provided by the revolution in Spain. AVP RI, f. 133, op. 468, d. 2992, Doklady, ll. 3–4, summary of reports received from Russia's missions abroad from the end of the last year to the present day (30 March/11 April 1820); *VPR*, v. 3 (11), doc. 108 (30 March/11 April 1820), pp. 337–43, memorandum from Kapodistrias to Alexander.

15. AVP RI, f. 133, op. 468, d. 2992, Doklady, ll. 12–140b., agenda of 6 April 1820.

16. *VPR*, v. 3 (11), doc. 102 (3/15 March 1820), pp. 315–18, Nesselrode to Lieven. The same communication was sent to minister plenipotentiary in Paris Pozzo di Borgo, envoy in Berlin Alopeus, envoy in Vienna Golovkin, envoy in Constantinople Stroganov, general consul in Bucharest Pini, governor-general of the Kingdom of Poland Grand Duke Constantine Pavlovich, envoy in Copenhagen Nikolai, and commander-in-chief of troops in Georgia General Aleksei Petrovich Ermolov.

17. *VPR*, v. 3 (11), doc. 111 (13/25 April 1820), pp. 348–50, Golovkin to Nesselrode.

18. This communication also was sent to Pozzo di Borgo, Stroganov, Pini, Constantine Pavlovich, and Ermolov. *VPR*, v. 3 (11), doc. 113 (19 April/1 May 1820), pp. 351–53, Nesselrode to Golovkin, Lieven, and Alopeus. By the end of March, the Russian government sensed opposition to active intervention in Spain from Austria and Britain. AVP RI, f. 133, op. 468, d. 2992, Doklady, ll. 3–4, summary of reports received from Russia's missions abroad from the end of the last year to the present day (30 March/11 April 1820); *VPR*, v. 3 (11), doc. 108 (30 March/11 April 1820), pp. 337–43, memorandum from Kapodistrias to Alexander.

19. *VPR*, v. 3 (11), doc. 114 (19 April/1 May 1820), pp. 354–56, Nesselrode to Pozzo di Borgo.

20. *VPR*, v. 3 (11), annotation (19 April/1 May 1820), p. 357, memorial memorandum from the Russian cabinet to Austria, Britain, Prussia, and France; annotation (20 April/2 May 1820), p. 357, note from Nesselrode informing Cea Bermúdez, Spain's chargé d'affaires in Saint Petersburg, that the allies would respond collectively to the Spanish government.

21. *VPR*, v. 3 (11), doc. 119 (4/16 May 1820), pp. 374–81, Lieven to Nesselrode; AVP RI, f. 133, op. 468, d. 2992, Doklady, ll. 339–41, report from Nesselrode to Alexander (24 August 1820); Bew, *Castlereagh*, chap. 14.

22. In a state paper of 5 May 1820, Castlereagh argued that a joint intervention in Spain would violate the treaties and purposes of the alliance. Paul W. Schroeder, *The Transformation of European Politics 1763–1848* (New York: Oxford University Press, 1994), 607–8; Jennifer Mitzen, *Power in Concert: The Nineteenth-Century Origins of Global Governance* (Chicago: University of Chicago Press, 2013), 106–10.

23. RGADA, f. 15, op. 1, d. 279, ll. 186–88ob., note from Cea Bermúdez to Nesselrode (7/19 April 1820).

24. Spanish resistance to Napoleonic rule began after Joseph Bonaparte became king (April 1808) and imposed the Bayonne constitution. In September 1808 the Supreme Central Junta, established in the town of Aranjuez, assumed leadership of the resistance, and the Cortes elected in 1810, which met in León and then Cadiz, called for the return of Ferdinand VII as a constitutional monarch. (In March 1808, Ferdinand had supported the forced abdication of Charles IV and had hoped to rule as Napoleon's protégé.) The 1812 constitution gave the king suspensive veto power over legislation but did not allow him to override or dissolve the Cortes. The king's power to cede territory or conclude aggressive alliances also was strictly limited. Finally, if the king left the country without permission, he abdicated the throne. The work of liberal politicians, the constitution also established a free press, equality before the law, the inviolability

of the individual, and an independent judiciary. The king appointed cabinet ministers, who were responsible to the Cortes, and a state council, chosen by the king and Cortes, monitored the monarch's actions. After Ferdinand returned to power in March 1814, he quickly abolished the Cortes and its ministries, restored censorship, purged the military, and ordered the arrest, imprisonment, and exile of liberal leaders. Stites, *Four Horsemen*, location 683–1329; Raymond Carr, "Spain and Portugal, 1793 to *c.* 1840," in *The New Cambridge Modern History. Vol. 9: War and Peace in an Age of Upheaval, 1793–1830*, ed. C. W. Crawley (Cambridge: Cambridge University Press, 1965), 443–47.

25. RGADA, f. 15, op. 1, d. 279, ll. 189–920b., note from Nesselrode to Cea Bermúdez (18 April 1820). Documents in the archive of the Russian Ministry of Foreign Affairs, including a report of 24 August 1820 from Nesselrode to Alexander, date the note to 20 April/2 May 1820. In the August report, prompted by the Spanish government's complaint about the note's publication in the Saint Petersburg press, Nesselrode praised the "noble and conservative language" of the document, as well as the "pure" perspective contained therein. According to the co-minister of foreign affairs, it had been necessary to inform the Russian public about the note, which already had been publicized throughout Europe. Nesselrode described the note as potentially decisive for the peace of Europe and as a statement that reflected well on Russia. The use and manipulation of the press in the conduct of diplomacy is another topic in need of comprehensive research. AVP RI, f. 133, op. 468, d. 2992, Doklady, ll. 352–530b., report from Nesselrode to Alexander (24 August 1820); ll. 385–860b., draft note from the Russian government to the Spanish government concerning Spain's complaint.

26. Dodolev dates the note to Cea Bermúdez to 2 May 1820 (NS), the date it was transmitted. Austria, Britain, France, and Prussia all reacted negatively to the Russian memorandum describing the exchange of notes. Dodolev, *Rossiia i Ispaniia*, 171–79. When Cea Bermúdez reported to the Spanish government, he expressed approval of the Russian note. The chargé d'affaires emphasized Alexander's unchanged support for liberal constitutions, as long as they emanated from the free sanction of "legitimate Princes." In other words, the monarch did not oppose the 1812 constitution, but the illegal event "that preceded its promulgation." RGADA, f. 15, op. 1, d. 377, Papers of Kapodistrias, ll. 107–210b., unsigned report to the Spanish ministry concerning negotiations with the Russian government (probably written by Cea Bermúdez); *VPR*, v. 3 (11), annotation (20 April/2 May 1820), p. 357, note from Nesselrode to Cea Bermúdez.

27. The version of the memorandum found in RGADA is dated 18/30 April 1820. RGADA, f. 15, op. 1, d. 279, ll. 193–202, memorandum sent to the ministers of H. I. M. for communication to foreign courts (18 April 1820). See also *VPR*, v. 3 (11), annotation (19 April/1 May 1820), p. 357, memorial memorandum from the Russian cabinet to Austria, Britain, Prussia, and France.

28. The constitution of 1812 envisioned a liberal nation state based on legal equality and proportional taxation, severely limited executive power, limits on the authority and property of the church, and the establishment of strong property rights, including freedom of enclosure. Carr, "Spain and Portugal," 443–47.

29. Emperor Alexander's "thoughts" on the Spanish crisis were sent out as instructions to Russia's diplomats abroad and also transmitted to the courts of Vienna, London, Paris, and Berlin. Collective allied discussion of the Spanish crisis did not materialize before the Verona conferences of 1822, and then only after multiple rebellions in Italy, Greece, and Portugal convinced the other powers of the need for a unified response.

30. RGADA, f. 3, op. 1, d. 78, Reports and correspondence of Sturdza to Kapodistrias, ll. 352–540b., account of Sturdza's official correspondence from 14 November 1819 to 12 December 1820.

31. RGADA, f. 3, op. 1, d. 78, ll. 222–280b., report from Sturdza to Kapodistrias (24 April 1820).

32. RGADA, f. 3, op. 1, d. 78, ll. 352–540b., account of Sturdza's official correspondence from 14 November 1819 to 12 December 1820.

33. RGADA, f. 3, op. 1, d. 78, ll. 222–280b., report from Sturdza to Kapodistrias (24 April 1820).

34. RGADA, f. 3, op. 1, d. 78, ll. 352–540b., account of Sturdza's official correspondence from 14 November 1819 to 12 December 1820.

35. *VPR*, v. 3 (11), doc. 118 (2/14 May 1820), pp. 371–74, Pozzo di Borgo to Nesselrode.

36. AVP RI, f. 133, op. 468, d. 2992, Doklady, ll. 258–61, report from Nesselrode to Alexander summarizing dispatches received from Madrid via France (20 July 1820).

37. William Spence Robertson, "Russia and the Emancipation of Spanish America, 1816–1826," *Hispanic American Historical Review* 21, no. 2 (May 1941): 196–221; Norman Saul, *Distant Friends: The United States and Russia, 1763–1867* (Lawrence: University Press of Kansas, 1991), 80–83; Bartley, *Latin American Independence*, chap. 6.

38. *VPR*, v. 2 (10), doc. 2 (2/14 October 1817), pp. 10–13, Tatishchev to Nesselrode. In October 1818, Nesselrode described the British proposals as "more harmful than useful to Spain." *VPR*, v. 2 (10), doc. 158 (not earlier than 13/25 October 1818), pp. 522–24, memorandum from Nesselrode to Alexander concerning discussions held in Aix-la-Chapelle on the mediation between Spain and its colonies.

39. See the protocol signed in Aix-la-Chapelle by Metternich, Richelieu, Castlereagh, Wellington, Hardenberg, Bernstorff, Nesselrode, and Kapodistrias. *VPR*, v. 2 (10), doc. 173 (10/22 November 1818), pp. 588–89, protocol of the meeting of the plenipotentiaries of Russia, Austria, Britain, Prussia, and France.

40. *VPR*, v. 2 (10), doc. 158 (not earlier than 13/25 October 1818), pp. 522–24, memorandum from Nesselrode to Alexander concerning discussions held in Aix-la-Chapelle on the mediation between Spain and its colonies. See also *VPR*, v. 2 (10), doc. 159 (20 October/1 November 1818), pp. 525–31, report from Kapodistrias to Alexander; doc. 170 (9/21 November 1818), p. 583, Alexander to Ferdinand VII; doc. 172 (9/21 November 1818), pp. 585–88, instruction from Nesselrode to Tuyll. See also, Robertson, "Russia and the Emancipation of Spanish America," 206–7.

41. *VPR*, v. 2 (10), doc. 177 (10/22 December 1818), pp. 596–98, Alexander to Ferdinand VII.

42. Historians date Ferdinand's explicit rejection of foreign intervention to December. Robertson, "Russia and the Emancipation of Spanish America," 206–7; Saul, *Distant Friends*, 87; Bartley, *Latin American Independence*, chap. 6.

43. *VPR*, v. 2 (10), doc. 179 (13/25 December 1818), pp. 602–10, Kapodistrias to Tatishchev.

44. Historians now recognize that Britain's opposition to intervention did not constitute opposition in principle (exactly the view of Alexander and his diplomatic agents). Rather, intervention should be carried out by interested parties on "a case-by-case basis" (exactly what had transpired in the Kingdom of the Two Sicilies and later in Spain). Wolfram Siemann, *Metternich: Strategist and Visionary*, trans. Daniel Steuer (Cambridge, MA: Harvard University Press, 2019), Kindle edition, 618–21.

45. *VPR*, v. 2 (10), doc. 185 (19/31 January 1819), pp. 639–45, Tatishchev to Nesselrode.

46. An illustration of this tactic can be found in *VPR*, v. 2 (10), doc. 185 (19/31 January 1819), pp. 639–45, Tatishchev to Nesselrode.

47. *VPR*, v. 2 (10), doc. 185 (19/31 January 1819), pp. 639–45.

48. *VPR*, v. 2 (10), doc. 190 (30 January/11 February 1819), pp. 656–61, Tatishchev to Alexander.

49. *VPR*, v. 2 (10), doc. 191 (31 January/12 February 1819), pp. 662–76, Tatishchev to Nesselrode.

50. The conditions for allied mediation enumerated by Britain included amnesty for the insurgents, neutrality on the part of the mediators, the suspension of hostilities, and the future independence of the colonies' commercial relations.

51. The Russian view held that a Spanish government morally supported by the five great powers would be better positioned to convince the Spanish American insurgents that promised reforms could be implemented. In other words, the moral force of allied unity would be more effective in promoting acceptance of Ferdinand VII's authority. *VPR*, v. 2 (10), doc. 185 (19/31 January 1819), pp. 639–45, Tatishchev to Nesselrode.

52. *VPR*, v. 2 (10), doc. 201 (19/31 March 1819), pp. 704–5, Tatishchev to Nesselrode; doc. 202 (25 March/6 April 1819), pp. 705–7, confidential letter from Tatishchev to Spain's minister of foreign affairs Casa Irujo; doc. 203 (28 March/9 April 1819), pp. 707–10, Pozzo di Borgo to Nesselrode.

53. On the proposed treaty between Spain and Portuguese Brazil, see *VPR*, v. 2 (10), n. 263, p. 824; n. 278, pp. 830–32.

54. *VPR*, v. 2 (10), doc. 204 (31 March/12 April 1819), pp. 710–12, circular dispatch from Nesselrode to Lieven, Golovkin, Alopeus, and Pozzo di Borgo. See the communication to Tatishchev of the same date, also approved by Alexander and sent to Alopeus, Golovkin, Lieven, and Pozzo di Borgo: *VPR*, v. 2 (10), doc. 208 (31 March/12 April 1819), pp. 722–24, Nesselrode to Tatishchev.

55. *VPR*, v. 2 (10), doc. 208 (31 March/12 April 1819), pp. 722–24.

56. Michael Broers, "The Quest for a 'Juste Milieu': The Restoration as a Silver Age?" in *Mächtepolitik und Friedenssicherung. Zur politischen Kultur Europas im Zeichen des Wiener Kongresses*, ed. Reinhard Stauber, Florian Kerschbaumer, and Marion Koschier (Berlin: LIT Verlag, 2014), 33–46.

57. *VPR*, v. 3 (11), doc. 75 (31 December 1819/12 January 1820), pp. 215–18, Tatishchev to Ferdinand VII.

58. RGADA, f. 15, op. 1, d. 377, Papers of Kapodistrias, ll. 45–1060b. This memorandum is preserved among the papers of Kapodistrias, though its authorship is not specified.

59. RGADA, f. 15, op. 1, d. 377, ll. 38–44. For the attribution, see Dodolev, *Rossiia i Ispaniia*, 176–77.

60. As early as 1811, the Russian periodical press described the disintegration of the Spanish Empire due to revolution and civil war. Diplomats likewise reported on the success of the independence movements in Spanish America, and by 1814 Tatishchev expected Spanish American independence. Robertson, "Russia and the Emancipation of Spanish America," 209–12; Bartley, *Latin American Independence*, chap. 5.

61. *VPR*, v. 3 (11), doc. 216 (2/14 February 1821), pp. 712–15, Nesselrode to Bulgari.

62. As early as 3/15 July 1820 the French government recognized the need for a common allied response to the crisis in Spain. In light of British opposition to collective action, French and Russian diplomats discussed the possibility of a common instruction (not necessarily an official communication) to regulate the language that allied agents would use to discuss their respective positions on Spain. The basis of the instruction would be the legitimacy and integrity of the Spanish monarchy, though decisions about the forms of government would be left to the king and his associates. AVP RI, f. 133, op. 468, d. 2992, Doklady, ll. 256–57, dispatch from Pozzo di Borgo concerning the French government's memorandum on Spain to be communicated to the Russian government by Count La Ferronnays (3/15 July 1820).

63. Prior to the disorders there had been talk of modifying the constitution to limit the franchise and enhance the king's power.

64. Gonzalo Butrón Prida, "From Hope to Defensiveness: The Foreign Policy of a Beleaguered Liberal Spain, 1820–1823," *English Historical Review* 133, no. 562 (June 2018): 567–96, here 573–85. See also Charles K. Webster, *The Foreign Policy of Castlereagh, 1815–1822. Vol. 2: Britain and the European Alliance* (London: G. Bell, 1963). Starting in October 1820, Ferdinand repeatedly appealed to the allies to save his kingdom and family. Stites, *Four Horsemen*, location 2265–2372; Dodolev, *Rossiia i Ispaniia*, 183–84; Schroeder, *Transformation*, 621–28. For a royalist account of the threat to Ferdinand VII and his family, see the *mémoire* of 1 December 1820 (NS) addressed to Alexander by the chevalier de Mésiére. RGADA, f. 15, op. 1, d. 290.

65. AVP RI, f. 133, op. 468, d. 11853, Vienna and Verona (1822), t. I, ll. 4–110b., acts of the conferences of Verona on the affairs of Spain. The *mémoire* of de Mésiére likewise reported on a military build-up by Spanish and Portuguese revolutionaries, that threatened all legitimate governments and sovereigns. RGADA, f. 15, op. 1, d. 290.

66. Some Russian diplomats explicitly stated that processes of change could not be controlled and that the revolutionary tempest had to play out. AVP RI, f. 133, op. 468, d. 2992, Doklady, ll. 163–600b., "Reflections on the Current State of Europe" (8 April 1820) sent as a *mémoire* to Kapodistrias from Prince Dmitrii Dolgorukii.

67. AVP RI, f. 133, op. 468, d. 11853, t. I, ll. 37–390b., 134–350b., proposals of Austria presented at the conferences of 31 October 1822.

68. AVP RI, f. 133, op. 468, d. 11853, t. I, ll. 136–37, response of Russia's plenipotentiaries to the proposals of Austria presented at the conferences of 31 October (21 October/2 November 1822); *VPR*, v. 4 (12), doc. 205 (21 October/2 November 1822), pp. 588–89, declaration of Russia's plenipotentiaries in response to Austria's proposals of 31 October.

69. AVP RI, f. 133, op. 468, d. 11853, t. I, ll. 2–20b., 108–12, coup d'oeil on the question of Spain (15 November 1822).

70. AVP RI, f. 133, op. 468, d. 11853, t. I, ll. 49–490b., 173–740b.; t. II, ll. 97–970b., verbal proceedings signed by the plenipotentiaries of Austria, France, Prussia, and Russia (19 November 1822); *VPR*, v. 4 (12), doc. 206 (7/19 November 1822), pp. 590–91, protocol signed by the plenipotentiaries of Russia, Austria, Prussia, and France.

71. AVP RI, f. 133, op. 468, d. 11853, t. I, ll. 47–480b., précis of the conferences of 18, 19, 20 November; *VPR*, v. 4 (12), doc. 209 (14/26 November 1822), pp. 594–96, Nesselrode to Bulgari; doc. 210 (14/26 November 1822), pp. 596–99, Nesselrode to Bulgari.

72. AVP RI, f. 133, op. 468, d. 11853, t. I, ll. 50–580b.; t. II, ll. 56–580b., dispatch to Bulgari approved in Verona 9/21 November 1822 and signed 14/26 November 1822; *VPR*, v. 4 (12), annotation (14/26 November 1822), p. 594, protocol signed by the plenipotentiaries of Russia, Austria, Prussia, and France.

73. On 7 July 1822 the Royal Guard revolted and marched on Madrid, though it was unclear whether they sought to modify the constitution or restore absolutism. The Cortes repressed the revolt, the king broke with Riego, and civil war ensued. The king also continued to complain to foreign envoys that he had become enslaved. Stites, *Four Horsemen*, location 2211–2372.

74. AVP RI, f. 133, op. 468, d. 11853, t. I, ll. 59–620b., dispatch to Bulgari; *VPR*, v. 4 (12), doc. 209 (14/26 November 1822), pp. 594–96, Nesselrode to Bulgari.

75. France did not adhere to the same sequence of actions, and in a December communication to Pozzo di Borgo, Nesselrode expressed concern about the French commitment to act in Spain. At the same time, he affirmed the intention of Austria, Prussia, and Russia to break relations with Spain. *VPR*, v. 4 (12), doc. 214 (2/14 December 1822), pp. 607–11, Nesselrode to Pozzo di Borgo.

76. Prida, "From Hope to Defensiveness," 584–96; Stites, *Four Horsemen*, location 2510–2724; Schroeder, *Transformation*, 621–28; Dodolev, *Rossiia i Ispaniia*, 166–93; Bartley, *Latin American Independence*, location 2971–3206.

77. AVP RI, f. 133, op. 468, d. 11853, t. I, ll. 457–67, circular on Italian affairs to be sent by the courts of Russia, Austria, and Prussia to their diplomatic agents as a common instruction (2/14 December 1822), unsigned lithographic copy; *VPR*, v. 4 (12), annotation (2/14 December 1822), p. 607, circular from the governments of Russia, Austria, and Prussia to their representatives abroad; n. 289, pp. 719–24.

78. See also *VPR*, v. 4 (12), doc. 211 (2 December 1822), pp. 600–3, protocol of the meeting of the plenipotentiaries of Russia, Austria, and Prussia with the participation of the plenipotentiary of the Sardinian kingdom; annotation (20 November/2 December 1822), p. 603, convention concluded by Russia, Austria, and Prussia with the Sardinian kingdom on the timetable for withdrawal of the Austrian auxiliary corps.

79. See also *VPR*, v. 4 (12), annotation (8 December 1822), p. 604, protocol of the meeting of the plenipotentiaries of Russia, Austria, Prussia, and the Kingdom of the Two Sicilies; annotation (9 December 1822), p. 605, protocol of the confidential meeting of the plenipotentiaries of Russia, Austria, Britain, Prussia, and the Kingdom of the Two Sicilies.

80. AVP RI, f. 133, op. 468, d. 11853, t. I, ll. 457–67, circular on Italian affairs to be sent by the courts of Russia, Austria, and Prussia to their diplomatic agents as a common instruction (2/14 December 1822). Despite the apparent finality of the Verona circular, the allies remained concerned about ongoing revolutionary activity in Italy: *VPR*, v. 4 (12), annotation (11 December 1822), p. 607, declaration of the Russian, Austrian, and Prussian courts.

81. AVP RI, f. 133, op. 468, d. 11853, t. I, ll. 457–67, circular on Italian affairs to be sent by the courts of Russia, Austria, and Prussia to their diplomatic agents as a common instruction (2/14 December 1822).

82. AVP RI, f. 133, op. 468, d. 11853, t. I, ll. 457–67, circular on Italian affairs.

83. Humphreys, "Emancipation of Latin America," 612–38. On Russia's continuing hope for reconciliation between the Spanish colonies and the metropolis, see *VPR*, v. 4 (12), annotation (24 October 1822), p. 587, record of the conversation between the French minister of foreign affairs Montmorency and Alexander.

84. For recent analysis and summary of ongoing debates, see O'Meara, *Russian Nobility*, chap. 12.

85. Eric Hobsbawm, *The Age of Revolution, 1789–1848* (New York: Vintage Books, 1996).

86. Osterhammel describes the European system of states as "an action-guiding image in the heads of the foreign policy elites of individual countries." Jürgen Osterhammel, *The Transformation of the World: A Global History of the Nineteenth Century*, trans. Patrick Camiller (Princeton, NJ: Princeton University Press, 2014), Kindle edition, location 11996–12003.

87. According to Osterhammel, between 1853 and 1871 five wars involving the great powers shattered the post-Vienna cohesion among European states: the Crimean War (1853–56), France and Sardinia-Piedmont versus Austria (1859), Denmark versus Prussia (1864), Austria versus Prussia (1866), and France versus Prussia (1870–71). Osterhammel, *Transformation of the World*, location 12003–12085.

Conclusion: Russia's European Diplomacy

1. James Van Horn Melton, *The Rise of the Public in Enlightenment Europe* (Cambridge: Cambridge University Press, 2001).

2. Dominic Lieven, *Russia against Napoleon: The True Story of the Campaigns of War and Peace* (New York: Penguin Books, 2009).

3. *VPR*, v. 2 (10), doc. 83 (15/27 March 1818), pp. 265–68, Golovkin to Kapodistrias. Emperor Alexander also expressed satisfaction with the meetings between Golovkin

and Metternich in the spring of 1818. *VPR*, v. 2 (10), doc. 104 (19 April/1 May 1818), pp. 334–36, Kapodistrias to Metternich; doc. 110 (2/14 May 1818), pp. 354–58, Golovkin to Kapodistrias.

4. *VPR*, v. 2 (10), doc. 96 (4/16 April 1818), pp. 297–304, Golovkin to Kapodistrias. On the oligarchic tendency, see the objections raised by Bavaria, Hanover, and the Netherlands in connection with the meeting of the great powers in Aix-la-Chapelle. *VPR*, v. 2 (10), doc. 112 (6/18 May 1818), pp. 364–67, Lieven to Kapodistrias.

5. The communication from Alexander preserved in RGADA is dated 9/21 November 1818 and addressed to Christoph Lieven. RGADA, f. 15, op. 1, d. 284, On the establishment of the Holy Alliance, ll. 11–120b.

6. *VPR*, v. 2 (10), doc. 108 (22 April/4 May 1818), pp. 350–51, Pahlen to Nesselrode.

7. For this distinction, see *VPR*, v. 2 (10), doc. 185 (19/31 January 1819), pp. 639–45, Tatishchev to Nesselrode.

8. For perceptive analysis of the reinvented "old regime" in the Restoration era, see Ambrogio A. Caiani, "Re-inventing the *Ancien Régime* in Post-Napoleonic Europe," *European History Quarterly* 47, no. 3 (2017): 437–60.

9. *VPR*, v. 2 (10), doc. 94 (27 March/8 April 1818), pp. 292–93, Kapodistrias to Lieven; v. 3 (11), doc. 197 (29 November/11 December 1820), pp. 645–47, Nesselrode to Struve.

10. *VPR*, v. 2 (10), doc. 81 (2/14 March 1818), pp. 263–64, Pahlen to Nesselrode. Russia's diplomats received instructions forbidding them to comment on constitutional debates in German states. On Bavaria in particular, see *VPR*, v. 3 (11), doc. 67 (30 November/12 December 1819), pp. 190–92, Nesselrode to Pahlen.

11. AVP RI, f. 133, op. 468, d. 2992, Doklady, ll. 366–670b., report from Nesselrode to Alexander (17 September 1820). For Alexander's speech at the opening of the Polish Diet on 27 March 1818, see *Le Conservateur impartial*, no. 26 (29 March/10 April 1818): 113–15. The speech described the Polish Diet as a model for Russia and has been read by contemporaries and subsequent generations as a promise of further constitutional reform.

12. Throughout the nineteenth-century, high-level Russian officials developed projects for political reform, including constitutional reform, though none came to fruition. Historians likewise point out that the provisions of the Polish constitution were never fully implemented. Marc Raeff, ed., *Plans for Political Reform in Imperial Russia, 1730–1905* (Englewood Cliffs, NJ: Prentice-Hall, 1966); S. Bertolissi, A. N. Sakharov, and A. N. Medushevskii, eds., *Konstitutsionnye proekty v Rossii XVIII-nachalo XX v.* (Moscow: Institut rossiiskoi istorii RAN, 2000). For recent coverage of constitutionalist thinking in the reign of Alexander, see Patrick O'Meara, *The Russian Nobility in the Age of Alexander I* (London: Bloomsbury Academic, 2019,) 155–60. On Alexander's continuing interest in reform, see S. V. Mironenko, *Aleksandr i dekabristy: Rossiia v pervoi chetverti XIX veka. Vybor puti* (Moscow: Kuchkovo pole, 2017).

13. *VPR*, v. 2 (10), doc. 33 (6/18 December 1817), pp. 104–9, Nesselrode to envoy in Dresden Khanykov. On the importance of impartiality, see also *VPR*, v. 2 (10), doc. 47 (12/24 January 1818), pp. 154–56, Nesselrode to Pahlen.

14. Elise Kimerling Wirtschafter, *Social Identity in Imperial Russia* (DeKalb: Northern Illinois University Press, 1997), chap. 1; Elise Kimerling Wirtschafter, "The Ideal of Paternalism in the Pre-Reform Army," in *Imperial Russia, 1700–1917: State, Society, Opposition*, ed. Ezra Mendelsohn and Marshall S. Shatz (DeKalb: Northern Illinois University Press, 1988), 95–114.

15. It is useful here to recall Adam Smith's theory of empathy and moral sentiment. See Jerry Z. Muller, *Adam Smith in His Time and Ours: Designing the Decent Society* (New York: The Free Press, 1993).

16. *VPR*, v. 2 (10), doc. 48 (12/24 January 1818), pp. 156–58, rescript from Alexander to Golovkin.

17. *VPR*, v. 2 (10), doc. 49 (14/26 January 1818), pp. 158–67, memorandum of instruction from the Ministry of Foreign Affairs to Golovkin, on special mission in Vienna.

18. The secret alliance against Prussia and Russia arose from Austrian, British, and French efforts to thwart Alexander's policy on the Polish-Saxon question.

19. *VPR*, v. 2 (10), doc. 49 (14/26 January 1818), pp. 158–67, memorandum of instruction to Golovkin.

20. One should note here that in the dispute over Poland at the Congress of Vienna, the personal friendship between Frederick William III and Alexander I translated into a Prussian refusal to enter into agreements designed to block Russia's plans.

21. *VPR*, v. 2 (10), doc. 84 (15/27 March 1818), pp. 268–71, Golovkin to Kapodistrias.

22. *VPR*, v. 2 (10), doc. 112 (6/18 May 1818), pp. 364–67, Lieven to Kapodistrias.

23. *VPR*, v. 2 (10), doc. 187 (25 January/6 February 1819), pp. 647–49, circular dispatch from Nesselrode to Russia's diplomatic representatives abroad.

24. *VPR*, v. 3 (11), doc. 43 (4/16 October 1819), pp. 134–35, Alexander to Francis I; doc. 44 (6/18 October 1819), pp. 136–37, Kapodistrias to Alopeus.

25. AVP RI, f. 133, op. 468, d. 2992, Doklady, ll. 395–97, 405–10, report from Nesselrode and Kapodistrias to Alexander concerning Austria's analysis of how the allies should respond to the revolution in Naples and the Austrian proposal for a treaty of guarantee presented in Troppau (15 October 1820).

26. The harmful German universities included Giessen, Heidelberg, and Jena. The acts of the Committee of Ministers identified the students as Livonians, Estonians, and Courlanders. Alexander's decision is dated 11/23 November 1820 and addressed to Count Kochubei. AVP RI, f. 133, op. 468, d. 2990, Doklady, ll. 79–82, project for a dispatch approved by Alexander.

27. Alexander believed that because the Karlsbad Decrees had proven effective in Prussia and Hanover, it would be inappropriate to issue an explicit decree ordering the students to return home. Conditions had improved in Germany over the past two years, and persuasion should be sufficient to achieve the desired outcome.

28. Jonathan Israel, *Enlightenment Contested: Philosophy, Modernity, and the Emancipation of Man, 1679–1752* (New York: Oxford University Press, 2006). For the Russian case, see Elise Kimerling Wirtschafter, *Religion and Enlightenment in Catherinian Russia: The Teachings of Metropolitan Platon* (DeKalb: Northern Illinois University Press,

2013). On "human flourishing," see Charles Taylor, *A Secular Age* (Cambridge, MA: Harvard University Press, 2007); Charles Taylor, *Sources of the Self: The Making of the Modern Identity* (Cambridge, MA: Harvard University Press, 1989).

29. These include, among others: the reconciliation of "great power demands for influence and control with small-power requirements for independence"; the role of intermediary bodies or independent smaller states and territories in buffering, separating, and connecting great powers; the development of rules and concepts for cooperation and concert between the powers; ways to guarantee "the rights and status of all states while discriminating between their different functions and responsibilities, necessarily conditioned by divergent capacities and interests"; the idea of "a political equilibrium based on the tacit acceptance by smaller powers of a general great-power hegemony so long as their independence and rights were guaranteed"; innovative regulation of diplomatic precedent and procedure; abolition of the slave trade; and international regulation and navigation of waterways. See Paul W. Schroeder, *The Transformation of European Politics 1763–1848* (New York: Oxford University Press, 1994), 575–82.

30. Lieven, *Russia against Napoleon*.

31. AVP RI, f. 133, op. 468, d. 2992, Doklady, ll. 395–97, report from Nesselrode and Kapodistrias to Alexander concerning Austria's analysis of how the allies should respond to the revolution in Naples (15 October 1820).

32. RGADA, f. 15, op. 1, d. 377, Papers of Kapodistrias, ll. 107–210b., unsigned communication from April 1820 located in a subsection titled "Ministère Espagnol"; appears to be written by the Spanish envoy Cea Bermúdez and addressed to his government.

33. Later variants include Slavophile, Pan-Slav, and Eurasianist thought.

34. For statements acknowledging the inevitability of revolutionary change, see AVP RI, f. 133, op. 468, d. 2992, Doklady, ll.163–690b., letter and memorandum of Prince Dmitrii Dolgorukii to Kapodistrias (8 April 1820); ll. 405–10, report from Nesselrode and Kapodistrias to Alexander concerning Austria's proposal for a treaty of guarantee (15/27 October 1820).

Archives

Arkhiv vneshnei politiki Rossiiskoi Imperii (AVP RI)/Archive of the Foreign Policy
of the Russian Empire, Moscow
Fond 133: Kantseliariia ministra inostrannykh del, opis' 468, v. I–IV (1797–1836)
Fond 187: Rossiiskoe posol'stvo v Parizhe, opis' 524, v. 1 (1801–1924)

Additional AVP RI opisi consulted

Fond 167: Posol'stvo v Berline, opis' 509/I (1784–1916)
Fond 170: Rossiiskoe posol'stvo v Vashingtone, opis' 512/2 (1809–1921)
Fond 172: Posol'stvo v Vene, opis' 514/I (1785–1916)
Fond 180: Posol'stvo v Konstantinopole, opis' 517/1 (1798–1853)
Fond 183: Missiia v Lisbone, opis' 519 (1800–63)
Fond 184: Rossiiskoe posol'stvo v Londone, opis' 520, v. I (1801–1920)
Fond 196: Missiia v Turine, opis' 530 (1790–1865)
Fond 198: Missiia vo Frankfurt-na-Maine, opis' 531 (1814–66)
Fond 270/1: General'noe konsul'stvo v Neapole, opis' 523 (1799–1921)

Rossiiskii gosudarstvennyi arkhiv drevnikh aktov (RGADA)/Russian State Archive
of Ancient Acts, Moscow
Fond 1/Razriad I: Sekretnye pakety, opis' 1 (1729–1842)
Fond 3/Razriad III: Dela otnosiashchiesia do vnutrennei i vneshnei politiki Rossii,
opis' 1 (1708–1914)
Fond 4/Razriad IV: Perepiska lits imperatorskoi familii i drugikh vysochaishikh
osob (1689–1904)
Fond 15/Razriad XV: Diplomaticheskii otdel, opis' 1 (1235–1873)

National Archives and Records Administration (NARA), Washington, DC:
M–35: Despatches from U.S. Ministers to Russia, 1808–1906
M–39: Notes from the Russian Legation in the United States to the Department of
State, 1809–1906

Printed Primary and Secondary Sources

Airapetov, Oleg. *Istoriia vneshnei politiki Rossiiskoi imperii. 1801–1914. Volume 1: Vneshniaia politika Imperatora Aleksandra I, 1802–1825*. Moscow: Kuchkovo pole, 2017.

Alexandre Ier et le prince Czartoryski, 1801–1823. Edited by L. Czartoryski. Paris: Michel Lévy Frères, 1865.

Ancillon, M. F. *Tableau des revolutions du système politique de l'Europe depuis la fin du quinzième siècle*. 7 vols. Paris: Imprimerie de la Harpe, 1806–1807.

Anderson, M. S. *The Eastern Question 1774–1923: A Study in International Relations*. New York: Saint Martin's Press, 1966.

Andreev, Andrei Iu. "Nachalo 'novogo veka': Rozhdestvenskaia simvolika v tsarstvovanii Aleksandra I." *Vestnik PSTGU. II. Istoriia. Istoriia Russkoi Pravoslavnoi Tserkvi*. Vypusk 1 (44) (2012): 40–48.

——. "'Liturgika' Sviashchennogo soiuza: K voprosu o religioznykh vzgliadakh Aleksandra I." *Filaretovskii al'manakh*. Edited by A. I. Iakovlev. Vypusk 12. Moscow: Izdatel'stvo PSTGU, 2016.

——. "'Anbetung der drei Könige': Alexander I und seine Idee der Heiligen Allianz." In *Die Heilige Allianz. Entstehung—Wirkung—Rezeption*. Edited by Anselm Schubert and Wolfram Pyta. Stuttgart: W. Kohlhammer, 2018.

Andreeva, T. V. *Tainye obshchestva v Rossii v pervoi treti XIX v.: Pravitel'stvennaia politika i obshchestvennoe mnenie*. Saint Petersburg: Liki Rossii, 2009.

Armitage, David, and Sanjay Subrahmanyam, eds. *The Age of Revolutions in Global Context, c. 1760–1840*. Basingstoke: Palgrave Macmillan, 2010.

Armitage, David. *Foundations of Modern International Thought*. New York: Cambridge University Press, 2013.

Artizov, A. N., A. K Levykin, and Iu. A. Petrov, eds. *Epokha 1812 goda v sud'bakh Rossii i Evropy*. Moscow: Institut rossiiskoi istorii RAN, 2013.

Barratt, Glynn R. "Notice sur l'insurrection des Grecs contre l'Empire Ottoman: A Russian View of the Greek War of Independence." *Balkan Studies: Biannual Publication of the Institute for Balkan Studies* 14, no. 1 (1973): 47–115.

Bartley, Russell H. *Imperial Russia and the Struggle for Latin American Independence, 1808–1828*. Austin: University of Texas Press, 1978.

Bauer, Joachim, Stefan Gerber, and Christopher Spehr, eds. *Das Wartburgfest von 1817 als europäisches Ereignes*. Stuttgart: Franz Steiner Verlag, 2020.

Bayly, C. A. *The Birth of the Modern World, 1780–1914: Global Connections and Comparisons*. Malden, MA: Blackwell Publishing, 2004.

Bell, David A. *The Cult of the Nation in France: Inventing Nationalism, 1680–1800*. Cambridge, MA: Harvard University Press, 2001.

——. *The First Total War: Napoleon's Europe and the Birth of Warfare as We Know It*. New York: Houghton Mifflin Harcourt, 2007.

Bell, Duncan S. A. "International Relations: The Dawn of a Historiographical Turn?" *British Journal of Politics and International Relations* 3, no. 1 (April 2001): 115–26.

Benl, Rudolf, ed. *Der Erfurter Fürstenkongress 1808: Hintergründe, Ablauf, Wirkung.* Erfurt: Stadtarchiv, 2008.

Bergquist, Harold Edward, Jr. "Henry Middleton and the Arbitrament of the Anglo-American Slave Controversy by Tsar Alexander I." *South Carolina Historical Magazine* 82 (1981): 20–31.

Berlin, Isaiah. *Russian Thinkers.* Edited by Henry Hardy and Aileen Kelly. New York: Viking Press, 1978.

Bethell, Leslie, ed. *The Cambridge History of Latin America. Volume I: Colonial Latin America.* Cambridge: Cambridge University Press, 1984.

——. *The Cambridge History of Latin America. Volume 3: From Independence to c. 1870.* Cambridge: Cambridge University Press, 1985.

——. *The Cambridge History of Latin America. Volume 11: Bibliographical Essays.* Cambridge: Cambridge University Press, 1995.

Bew, John. *Castlereagh: A Life.* New York: Oxford University Press, 2012.

Bezotosnyi, V. M., ed. *Epokha 1812 goda: Issledovaniia. Istochniki. Istoriografiia.* 16 vols. Moscow: Istoricheskii muzei, Kuchkovo pole, 2002–19.

——. *Rossiia i Evropa v epokhu 1812 goda. Strategiia ili geopolitika.* Moscow: Veche, 2012.

——. *Rossiia v napoleonovskikh voinakh 1805–1815.* Moscow: ROSSPEN, 2014.

Bibikov, G. N., and L. V. Mel'nikova, eds. *Epokha 1812 goda v sud'bakh Rossii i Evropy.* Moscow: Institut rossiiskoi istorii RAN, 2013.

Bitis, Alexander. *Russia and the Eastern Question: Army, Government, and Society, 1815–1833.* Oxford: Oxford University Press, for the British Academy, 2006.

Blanning, Tim. *The Pursuit of Glory: The Five Revolutions That Made Modern Europe: 1648–1815.* New York: Penguin, 2007.

Bobbitt, Philip. *The Shield of Achilles: War, Peace, and the Course of History.* New York: Alfred A. Knopf, 2002.

Bogdanovich, M. I. *Istoriia voiny 1814 goda vo Frantsii i nizlozheniia Napoleona I.* Reprint, Saint Petersburg, 1865. Moscow: Kuchkovo pole, 2014.

Bokova, V. M. *Epokha tainykh obshchestv: Russkie obshchestvennye ob"edineniia pervoi treti XIX v.* Moscow: Realii–Press, 2003.

Bordachenkov, I., ed. *Epokha Napoleona: Russkii vzgliad. Kniga pervaia.* Moscow: Tsentr knigi Rudomino, 2013.

Bourquin, M. *Histoire de la sainte alliance.* Geneva: Librairie de l'Université Georg & Cie, S. A., 1954.

Branch, M., J. Hartley, and A. Maczak, eds. *Finland and Poland in the Russian Empire: A Comparative Study.* London: School of Slavonic and East European Studies, University of London, 1995.

Breunig, Charles. *The Age of Revolution and Reaction, 1789–1850.* 2nd ed. New York: W. W. Norton, 1977.

British and Foreign State Papers. Volume 1820–1821. London: J. Harrison and Son, 1830.

Broers, Michael, and Ambrogio A. Caiani, eds. *A History of the European Restorations. Volume I. Governments, States and Monarchy; Volume II. Culture, Society and Religion.* London: Bloomsbury Academic, 2020.

Broers, Michael, Peter Hicks, and Agustin Guimera, eds. *The Napoleonic Empire and the New European Political Culture*. New York: Palgrave, 2012.

Burbank, Jane, and Frederick Cooper. *Empires in World History: Power and the Politics of Difference*. Princeton, NJ: Princeton University Press, 2010.

Bushkovitch, Paul. "Henry Middleton and the Decembrist Revolt." *Zapiski russkoi akademicheskoi gruppy v S. Sh. A.* 38 (2013): 131–56.

———. *Peter the Great*, 2nd ed. Lanham, MD: Rowman and Littlefield, 2016.

Caiani, Ambrogio A. "Re-inventing the *Ancien Régime* in Post–Napoleonic Europe." *European History Quarterly* 47, no. 3 (2017): 437–60.

Capefigue, M. *La Baronne de Krudner. L'empereur Alexandre Ier au Congrès de Vienne et les traités de 1815*. Paris: Amyot, 1866.

Capo d'Istria, Jean. *Aperçu de ma carrière publique depuis 1798 jusqu'à 1822*. Reprint, 1868. Moscow: Kuchkovo pole, 2014.

Carr, Raymond, ed. *Spain: A History*. New York: Oxford University Press, 2000.

Chodźko, Léonard. *Le Congrès de Vienne et les traités de 1815: precede et suivi des actes diplomatiques qui s'y rattachent*. 4 vols. Paris: Amyot, 1864.

Conrad, Sebastian. "Enlightenment in Global History: A Historiographical Critique." *American Historical Review* 117, no. 4 (October 2012): 999–1027.

Conrad, Sebastian. *What Is Global History?* Princeton, NJ: Princeton University Press, 2016.

Contamine, Philippe, ed. *War and Competition between States*. Oxford: Clarendon Press, 2000.

Cowles, Loyal. "The Failure to Restrain Russia: Canning, Nesselrode, and the Greek Question, 1825–1827." *International History Review* 13, no. 4 (1990): 688–720.

Correspondence of the Massachusetts Peace Society, with the Emperor of Russia, and Prince Alexander Gallitzin. [London]: Bensley, 1817.

Cracraft, James. *The Revolution of Peter the Great*. Cambridge, MA: Harvard University Press, 2006.

Crawley, C. W., ed. *The New Cambridge Modern History. Volume 9: War and Peace in the Age of Upheaval, 1793–1830*. Cambridge: Cambridge University Press, 1965.

Davydov, Michail, and Elena Vishlenkova. "Hundert Jahre Streit um die Helden von 1812: Vom 'Vaterländischen' Krieg zum Ersten 'Weltkrieg.'" *Jahrbücher für Geschichte Osteuropas* 63, no. 4 (2015): 545–72.

de Graaf, Beatrice. "Second-Tier Diplomacy: Hans von Gagern and William I in Their Quest for an Alternative European Order, 1813–1818. *Journal of Modern European History* 12, no. 4 (2014): 546–66.

de Graaf, Beatrice, and Brian Vick, eds. *Securing Europe after Napoleon: 1815 and the New Security Order*. Cambridge: Cambridge University Press, 2018.

Delfiner, Henry A. "Alexander I, the Holy Alliance and Clemens Metternich: A Reappraisal." *East European Quarterly* 2 (2003): 127–50.

Dergacheva, L. D. *Ocherki istochnikovedeniia otechestvennoi periodicheskoi pechati XVIII–XX vekov*. Moscow: n.p., 2012.

Desan, Suzanne, Lynn Hunt, and William Max Nelson, eds. *The French Revolution in Global Perspective*. Ithaca, NY: Cornell University Press, 2013.

Diplomaticheskii slovar'. 3 vols. Moscow: Nauka, 1984–86.

Dodolev, M. A. *Rossiia i Ispaniia, 1808–1823: voina i revoliutsiia v Ispanii i russko-ispanskie otnosheniia*. Moscow: Nauka, 1984.

———. "Russia and the Spanish Revolution of 1820–1823." *Russian Studies in History* 8, no. 3 (Winter 1969–1970): 252–71.

———. *Venskii Kongress v istoriografii XIX i XX vekov*. Moscow: Institut vseobshchei istorii RAN, 2000.

Dokumenty dlia istorii diplomaticheskikh snoshenii Rossii s zapadnymi derzhavami evropeiskimi ot zakliucheniia vseobshchego mira v 1814 do kongressa v Verone v 1822 godu. 2 vols. Saint Petersburg: Voennaia tipografiia Glavnogo shtaba, 1823–5.

Dostian, I. S. *Russkaia obshchestvennaia mysl' i balkanskie narody: Ot Radishcheva do dekabristov*. Moscow: Nauka, 1980.

Duchhardt, Heinz. *Der Aachener Kongress 1818: Ein europäisches Gipfeltreffen im Vormärz*. Munich: Piper Verlag, 2018.

Eich, Ulrike. *Russland und Europa: Studien zur russischen Deutschlandpolitik in der Zeit des Wiener Kongresses*. Cologne and Vienna: Böhlau, 1986.

"1815: The Power of Balance." Edited by Jörn Leonhard. Special forum in the *Journal of European History* 13, no. 4 (2015): 427–74. Articles by Mark Jarrett, Eckart Conze, Beatrice de Graaf, Stella Ghervas, and Matthias Schulz.

Ermolov, A. P. *Kavkazskie pis'ma 1816–1860*. Edited by Ia. A. Gordin. Saint Petersburg: Zhurnal "Zvezda," 2014.

Ferguson, Niall. "The Meaning of Kissinger: A Realist Reconsidered." *Foreign Affairs* 94, no. 5 (September/October 2015): 134–43.

The Festal Menaion. Translated by Mother Mary and Archimandrite Kallistos Ware. South Canaan, PA: Saint Tikhon's Seminary Press, 1998.

Fischer-Galati, Stephen A. "The Nature and Immediate Origins of the Treaty of Holy Alliance." *History* 38, no. 132 (February 1953): 27–39.

Fladeland, Betty. "Abolitionist Pressures on the Concert of Europe, 1814–1822." *Journal of Modern History* 38, no. 4 (1966): 355–73.

Florovskii, Georgii. *Puti russkogo bogosloviia*. Reprint. Minsk: Izdatel'stvo Belorusskogo Ekzarkhata, 2006.

Forrest, Alan. *Napoleon: Life, Legacy, and Image: A Biography*. New York: Saint Martin's Press, 2013.

Forrest, Alan, Étienne François, and Karen Hagemann, eds. *War Memories: The Revolutionary and Napoleonic Wars in Modern European Culture*. New York: Palgrave, 2012.

Frary, Lucien J., and Mara Kozelsky, eds. *Russian-Ottoman Borderlands: The Eastern Question Reconsidered*. Madison: University of Wisconsin Press, 2014.

Fuller, William C., Jr. *Strategy and Power in Russia 1600–1914*. New York: The Free Press, 1992.

Fumaroli, Marc. *When the World Spoke French*. Translated by Richard Howard. New York: New York Review Books, 2011.

Ghervas, Stella. "Balance of Power vs. Perpetual Peace: Paradigms of European Order from Utrecht to Vienna, 1713–1815." *The International History Review* (2016). https://doi.org/10.1080/07075332.2016.1214613.

———. "La reception de *L'Esprit des Lois* en Russie: histoire de quelques ambiguïtés. In *Le Temps de Montesquieu*. Edited by Michel Porret and Catherine Volpilhac-Auger. Geneva: Librairie Droz S. A., 2002, 391–404.

———. *Réinventer la tradition: Alexandre Stourdza et l'Europe de la Sainte-Alliance*. Paris: Honoré Champion, 2008.

Glenny, Misha. *The Balkans: Nationalism, War, and the Great Powers 1804–2011*. New York: Penguin Books, 2012.

Griffiths, David M. "Introduction: Of Estates, Charters, and Constitutions." In *Catherine II's Charters of 1785 to the Nobility and the Towns*. Edited and translated by David Griffiths and George E. Munro. Bakersfield, CA: Charles Schlacks, Jr., 1991.

Grimsted, Patricia Kennedy. "Czartoryski's System for Russian Foreign Policy, 1803: A Memorandum, Edited with Introduction and Analysis." *California Slavic Studies* 5 (1970): 19–91.

———. *The Foreign Ministers of Alexander I: Political Attitudes and the Conduct of Russian Diplomacy, 1801–1825*. Berkeley and Los Angeles: University of California Press, 1969.

Gruner, Wolf D. "Was There a Reformed Balance of Power System or Cooperative Great Power Hegemony?" *American Historical Review* 97, no. 3 (June 1992): 725–32.

Hamburg, G. M. *Russia's Path toward Enlightenment: Faith, Politics, and Reason, 1500–1801*. New Haven, CT: Yale University Press, 2016.

Hansard, T. C., ed. *The Parliamentary Debates from the Year 1803 to the Present Time*. Series 1: 41 vols. London: Longman, 1812–1820, vol. 32.

Hartley, Janet M. *Alexander I*. New York: Longman, 1994.

———. "England 'Enjoys the Spectacle of a Northern Barbarian': The Reception of Peter I and Alexander I." In *A Window on Russia. Papers from the Fifth International Conference of the Study Group on Eighteenth-Century Russia, Gargnano, 1994*. Edited by Maria Di Salvo and Lindsey Hughes. Rome: La Fenice Edizioni, 1996, 11–18.

———. *Russia, 1762–1825. Military Power, the State, and the People*. Westport, CT: Praeger, 2008.

Hartley, Janet M., Paul Keenan, and Dominic Lieven, eds. *Russia and the Napoleonic Wars*. New York: Palgrave Macmillan, 2015.

Haynes, Christine. *Our Friends the Enemies: The Occupation of France after Napoleon*. Cambridge, MA: Harvard University Press, 2018.

H-Diplo Roundtable Review. Volume 17, Number 24 (2016). Discussion of Brian E. Vick, *The Congress of Vienna: Power and Politics after Napoleon*.

Hennings, Jan. *Russia and Courtly Europe: Ritual and the Culture of Diplomacy, 1648–1725*. Cambridge: Cambridge University Press, 2016.

Hippler, Thomas, and Miloš Vec, eds. *Paradoxes of Peace in Nineteenth-Century Europe*. Oxford: Oxford University Press, 2015.

Hobsbawm, Eric. *The Age of Revolution, 1789–1848*. New York: Vintage Books, 1996.

Hughes, Lindsey. *The Romanovs. Ruling Russia, 1613–1917*. London: Humbledon Continuum, 2008.

———. *Russia in the Age of Peter the Great*. New Haven, CT: Yale University Press, 2000.

Ianovskii, A. D., and V. M. Bezotosnyi, eds. *Epokha 1812 goda: Issledovaniia, dokumenty*. Moscow: Istoricheskii muzei, 2012.

Ikenberry, G. John. *After Victory: Institutions, Strategic Restraint, and the Rebuilding of Order after Major Wars*. Princeton, NJ: Princeton University Press, 2001.

———, ed. *Power, Order, and Change in World Politics*. Cambridge: Cambridge University Press, 2014.

Imperator Aleksandr i Frederik–Sezar Lagarp. Pis'ma. Dokumenty. Edited by A. Iu. Andreev and D. Tozato–Rigo. Translated by V. A. Mil'china. 3 vols. Moscow: Politicheskaia entsiklopediia, 2014–17.

Ingrao, Charles. "Paul Schroeder's Balance of Power: Stability or Anarchy?" *International History Review* 16, no. 4 (1994): 681–700.

Ischinger, Wolfgang. "The World According to Kissinger: How to Defend Global Order." *Foreign Affairs* 94, no. 2 (March–April 2015): 160–6.

Isabella, Maurizio. "Citizens or Faithful? Religion and the Liberal Revolutions of the 1820s in Southern Europe." *Modern Intellectual History* (January 2015): 1–24. Available on CJO 2015 doi.org/10.1017/S147924431400078X.

Iskiul', S. N. *Vneshniaia politika Rossii i germanskie gosudarstva, 1801–1812*. Moscow: Indrik, 2007.

Israel, Jonathan. *Enlightenment Contested: Philosophy, Modernity, and the Emancipation of Man, 1679–1752*. New York: Oxford University Press, 2006.

Jarrett, Mark. *The Congress of Vienna and Its Legacy: War and Great Power Diplomacy after Napoleon*. New York: I. B. Tauris, 2014.

Jeffery, Renée. "Tradition as Invention: The 'Traditions Tradition' and the History of Ideas in International Relations." *Millennium: Journal of International Studies* 34, no. 1 (2005): 57–84.

Jelavich, Barbara. *Russia and the Formation of the Romanian National State, 1821–1878*. Cambridge: Cambridge University Press, 1984.

———. *Russia's Balkan Entanglements, 1806–1914*. New York: Cambridge University Press, 1991.

Jelavich, Charles, and Barbara Jelavich. *The Establishment of the Balkan National States, 1804–1920*. Seattle: University of Washington Press, 1977.

Jervis, Robert. "A Political Science Perspective on the Balance of Power and the Concert." *American Historical Review* 97, no. 3 (June 1992): 716–24.

Kagan, Korina. "The Myth of the European Concert: The Realist-Institutionalist Debate and Great Power Behavior in the Eastern Question, 1821–41." *Security Studies* 7, no. 2 (1997/98): 1–57.

Kamenskii, Alexander. "Catherine the Great's Foreign Policy Reconsidered." *Journal of Modern Russian History and Historiography* 12 (2019): 169–87.

Kappeler, Andreas. *The Russian Empire: A Multiethnic History.* Translated by Alfred Clayton. Harlow, Eng.: Pearson, 2001.

Keene, Edward. *International Political Thought: A Historical Introduction.* Malden, MA: Polity Press, 2005.

Keep, John L. H. *Soldiers of the Tsar: Army and Society in Russia, 1462–1874.* New York: Oxford University Press, 1985.

Kelly, Laurence. *Diplomacy and Murder in Tehran: Alexander Griboyedov and Imperial Russia's Mission to the Shah of Persia.* New York: I. B. Tauris, 2002.

Kennedy, Paul. *The Rise and Fall of the Great Powers: Economic Change and Military Conflict from 1500 to 2000.* New York: Vintage Books, 1989.

Khodarkovsky, Michael. *Russia's Steppe Frontier: The Making of a Colonial Empire, 1500–1800.* Bloomington: Indiana University Press, 2002.

Kissinger, Henry. "The Congress of Vienna: A Reappraisal." *World Politics* 8, no. 2 (1956): 264–80.

——. *A World Restored: Metternich, Castlereagh and the Problems of Peace, 1812–1822.* Boston: Houghton Mifflin Company, 1957.

——. *World Order.* New York: Penguin Press, 2014.

Köbler, Gerhard. *Historisches Lexikon der deutschen Länder: Die deutschen Territorien und reichsunmittelbaren Geschlechter vom Mittelalter bis zur Gegenwart.* Darmstadt: Wissenschaftliche Buchgesellschaft; Munich: C. H. Beck, 1988.

Konstitutsionnye proekty v Rossii XVIII–nachalo XX v. Edited by S. Bertolissi, A. N. Sakharov, and A. N. Medushevskii. Moscow: Institut rossiiskoi istorii RAN, 2000.

Kotilaine, J. T. "Opening a Window on Europe: Foreign Trade and Military Conquest on Russia's Western Border in the Seventeenth Century," *Jahrbücher für Geschichte Osteuropas* 46 (1998): 494–530.

Kraehe, Enno E. "A Bipolar Balance of Power." *American Historical Review* 97, no. 3 (June 1992): 707–15.

Krüger, Peter, and Paul W. Schroeder, eds. *The Transformation of European Politics, 1763–1848: Episode or Model in Modern History?* New York: Palgrave Macmillan, 2002.

Kudriavtseva, E. P. *Russkie na Bosfore: Rossiiskoe posol'stvo v Konstantinopole v pervoi polovine XIX veka.* Moscow: Nauka, 2010.

Langhorne, Richard. "The Development of International Conferences, 1648–1830." *Studies in History and Politics* 2 (1981/82): 61–75.

——. "Establishing International Organizations: The Concert and the League." *Diplomacy and Statecraft* 1, no. 1 (1990): 1–18.

Lebedeva, O. V. *Istoriia diplomaticheskoi sluzhby Rossii. Monografiia.* Moscow: Aspekt Press, 2019.

Lebzeltern, Ludwig. *Les rapports diplomatiques de Lebzeltern, ministre d'Autriche à la cour de Russie (1816–1826).* Edited by Grand-Duc Nicolas Mikhailowitch. Saint Petersburg: Manufacture des papiers de l'état, 1913.

Le Conservateur impartial.

LeDonne, John P. *The Grand Strategy of the Russian Empire, 1650–1831.* New York: Oxford University Press, 2004.

LeDonne, John P. *The Russian Empire and the World, 1700–1917: The Geopolitics of Expansion and Containment.* New York: Oxford University Press, 1997.

Lenhoff, Gail, and Ann Kleimola, eds. *"The Book of Royal Degrees" and the Genesis of Russian Historical Consciousness.* Bloomington, IN: Slavica, 2010.

Lentz, Thierry. *Le congrès de Vienne. Une refondation de l'Europe 1814–1815.* Paris: Perrin, 2013.

Lesure, Michel. *Les sources de l'histoire de Russie aux Archives nationales.* Paris: Mouton, 1970.

Levy, Richard S., ed. *Antisemitism: A Historical Encyclopedia of Persecution.* 2 vols. Santa Barbara, CA: ABC–CLIO, 2005.

Ley, Francis. *Alexandre Ier et sa Sainte-Alliance (1811–1825) avec des documents inédits.* Paris: Librairie Fischbacher, 1975.

Liashenko, Leonid Mikhailovich. *Aleksandr I. Samoderzhavnyi respublikanets.* Moscow: Molodaia gvardiia, 2014.

Lieven, Dominic. *The End of Tsarist Russia: The March to World War I and Revolution.* New York: Penguin Books, 2015.

——. *Russia against Napoleon: The True Story of the Campaigns of* War and Peace. New York: Penguin Books, 2009.

——. "Russia and the Defeat of Napoleon (1812–1814)." *Kritika: Explorations in Russian and Eurasian History* 7, no. 2 (Spring 2006): 283–308.

Lukin, Alexander. "What the Kremlin Is Thinking: Putin's Vision for Eurasia." *Foreign Affairs* 93, no. 4 (July–August 2014): 85–93.

Maiofis, Mariia. *Vozzvanie k Evrope: Literaturnoe obshchestvo "Arzamas" i rossiiskii modernizatsionnyi proekt 1815–1818 godov.* Moscow: Novoe literaturnoe obozrenie, 2008.

Maistre, Joseph de. *Correspondance diplomatique, 1811–1817.* Edited by Albert Blanc. 2 vols. Paris: Michel Lévy Frères, 1860.

Mälksoo, L. *Russian Approaches to International Law.* Oxford: Oxford University Press, 2015.

Marquez, Gabriel Garcia. *The General in His Labyrinth.* Translated by Edith Grossman. New York: Alfred A. Knopf, 1990.

Martens, F. F. *Recueil des traités et conventions, conclus par la Russie avec les puissances étrangères.* 15 vols. Saint Petersburg: Tipografiia Ministerstva Putei Soobshcheniia, 1874–1909.

Martens, G. F. *Nouveau Recueil des principaux traités d'Alliance, de Paix, de Trêve, de Neutralité, de Commerce, de Limites, d'Échange etc.* 8 vols. Gottinge: Librairie de Dieterich, 1817–35.

Martin, Alexander M. "A. S. Sturdza i 'Svaishchennyi soiuz' (1815–1823 gg.)." *Voprosy istorii,* no. 11 (1994): 145–51.

——. "Die Suche nach dem Juste Milieu: Der Gedanke der Heiligen Allianz bei den Geschwistern Sturdza in Russland und Deutschland im Napoleonischen

Zeitalters." *Forschungen zur osteuropäischen Geschichte* 54 (Berlin: Harrassowitz Verlag, 1998): 81–126

——. *Romantics, Reformers, Reactionaries: Russian Conservative Thought and Politics in the Reign of Alexander I*. DeKalb: Northern Illinois University Press, 1997.

Massachusetts Peace Society. *Correspondence of the Massachusetts Peace Society with the Emperor of Russia and Prince Alexander Gallitzin*. [London]: Bensley, 1817.

Mazower, Mark. *Governing the World: The History of an Idea, 1815 to the Present*. New York: Penguin Books, 2012.

McConnell, Allen. *Tsar Alexander I: Paternalistic Reformer*. Arlington Heights, IL: Harlan Davidson, 1970.

Mearsheimer, John J. "Why the Ukraine Crisis Is the West's Fault: The Liberal Delusion That Provoked Putin." *Foreign Affairs* 93, no. 5 (September–October 2014): 77–89.

Mel'nikova, L. V. *Armiia i Pravoslavnaia Tserkov' Rossiiskoi imperii v epokhu napoleonovskikh voin*. Moscow: Kuchkovo pole, 2007.

——. *Osvoboditel'nye pokhody russkoi armii 1813–1814 gg. v istorii Rossii i Evropy*. Moscow: Institut rossiiskoi istorii RAN, 2014.

Mendelsohn, Ezra, and Marshall S. Shatz, eds. *Imperial Russia, 1700–1917: State, Society, Opposition*. DeKalb: Northern Illinois University Press, 1988.

Melton, James Van Horn. *The Rise of the Public in Enlightenment Europe*. Cambridge: Cambridge University Press, 2001.

Memoirs of Prince Adam Czartoryski and his Correspondence with Alexander I. Edited by A. Gielgud. 2 vols. London: Remington, 1888.

Menger, Philipp. *Die Heilige Allianz. Religion und Politik bei Alexander I. (1801–1825)*. Stuttgart: Steiner, 2014.

Metternich-Winneburg, C. L. W. *Lettres du prince de Metternich à la comtesse de Lieven, 1818–1819*. Edited by J. Hanoteau. Paris: Librairie Plon, 1909.

Ministerstvo inostrannykh del SSSR. *Vneshniaia politika Rossii XIX i nachala XX veka: Dokumenty Rossiiskogo ministerstva inostrannykh del*. Volumes 6–12. Moscow: Gosudarstvennoe izdatel'stvo politicheskoi literatury, Izdatel'stvo "Nauka," 1960–95.

Mironenko, S. V. *Aleksandr i dekabristy: Rossiia v pervoi chetverti XIX veka. Vybor puti*. Moscow: Kuchkovo pole, 2017.

Mitzen, Jennifer. *Power in Concert: The Nineteenth-Century Origins of Global Governance*. Chicago: University of Chicago Press, 2013.

Mogilevskii, N. A. *Ot Nemana do Seny: Zagranichnyi pokhod russkoi armii 1813–1814 gg.* Moscow: Kuchkovo pole, 2012.

Muller, Jerry Z. *Adam Smith in His Time and Ours: Designing the Decent Society*. New York: The Free Press, 1993.

Nadler, V. K. *Imperator Aleksandr I i ideia sviashchennogo soiuza*. Moscow: Kuchkovo pole, Russkoe Imperatorskoe Istoricheskoe Obshchestvo, 2011.

——. *Imperator Aleksandr I i ideia sviashchennogo soiuza*. 5 vols. Riga: N. Kimmel', 1886–92.

Neff, Stephen C. *Justice among Nations: A History of International Law.* Cambridge, MA: Harvard University Press, 2014.

Nesselrode, K. R., Count. *Lettres et papiers du chancelier comte de Nesselrode, 1760–1850.* Edited by Count A. de Nesselrode. 11 vols. Paris: A. Lahure, 1904–12.

Neumann, Iver, and Vincent Pouliot. "Untimely Russia: Hysteresis in Russian-Western Relations over the Past Millennium." *Security Studies* 20, no. 1 (2011): 105–37.

Nichols, Irby C. *The European Pentarchy and the Congress of Verona, 1822.* The Hague: Martinus Nijhoff, 1971.

Nikolai Mikhailovich, Grand Duke. *L'Empereur Alexandre Ier. Essai d'étude historique.* 2 vols. Saint Petersburg: Manufacture des papiers de l'état, 1912.

Nikolai Mikhailovich, Velikii Kniaz'. *Imperator Aleksandr I.* Reprint. Petrograd, 1914. Moscow: Bogorodskii pechatnik, 1999.

Nipperdey, Thomas. *Germany from Napoleon to Bismarck, 1800–1866.* Translated by Daniel Nolan. Princeton, NJ: Princeton University Press, 1996.

Ocherki istorii Ministerstva inostrannykh del Rossii. 1802–2002. 3 vols. Moscow: Olma-Press, 2002.

O'Meara, Patrick. "Recent Russian Historiography on the Decembrists: From 'Liberation Movement' to 'Public Opinion'." *Kritika: Explorations in Russian and Eurasian History* 14, no. 4 (Fall 2013): 805–22.

———. *The Russian Nobility in the Age of Alexander I.* London: Bloomsbury Academic, 2019.

Orlik, O. V., ed. *Istoriia vneshnei politiki Rossii. Pervaia polovina XIX veka (Ot voin Rossii protiv Napoleona do Parizhskogo mira 1856 g.).* Moscow: Mezhdunarodnye otnosheniia, 1995.

Orlik, O. V. *Rossiia v mezhdunarodnykh otnosheniiakh 1815–1829: Ot Venskogo kongressa do Adrianopol'skogo mira.* Moscow: Nauka, 1998.

Osiander, Andreas. "The Westphalian Myth." *International Organization* 55, no. 2 (2001): 251–88.

Osterhammel, Jürgen. *The Transformation of the World: A Global History of the Nineteenth Century.* Translated by Patrick Camiller. Princeton, NJ: Princeton University Press, 2014.

Paquette, Gabriel. *Enlightenment, Governance, and Reform in Spain and Its Empire, 1759–1808.* New York: Palgrave Macmillan, 2008.

———. *Imperial Portugal in the Age of Atlantic Revolutions: The Luso–Brazilian World, c. 1770–1850.* Cambridge: Cambridge University Press, 2013.

———. "The Intellectual Context of British Diplomatic Recognition of the South American Republics, c. 1800-1830." *Journal of Transatlantic Studies* 2, no. 1 (2004): 75–95.

Parsamov, Vadim S. "'Apoklipsis diplomatii' ('Akt o Sviashchennom soiuze' v interpretatsii K.-V. Metternikha, baronessy Kriudner, Zhozefa de Mestra i Aleksandra Sturdzy)." *Osvoboditel'noe dvizhenie v Rossii.* Vypusk 20. Saratov, 2003, pp. 44–66.

———. "Sviashchennyi soiuz Aleksandra I: na perekrestke voiny i mira." *Mir i voina: kul'turnye konteksty sotsial'noi agressii. Vyborgskie chteniia (1).* Moscow, 2005, pp. 91–106.

Pirenne, Henri. *La Sainte-Alliance: Organization européenne de la paix mondiale.* Neuchatel: Éditions de la Baconnière, 1946.

Petrukhintsev, Nikolai N. "The Baltic Strategy of Peter the Great." In *Russland an der Ostsee. Imperiale Strategien der Macht und kulturelle Wahrnehmungsmuster (16. bis 20. Jahrhundert).* Edited by Karsten Brüggemann and Bradley D. Woodworth. Vienna: Böhlau Verlag, 2012, 169–89.

Polnoe sobranie zakonov Rossiiskoi Imperii. First series, 1649–1825. 45 vols. Saint Petersburg: II Otdelenie Sobstvennoi E. I. V. Kantseliarii, 1830.

Poletika, Petr Ivanovich. *Aperçu de la situation intérieure des Etats-Unis d'Amérique et de leurs rapports politiques avec l'Europe.* London: J. Booth, 1826.

Polovtsov (Polovtsoff), A. A., ed. *Correspondance diplomatique des ambassadeurs et ministres de Russie en France et de France en Russie avec leurs gouvernements de 1814 à 1830.* 3 vols. Saint Petersburg: Société Imperial d'Histoire de Russie, 1902–7.

Pouncy, Carolyn Johnston, ed. and trans. *The Domostroi: Rules for Russian Households in the Time of Ivan the Terrible.* Ithaca, NY: Cornell University Press, 1994.

Pozzo di Borgo, C. A. *Correspondance diplomatique du comte Pozzo di Borgo.* 2 vols. Paris: Calmann Levy, 1890–7.

Prida, Gonzalo Butrón. "From Hope to Defensiveness: The Foreign Policy of a Beleaguered Liberal Spain, 1820–1823." *English Historical Review* 133, no. 562 (June 2018): 567–96.

Prokesch von Osten, Anton Freihern. *Geschichte des Abfalls der Griechen vom türkischen Reiche im Jahre 1821 und der Gründlung des Hellenischen Königreiches. Aus diplomatischem Standpuncte.* Volume 3. Vienna: C. Gerold's Sohn, 1867.

Prousis, Theophilus C. *Lord Strangford at the Sublime Porte (1821): The Eastern Crisis.* Volume 1. Istanbul: Isis Press, 2010.

——. *Lord Strangford at the Sublime Porte (1822): The Eastern Crisis.* Volume 2. Istanbul: Isis Press, 2012.

——. *Russian Society and the Greek Revolution.* DeKalb: Northern Illinois University Press, 1994.

Prutsch, Markus J. *Making Sense of Constitutional Monarchism in Post-Napoleonic France and Germany.* London: Palgrave Macmillan, 2013.

Putzger Historischer Weltatlas. Berlin: Cornelsen, 1997.

Raeff, Marc. "The Emergence of the Russian European: Russia as a Full Partner of Europe." In *Russia Engages the World, 1453–1825.* Edited by Cynthia Hyla Whittaker. Cambridge, MA: Harvard University Press, 2003, 118–37.

——. "The Enlightenment in Russia and Russian Thought in the Enlightenment." In *The Eighteenth Century in Russia.* Edited by J. G. Garrard. Oxford: Clarendon Press, 1973, 25–47.

——. *Michael Speransky: Statesman of Imperial Russia, 1772–1839.* The Hague: Martinus Nijhoff, 1957.

——, ed. *Plans for Political Reform in Imperial Russia, 1730–1905.* Englewood Cliffs, NJ: Prentice-Hall, 1966.

Reinerman, Alan J. "Metternich, Alexander I, and the Russian Challenge." *Journal of Modern History* 46 (1974): 262–76.

Rendall, Matthew. "Cosmopolitanism and Russian Near Eastern Policy, 1821–41: Debunking a Historical Canard." In *Das Europäische Machtekonzert: Friedens– und Sicherheitspolitik vom Wiener Kongress 1815 bis zum Krimkrieg 1853*. Edited by Wolfram Pyta. Vienna: Böhlau Verlag, 2009, 237–55.

———. "Defensive Realism and the Concert of Europe." *Review of International Studies* 32 (2006): 523–40.

———. "Restraint or Self–Restraint of Russia: Nicholas I, the Treaty of Unkiar Skelessi, and the Vienna System, 1832–1841." *International History Review* 24, no. 1 (2002): 37–63.

———. "Russia, the Concert of Europe, and Greece, 1821–1829: A Test of Hypotheses about the Vienna System." *Security Studies* 9, no. 4 (2000): 52–90.

Reviakin, A. V., and N. Iu. Vasil'eva. *Istoriia mezhdunarodnykh otnoshenii. T. I: Ot Vestfal'skogo mira do okonchaniia Pervoi mirovoi voiny*. Moscow: Aspekt Press, 2012.

Rey, Marie-Pierre. *Alexander I: The Tsar who Defeated Napoleon*. Translated by Susan Emanuel. DeKalb: Northern Illinois University Press, 2012.

———. "Chateaubriand, historien et memorialiste du tsar Alexandre Ier, le jugement d'une grande figure de la restauration française." *Quaestio Rossica* 7, no. 2 (2019): 556–70.

———. *Le Dilemme russe: la Russie et l'Europe occidentale d'Ivan le Terrible à Boris Eltsine*. Paris: Flammarion, 2002.

Robertson, William Spence. "Russia and the Emancipation of Spanish America, 1816–1826." *Hispanic American Historical Review* 21, no. 2 (May 1941): 196–221.

Rodogno, Davide. "European Legal Doctrines on Intervention and the Status of the Ottoman Empire within the 'Family of Nations' throughout the Nineteenth Century." *Journal of the History of International Law* 18 (2016): 1–37.

Rynning, Sten. "The False Promise of Continental Concert: Russia, the West and the Necessary Balance of Power." *International Affairs* 91, no. 3 (2015): 539–52.

Russkii biograficheskii slovar'. 25 vols. Saint Petersburg: I. N. Skorokhodov, 1896–1918.

Russkii invalid.

Sakharov, A. N. *Aleksandr I*. Moscow: Nauka, 1998.

Sarotte, Mary Elise. "A Broken Promise? What the West Really Told Moscow About NATO Expansion." *Foreign Affairs* 93, no. 5 (September–October 2014): 90–97.

Saul, Norman E. *Distant Friends: The United States and Russia, 1763–1867*. Lawrence: University Press of Kansas, 1991.

Sbornik Imperatorskogo Rossiiskogo istoricheskogo obshchestva. 148 vols. Saint Petersburg: Imperatorskoe Rossiiskoe istoricheskoe obshchestvo, 1867–1916.

Scharf, Klaus. "The Power of the Weak Opponent: The Diplomacy of Alexander I in Tilsit." *Journal of Modern Russian History and Historiography* 12 (2019): 209–23.

Schaub Marie-Karine. "Se comprendre avec difficulté: les practiques russes de négociation à l'époque muscovite." In *Negociar en la Edad Media/Négocier au Moyen–Âge*.

Edited by M. T. Ferrer Maillol, J.–M. Moeglin, S. Péquignot, and M. Sanchez Martinez. Barcelona and Madrid: CSIC, 2005, 369–87.

Schneewind, J. B. *The Invention of Autonomy: A History of Moral Philosophy*. New York: Cambridge University Press, 1998.

Schroeder, Paul W. "A Mild Rejoinder." *American Historical Review* 97, no. 3 (June 1992): 733–35.

——. "Did the Vienna Settlement Rest on a Balance of Power?" *American Historical Review* 97, no. 3 (June 1992): 683–706.

——. *The Transformation of European Politics 1763–1848*. New York: Oxford University Press, 1994.

Schubert, Anselm, and Wolfram Pyta, eds. *Die Heilige Allianz. Entstehung— Wirkung—Rezeption*. Stuttgart: W. Kohlhammer, 2018.

Schulz, Matthias. *Normen und Praxis: Das Europäische Konzert der Großmächte als Sicherheitsrat, 1815–1860*. Munich: De Gruyter Oldenbourg, 2009.

Šedivý, Miroslav. *Crisis among the Great Powers: The Concert of Europe and the Eastern Question*. London: I. B. Tauris, 2017.

Sheehan, James J. *German History 1770–1866*. New York: Oxford University Press, 1989.

Shil'der, N. K. *Imperator Aleksandr Pervyi. Ego zhizn' i tsarstvovanie*. 4 vols. Saint Petersburg: Izdanie A. S. Suvorina, 1897–98.

Siemann, Wolfram. *Metternich. Stratege und Visionär. Eine Biografie*. Munich: C. H. Beck, 2016.

——. *Metternich: Strategist and Visionary*. Translated by Daniel Steuer. Cambridge, MA: Harvard University Press, 2019.

Simms, Brendan. *The Struggle for Mastery in Germany, 1779–1850*. Basingstoke: Palgrave Macmillan, 1998.

——. *Europe: The Struggle for Supremacy, from 1453 to the Present*. New York: Basic Books, 2013.

Sked, Alan, ed. *Europe's Balance of Power 1815–1848*. New York: Harper and Row, 1979.

——. *Metternich and Austria: An Evaluation*. New York: Palgrave Macmillan, 2008.

Skinner, Quentin. *The Foundations of Modern Political Thought. Volume 1: The Renaissance. Volume 2: The Age of Reformation*. New York: Cambridge University Press, 1978.

Sluga, Glenda. "On the Historical Significance of the Presence, and Absence, of Women at the Congress of Vienna." *L'Homme* 25/2 (2014): 49–62.

——. "Madame de Staël and the Transformation of European Politics, 1812–1817." *The International History Review* 37, no. 1 (2015): 142–66.

——. "'Who Hold the Balance of the World?' Bankers at the Congress of Vienna and in International History." *American Historical Review* 122, no. 5 (December 2017): 1403–30.

Sluga, Glenda, and Carolyn James, eds. *Women, Diplomacy and International Politics since 1500*. New York: Routledge, 2016.

Smiley, William. "War without War: The Battle of Navarino, the Ottoman Empire, and the Pacific Blockade." *Journal of the History of International Law* 18 (2016): 42–69.

Smilianskaia, Elena B., ed. *Rossiia v Sredizemnomor'e. Arkhipelagskaia ekspeditsiia Ekateriny Velikoi.* Moscow: Indrik, 2011.

——. *Grecheskie ostrova Ekateriny II. Opyty imperskoi politiki Rossii v Sredizemnomor'e.* Moscow: Indrik, 2015.

Sobranie Vysochaishikh manifestov, gramot, ukazov, reskriptov, prikazov voiskam i raznykh izveshchenii posledovavshikh v techenii 1812, 1813, 1814, 1815 i 1816 godov. Saint Petersburg: Morskaia tipografiia, 1816.

Solov'ev, S. M. "Imperator Aleksandr I. Politika. Diplomatiia." In *Sochineniia.* Volume 17. Moscow: Mysl', 1996, 203–704.

——. "Potstso di Borgo i Frantsiia. Nachalo vtoroi chetverti XIX veka." In *Sochineniia.* Volume 23. Moscow: Mysl', 2000, 122–55.

Soni, Vivasvan. "A New Passion for Enlightenment." *Eighteenth–Century Studies* 48, no. 2 (2015): 239–48.

Speranskii, M. M. *Rukovodstvo k poznaniiu zakonov.* Saint Petersburg: Nauka, 2002.

Sperber, Jonathan, ed. *Germany, 1800–1870.* New York: Oxford University Press, 2004.

Stauber, Reinhard, Florian Kerschbaumer, and Marion Koschier, eds. *Mächtepolitik und Friedenssicherung. Zur politischen Kultur Europas im Zeichen des Wiener Kongresses.* Berlin: LIT Verlag, 2014.

Stites, Richard. *The Four Horsemen: Riding to Liberty in Post-Napoleonic Europe.* New York: Oxford University Press, 2014.

Stråth, Bo. *Europe's Utopias of Peace. 1815, 1919, 1951.* London: Bloomsbury Academic, 2016.

Stroop, Christopher. "Nationalist War Commentary as Russian Religious Thought: The Religious Intelligentsia's Politics of Providentialism." *Russian Review* 72 (January 2012): 94–115.

Sunderland, Willard. *Taming the Wild Field: Colonization and Empire on the Russian Steppe.* Ithaca, NY: Cornell University Press, 2004.

Suonpää, Mika, and Owain Wright, eds. *Diplomacy and Intelligence in the Nineteenth-Century Mediterranean World.* London: Bloomsbury Academic Publishing, 2019.

Syn otechestva.

Taylor, Charles. *A Secular Age.* Cambridge, MA: Harvard University Press, 2007.

——. *Sources of the Self: The Making of the Modern Identity.* Cambridge, MA: Harvard University Press, 1989.

Thiessen, H. v. "Diplomatie vom type ancien. Überlegungen zu einem Idealtypus des frühneuzeitlichen Gesandtschaftswesens." In *Akteure der Aussenbeziehungen: Netzwerke und Interkulturalität im historischen Wandel.* Edited by H. v. Thiessen and C. Windler. Böhlau: Cologne, 2010, 471–503.

Tolstoy, Leo. *War and Peace*. Translated by Louise Maude and Aylmer Maude. New York: Simon and Schuster, 1942.

Torkunov, A. V., and M. M. Narinskii, eds. *Evropeiskaia diplomatiia i mezhdunarodnye protsessy epokhi napoleonovskikh voin*. Moscow: Aspekt Press, 2012.

———, eds. *Istoriia mezhdunarodnykh otnoshenii. Tom I: Ot Vestfal'skogo mira do okonchaniia Pervoi mirovoi voiny*. Moscow: Aspekt Press, 2012.

Tourgueneff, N. *La Russie et les Russes*. Volume 1. Paris: Au comptoir des imprimeurs-unis, 1847.

Tsygankov, Andrei P. *Russia and the West from Alexander to Putin: Honor in International Relations*. New York: Cambridge University Press, 2012.

Turgenev, Nikolai. *Rossiia i russkie*. Translated by S. V. Zhitomirskaia. Commentary by A. R. Kurilkin. Moscow: OGI, 2001.

Vagts, Alfred. "The Balance of Power: Growth of an Idea." *World Politics* 1, no. 1 (1948): 82–101.

Vagts, Alfred, and Detlev Vagts. "The Balance of Power in International Law: A History of an Idea." *American Journal of International Law* 73 (1979): 555–80.

Vermeiren, Jan. "Problèmes et perspectives d'une histoire de l'idée européenne de la Révolution française au Printemps des peuples (1789–1848/48)." *Canadian Journal of History* 50, no. 1 (2015): 68–85.

Vestnik Evropy.

Vick, Brian E. *The Congress of Vienna: Power and Politics after Napoleon*. Cambridge, MA: Harvard University Press, 2014.

Vinogradov, V. N., ed. *Balkanskie issledovaniia. Vypusk 18. Aleksandr I, Napoleon i Balkany*. Moscow: Nauka, 1997.

Vysshie i tsentral'nye gosudarstvennye uchrezhdeniia Rossii. 4 vols. Saint Petersburg: Nauka, 2004.

Walker, Franklin A. "Enlightenment and Religion in Russian Education in the Reign of Tsar Alexander I." *History of Education Quarterly* 32, no. 3 (Fall 1992): 343–60.

Waresquiel, Emmanuel de. *Talleyrand, le prince immobile*. Paris: Fayard, 2006.

Weber, Eugen. *Peasants into Frenchmen: The Modernization of Rural France, 1870–1914*. Stanford, CA: Stanford University Press, 1976.

Webster, Charles K., ed. *British Diplomacy 1813–1815. Select Documents Dealing with the Reconstruction of Europe*. London: G. Bell and Sons, 1921.

———. "Disarmament Proposals in 1816." *The Contemporary Review*, no. 683 (November 1922): 621–7

———. *The Foreign Policy of Castlereagh 1815–1822. Vol. 2: Britain and the European Alliance*. London: G. Bell and Sons, 1963.

Werner, Michael, and Bénédicte Zimmermann. "Beyond Comparison: Histoire Croisée and the Challenge of Reflexivity." *History and Theory* 45, no. 1 (February 2006): 30–50.

White, Eugene N. "Making the French Pay: The Costs and Consequences of the Napoleonic Reparations." *European Review of Economic History* 5, no. 3 (2001): 337–65.

Whitman, James Q. *The Verdict of Battle: The Law of Victory and the Making of Modern War.* Cambridge, MA: Harvard University Press, 2012.

Whittaker, Cynthia Hyla. *Russian Monarchy: Eighteenth-Century Rulers and Writers in Political Dialogue.* DeKalb: Northern Illinois University Press, 2003.

Wirtschafter, Elise Kimerling. "The Congress of Aix-la-Chapelle (1818) and Russia's Proposal for a Treaty of Guarantee." *Journal of Modern Russian History and Historiography* 12 (2019): 245–62.

———. *From Serf to Russian Soldier.* Princeton, NJ: Princeton University Press, 1990.

———. *The Play of Ideas in Russian Enlightenment Theater.* DeKalb: Northern Illinois University Press, 2003.

———. *Religion and Enlightenment in Catherinian Russia: The Teachings of Metropolitan Platon.* DeKalb: Northern Illinois University Press, 2013.

———. "Russian Diplomacy as Enlightenment Project: The Holy Alliance and the Vienna Settlement, 1815–1823." In *Vek Prosveshcheniia. Vypusk 6: Chto takoe Prosveshchenie? Novye otvety na staryi vopros.* (Moscow: Nauka, 2018), 208–18.

———. *Russia's Age of Serfdom 1649–1861.* Malden, MA: Blackwell Publishing, 2008.

———. *Social Identity in Imperial Russia.* DeKalb: Northern Illinois University Press, 1997.

Woloch, Isser. *The New Regime: Transformations of the French Civic Order, 1789–1820s.* New York: Norton, 1994.

Wortman, Richard S. *Scenarios of Power: Myth and Ceremony in Russian Monarchy from Peter the Great to the Abdication of Nicholas II.* 1 vol. abridged. Princeton, NJ: Princeton University Press, 2006.

Zamoyski, Adam. *Rites of Peace: The Fall of Napoleon and the Congress of Vienna.* New York: HarperCollins, 2007.

Zorin, Andrei. *Kormia dvuglavogo orla . . . Literatura i gosudarstvennaia ideologiia v Rossii v poslednei treti XVIII–pervoi treti XIX veka.* Moscow: Novoe literaturnoe obozrenie, 2001.

Zürcher, Erik-Jan, ed. *Fighting for a Living: A Comparative History of Military Labour 1500–2000.* Amsterdam: Amsterdam University Press, 2013.

CPSIA information can be obtained
at www.ICGtesting.com
Printed in the USA
LVHW090503090621
689713LV00011B/712